Computer Organization

McGraw-Hill Series in Computer Science

SENIOR CONSULTING EDITOR
C. L. Liu, University of Illinois at Urbana-Champaign

CONSULTING EDITOR
Allen B. Tucker, Bowdoin College

Fundamentals of Computing and Programming
Computer Organization and Architecture
Computers in Society/Ethics
Systems and Languages
Theoretical Foundations
Software Engineering and Databases
Artificial Intelligence
Networks, Parallel and Distributed Computing
Graphics and Visualization
The MIT Electrical Engineering and Computer Science Series

Computer Organization

FOURTH EDITION

V. Carl Hamacher
Queen's University

Zvonko G. Vranesic
University of Toronto

Safwat G. Zaky
University of Toronto

THE McGRAW-HILL COMPANIES, INC.

New York   St. Louis   San Francisco   Auckland   Bogotá   Caracas
Lisbon   London   Madrid   Mexico City   Milan   Montreal   New Delhi
San Juan   Singapore   Sydney   Tokyo   Toronto

McGraw-Hill

A Division of The McGraw·Hill Companies

COMPUTER ORGANIZATION

This book is printed on acid-free paper.

3 4 5 6 7 8 9 0 DOC DOC 9 0 9 8

ISBN 0-07-025883-X

This book was set in Times Roman by Publication Services, Inc.
The editor was Eric M. Munson;
the production supervisor was Elizabeth J. Strange.
The cover was designed by Rafael Hernandez.
Project supervision was done by Publication Services, Inc.
R. R. Donnelley & Sons Company was printer and binder.

INTERNATIONAL EDITION

When ordering this title, use ISBN 0-07-114309-2.

Library of Congress Catalog Card Number:
95-81367

Step	Action
1.	$R1_{out}$, Y_{in}
2.	$R2_{out}$, Add, Z_{in}
3.	Z_{out}, $R3_{in}$

The signals whose names are given in any step are activated, or set to 1, for the duration of the clock cycle corresponding to that step. All other signals are inactive. Hence, in step 1, the output of register R1 and the input of register Y are enabled, causing the contents of R1 to be transferred to Y. In step 2, the contents of register R2 are gated onto the bus and, hence, to input B of the ALU. The contents of register Y are always available at input A. The function performed by the ALU depends on the signals applied to the ALU control lines. In this case, the Add line is set to 1, causing the output of the ALU to be the sum of the two numbers at inputs A and B. This sum is loaded into register Z, because its input is enabled (Z_{in}). In step 3, the contents of register Z are transferred to the destination register, R3. This last transfer cannot be carried out during step 2, because only one register output can be meaningfully connected to the bus at any given time.

3.1.5 Register Gating and Timing of Data Transfers

Before we discuss the execution of machine instructions, we present some of the implementation details required for gating data to and from the common bus in Figure 3.1. We also present a brief overview of the required timing for the control signals involved in transferring data between registers.

Consider the case in which each bit of the registers in Figures 3.1 and 3.2 consists of a flip-flop like the one shown in Figure 3.3 (see also Appendix A). The flip-flop shown is assumed to be one of the bits of register Z. While the control input Z_{in} is equal to 1, the state of the flip-flop changes to correspond to the data on the bus. Following a 1 to 0 transition at the Z_{in} input, the data stored in the flip-flop immediately before this transition is locked in until Z_{in} is again set to 1. Thus, the two input gates of the flip-flop perform the function of the input control switch in Figure 3.2.

Conceptually, the output switches in Figure 3.2 act as mechanical On/Off switches. When a switch is in the On state, it transfers the contents of its corresponding register to the bus. When it is in the Off state, the register output is electrically disconnected from the bus, allowing another register to place data on the bus. In other words, the output of the register-switch circuit can be in one of the three states—1, 0, or open circuit.

In actual implementations, electronic switches are used. The output gate of a register is capable of being electrically disconnected from the bus or of placing a 0 or a 1 on the bus. Because it supports these three possibilities, such a gate is said to have a *three-state* output. A separate control input is used either to enable the gate output to drive the bus to 0 or 1 or to put it in a high-impedance (electrically disconnected) state. The latter state corresponds to the open-circuit state of a mechanical switch.

We now discuss some aspects of the timing of data transfers inside the CPU. Consider the addition operation in step 2 of Section 3.1.4. After the signal $R2_{out}$ is set to 1,

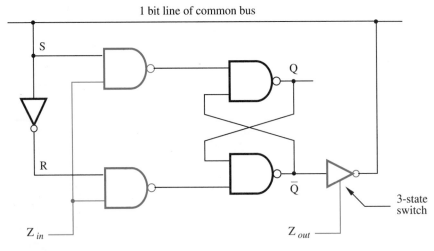

FIGURE 3.3
Input and output gating for one register bit.

a finite delay is encountered for the gate to open and then for the data to travel along the bus to the input of the ALU. Further delay is introduced by the ALU adder circuits. For the result to be properly stored in register Z, data must be maintained on the bus for an additional period of time equal to the setup and hold times for this register (see Appendix A). This situation is depicted in the timing diagram in Figure 3.4. The sum of the five delay times shown defines the minimum duration of the signal $R2_{out}$.

3.2
EXECUTION OF A COMPLETE INSTRUCTION

Let us now try to put together the sequence of elementary operations required to execute one instruction. Consider the instruction

Add   (R3),R1

which adds the contents of a memory location to register R1. The address of the memory operand is the contents of register R3 (register indirect mode). Executing this instruction requires the following actions:

1. Fetch the instruction.
2. Fetch the first operand (the contents of the memory location pointed to by R3).
3. Perform the addition.
4. Load the result into R1.

Figure 3.5 gives the sequence of control steps required to perform these operations for the single-bus architecture of Figure 3.1. Instruction execution proceeds as follows: In step 1, the instruction fetch operation is initiated by loading the contents of the PC into the MAR and sending a Read request to the memory. While waiting for a response from the memory, the PC is incremented by 1 by setting one of the inputs to the ALU

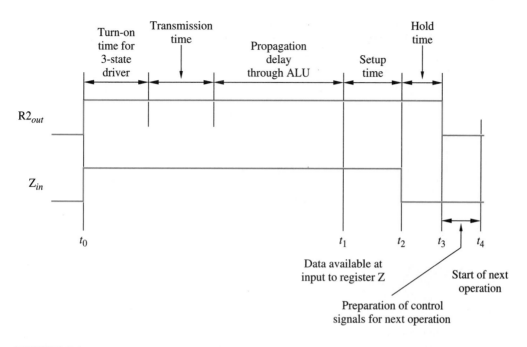

FIGURE 3.4
Timing of the control signals during the Add step.

(register Y) to 0 and the other input (CPU bus) to the current value in the PC. At the same time, the carry-in to the ALU is set to 1, and an Add operation is specified. The updated value is moved from register Z back into the PC during step 2. Of course, this way of incrementing the PC by using the adder circuit in the ALU is not the fastest approach; instead, the PC can be implemented as a counter circuit with a parallel-load capability. Our approach, however, uses the simplest structure to explain the basic concepts. Note that step 2 begins immediately after the memory Read is requested, without waiting for the memory function to be completed. Step 3, however, has to be delayed until the MFC signal is received. This is indicated by the WMFC (Wait for MFC) control signal in step

Step	Action
1	PC_{out}, MAR_{in}, Read, Clear Y, Set carry-in to ALU, Add, Z_{in}
2	Z_{out}, PC_{in}, WMFC
3	MDR_{out}, IR_{in}
4	$R3_{out}$, MAR_{in}, Read
5	$R1_{out}$, Y_{in}, WMFC
6	MDR_{out}, Add, Z_{in}
7	Z_{out}, $R1_{in}$, End

FIGURE 3.5
Control sequence for execution of the instruction Add (R3),R1.

2. In step 3, the word fetched from the memory is loaded into the IR. The instruction decoding circuit interprets the contents of the IR at the beginning of step 4. This enables the control circuitry to choose the appropriate signals for the remainder of the control sequence, steps 4 through 7, which constitute the execution phase. Steps 1 through 3 constitute the instruction fetch phase of the control sequence. Of course, this portion is the same for all instructions.

In step 4, the contents of register R3 are transferred to the MAR, and a memory Read operation is initiated. Then the contents of R1 are transferred to register Y. When the Read operation is completed, the memory operand is available in register MDR. The addition operation is performed in step 6, and the result is transferred to R1 in step 7. The End signal in step 7 indicates that this is the last step of the current instruction, and it causes a new fetch cycle to begin by returning to step 1.

3.2.1 Branching

As Chapter 2 describes, branching is accomplished by replacing the current contents of the PC with the branch address, that is, the address of the instruction to which the program must branch. The branch address is usually obtained by adding an offset X, which is given in the branch instruction, to the current value of the PC. Figure 3.6 gives a control sequence for an unconditional branch using the single-bus organization of Figure 3.1. Processing starts, as usual, with the fetch phase. This phase ends when the instruction is loaded into the IR in step 3 and decoded at the beginning of step 4. To execute the branch instruction, the contents of the PC are transferred to register Y in step 4. Then the offset X is gated onto the bus, and the addition operation is performed. The result, which is the branch address, is loaded into the PC in step 6.

Note that, in this example, the PC is incremented during the fetch phase, before knowing the type of instruction being executed. Thus, when the offset X is added to the contents of the PC in steps 4 and 5, these contents have already been updated to point to the instruction following the Branch instruction in the program. Therefore, the offset X is the difference between the branch address and the address immediately following the Branch instruction. For example, if the Branch instruction is at location 1000, and it is required to branch to location 1050, the value of X must be 49.

Now consider a conditional branch. The only difference between the control sequence of a conditional branch and that of an unconditional branch is that in a

Step	Action
1	PC_{out}, MAR_{in}, Read, Clear Y, Set carry-in to ALU, Add, Z_{in}
2	Z_{out}, PC_{in}, WMFC
3	MDR_{out}, IR_{in}
4	PC_{out}, Y_{in}
5	Offset-field-of-IR_{out}, Add, Z_{in}
6	Z_{out}, PC_{in}, End

FIGURE 3.6
Control sequence for an unconditional branch instruction.

conditional branch we need to check the status of the condition codes before loading a new value into the PC. For example, if the instruction decoding circuitry interprets the contents of the IR as a Branch-on-negative instruction, step 4 in Figure 3.6 is replaced with

$$PC_{out}, Y_{in}, \text{If } N=0 \text{ then End}$$

As before, the contents of the PC are copied into register Y, just in case they may be needed to compute the branch address. Meanwhile, the N flag is checked. If it is equal to 0, the End signal is issued, terminating execution of that instruction. If $N = 1$, steps 5 and 6 are performed to complete the branch operation.

3.3
HARDWIRED CONTROL

To execute instructions, the CPU must have some means of generating the control signals discussed in Section 3.2 in the proper sequence. Computer designers have used a wide variety of techniques to solve this problem. Most of these techniques, however, fall into one of two categories: hardwired control and microprogrammed control. We discuss each of these techniques in detail, starting with hardwired control in this section.

Consider the sequence of control signals given in Figure 3.5. Seven nonoverlapping time slots are required for executing the instruction represented by this sequence. Each time slot must be at least long enough for the functions specified in the corresponding step to be completed. Let us assume, for the moment, that all time slots are equal in duration. Therefore, the required control unit may be based on the use of a counter driven by a clock signal, CLK, as shown in Figure 3.7. Each state, or count, of this counter corresponds to one of the steps in Figures 3.5 and 3.6. Hence, the required control signals are uniquely determined by the following information:

- Contents of the control step counter
- Contents of the instruction register
- Contents of the condition code and other status flags

By status flags, we mean the signals representing the states of various sections of the CPU and of various control lines connected to it. An example is the MFC status signal used in Figure 3.5.

To gain insight into the structure of the control unit, we start with a simplified view of the hardware involved. The decoder/encoder block in Figure 3.7 is a combinational circuit that generates the required control outputs, depending on the state of all its inputs. By separating the decoding and encoding functions, we obtain the more detailed block diagram in Figure 3.8. The step decoder provides a separate signal line for each step, or time slot, in the control sequence. Similarly, the output of the instruction decoder consists of a separate line for each machine instruction. That is, for any instruction loaded in the IR, one of the output lines INS_1 through INS_m is set to 1, and all other lines are set to 0. (For design details of such decoders, refer to Appendix A.) All input signals to the encoder block in Figure 3.8 should be combined to generate the individual control signals Y_{in}, PC_{out}, Add, End, and so on. An example of encoder

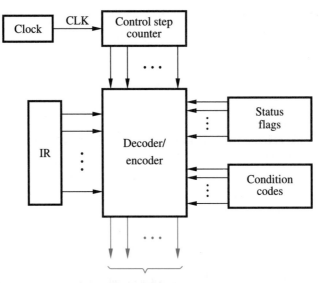

FIGURE 3.7
Control unit organization.

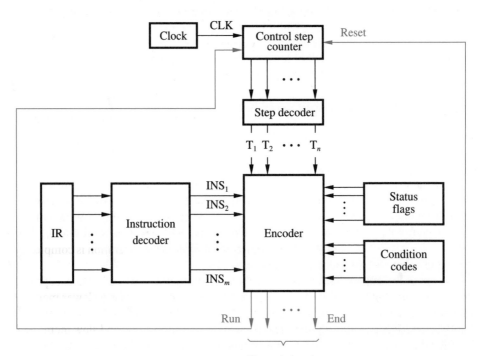

FIGURE 3.8
Separation of the decoding and encoding functions.

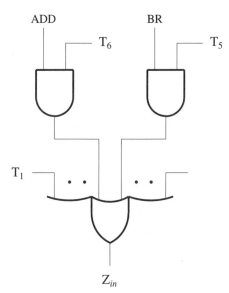

FIGURE 3.9
Generation of the Z_{in} control signal

structure is the circuit diagrammed in Figure 3.9. This circuit implements the logic function

$$Z_{in} = T_1 + T_6 \cdot ADD + T_5 \cdot BR + \cdots \tag{3.1}$$

Thus, the control signal Z_{in}, which enables the input to register Z, is turned on during time slot T_1 for all instructions, during T_6 for an ADD instruction, and so on. This part of the Z_{in} function is compiled from the control sequences in Figures 3.5 and 3.6. The term T_1 is common to all instructions, because it occurs during the fetch phase. Similarly, the End control signal, shown in Figure 3.10, is generated from the logic function

$$End = T_7 \cdot ADD + T_6 \cdot BR + (T_6 \cdot N + T_4 \cdot \overline{N}) \cdot BRN + \cdots \tag{3.2}$$

Figure 3.8 shows how the End signal can be used to start a new instruction fetch cycle by resetting the control step counter to its starting value.

3.3.1 CPU-Memory Interaction

The interaction between the internal signals in the CPU and the external bus deserves special attention. In our earlier discussion, we assumed that a Read or a Write control signal inside the CPU initiates a data transfer between the main memory and register MDR. The memory activates the MFC signal when the transfer operation is completed. Let us now examine this exchange in more detail.

A versatile CPU can communicate with main memory modules of different speeds. A fast memory can be accessed within a single clock cycle, whereas a slower memory may require several clock cycles. Figure 3.11 shows a possible circuit for dealing with the Read and Write control signals. The circuit can handle both fast and slow memories. Recall that the internal control signals generated during a given control step are active only for the duration of that step. A slow memory has to see these signals for more than one clock cycle. This is accomplished by the two positive-edge-triggered flip-flops

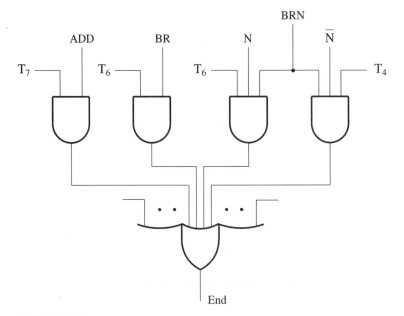

FIGURE 3.10
Generation of the End control signal.

in the figure. The control signals sent to the memory are Memory Read request (MR) and Memory Write request (MW). To explain the operation of the circuit, let us consider the case of a read request.

Figure 3.11b gives the timing diagram for a read access to a slow memory. This diagram assumes that the main memory is controlled by the same clock as the CPU. Moreover, it assumes that all control signals in the CPU are generated on the positive edge of the clock, whereas the memory responds with its control signal, MFC, on the negative edge of the clock. When the Read signal is activated at time t_1 as part of the control step i, the MR signal is also activated with only a small delay caused by propagation through the AND and OR gates. Note that MFC is low at this time. The next positive edge of the clock, t_2, advances the control step counter to $i + 1$ and sets the Memory Read flip-flop to 1, thus ensuring that the MR signal continues in the active state. Our example assumes that no further operations within the CPU can be performed until the memory responds. Hence, the WMFC signal is activated in step $i + 1$, causing the RUN signal to go low. The counter is advanced one step at each positive edge of the clock signal if RUN is equal to 1. Thus, the counter will not be advanced again until RUN returns to 1. This happens sometime later, at t_3, when the memory responds by activating MFC at a negative edge of the clock. At the next positive edge of the clock, t_4, the Memory Read flip-flop is reset, the step counter is advanced, and step $i + 2$ begins. Note that the memory keeps MFC equal to 1 for one clock cycle, until t_5.

In order to accommodate fast memories, the circuit must function correctly even if MFC goes high during step i in Figure 3.11b. In this case, the Memory Read flip-flop is not set to 1 at t_2, because its J input will be equal to 0. As a result, the RUN signal is

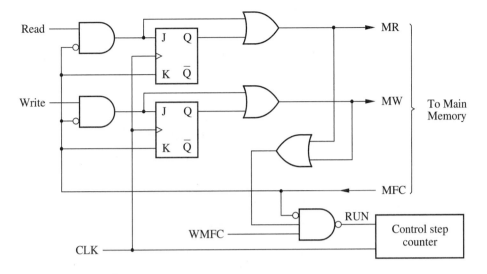

(a) Generation of Read and Write requests

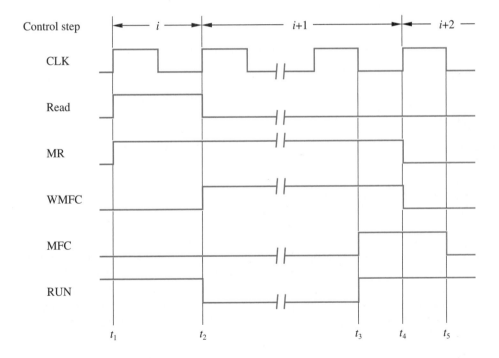

(b) Timing diagram of a Read operation

FIGURE 3.11
Control of external bus transfers.

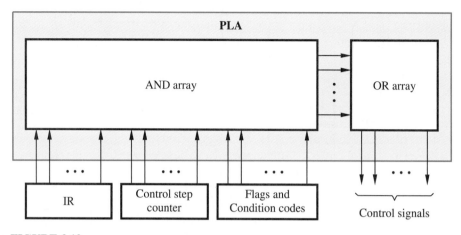

FIGURE 3.12
Implementation of a sequence controller on a VLSI chip.

equal to 1 when step $i + 1$ begins, and normal operation continues. Note that, as long as WMFC is not set to 1 by a control step, the counter remains enabled. Thus, while a memory access is taking place, the CPU can perform other internal operations that may span one or more clock cycles.

3.3.2 Practical Aspects of Circuit Implementation

The preceding discussion presents a simplified view of the way in which the sequence of control signals needed to fetch and execute instructions can be generated. The overall organization depicted in Figures 3.7 and 3.8 can be used to implement an arbitrary instruction set. We now consider some practical aspects of realizing such circuitry.

By necessity, the approach used in the design of a digital system must take into account the capabilities and limitations of the chosen implementation technology. The circuits of Figures 3.9 and 3.10 are easy to understand and to design; however, the size and complexity of the circuits needed may make this direct approach impractical. The implementation of modern computers is based on the use of very-large-scale-integration (VLSI) technology. In VLSI chips, structures that involve regular interconnection patterns are much easier to fabricate than the random connections used in the circuits just discussed. One such structure is a *programmable logic array* (PLA) (described in Appendix A). A PLA consists of an array of AND gates followed by an array of OR gates; it can be used to implement combinational logic functions of several variables. The entire decoder/encoder block in Figure 3.7 can be implemented in the form of a single PLA. Thus, the control section of a CPU can be organized as shown in Figure 3.12.

3.4
PERFORMANCE CONSIDERATIONS

Performance of a computer depends on many factors, some of which are related to the design of the CPU. Three of the most important factors are the power of the instructions, the clock cycle time, and the number of clock cycles per instruction. A powerful instruction performs a complex multistep task. Such instructions need several clock cycles for execution, but they accomplish more than simple instructions. The question is whether having such complex instructions leads to better overall performance in executing complete programming tasks. The evolution of RISC processors has demonstrated that it may be advantageous to use relatively simple instructions that are suitable for pipelined execution. This concept is examined in Chapter 7.

Clock speed has a major influence on performance. The clock speed depends on the technology used to implement the electronic circuits and the complexity of functional units such as the ALU. Using densely packed, small transistors to fabricate the desired circuits leads to high operating speed. Thus, implementing the entire CPU on a single VLSI chip allows much higher clock speeds than would be possible if several chips were used. The time required to perform an arithmetic operation, such as addition or multiplication, has a dominant effect on the achievable clock rate. Many clever schemes have been devised to optimize the logic circuits that perform these operations and reduce the time required for execution. We examine some of these schemes in Chapter 6.

The speed of processors has improved phenomenally during the past two decades. Microprocessors have evolved from chips clocked at a frequency of one MHz to present-day chips that run at several hundred MHz.

So far, we have concentrated on explaining the basic mechanisms of control in the CPU. We have used a simple model for this purpose, consisting of a CPU that has a single internal bus, as shown in Figure 3.1. We now consider more complex structures that lead to better performance. It is always desirable to use as few clock cycles as possible—a single clock cycle per instruction is ideal. This cannot be achieved with the simple single-bus structure of Figure 3.1, because the bus allows only one data item to be transferred during one clock cycle. Therefore, we should consider the use of multiple buses within the CPU.

3.4.1 Multiple-Bus Organization

Figure 3.13 depicts a three-bus structure used to connect the registers and the ALU of a CPU. All general-purpose registers are combined into a single block called the *register file*. Modern processors include many general-purpose registers; Chapter 2 explains that the PowerPC has 32 and the Motorola 68000 has 16 such registers. In VLSI technology, the most efficient way to implement these registers is in the form of an array of memory cells similar to those used to implement random-access memory (RAM), which is discussed in Chapter 5. The register file in Figure 3.13 has two outputs, allowing the contents of two registers to be placed on buses A and B simultaneously.

Compared to Figure 3.1, the structure in Figure 3.13 requires significantly fewer control steps to execute instructions. Consider a three-operand instruction of the form

OP   Rsrc1,Rsrc2,Rdst

in which an operation is performed on the contents of two source registers, and the result is placed into a destination register. Buses A and B are used to transfer the source

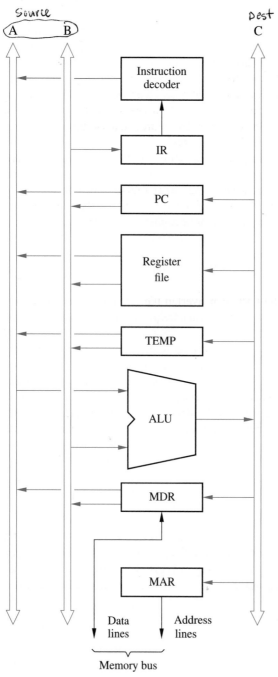

FIGURE 3.13
Three-bus organization of the CPU.

operands, and bus C provides the path to the destination. The path from the source
buses to the destination bus goes through the ALU, where the required operation is
performed. Thus, assuming that the operation to be performed can be completed in one
pass through the ALU, the structure of Figure 3.13 allows the execution phase of an
instruction to be performed in one clock cycle. Note that if it is merely necessary to

copy the contents of one register into another, then the transfer is also done through the ALU, but no arithmetic or logic operation is performed.

The temporary storage registers Y and Z in Figure 3.1 are not required in Figure 3.13. Register Y is not needed because both inputs to the ALU are provided simultaneously via buses A and B. Register Z is not needed because the output from the ALU is transferred to the destination register via the third bus, C. In this structure, it is essential to ensure that the same register can serve as both the source and the destination in a given instruction. This would not be possible if the registers were simple latches, as in Figure 3.3. Instead, the register file must be implemented using either edge-triggered or master-slave circuits (see Appendix A).

The three-bus structure allows execution of register-to-register operations in a single clock cycle. This is particularly well suited to the requirements of RISC processors, in which most arithmetic and logic instructions have register operands.

3.4.2 Other Enhancements

Performance improves greatly if the CPU can overlap the fetch and execute phases of instructions. While one instruction is being executed, the next instruction can be prefetched from the memory. Modern processors include a special unit, often called the *instruction unit,* whose main function is to fetch instructions and place them into a queue ready for execution. The instruction unit generates memory addresses based on the address of the last instruction fetched. In doing so, it attempts to ensure that correct instructions are prefetched when a branch instruction is encountered. It does this, with good success, by predicting which of the two possible paths will be taken following a conditional branch instruction. Prefetching is a form of pipelining, which is discussed in Chapter 7.

In Section 3.2, we introduced a WMFC signal to wait for the response from a main memory that is slower than the CPU. From the performance point of view, it would be best if the main memory could respond within a single clock cycle. Although it is unrealistic to attempt to construct such a main memory (unless the clock period is undesirably long), it is possible to include a fast cache memory on the same chip as the CPU, as suggested in Section 1.5. Data can be accessed from the cache in one clock cycle. Hence, if the required instructions and data are usually found in the cache, the apparent memory access time (as seen by the CPU) will be short. If the desired data are not found in the cache, that is, if a *cache miss* occurs, it is necessary to access the data in the main memory, which takes more time. A full discussion of the cache concept is presented in Chapter 5.

3.4.3 A Complete CPU

The preceding discussion suggests that a powerful CPU can be designed using the structure shown in Figure 3.14. This structure has an instruction unit that fetches instructions from an instruction cache, or from the main memory in case the desired instructions are not already in the cache. It has separate processing units to deal with integer data and floating-point data. Each of these units can be organized as described in Figure 3.13.

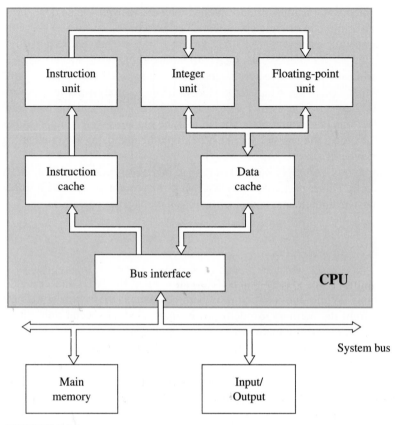

FIGURE 3.14
Block diagram of a complete CPU.

A data cache is inserted between these units and the main memory. We have included separate caches for instructions and data, as found in some processors. Other processors use a single cache that stores both instructions and data. The CPU is connected to the system bus and, hence, to the rest of the computer, by means of a bus interface.

Although we have shown just one integer and one floating-point unit in Figure 3.14, a CPU may include several units of each type to increase the potential for parallelism. Using multiple units and pipelining, it is possible to produce very powerful processors. Since fetching and execution of several instructions can be overlapped in a pipelined processor, an effective execution rate of several instructions per clock cycle can be achieved. Processors that execute instructions at a rate exceeding one instruction per clock cycle are called *superscalar* processors.

3.5
MICROPROGRAMMED CONTROL

In Section 3.3, we saw how all the control signals required inside the CPU can be generated using a control step counter and a PLA circuit. Now we discuss an alternative

Micro-instruction	..	PC_{in}	PC_{out}	MAR_{in}	Read	MDR_{out}	IR_{in}	Y_{in}	Clear Y	Carry-in	Add	Z_{in}	Z_{out}	$R1_{out}$	$R1_{in}$	$R3_{out}$	WMFC	End	..
1		0	1	1	1	0	0	0	1	1	1	1	0	0	0	0	0	0	
2		1	0	0	0	0	0	0	0	0	0	0	1	0	0	0	1	0	
3		0	0	0	0	1	1	0	0	0	0	0	0	0	0	0	0	0	
4		0	0	1	1	0	0	0	0	0	0	0	0	0	0	1	0	0	
5		0	0	0	0	0	0	1	0	0	0	0	0	1	0	0	1	0	
6		0	0	0	0	1	0	0	0	0	1	1	0	0	0	0	0	0	
7		0	0	0	0	0	0	0	0	0	0	0	1	0	1	0	0	1	

FIGURE 3.15
An example of microinstructions for Figure 3.5.

scheme called *microprogrammed control,* in which control signals are generated by a program similar to machine language programs.

First, we introduce some common terms. A *control word* (CW) is a word whose individual bits represent the various control signals in Figure 3.8. Each of the control steps in the control sequence of an instruction defines a unique combination of 1s and 0s in the CW. The CWs corresponding to the 7 steps of Figure 3.5 are shown in Figure 3.15. A sequence of CWs corresponding to the control sequence of a machine instruction constitutes the *microroutine* for that instruction, and the individual control words in this microroutine are referred to as *microinstructions.*

Let us assume that the microroutines for all instructions in the instruction set of a computer are stored in a special memory called the *control store.* The control unit can generate the control signals for any instruction by sequentially reading the CWs of the corresponding microroutine from the control store. This suggests organizing the control unit as shown in Figure 3.16. To read the control words sequentially from the

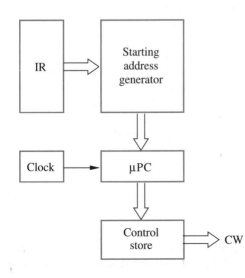

FIGURE 3.16
Basic organization of a microprogrammed control unit.

Address	Microinstruction
0	PC_{out}, MAR_{in}, Read, Clear Y, Set carry-in to ALU, Add, Z_{in}
1	Z_{out}, PC_{in}, WMFC
2	MDR_{out}, IR_{in}
3	Branch to starting address of appropriate microroutine.
. . .	. . . .
25	PC_{out}, Y_{in}, if $N = 0$ then branch to microinstruction 0
26	Offset-field-of-IR_{out}, Add, Z_{in}
27	Z_{out}, PC_{in}, End

FIGURE 3.17

Microroutine for the instruction Branch-on-negative.

control store, a *microprogram counter* (μPC) is used. Every time a new instruction is loaded into the IR, the output of the block labeled "starting address generator" is loaded into the μPC. The μPC is then automatically incremented by the clock, causing successive microinstructions to be read from the control store. Hence, the control signals are delivered to various parts of the CPU in the correct sequence.

One important function of the control unit has not been discussed yet, and, in fact, it cannot be implemented by the simple organization in Figure 3.16. This is the situation that arises when the control unit is required to check the status of the condition codes or status flags in order to choose between alternative courses of action. In the case of hardwired control, this situation is handled by including an appropriate logic function, as in Equation 3.2, in the encoder circuitry. In microprogrammed control, an alternative approach is to use conditional branching. In this case, the microinstruction set is expanded to include some conditional branch microinstructions. In addition to the branch address, these microinstructions specify which of the status flags, condition codes, or, possibly, bits of the instruction register, should be checked as a condition for branching to take place.

The instruction Branch-on-negative may now be implemented by a microroutine such as that shown in Figure 3.17. After loading this instruction into IR, a branch microinstruction transfers control to the corresponding microroutine, which is assumed to start at location 25 in the control store. This address is the output of the starting address generator block in Figure 3.16. At location 25, a conditional branch microinstruction tests the N bit of the condition codes. If this bit is equal to 0, a branch takes place to location 0 to fetch a new machine instruction. Otherwise, the microinstructions in locations 26 and 27 are executed to load a new value into the PC.

To support microprogram branching, the organization of the control unit should be modified as shown in Figure 3.18. The starting address generator block of Figure 3.16 becomes the starting and branch address generator. This block loads a new address into the μPC when a microinstruction instructs it to do so. To allow implementation of a conditional branch, inputs to this block consist of the status flags and condition codes as well as the contents of the instruction register. In this control unit, the μPC is incremented every time a new microinstruction is fetched from the microprogram memory, except in the following situations:

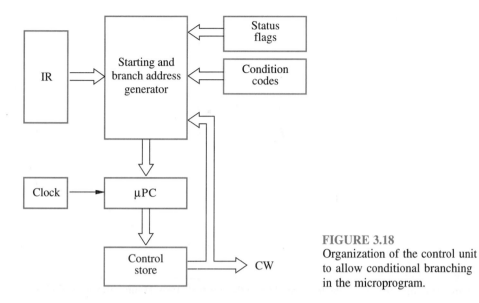

FIGURE 3.18
Organization of the control unit
to allow conditional branching
in the microprogram.

1. When an End microinstruction is encountered, the μPC is loaded with the address of the first CW in the microroutine for the instruction fetch cycle (this address is 0 in Figure 3.17).
2. When a new instruction is loaded into the IR, the μPC is loaded with the starting address of the microroutine for that instruction.
3. When a Branch microinstruction is encountered and the branch condition is satisfied, the μPC is loaded with the branch address.

3.5.1 Microinstructions

Having described a scheme for sequencing microinstructions, we now take a closer look at the format of individual microinstructions. A straightforward way to structure microinstructions is to assign one bit position to each control signal required in the CPU, as in Figure 3.15. However, this scheme has one serious drawback—assigning individual bits to each control signal results in long microinstructions, because the number of required signals is usually large. Moreover, only a few bits are set to 1 (to be used for active gating) in any given microinstruction, which means the available bit space is poorly used. Consider again the single-bus CPU of Figure 3.1, and assume that it contains only four general-purpose registers, R0, R1, R2, and R3. Some of the connections in this CPU are permanently enabled, namely, the output of the IR to the decoding circuits and both inputs to the ALU. The remaining connections to various registers require a total of 20 gating signals. Additional control signals not shown in the figure are also needed, including the Read, Write, Clear Y, Set Carry-in, WMFC, and End signals. Finally, we must specify the function to be performed by the ALU. Let us assume that 16 functions are provided, including Add, Subtract, AND, and XOR. These functions depend on the particular ALU used and do not necessarily show a one-to-one correspondence with the machine instruction OP codes. In total, 42 control signals are needed.

In the simple encoding scheme described earlier, the need for 42 control signals means that at least 42 bits are needed in each microinstruction. Fortunately, the length of the microinstructions can be reduced easily. Most signals are not needed simultaneously, and many signals are mutually exclusive. For example, only one function of the ALU can be activated at a time. The source for a data transfer must be unique, because it is not possible to gate the contents of two different registers onto the bus at the same time. Read and Write signals to the memory cannot be active simultaneously. This suggests that signals can be grouped so that all mutually exclusive signals are placed in the same group. Thus, at most one *microoperation* per group is specified in any microinstruction. Then it is possible to use a binary coding scheme to represent the signals within a group. For example, four bits suffice to represent the 16 available functions in the ALU. Register output control signals can be placed in a group consisting of PC_{out}, MDR_{out}, Z_{out}, $Address_{out}$, $R0_{out}$, $R1_{out}$, $R2_{out}$, $R3_{out}$, and $TEMP_{out}$. Any one of these can be selected by a unique 4-bit code.

Further natural groupings can be made for the remaining signals. Figure 3.19 shows an example of a partial format for the microinstructions, in which each group occupies a field large enough to contain the required codes. Most fields must include one inactive code for the case in which no action is required. For example, the all-zero pattern in F1 indicates that none of the registers that may be specified in this field should have its contents placed on the bus. An inactive code is not needed in all fields. For example, F4 contains 4 bits that specify one of the 16 operations performed in the ALU. Since no spare code is included, the ALU is active during the execution of every microinstruction. However, its activity is monitored by the rest of the machine through register Z, which is loaded only when the Z_{in} signal is activated.

Grouping control signals into fields requires a little more hardware, because decoding circuits must be used to decode the bit patterns of each field into individual control signals. The cost of this additional hardware is more than offset by the reduced number of bits in each microinstruction, which results in a smaller control store. Note that in Figure 3.19, only 20 bits are needed to store the patterns for the 42 signals.

So far we have considered grouping and encoding only mutually exclusive control signals. We can extend this idea by enumerating the patterns of required signals in all possible microinstructions. Each meaningful combination of active control signals can then be assigned a distinct code that represents the microinstruction. Such full encoding is likely to further reduce the length of microwords but also to increase the complexity of the required decoder circuits.

Highly encoded schemes that use compact codes to specify only a small number of control functions in each microinstruction are referred to as a *vertical organization.* On the other hand, the minimally encoded scheme of Figure 3.15, in which many resources can be controlled with a single microinstruction, is called a *horizontal organization.* The horizontal approach is useful when higher operating speed is desired and when the machine structure allows parallel use of resources. The vertical approach results in considerably slower operating speeds because more microinstructions are needed to perform the desired control functions. Although fewer bits are required for each

Microinstruction

F1	F2	F3	F4	F5

F1 (4 bits)	F2 (3 bits)	F3 (3 bits)	F4 (4 bits)	F5 (2 bits)
0000: No transfer	000: No transfer	000: No transfer	0000: Add	00: No action
0001: PC_{out}	001: PC_{in}	001: MAR_{in}	0001: Sub	01: Read
0010: MDR_{out}	010: IR_{in}	010: MDR_{in}	$\vdots$	10: Write
0011: Z_{out}	011: Z_{in}	011: $TEMP_{in}$		
0100: $R0_{out}$	100: $R0_{in}$	100: Y_{in}	1111: XOR	
0101: $R1_{out}$	101: $R1_{in}$		$\underbrace{\hspace{2cm}}$	
0110: $R2_{out}$	110: $R2_{in}$		16 ALU	
0111: $R3_{out}$	111: $R3_{in}$		functions	
1010: $TEMP_{out}$				
1011: $Address_{out}$				

F6	F7	F8	F9	$\cdots$

F1 (1 bit)	F2 (1 bit)	F3 (1 bit)	F4 (1 bit)
0: No action	0: Carry-in = 0	0: No action	0: Continue
1: Clear Y	1: Carry-in = 1	1: WMFC	1: End

FIGURE 3.19
An example of a partial format for field-encoded microinstructions.

microinstruction, this does not imply that the total number of bits in the control store is smaller. The significant factor is that less hardware is needed to handle the execution of microinstructions.

Horizontal and vertical organizations represent the two organizational extremes in microprogrammed control. Many intermediate schemes are also possible, in which the degree of encoding is a design parameter. The layout in Figure 3.19 is a horizontal organization, since it groups only mutually exclusive microoperations in the same fields. As a result, it does not limit in any way the CPU's ability to perform various microoperations in parallel.

The example used in this section is based on the structure in Figure 3.1. We have omitted some details that are not essential for understanding the principles of operation. Although we have considered only a subset of all the possible control signals, this subset is representative of actual requirements.

3.5.2 Microprogram Sequencing

The simple microprogram example in Figure 3.15 requires only straightforward sequential execution of microinstructions, except for the branch at the end of the fetch phase. If each machine instruction is implemented by a microroutine of this kind, effective use is made of the microcontrol structure suggested in Figure 3.18, in which a μPC governs the sequencing. A microroutine is entered by decoding the machine instruction into a starting address that is loaded into the μPC. Some branching capability within the microprogram can be introduced through special branch microinstructions that specify the branch address, similar to the way branching is done in machine-level instructions.

With the approach just described, writing microprograms is fairly simple, because standard software techniques can be used. However, this advantage is countered by two major disadvantages. Having a separate microroutine for each machine instruction results in a large total number of microinstructions and a large control store. If most machine instructions involve several addressing modes, there can be many instruction and addressing mode combinations. A separate microroutine for each of these combinations would produce considerable duplication of common parts. We want to organize the microprogram so that the microroutines share as many common parts as possible. This requires many branch microinstructions to transfer control among the various parts. Hence, a second disadvantage arises—execution time is longer because it takes more time to carry out the required branches.

Consider a more complicated example of a complete machine instruction. In Chapter 2, we used instructions of the type

$$\text{ADD} \qquad \text{src,Rdst}$$

which adds the source operand to the contents of register Rdst and places the sum in Rdst, the destination register. Let us assume that the source operand can be specified in the following addressing modes: register, autoincrement, autodecrement, and indexed, as well as the indirect forms of these four modes. We now use this instruction in conjunction with the CPU structure in Figure 3.1 to demonstrate a possible microprogrammed implementation.

A suitable microprogram is presented in flowchart form, for easier understanding, in Figure 3.20. Each box in the chart corresponds to a microinstruction that controls the transfers and operations indicated within the box. The microinstruction is located at the address indicated by the octal number above the upper right-hand corner of the box. Each octal digit represents three bits. We use the octal notation in this example as a convenient shorthand notation for binary numbers. Most of the flowchart in the figure is self-explanatory, although some details warrant elaboration.

Branch Address Modification Using Bit-ORing

The microprogram in Figure 3.20 shows that branches are not always made to a single branch address. This is a direct consequence of combining simple microroutines by sharing common parts. Consider the point labeled α in the figure. At this point, it is necessary to choose between actions required by direct and indirect addressing modes. If the indirect mode is specified in the instruction, then the microinstruction in location 170 is performed to fetch the operand from the memory. If the direct mode is specified,

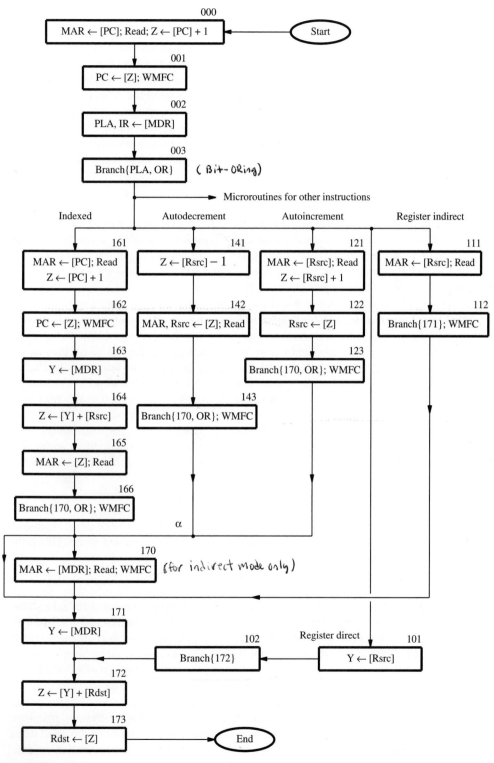

FIGURE 3.20
Flowchart of a microprogram for the ADD src,Rdst instruction.

this fetch must be bypassed by branching immediately to location 171. The most efficient way to bypass microinstruction 170 is to have the preceding branch microinstructions specify the address 170 and then use an OR gate to change the least-significant bit of this address to 1 if the direct addressing mode is involved. This is known as the *bit-ORing* technique for modifying branch addresses. An alternative to the bit-ORing approach is to use two conditional branch microinstructions at locations 123, 143, and 166. Another possibility is to include two fields within a branch microinstruction, where each field is used to generate a particular branch address. Both of these alternatives are inferior to the bit-ORing technique.

Wide-Branch Addressing

Generating branch addresses means the circuitry becomes more complex as the number of branches increases. A particularly complex case arises when the machine instruction fetch is completed and it is necessary to decide which microroutine corresponds to the instruction. It is not unusual to have 30 or more possible branches at this point, depending on the organization of the microprogram.

A simple and inexpensive way of generating the required branch addresses is to use a programmable logic array (PLA). In this case of wide-branch addressing, the OP code of a machine instruction must be translated into the starting address of the corresponding microroutine. This can be done by connecting the OP-code bits of the instruction register as inputs to the PLA, which acts as a decoder. The output of the PLA is the address of the desired microroutine. An example of such use of a PLA appears at microinstruction address 003 in Figure 3.20. Note that at this point, it is also necessary to derive the source operand address and fetch the operand for our ADD instruction. The figure shows five possible branches which, from left to right, correspond to indexed, autodecrement, autoincrement, register direct, and register indirect addressing modes. The choice can again be made by using the bit-ORing technique, as illustrated in the example that follows.

Detailed Example

Let us examine one path of the flowchart in Figure 3.20 in more detail. Consider the case in which the source operand is accessed in the autoincrement mode. This is the path needed to execute the instruction

$$\text{ADD} \qquad \text{(Rsrc)+,Rdst}$$

where Rsrc and Rdst are general-purpose registers in the machine. Figure 3.21 shows the microroutine for this instruction. We assume that the instruction has a 3-bit field used to specify the addressing mode for the source operand, as shown. Bits 10 and 9 denote the indexed, autodecrement, autoincrement, and register modes, using bit patterns 11, 10, 01, and 00, respectively. Bit 8 is used to specify the indirect version of the addressing mode in question. That is, 010 in the mode field means that the direct version of the autoincrement mode is specified, whereas 011 denotes the indirect version of this mode. We also assume that the CPU has 16 registers that can be used for addressing purposes; these are specified using 4-bit codes. Thus, the source operand is fully specified using the mode field and the register indicated by bits 7 through 4. The destination operand in this example is in the register specified by bits 3 through 0.

why is 170 included here since it is direct mode other instructs that are not used are NOT shown

Mode

Contents of IR : | OP code | 0 1 0 | Rsrc | Rdst |

11 10   8 7   4 3   0

machine Instr.

Address (octal)	Microinstruction
000	PC_{out}, MAR_{in}, Read, Clear Y, Set carry-in, Add, Z_{in}
001	Z_{out}, PC_{in}, WMFC
002	MDR_{out}, IR_{in} *300* *HW9*
003	μBranch {$\mu PC \leftarrow 101$ (from PLA); $\mu PC_{5,4} \leftarrow [IR_{10,9}]$; $\mu PC_3 \leftarrow \overline{[IR_{10}]} \cdot \overline{[IR_9]} \cdot [IR_8]$}
121	$Rsrc_{out}$, MAR_{in}, Read, Clear Y, Set carry-in, Add, Z_{in}
122	Z_{out}, $Rsrc_{in}$
123	μBranch {$\mu PC \leftarrow 170$; $\mu PC_0 \leftarrow \overline{[IR_8]}$}, WMFC
170	MDR_{out}, MAR_{in}, Read, WMFC
171	MDR_{out}, Y_{in}
172	$Rdst_{out}$, Add, Z_{in}
173	Z_{out}, $Rdst_{in}$, End

(handwritten annotations beside table)

1   0   0

μPC [170]   set to 170; then changed to 1 by the $\mu PC_0 \leftarrow \overline{[IR_8]}$ part

001|111|00$\cancel{0}$

1 change to 1

$IR_8 = 0$ (bit 8)

$\overline{IR_8} = 1$ (complement)

IR_8 is the variable input

FIGURE 3.21
Microroutine for ADD (Rsrc)+,Rdst.
Note: Microinstruction at location 170 is not executed in this specific example.

Figure 3.21 shows the control signals that are activated by the microinstructions needed to fetch and execute our ADD instruction. Actual signals are shown, instead of encoded bit patterns, to aid understanding. The corresponding codes are similar to those in Figure 3.19.

Since any of the 16 general-purpose registers may be involved in determining the source and destination operand locations, the microinstructions refer to the respective control signals only as $Rsrc_{out}$, $Rsrc_{in}$, $Rdst_{out}$, and $Rdst_{in}$. These signals must be translated into specific register transfer signals by the decoding circuitry connected to the Rsrc and Rdst address fields of the IR. Note that this involves a two-level decoding process. First, the microinstruction field must be decoded to determine that an Rsrc or Rdst register is involved. The decoded output is then used to gate the contents of the Rsrc or Rdst fields in the IR into a second decoder, which produces the gating signals for the actual registers R0 to R15.

The microprogram in Figure 3.20 is derived by combining separate microroutines to save space in the control store; this results in a structure that requires many branch points. Our example in Figure 3.21 has two branch points, so two branch microinstructions are required. In each case, the expression in brackets indicates the branch address that is to be loaded into the μPC and how this address is modified according to the bit-ORing scheme. Consider the microinstruction in location 123 as an illustration: Its unmodified version causes a branch to the microinstruction in 170, which causes another fetch from the main memory corresponding to an indirect addressing mode. When a direct addressing mode appears, this fetch is bypassed by ORing the inverse of the indirect bit in the src address field (that is, bit 8 in the IR) with the 0 bit position of the μPC.

An example of a multiple branch is the microinstruction in location 003. In this case, the five branch addresses differ in the middle octal digit only. Therefore, the octal pattern 101 is obtained from the PLA and loaded into the μPC, and the 3 bits to be ORed with the middle octal digit are supplied by the decoding circuitry connected to the src address mode field (bits 8, 9, and 10 of the IR). Microinstruction addresses have been chosen to make this modification easy to implement; bits 4 and 5 of the μPC are set directly from bits 9 and 10 in the IR. This suffices to select the appropriate microinstruction for all src address modes except the register indirect mode. This mode is covered by setting bit 3 of the μPC to 1 using the AND gate $[\overline{IR_{10}}] \cdot [\overline{IR_9}] \cdot [IR_8]$. Register indirect is a special case, because it is the only indirect mode that does not use the microinstruction at 170.

3.5.3 Microinstructions with Next-Address Field

The microprogram in Figure 3.20 requires several branch microinstructions. These microinstructions perform no useful operation in the datapath; they are needed only to determine the address of the next microinstruction. Thus, they detract from the operating speed of the computer. The situation can become significantly worse when other microroutines are considered. The increase in branch microinstructions stems partly from limitations in the ability to assign successive addresses to all microinstructions that are generally executed in consecutive order.

This problem prompts us to reevaluate the sequencing technique built around an incrementable μPC. A powerful alternative is to include an address field as a part of every microinstruction to indicate the location of the next microinstruction to be fetched. This means, in effect, that every microinstruction becomes a branch microinstruction, in addition to its other functions.

The flexibility of this approach comes at the expense of additional bits for the address field. The severity of this penalty can be assessed as follows: In a typical computer, it is possible to design a complete microprogram with fewer than 4K microinstructions, employing perhaps 50 to 80 bits per microinstruction. This implies that an address field of 12 bits is required. Therefore, approximately one-sixth of the control store capacity would be devoted to addressing. Even if more extensive microprograms are needed, the address field would be only slightly larger.

The most obvious advantage of this approach is that separate branch microinstructions are virtually eliminated. Furthermore, there are few limitations in assigning addresses to microinstructions. These advantages more than offset any negative attributes and make the scheme very attractive. The μPC is replaced with a *microinstruction address register* (μAR), which holds the address of the microinstruction to be fetched. A new control structure that incorporates this feature and supports bit-ORing is shown in Figure 3.22. The next-address bits are fed through the OR gates to the μAR, so that

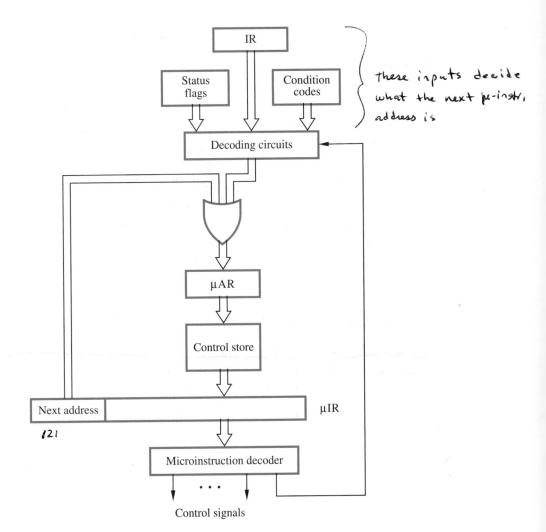

these inputs decide
what the next µ-instr.
address is

FIGURE 3.22
Microinstruction-sequencing organization.

the address can be modified on the basis of the data in the IR, status flags, and condition codes. The decoding circuits include a PLA decoder that is used to generate the starting address of a given microroutine on the basis of the OP code in the IR.

Let us now reconsider the example of Figure 3.21 to see how a microroutine for the machine instruction

$$\text{ADD} \qquad (\text{Rsrc})+,\text{Rdst}$$

can be arranged in light of the ideas introduced in this section. We assume that the CPU has 16 general-purpose registers and that it is structured essentially the same as the block diagram in Figure 3.1. Further, we assume that its microprogrammed control follows the pattern of Figure 3.22.

We need several control signals that are not included in Figure 3.19. Instead of referring to registers R0 to R15 explicitly, we use the names Rsrc and Rdst, which can be decoded into the actual control signals with the data in the src and dst fields of the IR. Branching with the bit-ORing technique requires that we include the appropriate commands in the microinstructions. In the flowchart of Figure 3.20, bit-ORing is needed in microinstructions 003, 123, 143, and 166. In microinstruction 003, the bit-ORing is used to determine the address of the next microinstruction based on the addressing mode of the source operand. The addressing mode is indicated by bits 8 through 10 of the instruction register, as shown in Figure 3.21. Let the signal OR_{mode} control whether or not this bit-ORing is used. In microinstructions 123, 143, and 166, bit-ORing is used to decide if indirect addressing of the source operand is to be used. We use the signal OR_{indsrc} for this purpose. For simplicity, we use separate bits in the microinstructions to denote these signals. Since a PLA is used initially to decode the instruction OP codes, one bit in a microinstruction is used to indicate when the output of the PLA is to be gated into the μAR. Finally, each microinstruction contains an 8-bit field that holds the address of the next microinstruction. Figure 3.23 shows a complete format for these microinstructions. This format is an expansion of the format in Figure 3.19.

Using such microinstructions, we can implement the microroutine of Figure 3.21 as shown in Figure 3.24. In this case, fewer microinstructions are needed because the branch microinstructions are no longer required. The branch microinstructions at locations 003 and 123 have been combined with the microinstructions immediately preceding them. When microinstruction sequencing is controlled by a μPC, the End signal is used to reset the μPC to point to the starting address of the microinstruction that fetches the next machine instruction to be executed. In our example, this starting address is 000_8. However, the microroutine in Figure 3.24 does not terminate by producing the End signal. In an organization such as this, the starting address is not specified by a resetting mechanism triggered by the End signal—instead, it is specified explicitly in the F0 field.

Figure 3.25 gives a more detailed diagram of the control structure of Figure 3.22. It shows how control signals can be decoded from the microinstruction fields and used to control the sequencing. Detailed circuitry for bit-ORing is shown in Figure 3.26.

3.5.4 Prefetching Microinstructions

The major drawback of microprogrammed control is the inherently slower operating speed of the computer. Fetching a microinstruction from the control store takes considerably longer than generating control signals using hardwired circuits. It is unlikely that microprogrammed machines will ever match the speed of hardwired ones.

Having decided to use microprogramming, the designer may still wish to produce as fast a machine as possible, probably by choosing the fastest available control store and using long microinstructions to simultaneously generate as many control signals as possible. The designer may also use prefetching, which we introduced in Section 3.4.2. Much faster operation is achieved if the next microinstruction is prefetched while the current one is being executed. In this way, most of the execution time can be overlapped with the fetch time. Thus, the overall machine speed depends on the fetch times.

Microinstruction

F0	F1	F2	F3

F0 (8 bits)	F1 (3 bits)	F2 (3 bits)	F3 (3 bits)
Address of next microinstruction	000: No transfer	000: No transfer	000: Add
	001: PC_{out}	001: PC_{in}	001: Sub
	010: MDR_{out}	010: IR_{in}	010: MDR_{in}
	011: Z_{out}	011: Z_{in}	011: $Temp_{in}$
	100: $Rsrc_{out}$	100: $Rsrc_{in}$	100: Y_{in}
	101: $Rdst_{out}$	101: $Rdst_{in}$	
	110: $TEMP_{out}$		

F4	F5	F6	F7

F4 (4 bits)	F5 (2 bits)	F6 (1 bit)	F7 (1 bit)
0000: Add	00: No action	0: No action	0: Carry-in = 0
0001: Sub	01: Read	1: Clear Y	1: Carry-in = 1
⋮	10: Write		
1111: XOR			

F8	F9	F10	F11

F8 (1 bit)	F9 (1 bit)	F10 (1 bit)	F11 (1 bit)
0: No action	0: No action	0: No action	0: No action
1: WMFC	1: PLA_{out}	1: OR_{mode}	1: OR_{indsrc}

FIGURE 3.23
Format for microinstructions in the example of Section 3.5.3.

Prefetching microinstructions presents some organizational difficulties. Sometimes the status flags and the results of the currently executed microinstruction are needed to determine the address of the next microinstruction. Thus, straightforward prefetching occasionally prefetches a wrong microinstruction. In these cases, the fetch must be repeated with the correct address, which requires more complex hardware. However, the disadvantages are minor, and the prefetching technique is often used.

Handwritten notes (top right):
F9 : 1 ⇒ use PLA_out
F10 : 1 ⇒ OR mode
F11 : 1 ⇒ OR in adrc

Octal address	F0	F1	F2	F3	F4	F5	F6	F7	F8	F9	F10	F11
0 0 0	0 0 0 0 0 0 0 1	0 0 1	0 1 1	0 0 1	0 0 0 0	0 1	1	1	0	0	0	0
0 0 1	0 0 0 0 0 0 1 0	0 1 1	0 0 1	0 0 0	0 0 0 0	0 0	0	0	1	0	0	0
0 0 2	0 0 0 0 0 0 0 0	0 1 0	0 1 0	0 0 0	0 0 0 0	0 0	0	0	0	1	1	0
1 2 1	0 1 0 1 0 0 1 0	1 0 0	0 1 1	0 0 1	0 0 0 0	0 1	1	1	0	0	0	0
1 2 2	0 1 1 1 1 0 0 0	0 1 1	1 0 0	0 0 0	0 0 0 0	0 0	0	0	1	0	0	1
1 7 0	0 1 1 1 1 0 0 1	0 1 0	0 0 0	0 0 1	0 0 0 0	0 1	0	0	1	0	0	0
1 7 1	0 1 1 1 1 0 1 0	0 1 0	0 0 0	1 0 0	0 0 0 0	0 0	0	0	0	0	0	0
1 7 2	0 1 1 1 1 0 1 1	1 0 1	0 1 1	0 0 0	0 0 0 0	0 0	0	0	0	0	0	0
1 7 3	0 0 0 0 0 0 0 0	0 1 1	1 0 1	0 0 0	0 0 0 0	0 0	0	0	0	0	0	0

Handwritten annotations: fetch (bracketing rows 000, 001, 002); ↑ marks at 002, 122, 173; "go back to start fetch cycle →" pointing to row 173; "F0: Addr. of next instr. (000₈ indicates the start addr)"; "003 multiple branch instruc"; "★ combined w/ next address field".

FIGURE 3.24

Implementation of the microroutine of Figure 3.21, using a next-microinstruction address field. (See Figure 3.23 for encoded signals)

3.5.5 Emulation

The main function of microprogrammed control is to provide a means for simple, flexible, and relatively inexpensive execution of machine instructions. However, it also offers other interesting possibilities. Its flexibility in using a machine's resources allows diverse classes of instructions to be implemented. Given a computer with a certain instruction set, it is possible to define additional machine instructions and implement them with extra microroutines.

An extension of the preceding idea leads to another interesting possibility. Suppose we add to the instruction repertoire of a given computer, M_1, an entirely new set of instructions that is in fact the instruction set of a different computer, M_2. Programs written in the machine language of M_2 can then be run on computer M_1; that is, M_1 *emulates* M_2. Emulation allows us to replace obsolete equipment with more up-to-date machines. If the replacement computer fully emulates the original one, then no software changes have to be made to run existing programs. Thus, emulation facilitates transitions to new computer systems with minimal disruption.

Emulation is easiest when the machines involved have similar architectures. However, emulation can also succeed using machines with totally different architectures.

3.6
CONCLUDING REMARKS

In this chapter, we have presented an overview of the organization of the computer's central processing unit. Commercially available machines use many variations of the organizations presented here. The choice of a particular organization involves trade-offs between speed of execution and cost of implementation. Other factors also come into play, such as the technology used, the flexibility for modification, and the need for special capabilities in the instruction set of the computer.

Two approaches were presented for implementing the control unit of a CPU—hardwired control and microprogrammed control. Hardwired control is the best approach when speed of operation is most important. Microprogrammed control results in

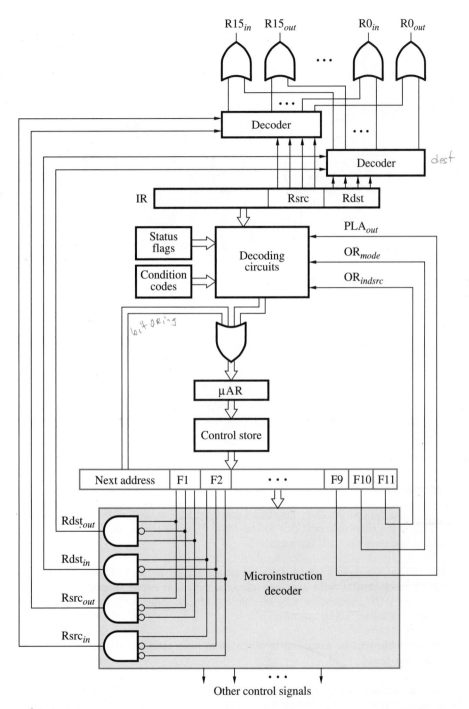

FIGURE 3.25

Details of the circuitry that generates the control signals in Figure 3.22.

145

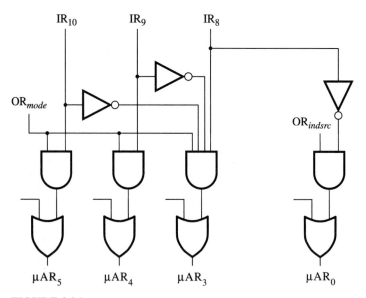

FIGURE 3.26
Control circuitry for bit-ORing (part of the decoding circuits in Figure 3.25).

slower CPUs, but it provides considerable flexibility in implementing instruction sets and facilitates adding new instructions to existing machines.

Today's computing requirements place a premium on speed, even in relatively inexpensive personal computers. For this reason, most present-day processors use hardwired control.

PROBLEMS

3.1. Why is the Wait-for-Memory-Function-Completed step needed when reading from or writing to the main memory? Can the circuit in Figure 3.11a be used regardless of the relative speeds of the CPU and memory?

3.2. The CPU of a computer uses a control sequence similar to that in Figure 3.5. Assume that a memory read or write operation takes the same time as one internal CPU step and that both the CPU and the memory are controlled by the same clock. Rewrite the control sequence of Figure 3.5 for this machine.

3.3. Repeat Problem 3.2 for a machine in which the memory access time is equal to twice the CPU clock period.

3.4. Assume that propagation delays along the bus and through the ALU of Figure 3.1 are 2 and 20 ns, respectively. The setup time for the registers is 1 ns, and the hold time is 0. What is the minimum time that must be allowed for performing each of the following operations?

(a) Transfer data from one register to another.
(b) Increment the program counter.

3.5. Write the sequence of control steps required for the bus structure in Figure 3.1 for each of the following instructions:

(*a*) Add the (immediate) number NUM to register R1.
(*b*) Add the contents of memory location NUM to register R1.
(*c*) Add the contents of the memory location whose address is at memory location NUM to register R1.

Assume that each instruction consists of two words and that each word occupies one address location. The first word of an instruction specifies the operation and the addressing mode, and the second word contains the number NUM.

3.6. The three instructions in Problem 3.5 have many common control steps. However, some of these control steps occur at different counts of the control step counter. Show a scheme that exploits these common steps to reduce the complexity of the encoder block in Figure 3.8.

3.7. Consider the Add instruction that has the control sequence given in Figure 3.5. The CPU is driven by a continuously running clock, such that each control step is 20 ns in duration. How long will the CPU have to wait in steps 2 and 5, assuming that a memory read operation takes 80 ns to complete? What percentage of time is the CPU idle during execution of this instruction?

3.8. In a 32-bit, byte-addressable machine, the PC should be incremented by 4 after fetching an instruction word from memory. Suggest some modification to Figure 3.1 to simplify this operation.

3.9. Show the control steps for the Add (R3),R1 instruction considered in Figure 3.5, but assume that the CPU has the structure given in Figure 3.13.

3.10. Show the control steps for the Branch-on-Negative instruction discussed in Section 3.2.1, but assume that the CPU has the structure given in Figure 3.13.

3.11. Assume that one of the registers, R*i*, in Figure 3.1 serves as a stack pointer, SP. Show the control steps needed to implement the Branch-to-Subroutine instruction of the 68000 processor in this simple CPU. See Table C.5 for details of the BSR instruction. Note that both the program counter and the stack pointer need to be modified by the constant 4.

3.12. Repeat Problem 3.11 for the CPU in Figure 3.13. Suggest an appropriate mechanism for dealing with the constant 4.

3.13. Section 3.4.1 states that simple latches of Figure 3.3 cannot be used to implement the registers in Figure 3.13. Instead, edge-triggered or master-slave circuits are needed. However, would it be possible to use the latches of Figure 3.3 if a Z register were included between the output of the ALU and the C bus, similar to Figure 3.1? How would this affect performance?

3.14. Show how master-slave flip-flops can be used to implement the registers in Figure 3.13 in order to allow the operation R1 ← [R1] + [R2] to be performed in one clock cycle. Sketch a circuit that shows how flip-flops must be connected to accomplish this task. Draw a timing diagram that indicates when the changes in control signals and in the state of R1 occur. How does your circuit affect the performance of the system?

3.15. Repeat Problem 3.14 using positive-edge-triggered D flip-flops, such as those illustrated in Figure A.28. (*Hint:* At the positive edge of each clock cycle, set the new state of the flip-flop to be equal to the old state, unless $R1_{in}$ is active, in which case the value from bus C should be used to set the flip-flop.)

3.16. Consider a 16-bit, byte-addressable machine that has the organization of Figure 3.1. Bytes at even and odd addresses are transferred on the high- and low-order 8 bits of the memory bus, respectively. Show a suitable gating scheme for connecting register MDR to the memory bus and to the internal CPU bus to allow byte transfers to occur. When a byte is being handled, it should always be in the low-order byte position inside the CPU.

3.17. Design an oscillator using an inverter and a delay element. Assuming that the delay element introduces a delay T, what is the frequency of oscillation?

Modify the oscillator circuit such that oscillations can be started and stopped under the control of an asynchronous input RUN. When the oscillator is stopped, the width of the last pulse at its output must be equal to T, independent of the time at which RUN becomes inactive.

3.18. Some operations in an ALU circuit, such as Multiply, may take longer to complete than simple operations such as Add and Subtract. For performance reasons, it can be arranged to have the CPU clock period correspond to the time needed to perform simple operations and to extend the clock period when a complex operation is encountered. Assume that one of the control signals generated by the encoder block in Figure 3.8 is called $\overline{\text{Long}}$/Short. When this line is equal to 1, the control step counter is advanced at successive positive edges of the clock. When the line is equal to 0, the length of the time slot is doubled. Assume that the counter has an Enable input and that it is advanced on the positive edge of the clock if Enable $= 1$. Design a circuit that generates the Enable signal to vary the size of the control steps as needed.

3.19. The output of a shift register is inverted and fed back to its input, to form a counting circuit known as a Johnson counter.

(a) What is the count sequence of a 4-bit Johnson counter, starting with the state 0000?
(b) Show how you can use a Johnson counter to generate the timing signals T_1, T_2, and so on in Figure 3.8, assuming there is a maximum of 10 timing intervals.

3.20. An ALU of a processor uses the shift register shown in Figure P3.1 to perform shift and rotate operations. Inputs to the control logic for this register consist of

ASR	Arithmetic Shift Right
LSR	Logic Shift Right
SL	Shift Left
ROR	Rotate Right
LD	Parallel Load

All shift and load operations are controlled by one clock input. The shift register is implemented with edge-triggered D flip-flops. Give a complete logic diagram for the control logic and for bits r_0, r_1, and r_{15} of the shift register.

3.21. A digital controller in Figure P3.2 has three outputs, X, Y, and Z, and two inputs, A and B. It is externally driven by a clock. The controller is continuously going through the following sequence of events: At the beginning of the first clock cycle, line X is set to 1. At the beginning of the second clock cycle, either line Y or Z is set to 1, depending on whether line A is equal to 1 or 0, respectively. The controller then waits until line B is set to 1. On the following positive edge of the clock, the controller sets output Z to 1 for the duration of one clock cycle, then resets all output signals to 0 for one clock cycle. The

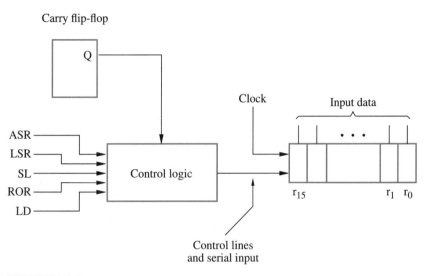

FIGURE P3.1
Organization of shift-register control for Problem 3.20.

sequence is repeated, starting at the next positive edge of the clock. Give a suitable logic design for this controller.

3.22. Write a microroutine, such as the one shown in Figure 3.21, for the instruction

$$\text{MOV} \qquad \text{X(Rsrc),Rdst}$$

where the source and destination operands are specified in indexed and register addressing modes, respectively.

3.23. A BGT (Branch if > 0) machine instruction has the expression $Z + (N \oplus V) = 0$ as its branch condition, where Z, N, and V are the zero, negative, and overflow condition flags, respectively. Write a microroutine that can implement this instruction. Show the circuitry needed to test the condition codes appropriately.

3.24. Write a combined microroutine that can implement the BGT (Branch if > 0), BPL (Branch if Plus), and BR (Branch Unconditionally) instructions. The branch conditions for the BGT and BPL instructions are $Z + (N \oplus V) = 0$ and $N = 0$, respectively. What is the total number of microinstructions required? How many microinstructions are needed if a separate microroutine is used for each machine instruction?

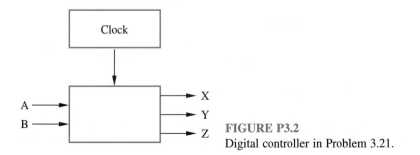

FIGURE P3.2
Digital controller in Problem 3.21.

3.25. Figure 3.21 shows an example of a microroutine in which bit-ORing is used to modify microinstruction addresses. Write an equivalent routine, without using bit-ORing, in which conditional branch microinstructions are used. How many additional microinstructions are needed? Assume that the conditional branch microinstructions can test some of the bits in the IR.

3.26. Can the microprogram in Figure 3.20 be modified to implement the general 68000 microprocessor instruction

MOVE   src,dst

Show a detailed flowchart.

3.27. Is the microprogram in Figure 3.20 suitable for implementing the 68000 microprocessor instruction

ADD   src,dst

If not, show how it should be modified.

3.28. Figure P3.3 gives part of the microinstruction sequence corresponding to one of the machine instructions of a microprogrammed computer. Microinstruction B is followed by C, E, F, or I, depending on bits b_6 and b_5 of the machine instruction register. Compare the three possible implementations described below.

(a) Microinstruction sequencing is accomplished by means of a microprogram counter. Branching is achieved by microinstructions of the form

If b_6b_5 branch to X

where b_6b_5 is the branch condition and X is the branch address.

(b) Same as part a except that the branch microinstruction has the form

Branch to X

where X is a base branch address. The branch address is modified by bit-ORing of bits b_5 and b_6 with the appropriate bits within X.

(c) A field in each microinstruction specifies the address of the next microinstruction, which has bit-ORing capability.

Assign suitable addresses for all microinstructions in Figure P3.3 for each of the implementations in parts a through c. Note that you may need to insert branch instructions in some cases. You may choose arbitrary addresses, as long as they are consistent with the method of sequencing used. For example, in part a, you could choose addresses as follows:

Address	Microinstruction
00010	A
00011	B
00100	If $b_6b_5 = 00$ branch to XXXXX
. . .	. . .
XXXXX	C

3.29. Assume you want to reduce the number of bits needed to encode the control signals in Figure 3.19. Show a possible format for encoding these signals that requires a maximum

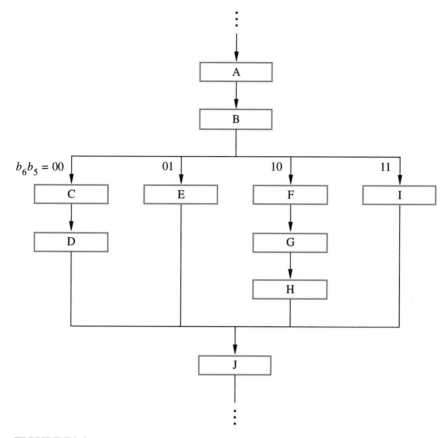

FIGURE P3.3
A microinstruction-sequence pattern.

of 18 bits, instead of the 20 in the figure. No two signals may be in the same field if both of them are likely to be specified in any one microinstruction.

3.30. Can the control signals in Figure 3.19 be encoded using only 12 bits in a microinstruction? If they can, what is the effect of such encoding on microroutines corresponding to the Add and Branch machine instructions in Figures 3.5 and 3.6, respectively?

3.31. Suggest a format for microinstructions, similar to Figure 3.19, if the CPU is organized as shown in Figure 3.13.

3.32. What are the relative merits of horizontal and vertical microinstruction formats? Relate your answer to the answers to Problems 3.29 and 3.30.

3.33. What are the advantages and disadvantages of hardwired and microprogrammed control?

CHAPTER 4

Input-Output Organization

One of the basic features of a computer is its ability to exchange data with other devices. This communication capability allows a user, for example, to enter a program and its data via the keyboard of a video terminal and receive results on a display or a printer. A computer may be required to communicate with a variety of equipment, such as video terminals, printers, and plotters, as well as magnetic disk and magnetic tape drives. In addition to these standard I/O devices, a computer may be connected to other types of equipment. For example, in industrial control applications, input to a computer may be the digital output of a voltmeter, a temperature sensor, or a fire alarm. Similarly, the output of a computer may be a digitally coded command to change the speed of a motor, open a valve, or cause a robot to move in a specified manner. A general-purpose computer should have the ability to deal with a wide range of device characteristics in varying environments.

In this chapter, we consider in detail various ways I/O operations are performed. First, we consider these operations from the point of view of the programmer. Then we present some of the hardware needed for buses and I/O interfaces.

4.1
ACCESSING I/O DEVICES

Most modern computers use a single bus arrangement, as shown in Figure 4.1. The processor, memory, and I/O devices are connected to this bus, which consists of three sets of lines used to carry address, data, and control signals. Each I/O device is assigned a unique set of addresses. When the processor places a particular address on the address lines, the device that recognizes this address responds to the commands issued on the control lines. The processor requests either a read or a write operation, and the requested data are transferred over the data lines. As Section 2.6 explains, when I/O devices and the memory share the same address space, the arrangement is called memory-mapped I/O.

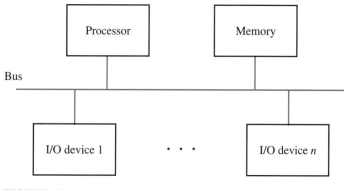

FIGURE 4.1
A single bus structure.

With memory-mapped I/O, any machine instruction that can access memory can be used to transfer data to or from an I/O device. For example, if DATAIN is the address of the input buffer associated with the keyboard, the instruction

Move   DATAIN,R0

reads the data from DATAIN and stores them in processor register R0. Similarly, the instruction

Move   R0,DATAOUT

sends the contents of register R0 to location DATAOUT, which may be the output data buffer of a display unit or a printer.

Many processors, such as the 68000, use memory-mapped I/O. Others, however, use alternative approaches for handling I/O operations. Some processors have special instructions, such as In and Out, to perform I/O transfers. For example, Intel microprocessors have special I/O instructions and a separate 16-bit address space for I/O devices; but, an I/O device can also be connected to the processor in a memory-mapped fashion. In the PowerPC, I/O devices can be placed in the same address space as the memory or in a separate address space. Although the PowerPC does not have special I/O instructions, it has a special control register that can be used to switch from one address space to another.

Figure 4.2 illustrates the hardware required to connect an I/O device to the bus. The address decoder enables the device to recognize its address when it appears on the address lines. The data register holds data to be transferred to the processor from an input device or receives data from the processor for transfer to an output device. The status register contains information relevant to the operation of the I/O device. Such registers are also connected to the data bus and assigned unique addresses. The address decoder, the data and status registers, and the control circuitry required to coordinate I/O transfers constitute the device's *interface circuit*.

I/O devices operate at speeds vastly different from that of the processor. For example, when a human operator enters characters at a keyboard, the processor can execute millions of instructions between successive character entries. Hence, we must ensure that an instruction to read a character from the keyboard is executed only when a

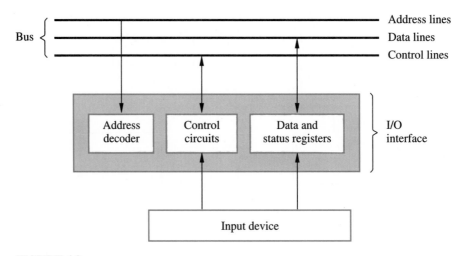

FIGURE 4.2
I/O interface for an input device.

character is available in the input buffer of the keyboard interface. We must also ensure that an input character is read only once.

The basic ideas used in input and output operations are introduced in Section 2.6. If the input device is a keyboard, a synchronization control flag, SIN, is included in the interface circuit as part of the status register. This flag is set to 1 when a character is entered at the keyboard and cleared to 0 when this character is read by the processor. The required synchronization between the processor and the input device is achieved by a program loop that repeatedly reads the status register until SIN becomes equal to 1. Then the program reads the input data register. A similar procedure can be used to control output operations, using an output synchronization flag, SOUT.

To review the basic concepts, consider the example of I/O operations involving a keyboard and a video display in a computer system. The three registers shown in Figure 4.3 are used in the data transfer operations. The STATUS register contains the two

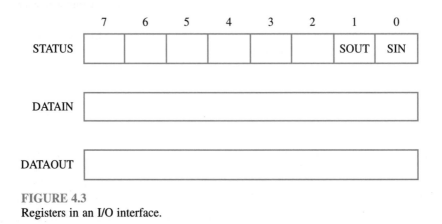

FIGURE 4.3
Registers in an I/O interface.

	Move	#LINE,R1	Initialize memory pointer.
WAITK	TestBit	#0,STATUS	Test SIN.
	Branch=0	WAITK	Wait for character to be entered.
	Move	DATAIN,R0	Read character.
WAITD	TestBit	#1,STATUS	Test SOUT.
	Branch=0	WAITD	Wait for display to become ready.
	Move	R0,DATAOUT	Send character to display.
	Move	R0,(R1)+	Store character and advance pointer.
	Compare	#$0D,R0	Check if carriage return.
	Branch≠0	WAITK	If not, get another character.
	Call	PROCESS	Call a subroutine to process the input line.

FIGURE 4.4

A program that reads one line from the keyboard and sends it to the display.

control flags, SIN and SOUT, which provide status information for the keyboard and the display unit, respectively. Data from the keyboard are held in the DATAIN register until they are sent to the processor, and data received from the processor to be sent to the display are stored in the DATAOUT register.

Figure 4.4 gives a program that reads a line of characters from the keyboard, stores it in a memory buffer starting at location LINE, and calls a subroutine to process these data. As each character is read, it is *echoed back* to the display. Register R1 is used as a pointer to the memory. The contents of R1 are updated using the autoincrement addressing mode so that successive characters are stored at successive memory locations.

Each character is checked to see if it is the Carriage Return character, which has the ASCII code 0D (hex). If it is, the subroutine PROCESS is called; otherwise, the program waits for another character from the keyboard.

This example illustrates *program-controlled I/O*, in which the processor repeatedly checks a status flag to achieve the required synchronization between the processor and the input device. Two other mechanisms are commonly used for implementing I/O operations—interrupts and direct memory access. With interrupts, synchronization is implemented by having the I/O device send a special interrupt signal over the bus whenever the device is ready for a data transfer operation. In direct memory access, a technique used for high-speed I/O devices, the device interface transfers data directly to or from the memory, without continuous involvement by the processor. We discuss these two mechanisms in the next two sections. Then we examine the hardware involved, which includes the processor bus and the I/O device interface.

4.2
INTERRUPTS

In the example of Figure 4.4, the program enters a wait loop in which it repeatedly tests the device status. During this period, the processor is not performing any useful computation. In many situations, other tasks can be performed while the processor waits for an I/O device to become ready. To do this, we can arrange for the I/O device to alert the processor when it is ready. It does so by sending a hardware signal called an *interrupt* to the processor. At least one of the bus control lines, called an *interrupt-request* line, is usually dedicated for this purpose. The processor can instruct an I/O device interface to activate this line as soon as it is ready for a data transfer. Since the processor is no longer required to continuously check the status of external devices, it can perform other useful functions while waiting. Indeed, by using interrupts, such waiting periods can ideally be eliminated.

Consider a task that requires some computations to be performed and the results to be printed on a line printer. This is followed by more computations and output, and so on. Let the program consist of two routines, COMPUTE and PRINT. Assume that COMPUTE produces n lines of output, to be printed by the PRINT routine.

The required task can be performed by repeatedly executing first the COMPUTE routine and then the PRINT routine. The printer accepts only one line of text at a time. Hence, the PRINT routine must send one line of text, wait for it to be printed, then send the next line, and so on, until all the results have been printed. The disadvantage of this simple approach is that the processor spends a considerable amount of time waiting for the printer to be ready. If it is possible to overlap printing and computation, that is, to execute the COMPUTE routine while printing is in progress, a faster overall speed of execution results. This is done as follows: First, the COMPUTE routine is executed to produce the first n lines of output. Then the PRINT routine is executed to send the first line of text to the printer. At this point, instead of waiting for the line to be printed, the PRINT routine can be temporarily suspended and execution of the COMPUTE routine can continue. Whenever the printer becomes ready, it alerts the processor by sending an interrupt-request signal. In response, the processor interrupts execution of the COMPUTE routine and transfers control to the PRINT routine. The PRINT routine sends the second line to the printer and is again suspended. Then the interrupted COMPUTE routine resumes execution at the point of interruption. This process continues until all n lines have been printed.

The PRINT routine is restarted whenever the next set of n lines is available for printing. If COMPUTE takes longer to generate n lines than the time required to print them, the processor will be performing useful computations all the time.

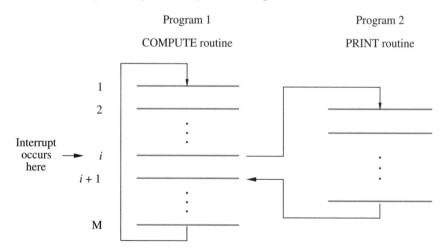

FIGURE 4.5
Transfer of control through the use of interrupts.

The routine executed in response to an interrupt request is called the *interrupt-service routine*. This is the PRINT routine in our example. Interrupts resemble subroutine calls. Assume that an interrupt request arrives during execution of instruction i in Figure 4.5. The processor first completes execution of instruction i. Then it loads the program counter with the address of the first instruction of the interrupt-service routine. For the time being, let us assume that this address is hardwired in the processor. After executing the interrupt-service routine, the processor has to return to instruction $i + 1$. Therefore, when an interrupt occurs, the current contents of the PC, which point to instruction $i + 1$, must be put in temporary storage. A Return-from-interrupt instruction at the end of the interrupt-service routine reloads the PC from that temporary storage location, causing execution to resume at instruction $i + 1$. In many processors, the return address is saved on the processor stack. Alternatively, it can be saved in a special location, such as a register provided for this purpose.

Note that, as part of handling interrupts, the processor must inform the device that its request has been recognized so that it can remove its interrupt-request signal. A special control signal on the bus called an *interrupt-acknowledge* signal, used in some of the interrupt schemes we discuss later, serves this function. A common alternative is to have the transfer of data between the processor and the I/O device interface accomplish the same purpose. The execution of an instruction in the interrupt-service routine that accesses a status or data register in the device interface implies to the device that its interrupt request has been recognized.

So far, an interrupt-service routine is treated much like a subroutine. An important difference is that a subroutine performs a function required by the program from which it is called, whereas the interrupt-service routine may have nothing in common with the program being executed at the time the interrupt request is received. In fact, the two programs often belong to different users. Therefore, before starting execution of the interrupt-service routine, any information that may be altered during the execution of that routine must be saved. This information must be restored before execution of the interrupted program is resumed. In this way, the original program can continue execution without being affected in any way by the interruption, except for the time delay. The information that must be saved and restored typically includes the condition code flags and the contents of any registers used by both the interrupted program and the interrupt-service routine.

The task of saving and restoring information can be done automatically by the processor or by program instructions. Most modern processors save only the minimum amount of information needed to maintain the integrity of program execution. This is because the process of saving and restoring registers involves memory transfers that increase the total execution time and, hence, represent execution overhead. Saving registers also increases the delay between the time an interrupt request is received and the start of execution of the interrupt-service routine. This delay is called *interrupt latency*. In some applications, a long interrupt latency is unacceptable. For these reasons, the amount of information saved automatically by the processor when an interrupt request is accepted should be kept to a minimum. Typically, the processor saves only the contents of the program counter and the processor status register. Any additional information to be saved must be saved by program instructions at the beginning of the interrupt-service routine and restored at the end of the routine.

In some early processors, particularly those with a small number of registers, all registers are saved automatically by the processor hardware. The data saved are restored to their respective registers as part of the execution of the Return-from-interrupt instruction. To minimize the interrupt overhead, some computers provide two types of interrupts. One saves all register contents, and the other does not. A particular I/O device may use either type, depending on its response time requirements. Another interesting approach is to provide duplicate sets of processor registers. In this case, a different set of registers can be used by the interrupt-service routine, thus eliminating the need to save and restore registers.

An interrupt is more than a simple mechanism for coordinating I/O transfers. In general, interrupts enable the transfer of control from one program to another to be initiated by an event outside the computer. Execution of the interrupted program resumes after execution of the interrupt-service routine is completed. Interrupt handling is an important function in operating systems. Interrupts are also used in many control applications in which the processing of certain routines must be accurately timed relative to external events. This type of application is referred to as *real-time processing*.

4.2.1 Enabling and Disabling Interrupts

The facilities provided in a computer must give the programmer complete control over the events that take place during program execution. The arrival of an interrupt request from an external device causes the processor to suspend the execution of one program and start the execution of another. Interrupts can arrive at any time and may alter the sequence of events envisaged by the programmer. Hence, the interruption of program execution must be carefully controlled. All computers provide the programmer with the ability to enable and disable such interruptions at various times during program execution. We now examine this capability in some detail.

There are many situations in which the processor should ignore interrupt requests. For example, in the Compute-Print program in Figure 4.5, an interrupt request from the printer should be accepted only if there are output lines to be printed. After the last line of a set of *n* lines is printed, interrupts should be disabled until another set of lines is available for printing. In another case, it may be necessary to guarantee that a particular sequence of instructions is executed to the end without interruption, because the interrupt-service routine may change some of the data used by those instructions. For these reasons, the programmer must be able to enable and disable interrupts. One way is to provide machine instructions, such as Interrupt-enable and Interrupt-disable, that perform these functions.

Let us consider in detail a single interrupt request from one device. When a device activates the interrupt-request signal, it keeps this signal activated until it learns that the processor has accepted its request. This means that the interrupt-request signal is active during execution of the interrupt-service routine, perhaps until it reaches an instruction that accesses the device. It is essential to ensure that this active request signal does not lead to successive interruptions, causing the system to enter an infinite loop from which it cannot recover. Several mechanisms can solve this problem. We describe three basic possibilities here; other schemes that can handle more than one interrupting device are presented later.

The first possibility is to have the processor hardware ignore the interrupt-request line until the first instruction of the interrupt-service routine has been completely executed. By using an Interrupt-disable instruction as the first instruction in the interrupt-service routine, the programmer can ensure that no further interruptions occur until an Interrupt-enable instruction is executed. Typically, this is the last instruction in the interrupt-service routine before the Return-from-interrupt instruction. The processor must guarantee that the Return-from-interrupt instruction is completely executed before further interruption can occur.

The second option, which is in common practice, is to have the processor automatically disable interrupts before it starts executing the interrupt-service routine. That is, after saving the contents of the PC and the processor status (PS), the processor automatically performs the equivalent of executing an Interrupt-disable instruction. Often, one bit in the PS register, the *interrupt mask*, indicates whether interrupts are disabled. The processor sets this bit to disable interrupts before it starts execution of the interrupt-service routine. Similarly, the processor may automatically enable interrupts when a Return-from-interrupt instruction is executed. This is one of the results of restoring the old contents of the PS register. The interrupt mask bit in the copy of the PS that was saved must be equal to 0. Otherwise, interruption would not have occurred.

The third approach is to arrange the interrupt-handling circuit in the processor so that it responds only to the leading edge of the interrupt-request signal. Since only one such transition is seen by the processor for every request generated by the device, no further interruption will occur. Such interrupt-request lines are said to be *edge-triggered*.

Before we proceed to more complex aspects of interrupts, let us summarize the sequence of events in handling an interrupt request from a single device. Assuming that interrupts are enabled, the following is a typical scenario:

1. The device raises an interrupt request.
2. The processor interrupts the program currently being executed.
3. Interrupts are disabled.
4. The device is informed that its request has been recognized, and in response, it deactivates the interrupt-request signal.
5. The action requested by the interrupt is performed by the interrupt-service routine.
6. Execution of the interrupted program is resumed, with interrupts enabled.

4.2.2 Handling Multiple Devices

We now consider the situation in which several devices capable of initiating interrupts are connected to the processor. Because these devices operate independently, there is no specific order in which they generate interrupts. For example, device X may request an interrupt while an interrupt caused by device Y is being serviced, or all devices may request interrupts at exactly the same time. This leads to several questions:

1. How can the processor recognize the device requesting an interrupt?
2. Because different devices probably require different interrupt-service routines, how can the processor obtain the starting address of the appropriate routine?

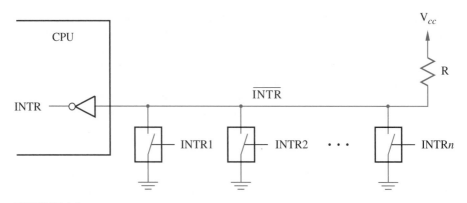

FIGURE 4.6

An equivalent circuit for an open-collector bus used to implement a common interrupt-request line.

3. Should a device be allowed to interrupt the processor while another interrupt is being serviced?
4. How should two or more simultaneous interrupt requests be handled?

The ways these problems are resolved vary considerably from one machine to another. The approach taken in any machine is an important consideration in determining the machine's suitability for a given application. We now discuss some of the more common techniques.

Device Identification

Consider the case in which an external device requests an interrupt by activating an interrupt-request line that is common to all devices. A single line can be used to serve several devices by means of the organization depicted in Figure 4.6. All n devices are connected to a common line via switches to ground. To raise an interrupt request, a device closes its switch. Thus, if all interrupt-request signals $INTR_1$ to $INTR_n$ are inactive, that is, in the 0 state, the interrupt-request line is maintained in the high-voltage state by resistor R. This is the inactive state of the line. When a device requests an interrupt by closing its switch, the voltage on the line drops to 0, causing INTR to go to 1. Hence, the interrupt request signal received by the processor is given by

$$INTR = INTR_1 + \cdots + INTR_n$$

It is customary to use the complemented form, $\overline{INTR}$, to name the interrupt-request signal on the common line because this signal is low when the line is active.

In the electronic implementation of the circuit in Figure 4.6, special gates are used as switches. These gates are known as *open-collector* gates, for bipolar circuits, or *open-drain* gates, for MOS circuits. The output of such a gate is equivalent to a switch to ground. The switch is open when the gate's input is in the 0 state and closed when it is in the 1 state. The voltage level, and hence the logic state, at the output of the gate is determined by the data applied to all the gates connected to the bus, according to the preceding equation.

When a request is received over the common interrupt-request line, additional information is needed to identify the particular device that activated the line. The required information is provided in the status registers of the devices. When a device raises an interrupt request, it sets a bit in its status register, which we call the Interrupt-Request (IRQ) bit. The interrupt-service routine begins by polling the devices in some order. The first device encountered with its IRQ bit set is the device that is serviced, and an appropriate subroutine is called to provide the requested service.

The polling scheme is simple and easy to implement. Its main disadvantage is the time spent interrogating the IRQ bits of all the devices that may not be requesting any service. An alternative approach is to use vectored interrupts, as we describe next.

Vectored Interrupts

To reduce the time involved in the polling process, a device requesting an interrupt may identify itself directly to the processor. Then the processor can immediately start executing the corresponding interrupt-service routine. The term *vectored interrupts* refers to all interrupt-handling schemes based on this approach.

A device requesting an interrupt can identify itself by sending a special code to the processor over the bus. This technique enables the processor to identify individual devices even if they share a single interrupt-request line. The code supplied by the device may represent the starting address of the interrupt-service routine for that device. In some cases, only a few bits of the address are supplied, and the remainder of the address is fixed. This reduces the number of bits that the I/O device needs to transmit, thus simplifying the design of its interface circuit. However, having a code with only a few bits limits the number of devices that can be automatically identified by the processor. For example, if four bits are supplied by the device, only 16 different devices can be recognized by the processor. To accommodate a larger number of devices, each code can be assigned to a group of devices; when a given code is received, the interrupt-service routine can identify the device that generated the interrupt by polling the devices in the group represented by that code.

This arrangement implies that the interrupt-service routine for a given device must always start at the same location. The programmer can gain some flexibility by storing in this location an instruction that causes a jump or a branch to the appropriate routine. In many machines, this is done automatically by the interrupt-handling mechanism. The processor uses the code received from the interrupting device as an indirect specification of the starting address of the interrupt-service routine. That is, this code is an address of a memory location that contains the required starting address. The contents of this location, which constitute a new value for the PC, are referred to as the *interrupt vector*. In some machines, the interrupt vector also includes a new value for the processor status register.

Consider now the hardware needed to support vectored interrupts. The processor may not respond immediately when it receives an interrupt request. Some delay occurs because the processor is required to complete execution of the current instruction. Further delays may occur if interrupts happen to be disabled at the time the request is generated. Because the processor may require the use of the bus during this delay, the interrupting device must not be allowed to put data on the bus until the processor is ready to receive it. Coordination is achieved through the interrupt-acknowledge (INTA) control signal mentioned in Section 4.2. As soon as the processor is ready to service the interrupt, it activates the INTA line. This, in turn, causes the device interface to place the interrupt-vector code on the data lines of the bus and to turn off the INTR signal.

Interrupt Nesting

Section 4.2.1 suggests that interrupts should be disabled during the execution of an interrupt-service routine to ensure that an interrupt request from one device does not cause more than one interruption. The same arrangement is often used when several devices are involved, in which case execution of a given interrupt-service routine, once started, always continues to completion before a second interrupt request is accepted by the processor. Interrupt-service routines are typically short, and the delay they may cause in responding to a second request is acceptable for most simple devices.

For some devices, however, a long delay in responding to an interrupt request may cause errors in the operation of the computer. Consider, for example, a computer that keeps track of the time of day using a real-time clock. This clock sends interrupt requests to the processor at regular intervals. For each of these requests, the processor executes a short interrupt-service routine to increment a set of counters in the memory that keep track of time in seconds, minutes, and so on. Proper operation requires that the delay in responding to an interrupt request from the real-time clock be small compared to the interval between two successive requests. To satisfy this requirement in the presence of other interrupting devices, the processor may have to accept an interrupt request from the clock during the execution of an interrupt-service routine for another device.

This example suggests that I/O devices should be organized in a priority structure. An interrupt request from a high-priority device should be accepted while the processor is servicing another request from a low-priority device.

A multilevel priority organization means that during execution of an interrupt-service routine, interrupt requests are accepted from some devices but not from others, depending on the device's priority. To implement this scheme, we can assign to the processor a priority level that can be changed under program control. The priority level of the processor is the priority of the program that is currently being executed. The processor accepts interrupts only from devices that have priorities higher than its own. When the execution of an interrupt-service routine for some device begins, the priority of the processor is raised to that of the device. This action disables interrupts from devices at the same level of priority or lower. However, interrupt requests from higher-priority devices continue to be accepted.

The processor's priority is usually encoded in a few bits of the processor status word. It can be changed by a program instruction that writes into the PS. Such instructions are privileged; that is, they can be executed only while the processor is running in the supervisor mode, as determined by the contents of the processor status word. The processor is in the supervisor mode only when it is executing operating system routines. It switches to the user mode before it begins to execute application programs. Thus, a user program cannot accidentally, or intentionally, change the priority of the processor and disrupt the system's operation. An attempt to execute a privileged instruction while in the user mode leads to a special type of interrupt called privilege exception, which we describe in Section 4.2.4.

The hardware for a multiple-priority scheme can be implemented easily by using separate interrupt-request and interrupt-acknowledge lines for each device. Such an arrangement is shown in Figure 4.7. Each of the interrupt-request lines is assigned a different priority level. Interrupt requests received over these lines are sent to a priority

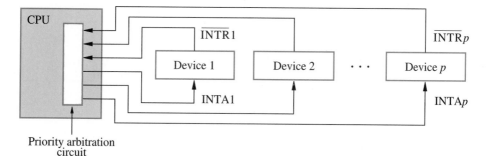

FIGURE 4.7
Implementation of interrupt priority using individual interrupt-request and acknowledge
lines.

arbitration circuit in the processor. A request is accepted only if it has a higher priority
level than that currently assigned to the processor.

Simultaneous Requests

We now consider the problem of interrupt requests arriving from two or more devices simultaneously. The processor should have some means for deciding which request is serviced and which are delayed. In a priority scheme such as that in Figure 4.7,
the solution to this problem is straightforward; the processor simply accepts the request
having the highest priority. However, if several devices share one interrupt-request line,
some other mechanism must be employed to assign relative priority to these devices.

When polling is used to identify the interrupting device, priority is automatically
assigned by the order in which devices are polled. Therefore, no further treatment is
required to accommodate simultaneous interrupt requests. In the case of vectored interrupts, the priority of any device is usually determined by the way the device is connected
to the processor. A widely used scheme is to connect the devices to form a *daisy chain*,
as shown in Figure 4.8a. The interrupt-request line, $\overline{INTR}$, is common to all devices.
However, the interrupt-acknowledge line, INTA, is connected in a daisy-chain fashion,
allowing its signal to propagate serially through the devices. When several devices issue an interrupt request and the $\overline{INTR}$ line is activated, the processor responds, after
some delay, by setting the INTA line to 1. This signal is received by device 1. Device
1 passes the signal on to device 2 only if it does not require any service. If device 1
has a pending request for interrupt, it blocks the acknowledgment signal and proceeds
to put its identifying code on the data lines. Therefore, in the daisy-chain arrangement,
the device that is electrically closest to the processor has the highest priority, the second
device along the chain has second highest priority, and so on.

The scheme in Figure 4.8a has the advantage that it requires considerably fewer
wires than the individual connections in Figure 4.7. The main advantage of the scheme
in Figure 4.7 is that the processor can accept interrupt requests from some devices but
not from others, depending on their priorities. The two schemes may be combined to
produce the more general structure in Figure 4.8b. This organization is used in many
computer systems.

Note that the general organization in Figure 4.8b makes it possible for a device
to be connected to several priority levels. At any given time, the device requests an

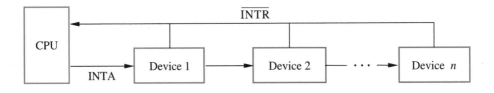

(a) Daisy chain

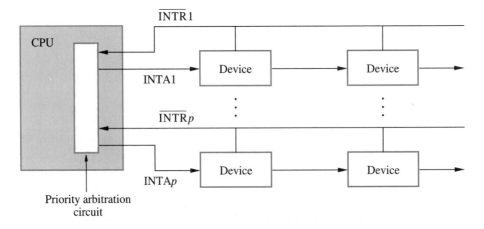

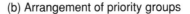

(b) Arrangement of priority groups

FIGURE 4.8
Interrupt priority schemes.

interrupt at a priority level consistent with the urgency of the service requested. This approach offers additional flexibility at the expense of more complex control circuitry in the device interface.

4.2.3 Controlling Device Requests

Until now, we have assumed that an I/O device interface generates an interrupt request whenever it is ready for an I/O transfer, that is, whenever the SIN or SOUT bit in its status register is equal to 1. It is important to ensure that interrupt requests are generated only by the I/O devices that some program is using. Idle devices must not be allowed to generate interrupt requests even though they may be ready to participate in I/O transfer operations. Hence, we need a way to enable and disable interrupts in the interface circuit of individual devices, in order to control whether the device is allowed to generate an interrupt request. Usually this is done through an Interrupt-enable (IE) bit in the device's interface circuit, which can be set or cleared by the processor. The IE bit may be part of a control or status register into which the processor can write. When this bit is set, the interface circuit generates an interrupt request and sets its IRQ bit whenever its SIN or SOUT bit is set. If IE is equal to 0, the interface circuit does not generate an interrupt request, regardless of the state of SIN or SOUT. In practice, two Interrupt-enable bits, IE_{SIN} and IE_{SOUT}, are often used. The first enables interrupts when SIN is equal to 1 and the second does the same when SOUT equals 1.

To summarize, there are two independent means of controlling interrupt requests. At the device end, an Interrupt-enable bit in a control register determines whether the device is allowed to generate an interrupt request. At the processor end, a priority structure and an interrupt mask in the PS determine whether a given interrupt request is accepted.

4.2.4 Exceptions

An interrupt is an event that suspends the execution of one program and begins the execution of another program. So far, we have assumed that an interrupt is caused by a request received from an I/O device in the form of a hardware signal sent over the computer bus. In fact, many events can cause an interrupt. All such events are called *exceptions*. Thus, I/O interrupts are one example of an exception. We now describe a few other kinds of common exceptions.

Recovery from Errors

Computers use a variety of techniques to ensure that all hardware components are operating properly. For example, many computers include a parity check code in the main memory, which allows the computer to detect errors in the stored data. If an error occurs, the control hardware detects it and informs the processor by raising an interrupt.

The processor may also interrupt a program if it detects an error or an unusual condition while executing the instructions of this program. For example, the OP-code field of an instruction may not correspond to any legal instruction, or an arithmetic instruction may attempt to divide by zero.

When exception processing is initiated as a result of such errors, the processor responds in exactly the same manner as it does for an I/O interrupt request; it suspends the program being executed and starts an exception-service routine. This routine takes appropriate action to recover from the error, if possible, or informs the user about it. Recall that in the case of an I/O interrupt, the processor completes execution of the instruction in progress before accepting the interrupt. When an interrupt is caused by an error, however, execution of the interrupted instruction cannot usually be completed, and the processor begins exception processing immediately.

Debugging

Another important exception is used as an aid in debugging programs. System software usually includes a program called a *debugger*, which helps the programmer find errors in a program. The debugger uses exceptions to provide two important capabilities: trace mode and breakpoints.

When a processor is operating in the *trace* mode, an exception occurs after execution of every instruction. The service routine for this exception is the debugging program, which allows the user to examine the contents of registers, memory locations, and so on. After the computer returns from the debugging program, the next instruction of the program being debugged is executed, and the debugging program is activated again. During execution of the debugging program, the trace exception is disabled.

Breakpoints provide a similar capability, except that the program being debugged is interrupted only at specific points selected by the user. An instruction called Trap or Software-interrupt is usually provided for this purpose. Executing this instruction results in exactly the same actions as when a hardware interrupt request is received. While debugging a program, the user may wish to interrupt program execution after instruction i, for example. The debugging routine replaces instruction $i + 1$ in the assembled code in the memory with a Software-interrupt instruction. When program execution reaches this point, it is interrupted, and the debugging routine is activated. This gives the user a chance to examine memory and register contents. When the user is ready to continue executing the program being debugged, the debugging routine restores the instruction that was at location $i + 1$ and executes a Return-from-interrupt instruction.

Software-interrupt instructions are also used by the operating system to communicate with and control the execution of other programs, as Section 4.2.5 explains.

Privilege Exception

To protect the operating system of a computer from being corrupted by user programs, certain instructions can be executed only while the processor is in the supervisor mode. In particular, when the processor is running in the user mode, it cannot execute an instruction that changes the priority level of the processor or that enables the user program to access areas in the main memory that have been allocated to other users. (Memory management is discussed in Chapter 5.) An attempt to execute a privileged instruction while the processor is in user mode causes a privilege exception. As a result, the processor switches to the supervisor mode and begins to execute an appropriate routine in the operating system.

4.2.5 Use of Interrupts in Operating Systems

The preceding discussion presents the details of interrupt mechanisms in modern computers, concentrating on interrupt handling at the machine level. Let us now consider how interrupts are handled in an environment in which application programs run under the control of an operating system.

All activities within a computer are coordinated by the operating system. Among other things, the operating system performs all input and output operations. It incorporates interrupt-service routines for all devices connected to the computer. An application program requests an I/O operation by issuing a software interrupt. The operating system suspends the execution of that program temporarily and performs the steps necessary for the requested operation. When the operation is completed, the operating system transfers control back to the application program.

Software interrupts, also known as traps, are the mechanism by which application programs request services from the operating system. To facilitate the implementation of the variety of services provided, most processors have several different software interrupt instructions, each with its own interrupt vector. Thus, these instructions can be used to call different parts of the operating system.

In a computer that has both a supervisor and a user mode, the processor switches its operation to supervisor mode at the time it accepts an interrupt request. It does so by setting a bit in the processor status register after saving the old contents of that register. Thus, when an application program calls the operating system by a software interrupt instruction, the processor automatically switches to supervisor mode, giving the operating system complete access to the machine's resources. When the operating system executes a Return-from-interrupt instruction, the processor status word belonging to the application program is restored. As a result, the processor switches back to the user mode.

To illustrate the interaction between application programs and the operating system, let us consider an example that involves multitasking. *Multitasking* is a mode of operation in which a processor executes several user programs at the same time. A common operating system technique that makes this possible is called *time slicing*; a program runs for a short period called a time slice, then another program runs for its time slice, and so on. The period, τ, is determined by a continuously running hardware clock, which generates an interrupt every τ seconds.

Figure 4.9 describes a few routines needed to implement some of the essential functions in a multitasking environment. The time-slice interrupt causes an OS scheduling routine, called SCHEDULER in the figure, to be executed. The starting address of this routine is stored in the corresponding interrupt vector by the OSINIT routine at the time the operating system is started. The scheduler routine saves all information relating to the program that was just interrupted, say, program A. The information saved, which is called the *program state*, includes the register contents, the processor status word, and so on. The scheduler selects for execution another program, B, that was suspended earlier.

A program and any information that describes its current state of execution are regarded by the operating system as an entity called a *process*. A process can be in one of three states—Running, Runnable, or Blocked. The Running state means that the program is currently being executed. The process is Runnable if the program is ready for execution but is waiting to be selected by the scheduler. The third state, Blocked, means that the program is not ready to resume execution for some reason. For example, it may be waiting for completion of an I/O operation that it requested earlier.

Having selected process B, the scheduler restores all information saved at the time program B was suspended, including the contents of PS and PC, and executes a Return-from-interrupt instruction. As a result, program B resumes execution for τ seconds, at the end of which the clock raises an interrupt again, and a *context switch* to another runnable process takes place.

Assume that program A wishes to read an input line from the keyboard of a video terminal. Instead of performing the operation itself, it requests I/O service from the operating system. The program uses the stack or the processor registers to pass information to the operating system; this information describes the required operation, the I/O device, and the address of a buffer in the program data area where the line should be placed. The program calls the operating system by executing a software interrupt instruction whose interrupt vector points to the OSSERVICES routine in Figure 4.9. This routine examines the information on the stack or in the registers and initiates the requested operation by calling an appropriate OS routine. In our example, it calls IOINIT in Figure 4.9*b*, which is a routine responsible for starting I/O operations.

While an I/O operation is in progress, the program that requested it cannot continue execution. Hence, the IOINIT routine sets the process associated with program A into the Blocked state, indicating to the scheduler that the program cannot resume execution at this time. Then IOINIT starts the requested I/O operation. It carries out any

OSINIT	Set interrupt vectors
	Time-slice clock ← Scheduler
	Trap ← OSSERVICES
	VDT interrupts ← IOData
	⋮
OSSERVICES	Examine stack to determine requested operation.
	Call appropriate routine.
SCHEDULER	Save current context.
	Select a runnable process.
	Restore saved context of new process.
	Push new values for PS and PC on stack.
	Return from interrupt.

(a) OS initialization, services, and scheduler

IOINIT	Set process status to Blocked.
	Initialize memory buffer address pointer and counter.
	Call device driver to initialize device and enable interrupts in the device interface.
	Return from subroutine.
IODATA	Poll devices to determine source of interrupt.
	Call appropriate driver.
	If END = 1, then set process status to Runnable
	Return from interrupt.

(b) I/O routines

VDTINIT	Initialize device interface (select baud rate, etc.).
	Enable interrupts.
	Return from subroutine.
VDTDATA	Check device status.
	If ready, then transfer character.
	If character = CR, then set END = 1;
	else set END = 0.
	Return from subroutine.

(c) VDT driver

FIGURE 4.9
A few operating system routines.

preparations needed, such as initializing address pointers, byte count, and so on, and then it calls a routine that performs the I/O transfers.

It is common practice in operating system design to encapsulate all software pertaining to a particular device into a self-contained module called the *device driver*. Such a module can be easily added to or deleted from the operating system. We have assumed that the device driver for the video terminal consists of two routines, VDTINIT and VDTDATA, as shown in Figure 4.9*c*. IOINIT calls VDTINIT to perform any initialization operations needed by the device or its interface circuit, such as selecting the data transmission format or transfer rate. Then VDTINIT enables interrupts in the interface circuit by setting the appropriate bit in the status register. Once these actions are completed, the device is ready to participate in a data transfer operation. It will generate an interrupt request whenever a character is entered at the keyboard.

Following the return to OSSERVICES, the SCHEDULER routine selects a user program to run. Of course, the scheduler does not select program A, because that program is now in the Blocked state. The Return-from-interrupt instruction that causes the selected user program to begin execution also lowers the processor's priority to the user level. Thus, an interrupt request generated by the video terminal's interface will be accepted. The interrupt vector for the terminal points to an operating system routine called IODATA. Because there could be several devices connected to the same interrupt request line, IODATA begins by polling these devices to determine the one requesting service. Then it calls the appropriate device driver to service the request. In our example, the driver, called VDTDATA, transfers one character of data. If the character is a carriage return, it also sets to 1 a flag called END, which informs IODATA that the requested I/O operation has been completed. When the IODATA routine observes that the END flag is equal to 1, it changes the state of process A from Blocked to Runnable, so that the scheduler selects it for execution in some future time slice.

4.3
PROCESSOR EXAMPLES

We have discussed the organization of interrupts in general. Commercially available processors provide many of the features and control mechanisms just described, but not necessarily all of them. For example, vectored interrupts may be supported to enable the processor to branch quickly to the interrupt-service routine of a particular device. Alternatively, the task of identifying the device and determining the starting address of the interrupt-service routine may be left for implementation in software using polling. Next, we describe the interrupt-handling mechanisms of the 68000 and PowerPC processors as examples.

4.3.1 68000 Interrupt Structure

The 68000 has eight interrupt priority levels. The priority at which the processor is running at any given time is encoded in three bits of the processor status word, as shown in Figure 4.10, with level 0 being the lowest priority. I/O devices are connected to the 68000 using an arrangement similar to that in Figure 4.8*b*, in which interrupt requests

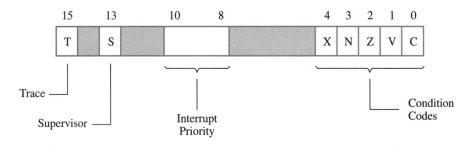

FIGURE 4.10
Processor status register in the 68000 processor.

are assigned priorities in the range 1 through 7. A request is accepted only if its priority is higher than that of the processor, with one exception: An interrupt request at level seven is always accepted. This is a *nonmaskable* interrupt. When the processor accepts an interrupt request, the priority level indicated in the PS is automatically raised to that of the request, before the interrupt-service routine is executed. Thus, requests of equal or lower priority are disabled, except for level seven interrupts, which are always enabled.

The processor automatically saves the contents of the program counter and the processor status word at the time of interruption. The PC is pushed onto the processor stack followed by the PS, using register A7 as the stack pointer. A Return-from-interrupt instruction, called Return-from-exception (RTE) in the 68000 assembly language, pops the top element of the stack into the PS, and pops the next element into the PC. As shown in Figure 4.10, the PS register contains a Supervisor bit, S, and a Trace bit, T. The S bit determines whether the processor is running in the Supervisor (S = 1) or User (S = 0) mode. The T bit enables a special type of interrupt called a trace exception, as described in Section 4.2.4. This information is saved automatically at the time an interrupt is accepted and restored at the end of interrupt servicing. Any additional information to be saved, such as the contents of general-purpose registers, must be saved and restored explicitly inside the interrupt-service routine.

The 68000 processor uses vectored interrupts. When it accepts an interrupt request, it obtains the starting address of the interrupt-service routine from an interrupt vector stored in the main memory. There are 256 interrupt vectors, numbered 0 through 255. Each vector consists of 32 bits that constitute the required starting address. When a device requests an interrupt, it may point to the vector that should be used by sending an 8-bit vector number to the processor, in response to the interrupt acknowledge signal. As an alternative, the 68000 also provides an *autovector* facility. Instead of sending a vector number, the device can activate a special bus control line to indicate that it wishes to use the autovector facility. In this case, the processor chooses one of seven vectors provided for this purpose, based on the priority level of the interrupt request.

4.3.2 PowerPC Interrupt Structure

The PowerPC has many different types of exceptions to handle conditions such as addressing errors, privilege violations, illegal instructions, and hardware errors. One type of exceptions is external interrupt requests received over the processor bus. There

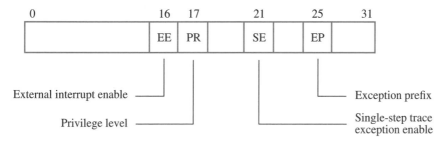

FIGURE 4.11
Machine State Register (MSR) in the PowerPC.

is only one interrupt request line on the bus, which can be activated by any device connected to the bus. Whether a request on this line is accepted is determined by an External-interrupt-Enable (EE) bit in a register called the Machine State Register (MSR). When this bit is equal to 1, an interrupt request is accepted by the processor.

Figure 4.11 shows some of the control bits in the MSR. This register plays an important role in controlling the operation of the processor. Bit SE is used to enable trace interrupts, which are explained in Section 4.2.4. Bit PR determines the privilege level. When PR = 1, the processor is in the Supervisor mode; otherwise, it is in the User mode. The contents of the MSR register are saved at the time of interruption, as we describe next.

The PowerPC uses two special registers called the Save/Restore registers, SRR0 and SRR1, to store the information that must be saved when an interrupt request is accepted. In register SRR0, the processor saves the address of the instruction that would have been executed had the interrupt not occurred. This is the return address at which execution should resume when a Return-from-interrupt (RFI) instruction is executed. The low-order half of the second register, SRR1, is used to save bits 16 through 31 of the MSR. The remaining bits of the MSR are not saved because they are always equal to 0. The high-order bits of register SRR1 are cleared to 0 for most exceptions. In some cases, they are used to record additional information about the cause of the exception.

After saving the return address and the contents of the MSR, the processor clears the interrupt-enable bit in MSR to 0. This guarantees that no further interrupts will be accepted until the interrupt-service routine has been entered and has had a chance to save any other critical information. The processor loads the starting address of the interrupt-service routine in the program counter and resumes execution.

The interrupt-service routines for different exceptions are stored in a table whose starting address is determined by the value of the Exception Prefix (EP) bit in the MSR register. When this bit is equal to 0, the table starts at location 0, otherwise the table starts at location FFF00000. The interrupt-service routine for external interrupts has an offset of 500 (hex) relative to the beginning of the table. Thus, it starts at either 00000500 or FFF00500, depending on the value of EP. The table is 16K bytes long, where 40 words are provided for each routine. If more space is needed for a given routine, a branch should be made to another suitable area in the memory.

Before allowing other interrupts to be accepted, the interrupt-service routine must save the contents of registers SRR0 and SRR1 in a convenient location, such as a stack. Recall that these registers contain the return address and the machine state information that were saved at the time of interruption. The routine must also save any other registers that it needs to use, such as CR, CTR, Link, or any general-purpose register.

4.3.3 Example of an Interrupt Program

Let us now consider an example of an interrupt-service routine. Assume that, at some point in a program MAIN, we want to read an input line from the keyboard. The input characters are to be stored in a buffer area in the main memory, starting at location LINE. When a complete line is read, as a Carriage Return character indicates, the program calls a subroutine called TEXT to perform the necessary processing. Let us assume that bit b_6 of register STATUS in Figure 4.3 is the interrupt-enable bit. While b_6 is set, an interrupt request is generated by the interface whenever the SIN flag is set, that is, whenever a key is pressed, causing an input character to be deposited in the DATAIN register.

Figures 4.12 and 4.13 give examples of two routines for reading an input line from the keyboard using interrupts, for the 68000 and the PowerPC, respectively. In

INTVEC	EQU	$68	Interrupt-vector address.
INTEN	EQU	$40	Keyboard interrupt-enable
INTDIS	EQU	0	and disable masks.
NEWPS	EQU	$0100	Contents of PS to set priority to 1.
RTRN	EQU	$0D	ASCII code for carriage return.

Initialization

	MOVE.L	#LINE,PNTR	Initialize buffer pointer.
	MOVE.B	#INTEN,STATUS	Enable keyboard interrupts.
	MOVE.L	#READ,INTVEC	Set interrupt vector.
	MOVE.L	#MAIN, −(A7)	Push new PC onto the stack.
	MOVE.W	#NEWSP, −(A7)	Push new PS onto the stack.
	RTE		Load PC and PS from the stack.

         ⋮

MAIN	main program

         ⋮

Interrupt-service routine

READ	MOVEA.L	A0, −(A7)	Save register A0 on the stack.
	MOVEA.L	PNTR,A0	Load address pointer.
	MOVE.B	DATAIN, (A0)+	Get input character.
	MOVEA.L	A0,PNTR	Update pointer.
	CMPI.B	#RTRN, −1(A0)	Check if carriage return.
	BNE	DONE	
	MOVE.B	#INTDIS,STATUS	Disable keyboard interrupts.
	BSR	TEXT	Process input line.
DONE	MOVEA.L	(A7)+, A0	Restore register A0.
	RTE		

FIGURE 4.12
A 68000 interrupt-service routine to read one line from a keyboard.

INTVEC	EQU	$1F4	Interrupt-vector address.
INTEN	EQU	$40	Keyboard interrupt-enable
INTDIS	EQU	0	and disable masks.
NEWMSR	EQU	$8000	Desired contents of MSR.
RTRN	EQU	$0D	ASCII code for carriage return.

Initialization

START	ADDI	R2,0,LINE	Get the address LINE.
	STW	R2,PNTR(0)	Store it at PNTR.
	ADDI	R2,0,INTEN	Load interrupt-enable mask.
	STW	R2,STATUS(0)	Set interrupt-enable in STATUS.
	ADDI	R2,0,NEWMSR	Load desired contents of MSR.
	MTSRR1	R2	Transfer to SRR1.
	ADDI	R2,0,MAIN	Load address of main program.
	MTSRR0	R2	Transfer to SRR0.
	RFI		Go to main program.
	$\vdots$		
MAIN	Main program		
	$\vdots$		

Interrupt-service routine

READ	. . .		Save registers R30, R31, and CR.
	LBZ	R30,DATAIN(0)	Get input character.
	LWZ	R31,PNTR(0)	Load value at PNTR.
	STBU	R30,1(R31)	Store character in line buffer and update R31.
	STW	R31,PNTR(0)	Update PNTR.
	CMPWI	CR1,R30,RTRN	Check if Carriage Return.
	BNE	CR1,DONE	
	ADI	R2,0,INTDIS	Load interrupt-disable mask.
	STW	R2,STATUS(0)	Clear interrupt-enable in STATUS.
	BL	TEXT	Call subroutine to process line.
DONE	. . .		Restore saved registers.
	RFI		Return from interrupt.

A PowerPC interrupt-service routine to read one line from a keyboard.

FIGURE 4.13

each case, initialization is followed by execution of a program called MAIN. When an interrupt request is received, execution of MAIN is interrupted and the interrupt-service routine READ is executed.

The initialization section loads the address LINE into location PNTR, which will be used as a pointer for storing input characters in the memory buffer. Interrupts from the keyboard are enabled by setting bit b_6 of STATUS to 1. In the case of the 68000, the initialization section also loads the address READ into the interrupt vector at location INTVEC in the main memory. This step is not needed in the PowerPC because the interrupt vector location contains the first instruction of the interrupt-service routine. Finally, interrupts are enabled in the processor and execution of program

MAIN begins. The details differ somewhat between the 68000 and the PowerPC, as explained in the following sections.

68000

For the 68000, we have assumed that the keyboard uses the autovector facility at priority level 2. The corresponding interrupt vector is number 26. Because the vector table in the 68000 starts at location 0 and each vector is four bytes long, the value assigned to INTVEC is four times the vector number. During initialization, the processor is running in the supervisor mode, at priority 7. When the processor is executing program MAIN, it should be in the user mode and at a priority level of 1 or less. The desired new values for PC and PS are pushed onto the processor stack. Then these values are loaded into the corresponding registers using the RTE instruction. As a result, execution of program MAIN begins, with the new PS word. This program should not change the contents of PNTR or use the contents of the main memory data buffer at LINE until a complete input line has been read.

When a key is pressed on the keyboard, program MAIN is interrupted and routine READ is executed. The routine starts by saving the contents of register A0, which it needs to use; then it transfers the input character to the memory buffer. If the character is Carriage Return, interrupts from the keyboard interface are disabled by clearing b_6 in the interface's status register, and subroutine TEXT is called to process the input line in the memory data buffer. Otherwise, the contents of A0 are restored and a Return-from-exception instruction is executed.

PowerPC

For this example, we have chosen simple address assignments for all variables to make it possible to concentrate on the concepts involved in interrupt servicing. The variables PNTR and LINE are assumed to be in the low 32K of the addressable space. The status register of the keyboard interface is assumed to be in the high 32K. Thus, in all cases, sign extension of a 16-bit quantity can be used to provide the correct address. We have also assumed that the entire interrupt-service routine is stored in the interrupt table.

When the machine status register, MSR, is loaded, bit EP is set to 0. As a result, the interrupt vector for external interrupts is at location 500. To load new data into MSR and PC, the desired values are first loaded into the Save/Restore registers, SRR1 and SRR0. Then the Return-from-interrupt instruction, RFI, is used to transfer these values into the MSR and PC. As a result, the processor begins to execute program MAIN, with EP equal to 0 and EE equal to 1 in MSR.

When a character is entered at the keyboard and the interrupt is accepted, the interrupt-service routine begins by saving the registers it needs to use. We have not shown the details of this step in the figure. One of the registers that must be saved is the condition register, CR, because this register is used in the compare instruction. Although we have not indicated this in the example, registers SRR0 and SRR1 must also be saved if interrupts are enabled before the return from this routine, that is, if interrupt nesting is allowed.

The input character is read from DATAIN and stored in the memory using the immediate index with update mode. Note that, with this mode, the first character is actually stored in location LINE+1. If the input character is a Carriage Return, the interrupt-enable bit in the keyboard status register is cleared, and subroutine TEXT is called. Otherwise, the saved registers are restored and a Return-from-interrupt instruction is executed.

4.4
DIRECT MEMORY ACCESS

The discussion in the previous sections concentrates on data transfer between the processor and I/O devices. Data are transferred by executing instructions such as

$$\text{Move} \qquad \text{DATAIN,R0}$$

An instruction to transfer input or output data is executed only after the processor determines that the I/O device is ready. To do this, the processor either polls a status flag in the device interface or waits for the device to send an interrupt request. In either case, considerable overhead is incurred, because several program instructions must be executed for each data word transferred. In addition to polling the status register of the device, instructions are needed for tasks such as incrementing the memory address and keeping track of the word count. When interrupts are used, there is the additional overhead associated with saving and restoring the program counter and other state information.

To transfer large blocks of data at high speed, we can use an alternative approach. A special control unit may be provided to allow transfer of a block of data directly between an external device and the main memory, without continuous intervention by the processor. This approach is called *direct memory access*, or DMA.

DMA transfers are performed by a control circuit associated with the I/O device. We refer to this circuit as a *DMA controller*. The DMA controller allows direct data transfer between the device and the main memory without involving the processor. This means that it performs the functions that would normally be performed by the processor when accessing the main memory. For each byte or word transferred, it must provide the memory address and all the bus signals that control data transfer. Since it has to transfer blocks of data, the DMA controller must increment the memory address as appropriate for successive bytes or words and keep track of the number of transfers.

Although the DMA controller can transfer data without intervention from the processor, its operation must be under the control of a program executed by the processor. To initiate the transfer of a block of words, the processor sends the following data to the controller: the starting address, the number of words in the block, and the direction of the transfer. On receiving this information, the DMA controller proceeds to perform the requested transfer. When the entire block has been transferred, the controller informs the processor by raising an interrupt signal.

Figure 4.14 shows an example of the registers in a DMA controller that the programmer sees. These registers are accessed in the same way as in any other I/O device interface. Two registers are used for storing the starting address and the word count. The third register contains status and control flags. The $R/\overline{W}$ bit determines the direction of the transfer and is used to control the corresponding line on the bus. When this bit is set to 1 by a program instruction, the controller performs a read operation; that is, it transfers data from the memory to the I/O device. Otherwise, it performs a write

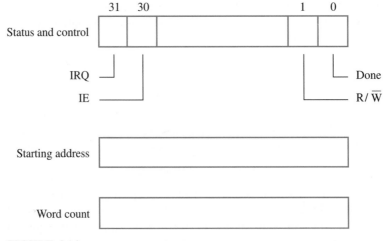

FIGURE 4.14

Registers in a DMA interface.

operation. When the controller has completed transferring a block of data and is ready to receive another command, it sets the Done flag to 1. Bit 30 is the Interrupt-enable flag. When set to 1, this flag causes the controller to raise an interrupt after it has completed transferring a block of data. Finally, the controller sets the IRQ bit to 1 when it has requested an interrupt.

Figure 4.15 shows an example of a DMA controller used in conjunction with two I/O devices, a disk drive and a high-speed printer. In this case, the controller is said to provide two DMA channels. The registers needed to store the memory address, the word count, and so on are duplicated, so that one set can be used with each device. A connection is also provided for each channel between the DMA controller and one of the I/O devices.

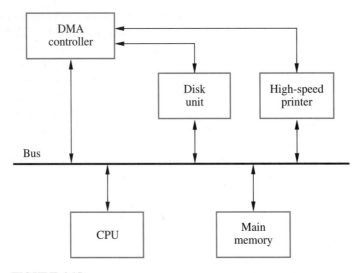

FIGURE 4.15

A two-channel DMA controller.

To start a DMA transfer of a block of data from the main memory to the printer, a program, usually a routine in the operating system, writes the following information into the registers of the DMA channel assigned to the printer:

- Memory address
- Word count
- Function to be performed (Read or Write)

The DMA controller then proceeds independently to implement the specified function. It uses its connection to the printer to determine when the printer is ready. Whenever the printer is ready, the DMA controller sends a read request to the memory and instructs the printer to receive the data from the bus. Then it waits for the printer to be ready again. When the DMA transfer is completed, this fact is recorded in the status and control register of the DMA controller by setting the Done bit. At the same time, if the IE bit is set, the controller sends an interrupt request to the processor and sets the IRQ bit. The status register can also be used to record other information, such as whether the transfer took place correctly or errors occurred.

While the DMA transfer is taking place, the program that requested the transfer cannot continue. However, the processor can be used to execute another program. After the DMA transfer is completed, the processor can return to the program that requested the transfer.

I/O operations are always performed by the operating system of the computer in response to a request from an application program. The operating system is also responsible for suspending the execution of one program and starting another. Thus, for an I/O operation involving DMA, the operating system puts the program that requested the transfer in the Blocked state (see Section 4.2.5), initiates the DMA operation, and starts the execution of another program. When the transfer is completed, the DMA controller informs the processor by sending an interrupt request. In response, the operating system puts the suspended program in the Runnable state so that it can be selected by the scheduler to continue execution.

Note that a conflict may arise if both the processor and a DMA controller try to use the bus at the same time to access the main memory. In fact, several DMA controllers serving different I/O devices may be connected to the bus. In this case, two or more controllers may attempt to use the bus simultaneously. To resolve these conflicts, a special circuit called the *bus arbiter* is provided to coordinate the activities of all devices requesting memory transfers. The arbiter implements a priority system for gaining access to the bus. Memory accesses by the processor and the DMA controllers are interwoven, with top priority given to DMA transfers involving synchronous, high-speed peripherals such as disk and tape drives. Since the processor originates most memory access cycles, the DMA controller can be said to "steal" memory cycles from the processor. Hence, this interweaving technique is usually called *cycle stealing*. Alternatively, the DMA controller may be given exclusive access to the main memory to transfer a block of data without interruption. This is known as *block* mode.

4.4.1 Bus Arbitration

A DMA transfer uses the same address, data, and control lines used by the processor to communicate with the memory and the I/O devices. Therefore, we need some means

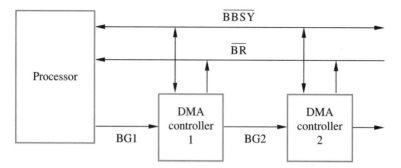

FIGURE 4.16
A simple arrangement for bus arbitration using a daisy chain.

of coordinating the use of these lines, to prevent two devices from initiating transfers at the same time.

The device that is allowed to initiate data transfers on the bus is called the *bus master*. Clearly, only one bus master can exist at any given time. When the master relinquishes its control, other devices can acquire this status. The process of transferring bus mastership from one device to another must be carefully coordinated to take into account the needs of various devices. The bus arbiter performs the required scheduling function. This circuit may be a part of the processor itself or may be a separate unit connected to the bus.

Figure 4.16 illustrates a basic arrangement in which the processor contains the bus arbiter circuitry. In this case, the processor is normally the bus master, unless it grants bus mastership to one of the DMA controllers. A DMA controller indicates that it needs to become the bus master by activating the Bus-Request line, $\overline{BR}$. This is an open-collector line for the same reasons that the Interrupt-Request line in Figure 4.6 is an open-collector line. The signal on the Bus-Request line is the logical OR of the bus requests from all the devices connected to it. When Bus Request is activated, the processor activates the Bus Grant signal, BG1, indicating to the DMA controllers that they may use the bus when it becomes free. This signal is connected to all DMA controllers using a daisy-chain arrangement. Thus, if DMA controller 1 is requesting the bus, it blocks the propagation of the grant signal to other devices. Otherwise, it passes the grant downstream by asserting BG2. The current bus master indicates to all devices that it is using the bus by activating another open-collector line called Bus Busy, $\overline{BBSY}$. Hence, after receiving the Bus Grant signal, a DMA controller waits for Bus Busy to become inactive, indicating that the bus is free. When this happens, the DMA controller assumes mastership of the bus. It activates Bus Busy to prevent other devices from using the bus at the same time.

The timing diagram in Figure 4.17 shows the sequence of events for the devices in Figure 4.16 as DMA controller 2 requests and acquires bus mastership and later releases the bus. During its tenure as the bus master, it may perform one or more data transfer operations, depending on whether it is operating in the cycle stealing or block mode. After it releases the bus, the processor resumes bus mastership. This figure shows the causal relationships among the signals involved in the arbitration process. Details of timing, which vary significantly from one processor bus to another, are not shown. The

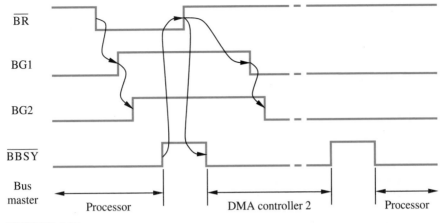

FIGURE 4.17
Sequence of signals during transfer of bus mastership for the devices in Figure 4.16.

signals generated by the processor are always synchronized with the processor clock. A clock signal is often included on the bus and used by the I/O device interfaces to control their own operation.

Figure 4.16 shows one bus request line and one bus grant line forming a daisy chain. Several such pairs may be provided, in an arrangement similar to that used for multiple interrupt requests in Figure 4.8*b*. This arrangement leads to considerable flexibility in determining the order in which requests from different devices are serviced. An arbiter circuit ensures that only one request is granted at any given time, according to a predefined priority scheme. For example, if there are four bus request lines, BR1 through BR4, a fixed priority scheme may be used in which BR1 is given top priority and BR4 is given lowest priority. Alternatively, a rotating priority scheme may be used to give all devices an equal chance, on average, at being serviced. Rotating priority means that, after a request on line BR1 is granted, the priority order becomes 2, 3, 4, 1.

The arbitration scheme just described is called *centralized arbitration*, because a single arbiter is used. Other arbitration schemes exist in which equal responsibility is given to all devices to carry out the arbitration process, without using a central arbiter. Such schemes are said to use *distributed arbitration*.

A simple, common method for distributed arbitration is illustrated in Figure 4.18. Each device on the bus is assigned a 4-bit identification number. When one or more devices request the bus, they assert the $\overline{\text{Start-Arbitration}}$ signal and place their 4-bit ID numbers on the four open-collector lines, $\overline{\text{ARB0}}$ through $\overline{\text{ARB3}}$. A winner is selected as a result of interaction among the signals transmitted over these lines by all contenders. The net outcome of this interaction is that the code on the four lines represents the request that has the highest ID number.

Assume that two devices, A and B, are requesting the use of the bus; let their ID numbers be 5 and 6, respectively. Device A transmits the pattern 0101, and device B transmits the pattern 0110. Because the arbitration lines are active when low (that is, a logic 1 drives the line low), the code seen by either of the two devices is 0111. Each device compares the pattern on the arbitration lines to its own ID, starting from the most significant bit. If it detects a difference at any bit position, it disables its drivers

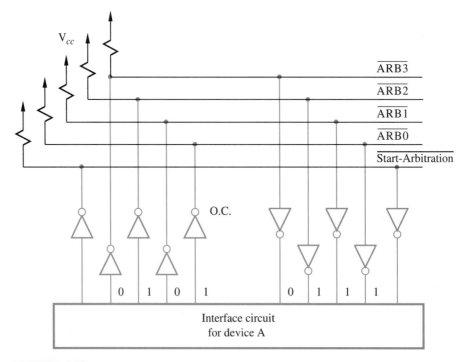

FIGURE 4.18
Connection of device interface circuit to priority arbitration lines.

at that bit position and for all lower-order bits. It does so by placing a 0 at the input of these drivers. (Recall that the drivers are the open-collector type. Their output consists of a switch to ground, which is closed when the driver's input equals 1.) In the case of our example, device A detects a difference on line $\overline{\text{ARB1}}$. Hence, it disables its drivers on lines $\overline{\text{ARB1}}$ and $\overline{\text{ARB0}}$. This causes the pattern on the arbitration lines to change to 0110, which means that B has won the contention. Note that, since the code on the priority lines is 0111 for a short period, device B may temporarily disable its driver on line $\overline{\text{ARB0}}$. However, it will enable its driver again once it sees a 0 on line $\overline{\text{ARB1}}$ resulting from the action by device A.

4.5
I/O HARDWARE

The processor, main memory, and I/O devices are interconnected by means of a common bus. The primary function of the bus is to provide a communications path over which data can be transferred among the processor, the main memory, and the I/O devices. In addition to data transfer lines, the bus includes the lines needed to support interrupts and to implement the arbitration functions that enable DMA controllers to acquire bus mastership.

In this section, we discuss some details of I/O interface circuits. We limit our discussion to the circuits needed for transferring data over the bus.

4.5.1 Processor Bus

A typical bus consists of three sets of lines: data, address, and control lines. The control signals involved in data transfers specify two types of information, namely, the nature of the transfer and its timing. The first of these, which we refer to as the *mode* of the transfer, involves the specification of whether a Read or a Write operation is to be performed. A Read/$\overline{\text{Write}}$ line specifies Read when set to 1 and Write when set to 0. When several operand sizes are possible, such as byte, word, or long word, the required size of data should also be indicated.

The second component of the bus control signals carries timing information. These signals specify the times at which the processor and the I/O devices may place data on the bus or receive data from the bus. A variety of schemes have been devised for the timing of data transfers over a bus. These can be broadly classified as either synchronous or asynchronous schemes.

Synchronous Bus

In a *synchronous* bus, all devices derive timing information from a common clock line. Equally spaced pulses on this line define equal time intervals; each interval constitutes a *bus cycle*, during which one data transfer can take place. Such a scheme is illustrated in Figure 4.19. Note that the address and data lines in this and subsequent figures are shown as high and low at the same time. This indicates that some lines are high and some low, depending on the particular address or data pattern being transmitted. The crossing points indicate the times at which these patterns change. A signal line in an indeterminate or high impedance state (see Section 3.1.5) is represented by an intermediate level half-way between the low and high signal levels.

Let us consider the sequence of events during an input (read) operation. At time t_0, the processor places the device address on the address lines and sets the mode control lines to indicate an input operation. This information travels over the bus at a

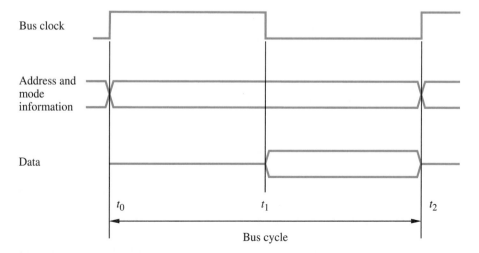

FIGURE 4.19
Timing of an input transfer on a synchronous bus.

speed determined by its physical and electrical characteristics. The clock pulse width, $t_1 - t_0$, should be chosen such that it is greater than the maximum propagation delay between the processor and any of the devices connected to the bus. It should also be wide enough to allow all devices to decode the address and control signals so that the addressed device can be ready to respond at time t_1. The addressed device, recognizing that an input operation is requested, places its input data on the data lines at time t_1. At the end of the clock cycle, that is, at time t_2, the processor *strobes* the data lines and loads the data into its input buffer (MDR in Figure 3.1). In this context, "strobe" means to determine the value of the data at a given instant. For data to be loaded correctly into any storage device, such as a register built with flip-flops, the data must be available at the input of that device for a period greater than the setup time of the device (see Appendix A). Hence, the period $t_2 - t_1$ must be greater than the maximum propagation time on the bus plus the setup time of the input buffer register of the processor.

The procedure for an output operation is similar to that for the input sequence. The processor places the output data on the data lines when it transmits the address and mode information. At time t_1, the addressed device strobes the data lines and loads the data into its data buffer.

The synchronous bus scheme is simple and results in a simple design for the device interface. The clock speed must be chosen such that it accommodates the longest delays on the bus and the slowest interface. Note that the processor has no way of determining whether the addressed device has actually responded. It simply assumes that, at t_2, the output data have been received by the I/O device or the input data are available on the data lines. If, because of a malfunction, the device does not respond, the error will not be detected.

Asynchronous Bus

An alternative scheme for controlling data transfers on the bus is based on the use of a *handshake* between the processor and the device being addressed. The common clock is eliminated; hence, the resulting bus operation is *asynchronous*. The clock line is replaced by two timing control lines, which we refer to as Ready and Accept. In principle, a data transfer controlled by a handshake protocol proceeds as follows: The processor places the address and mode information on the bus. Then it indicates to all devices that it has done so by activating the Ready line. When the addressed device receives the Ready signal, it performs the required operation and then informs the processor it has done so by activating the Accept line. The processor waits for the Accept signal before it removes its signals from the bus. In the case of a read operation, it also strobes the data into its input buffer.

An example of the timing of a data transfer using the handshake scheme is given in Figure 4.20; the figure depicts the following sequence of events:

t_0—The processor places the address and mode information on the bus.

t_1—The processor sets the Ready line to 1 to inform the I/O devices that the address and mode information is ready. The delay $t_1 - t_0$ is intended to allow for any *skew* that may occur on the bus. Skew occurs when two signals simultaneously transmitted from one source arrive at the destination at different times. This happens because different lines of the bus may have different propagation speeds. Thus, to guarantee that the Ready signal does not arrive at any device ahead of

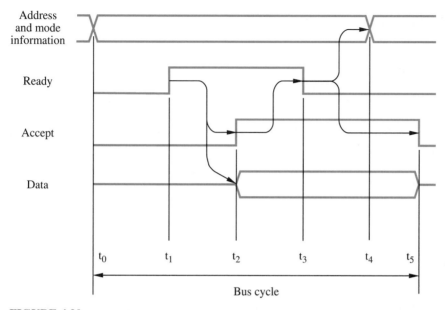

FIGURE 4.20

Handshake control of data transfer during an input operation.

the address and mode information, the delay $t_1 - t_0$ should be larger than the maximum possible bus skew. (Note that, in the synchronous case, bus skew is accounted for as a part of the maximum propagation delay.) When this address information arrives at any device, it is decoded by the interface circuitry. Sufficient time should be allowed for the interface circuitry to decode the address. This delay can be included in the period $t_1 - t_0$.

t_2—The interface of the addressed device receives the Ready signal, and, having already decoded the address and mode information, it recognizes that it should perform an input operation. Hence, it gates the data from its data register to the data lines. At the same time, it sets the Accept signal to 1. If extra delays are introduced by the interface circuitry before it places the data on the bus, it must delay the Accept signal accordingly. The period $t_2 - t_1$ depends on the distance between the processor and the device interface. It is also a function of the delays introduced by the interface circuitry. It is this variability that gives the bus its asynchronous nature.

t_3—The Accept signal arrives at the processor, indicating that the input data are available on the bus. However, since it was assumed that the device interface transmits the Accept signal at the same time that it places the data on the bus, the processor should allow for bus skew. After a delay equivalent to the maximum bus skew, the processor strobes the data into its input buffer. At the same time, it drops the Ready signal, indicating that it has received the data.

t_4—The processor removes the address and mode information from the bus. The delay between t_3 and t_4 is again intended to allow for bus skew. Erroneous addressing may take place if the address, as seen by some device on the bus, starts to change while the Ready signal is still equal to 1.

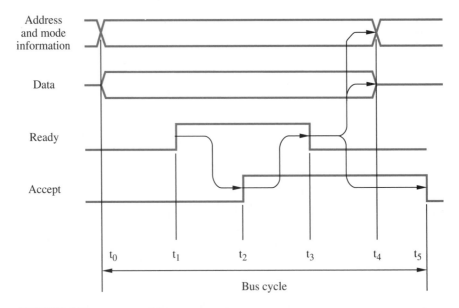

FIGURE 4.21
Handshake control of data transfer during an output operation.

t_5—When the device interface receives the 1 to 0 transition of the Ready signal, it removes the data and the Accept signal from the bus. This completes the input transfer.

The timing for an output operation, illustrated in Figure 4.21, is essentially the same as for an input operation. In this case, the processor places the output data on the data lines at the same time that it transmits the address and mode information. The addressed device strobes the data into its output buffer when it receives the Ready signal and indicates that it has done so by setting the Accept signal to 1. The remainder of the cycle is identical to the input operation.

In the timing diagrams in Figures 4.20 and 4.21, it is assumed that the compensation for bus skew and address decoding is performed by the processor. This simplifies the I/O interface at the device end, because the interface circuit can use the Ready signal directly to gate other signals to or from the bus.

Mixed Synchronous/Asynchronous Bus

Another practical alternative is to use an asynchronous bus, but with a provision that all signaling changes are synchronized with a clock. The time elapsed between successive handshake signals is an integral number of clock cycles. For example, the processor may send an address during one clock cycle. During that cycle, it asserts a signal indicating that the address is valid and that all devices on the bus should decode this address. The addressed device responds, when it is ready, by asserting an acknowledge signal and placing the data on the bus (in the case of a read operation). One or more clock cycles may separate the request and the response, depending on the speed of the device being addressed. Using the clock often leads to simpler designs of logic circuits in device interfaces.

Many variations of the bus techniques just described are found in commercial computers. For example, the bus in the 68000 family of processors has two modes of operation, one asynchronous and one synchronous. The PowerPC bus uses the mixed synchronous/asynchronous approach. The choice of design involves trade-offs among many factors. Some of the important considerations are:

- Simplicity of the device interface
- Ability to accommodate device interfaces that introduce different amounts of delay
- Total time required for a bus transfer
- Ability to detect errors resulting from addressing a nonexistent device or from an interface malfunction

The fully asynchronous scheme provides the highest degree of flexibility and reliability, but its device interface circuit is somewhat more complex than that of the synchronous or mixed synchronous/asynchronous bus. Asynchronous buses have an error-detection capability provided by interlocking the Ready and Accept signals. If the Accept signal is not received within a fixed time-out period after Ready is set to 1, the processor assumes that an error has occurred. A bus error can be used to cause an interrupt and execute a routine that either alerts the operator to the malfunction or takes some other appropriate action.

4.5.2 Interface Circuits

The I/O interface consists of the circuitry required to transfer data between the computer bus and an I/O device. Therefore, on one side of the interface we have the bus signals for address, data, and control. On the other side we have a data path with its associated controls, which enables transfer of data between the interface and the I/O device. This side is device-dependent. However, it can be classified as either a parallel or a serial interface. A parallel interface transfers data in the form of one or more bytes simultaneously to or from the device. A serial interface transmits and receives data one bit at a time. Communication with the bus is the same for both formats; the conversion from the parallel to the serial format, and vice versa, takes place inside the interface circuit.

Before discussing a specific example, let us recall the functions of an I/O interface. According to the discussion in Section 4.1, an I/O interface does the following:

1. Provides a storage buffer for one word of data (or one byte, in the case of byte-oriented devices)
2. Contains status flags that can be accessed by the processor to determine whether the buffer is full (for input) or empty (for output)
3. Contains address-decoding circuitry to determine when it is being addressed by the processor
4. Generates the appropriate timing signals required by the bus control scheme used
5. Performs any format conversion that may be necessary to transfer data between the bus and the I/O device (for example, parallel-serial conversion)

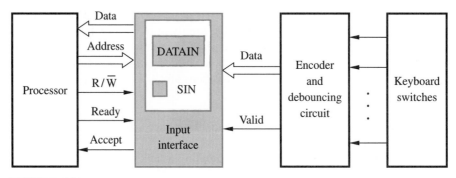

FIGURE 4.22
Keyboard connected to processor.

Parallel Interface

We now explain the key aspects of interface design with a practical example. First, we describe a circuit that can be used to connect a keyboard to a processor, to illustrate an input interface. Next, we present a circuit suitable for connecting a printer, to demonstrate an output interface. Finally, we combine the two circuits to show how a general-purpose parallel interface can be constructed. We assume that the interface is connected to a 32-bit processor that uses memory-mapped I/O and the asynchronous bus protocol depicted in Figures 4.20 and 4.21.

Figure 4.22 shows a scheme for connecting a keyboard to a processor. A typical keyboard consists of mechanical switches that are normally open. When a key is pressed, its switch closes and establishes a path for an electrical signal. This signal is detected by an encoder circuit that generates the ASCII code (see Appendix D) for the corresponding character. A difficulty with such push-button switches is that they bounce when pressed. Although bouncing may last only one or two milliseconds, this is long enough for the computer to observe a single pressing of a key as several distinct electrical events; this single pressing could be erroneously interpreted as the key being pressed and released rapidly several times. The effect of bouncing must be eliminated. We can do this in two ways: A simple debouncing circuit can be included, or a software approach can be used, in which the I/O routine that reads the characters from the keyboard waits long enough to ensure that bouncing has subsided. Figure 4.22 illustrates the hardware approach; debouncing circuits are included as a part of the encoder block.

The output from the encoder consists of the bits that represent the encoded character and one control signal, called Valid, which indicates that a key is being pressed. This information is sent to the input interface. The interface contains a data register, DATAIN, and a status flag, SIN. When a key is pressed, the Valid signal changes from 0 to 1. This causes the ASCII code to be loaded into DATAIN and SIN to be set to 1. The status flag SIN is cleared to 0 when the processor reads the contents of the DATAIN register. The I/O interface is connected to the asynchronous bus on which transfers are controlled using the handshake signals Ready and Accept, as indicated in Figure 4.20. The third control line, R/$\overline{\text{W}}$ distinguishes read and write transfers.

Figure 4.23 shows a suitable circuit for the input interface. The output lines of the DATAIN register are connected to the data lines of the bus by means of three-state drivers, which are turned on when the processor issues a read instruction with

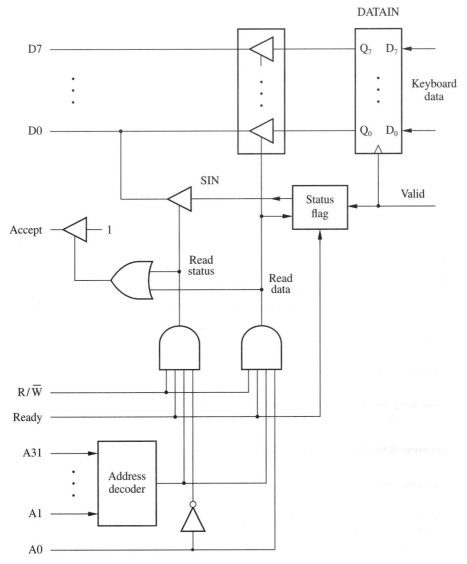

FIGURE 4.23
An input interface circuit connecting a keyboard to an asynchronous bus.

the address that selects this register. The SIN signal is generated by a status flag circuit. This signal is also sent to the bus through a three-state driver. An address decoder is used to select the input interface when the high-order 31 bits of an address correspond to addresses assigned to this interface. Address bit A0 determines whether the status or the data are to be read when the Ready signal is active. The control handshake is accomplished by activating the Accept signal when either Read-status or Read-data is equal to 1.

A possible implementation of the status flag circuit is shown in Figure 4.24. An edge-triggered D flip-flop is set to 1 by a rising edge on the Valid signal line.

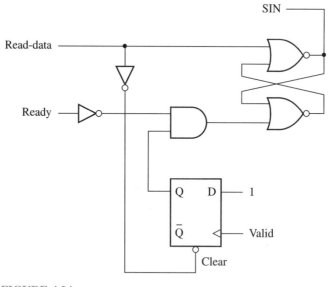

FIGURE 4.24
Circuit for the status flag block in Figure 4.23.

This event sets the NOR latch to indicate that SIN is equal to 1. The state of SIN must not change while the status is being read by the processor. The Ready signal ensures that SIN can be set only while Ready is equal to 0. In turn, this means that SIN can be set only when no read or write operations are in progress. Both the flip-flop and the latch are reset to 0 by an active Read-data signal, that is, when the processor reads the data from the interface.

Let us now consider an output interface that can be used to connect a printer. The desired connection is depicted in Figure 4.25. The printer operates under control of the handshake signals Valid and Idle, in a manner similar to the handshake used on the bus with the Ready and Accept signals. When it is ready to accept another character, the printer asserts its Idle signal. The I/O interface can then place a new character on the data lines and activate the Valid signal. The printer negates the Idle signal and starts

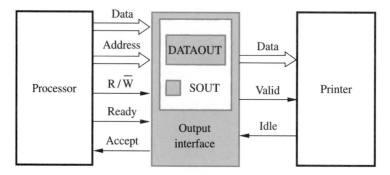

FIGURE 4.25
Printer connected to processor.

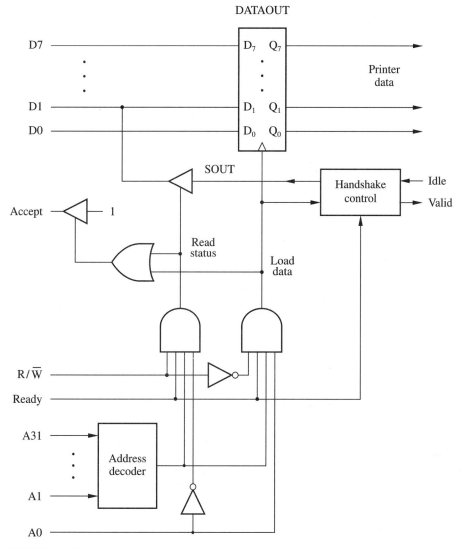

FIGURE 4.26
An output interface circuit connecting a printer to an asynchronous bus.

printing the new character, which in turn causes the interface to deactivate the Valid signal.

The interface contains a data register, DATAOUT, and a status flag, SOUT. The SOUT flag is set to 1 when the printer is ready to accept another character, and it is cleared to 0 when a new character is loaded into DATAOUT. Figure 4.26 shows an implementation of this interface. Its operation is similar to the input interface of Figure 4.26. The only significant difference is the handshake control circuit, the detailed design of which we leave as an exercise for the reader.

The input and output interfaces just described can be combined into a single interface, as shown in Figure 4.27. In this case, the overall interface is selected by

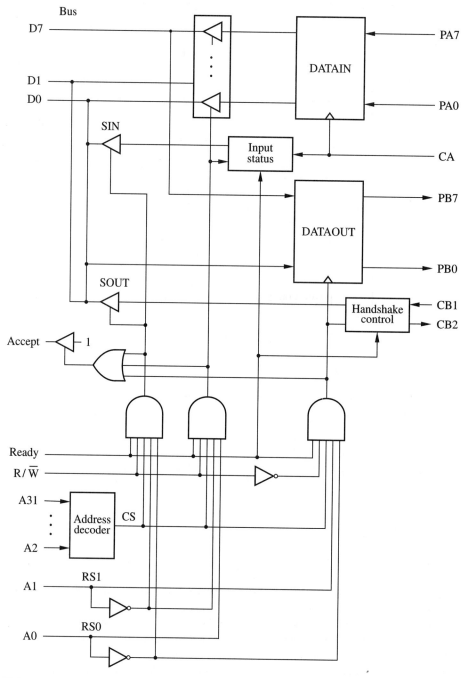

FIGURE 4.27
Combined input/output interface circuit.

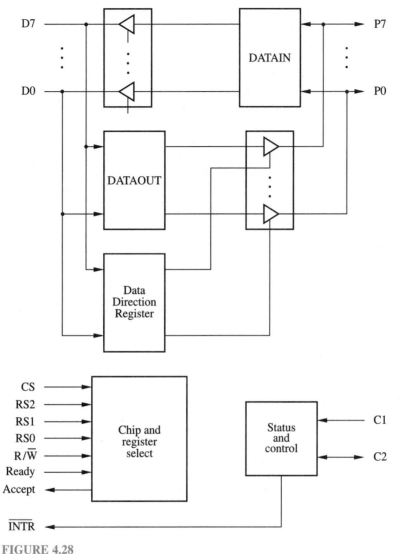

FIGURE 4.28
A bidirectional 8-bit parallel interface.

the high-order 30 bits of the address. Address bits A1 and A0 select one of the three addressable locations in the interface, namely, the two data registers and the STATUS register, which comprises the flags SIN and SOUT. Since all such locations are often referred to as registers, we have used the label Register Select, RS1 and RS0, to denote the two inputs to the decoding circuit that determine the addressed location.

The circuit in Figure 4.27 has separate input and output data lines for connection to an I/O device. A more general parallel I/O interface is created if the data lines to I/O devices are bidirectional, as in Figure 4.28. Data lines P7 through P0 can now be used for either input or output purposes. For increased flexibility, the circuit makes it possible for some lines to serve as inputs and some lines to serve as outputs, under program control. The DATAOUT register is connected to these lines via three-state drivers that are controlled by the data direction register, DDR. The processor can write any 8-bit pattern into DDR. For a given bit, if the DDR value is 1, then the corresponding data line acts as an output line; otherwise, it acts as an input line. Various locations in this interface are selected by the signals on lines RS2 through RS0, when the Chip Select (CS) input is activated. The interface has two lines, C0 and C1, to control its interaction with the I/O device it serves. It is customary to make at least one of these lines bidirectional and to provide several different modes of signaling, including the handshake. Not all the internal details are shown in the figure, but we can see how they may correspond to those in Figure 4.27. One extra control output is included in Figure 4.28, namely, interrupt request, $\overline{INTR}$, which may be used as shown in Figure 4.6.

A variety of commercial chips provide parallel interfaces that have the features illustrated in Figure 4.28. Instead of having just one set of data and control lines, or *port*, for connection to an I/O device, a commercial chip is likely to have two or more ports. In addition, many chips include timer circuits that can be driven either by a continuously running clock signal on the bus or by control signals from an I/O device. Such timers can be used for many purposes. For example, a timer incremented by the clock can be used to measure time. If the timer is incremented by a control signal from a connected I/O device, it can indicate how many times the events represented by this control signal have occurred. The timer registers can be read or written by the processor as any other register.

Serial Interface

A serial interface is used to connect the processor to I/O devices that require transmission of data one bit at a time. The key feature of a serial interface is a circuit capable of communicating in bit-serial fashion on the device side and in bit-parallel fashion on the bus side. Transformation between parallel and serial formats is achieved with shift registers that have parallel access capability. A block diagram of a typical serial interface is shown in Figure 4.29. It includes the familiar DATAIN and DATAOUT registers. The input shift register accepts bit-serial input from the I/O device. When all 8 bits of data have been received, the contents of this shift register are loaded in parallel into the DATAIN register. Similarly, output data in the DATAOUT register are loaded into the output shift register, from which the bits are shifted out and sent to the I/O device. The part of the interface that deals with the bus is the same as in the parallel interface just described. The only differences are the details of status and control circuitry. The status flags SIN and SOUT are used as follows: The SIN flag is set to 1 when new data are loaded in DATAIN; it is cleared to 0 when the processor reads the contents of DATAIN. As soon as the data are transferred from the input shift register into the DATAIN register, the shift register can start accepting the next 8-bit character from the I/O device. The SOUT flag indicates whether the output buffer is available. It is cleared to 0 when the processor writes new data into the DATAOUT register and set to 1 when data are transferred from DATAOUT into the output shift register.

The double buffering used in the input and output paths is important. A simpler interface could be implemented by turning DATAIN and DATAOUT into shift registers and eliminating the shift registers in Figure 4.29. However, this would impose awkward restrictions on the operation of the I/O device; after completing the serial transfer of

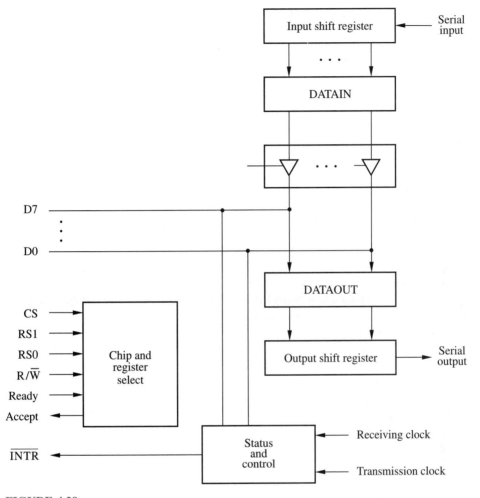

FIGURE 4.29
A serial interface.

a character, the device could not start transferring the next character until the processor read the contents of DATAIN. Thus, a pause would be needed between two characters to allow the processor to read the input data. With the double buffer, however, the transfer of the second character can begin as soon as the first character is loaded from the shift register into the DATAIN register. Thus, if the processor reads the contents of DATAIN before the serial transfer of the second character is completed, the interface can receive a continuous stream of serially transferred data. An analogous situation occurs in the output path of the interface.

The most common use of the serial interface is in connecting the computer to devices that are a considerable distance away. The communication link often involves a telephone line. The speed of transmission, often given as a *bit rate*, depends on the nature of the devices connected. To accommodate a range of devices, the serial interface must be able to use a range of clock speeds. Figure 4.29 indicates that two clock signals can be used. The receiving clock governs the shifting of data into the input shift register, and the transmission clock is used to shift data out of the output shift register.

Because serial interfaces play a vital role in connecting I/O devices, several widely used standards have been developed. A standard circuit that includes the features of our example in Figure 4.29 is known as a Universal Asynchronous Receiver Transmitter (UART). It is intended for use with low-speed serial devices, such as video terminals. Data transmission is performed using the asynchronous start-stop format, which we discuss in Chapter 9. To facilitate connection to communication links, a popular standard known as RS-232-C was developed. It is also described in Chapter 9.

4.6
STANDARD I/O INTERFACES

The previous sections point out that there are several alternative designs for the bus of a computer. This variety means that I/O devices fitted with an interface circuit suitable for one computer may not be usable with other computers. A different interface may have to be designed for every combination of I/O device and computer, resulting in many different interfaces. A better alternative is to standardize interface signals and protocols.

It is difficult to define a uniform standard for the main bus of a computer. The structure of the bus is closely tied to the architecture of the computer; therefore, it changes from one computer to another. It is equally difficult to develop a standard that covers all computer peripherals because of the extremely wide range of transfer speeds and other requirements. A workable solution is to define standards for certain classes of interconnection that are suitable for both computers and peripherals.

Figure 4.30 shows a typical arrangement in which different interfaces are used to connect various peripheral devices. The functions of parallel and serial interfaces are described in Section 4.5.2. A printer is usually connected via a parallel interface. Although a standard for a parallel interface connection to a printer has not been defined, some interfaces specified by particular manufacturers have become highly popular. One such interface is known as the Centronix Parallel Interface. It was first used by Centronix Corporation for its printers and has since been adopted by many other manufacturers.

Serial interfaces are typically used to connect video terminals. If the terminal is remotely located, the connection may involve the use of a telephone line, in which case a modem is needed at each end of the line. A widely used specification for a serial interface is the RS-232-C Standard, which we describe in Chapter 9.

The third interface in Figure 4.30 is the SCSI controller, which is used extensively for connecting bulk storage devices such as disks, tapes, and CD-ROMs. In the figure, two disk drives, a tape drive, and a CD-ROM reader are connected to the SCSI bus by means of their respective controllers. Note that more than one device can be controlled by a single controller. A detailed discussion of peripheral devices is given in Chapter 9. In the following section, we examine some of the important features of the SCSI bus.

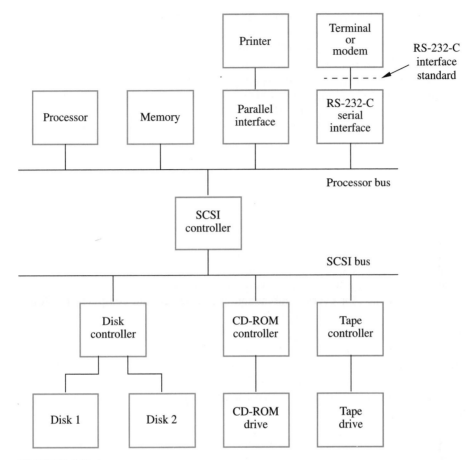

FIGURE 4.30
An example of a computer system using different interface standards.

4.6.1 SCSI Bus

The acronym SCSI stands for Small Computer System Interface. It refers to a standard bus defined by the American National Standards Institute (ANSI) under the designation X3.131.[1] It is widely used in small- to medium-sized computer systems. Devices such as disks are connected to a computer via a 50-wire cable, which can be up to 25 meters in length. Up to eight devices may be connected to the bus. Each device is connected through a controller, which implements the communication protocol needed to transfer information over the bus.

Communication with a disk drive differs substantially from communication with random access memory. As we describe in Chapter 9, data are stored on a disk in blocks called *sectors*, where each sector may contain several hundred bytes. A read or write request refers to one or more sectors. Furthermore, because of the constraints of the mechanical motion of the disk, a relatively long delay is involved in reaching the first sector to or from which data are to be transferred. When data transfer begins, the time at which individual words are transferred is dictated by the mechanical motion of the disk. The SCSI protocol is designed to take these characteristics into account.

There are two types of controllers—an *initiator* and a *target*. An initiator has the ability to select a particular target and to send commands specifying the operations to be performed. Clearly, the controller connected to a processor must be able to operate as an initiator. The disk controller operates as a target, which carries out the commands it receives from the initiator. Because of how disks operate, long delays may occur between the issuing of a command to access data on a disk and the beginning of data transfer. For this reason, the initiator establishes a *logical connection* with the intended target. Once this connection has been established, it can be suspended and restored as needed to transfer commands and blocks of data. While a particular connection is suspended, other devices can use the bus to transfer information.

An interesting feature of the SCSI bus is that data transfers are always controlled by the target controller. To send a command to a target, an initiator requests control of the bus, and, after winning arbitration, selects the controller it wants to communicate with and hands the bus over to it. Then the controller starts a data transfer operation to receive a command from the initiator. Here again, the nature of data transfer to or from I/O devices influences the design of the bus protocol. In many I/O devices, the exact timing of data transfer must be coordinated with certain aspects of the operation of the device, such as mechanical motion in a disk drive or a printer.

Let us examine a complete disk read operation as an example. In this discussion, we refer to the initiator and target controllers. Of course, the initiator performs these functions after receiving appropriate commands from the processor to which it is connected. Assume that the processor wishes to read a block of data from the disk drive and that these data are stored in two disk sectors that are not contiguous. The following sequence of events takes place:

1. The initiator contends for control of the bus.
2. When the initiator wins the arbitration process, it selects the target controller and hands over control of the bus to it.
3. The target starts an input operation (from initiator to target); in response to this, the initiator sends a command specifying the required read operation.
4. The target, realizing that it first needs to perform a disk-seek operation, sends a message to the initiator indicating that it will temporarily suspend the connection between them. Then it releases the bus.
5. The target controller sends a command to the disk drive to move the read head to the first sector involved in the requested read operation. When it is ready to begin transferring data, the target requests control of the bus. After it wins arbitration, it reselects the initiator controller, thus restoring the suspended connection.
6. The target transfers the contents of the first disk sector to the initiator, one byte at a time, and then suspends the connection again.
7. The target controller sends a command to the disk drive to perform another seek operation. Then it transfers the contents of the second disk sector to the initiator, as before. At the end of this transfer, the logical connection between the two controllers is terminated.

This scenario shows that the messages exchanged over the SCSI bus can be at a much higher level than those exchanged over the processor bus. In this context, a

TABLE 4.1
The SCSI bus signals

Category	Name	Function
Data	−DB(0) through −DB(7) −DB(P)	Data lines: Carry one byte of information during the information transfer phase and identify device during arbitration, selection, and reselection phases Parity bit for the data bus
Phase	−BSY −SEL	Busy: Asserted when the bus is not free Selection: Asserted during selection and reselection
Information type	−C/D −MSG	Control/Data: Asserted during transfer of control information (command, status, or message) Message: Indicates that the information being transferred is a message
Handshake	−REQ −ACK	Request: Asserted by a target to request a data transfer cycle Acknowledge: Asserted by the initiator when it has completed a data transfer operation
Direction of transfer	−I/O	Input/Output: Asserted to indicate an input operation (relative to the initiator)
Other	−ATN −RST	Attention: Asserted by an initiator when it wishes to send a message to a target Reset: Causes all device controls to disconnect from the bus and assume their start-up state

higher level means that the messages refer to operations that may require several steps to complete, depending on the device. However, the initiator controller, as well as the processor, need not be aware of the details of operation of the particular device involved in the data transfer. In the preceding example, the processor is unaware of the disk-seek operation and may even be unaware that the requested data are stored in two sectors. This is not necessarily always the case; a simpler disk controller may require individual seek and read commands to be generated by the processor.

The SCSI bus standard defines a wide range of control messages that can be exchanged between the controllers to handle different types of I/O devices. Messages are also defined to deal with various error or failure conditions that might arise during device operation or data transfer.

Bus Signals

We now describe the operation of the SCSI bus from the hardware point of view. The bus signals are summarized in Table 4.1. Note that all signal names are preceded by a minus sign. This indicates that the signals are active, or that a data line is equal to 1, when they are in the low-voltage state. The bus has no address lines. Instead, the data lines are used to identify the bus controllers involved during the selection or reselection process and during bus arbitration. There are eight possible controllers, numbered 0 through 7, and each is associated with the data line that has the same number. A

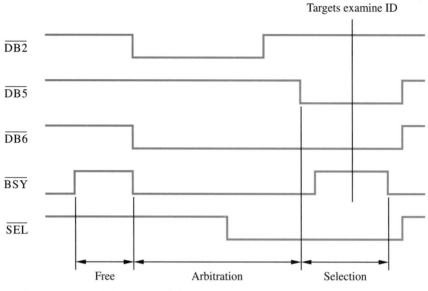

FIGURE 4.31

Arbitration and selection on the SCSI bus.

controller places its own address or the address of another controller on the bus by activating the corresponding data line. Thus, it is possible to have more than one address on the bus at the same time, as in the arbitration process we describe next. Once a connection is established between two controllers, there is no further need for addressing, and the data lines are used to carry data.

The main phases involved in the operation of the SCSI bus are arbitration, selection, data transfer, and reselection. We now examine each of these phases.

Arbitration

The bus is free when the $-$BSY signal is in the inactive (high-voltage) state. Any controller can request the use of the bus while it is in this state. Since two or more controllers may generate such a request at the same time, an arbitration scheme must be implemented. A controller requests the bus by asserting the $-$BSY signal and by asserting its associated data line to identify itself. The SCSI bus uses a simple distributed arbitration scheme. It is illustrated by the example in Figure 4.31, in which controllers number 2 and 6 request the use of the bus simultaneously.

Each controller on the bus is assigned a fixed priority, with number 7 having the highest priority. When $-$BSY becomes active, all controllers that are requesting the bus examine the data lines and determine whether a higher-priority device is requesting the bus at the same time. The controller using the highest-numbered line realizes that it has won the arbitration process. All other controllers disconnect from the bus and wait for $-$BSY to become inactive again.

In Figure 4.31, we have assumed that controller 6 is an initiator that wishes to establish a connection to a target. After winning arbitration, this controller proceeds to the selection phase.

Selection

Having won arbitration, controller 6 continues to assert −BSY and −DB6 (its address). It indicates that it wishes to select controller 5 by asserting the −SEL and then the −DB5 lines. Any other controller that may have been involved in the arbitration phase, such as controller 2 in the figure, must stop driving the data lines once the −SEL line becomes active, if it has not already done so. After placing the address of the target controller on the bus, the initiator releases the −BSY line.

The selected target controller responds by asserting −BSY. This informs the initiator that the connection it is requesting has been established, and it removes the address information on the data lines. The selection process is now complete, and the target controller (controller 5) is asserting −BSY. Thus, it has control of the bus, as required for the information transfer phase.

Information Transfer

The information transferred between two controllers may consist of commands from the initiator to the target, status responses from the target to the initiator, or data being transferred to or from the I/O device. Handshake signaling is used to control information transfers in the same manner as described in Section 4.5.1, with the target controller taking the role of the processor. The −REQ and −ACK signals replace the Ready and Accept signals in Figures 4.20 and 4.21. The target asserts −I/O during an input operation (target to initiator), and it asserts −C/D to indicate that the information being transferred is either a command or a status response.

Reselection

When a logical connection is suspended and the target is ready to restore it, it must first gain control of the bus. It starts an arbitration cycle, and after winning arbitration, it selects the initiator controller in exactly the same manner as just described. But with the roles of the target and initiator reversed, the initiator is now controlling the bus. Before data transfer can begin, the initiator must hand control over to the target. This is achieved by having the target controller assert −BSY after selecting the initiator. Meanwhile, the initiator waits for a short period after being selected, to make sure that the target has asserted −BSY, and then it releases the −BSY line. The connection between the two has now been reestablished, with the target in control of the bus as required for data transfer to proceed.

4.6.2 Backplane Bus Standards

Throughout this text, we use the single bus as the most representative way of connecting various functional units in a computer. In small computers, it is possible to place the processor, the memory, and the I/O interfaces on a single printed-circuit board. In this case, the bus is fully contained within the board, and it is defined by the requirements of the processor. In larger computers, however, it is not possible to place all components on a single board. Such systems comprise several circuit boards, typically housed in a card cage with connectors at the back, and the boards are plugged into these connectors. The pins on different connectors are wired together to form a bus, which is often referred to as a *system bus* or a *backplane*. The backplane of a computer may correspond fully to the processor bus, or it may be implemented as a different bus, perhaps conforming to some standard specification.

The main advantage of using a standard backplane is that the designer has a wide selection of readily available circuit boards that implement various functions and interfaces to different peripheral devices. Some common standards for backplane buses have been defined. A standard comprises a set of functional, electrical, and mechanical specifications of all lines and connectors in the backplane. It also specifies the protocol used for control and data transfer on the bus. The details of standard specifications can be obtained either from the manufacturers or from various organizations concerned with the development of these standards, such as the Institute of Electrical and Electronics Engineers (IEEE) or the American National Standards Institute (ANSI).

The backplane bus incorporates the data, address, and control lines needed for data transfers, interrupts, and DMA. We have already encountered examples of these signals in Sections 4.5.1, 4.2, and 4.4.1, respectively. Other lines are provided to deliver electrical power to the devices connected to the bus and to perform auxiliary functions such as testing and system start-up. A brief overview of the VMEbus Standard follows.

The VMEbus Standard[2,3] gives the functional, electrical, and mechanical specifications of an interconnection and packaging scheme for computer-based systems. This bus is suitable for small- to medium-sized systems and has been widely used in industry. Several options are available for the width of the data and address buses as well as for the size of the circuit boards. The full bus consists of 32 data lines, 32 address lines, and many control, power supply, and ground lines. Circuit boards are interconnected via a motherboard mounted at the back of a cage that fits on a 19-inch rack. Each circuit board has two 96-pin connectors that carry the bus signals. Smaller systems may have only 8 or 16 data lines and 24 address lines. These systems use smaller circuit boards with one 96-pin connector on each board.

Data transfers are controlled by handshake signaling, in a manner similar to that described in Section 4.5.1. Data rates approaching 30 Mbytes/s are possible. The bus supports seven levels of interrupt priority, and daisy-chain connections can be used to attach several devices on each level, as described in Section 4.2.2. Several processors may be connected to the bus. In this case, each of the seven interrupt levels must have one processor designated as the interrupt handler for that level. The designated processor is responsible for receiving the interrupt request, generating the interrupt acknowledge, and executing the interrupt-service routine. Bus arbitration has four levels of priority, again with the possibility of using daisy-chain connections on each level. The arbiter circuit must reside at one end of the bus, in slot number 1 in the card cage. It can implement either a fixed-priority or a rotating-priority scheme for servicing requests on the bus request lines.

Other lines on the bus include power supply lines for +5 volt, ±12 volt, and ground. They also include a line used by the system power supply to inform all devices of an imminent power failure. A few milliseconds are available for devices to save critical data before the system's operation must be shut down.

The VMEbus signals are closely related to those on the 68000 bus. As a result, this bus standard is frequently used in 68000-based computer systems. However, it is also used as an interconnection scheme with other processors or for systems that contain several different processors.

4.7
CONCLUDING REMARKS

In this chapter, we discussed three basic approaches to I/O transfers. The simplest technique is programmed I/O, in which the processor performs all the necessary control functions under direct control of program instructions. The second approach is based on the use of interrupts; this mechanism makes it possible to interrupt normal execution of programs in order to service higher-priority requests that require more urgent attention. Although all computers have a mechanism for dealing with such situations, the complexity and sophistication of interrupt-handling schemes vary from one computer to another. The third I/O scheme involves direct memory access; the DMA controller transfers data between an I/O device and the main memory without continuous processor intervention. Access to memory is shared between the DMA controller and the processor.

Finally, some issues related to interconnection standards were introduced, illustrated by the popular SCSI bus and VMEbus.

PROBLEMS

4.1. The input status bit in an interface circuit is cleared as soon as the input data buffer is read. Why is this important?

4.2. Write a program that displays the contents of 10 bytes of the main memory in hexadecimal format on a video display terminal. Use either the assembler instructions of a processor of your choice or pseudo instructions. Start at location LOC in the memory, and use two hex characters per byte. The contents of successive bytes should be separated by a space.

4.3. What is the difference between a subroutine and an interrupt-service routine?

4.4. Two magnetic disk units, a real-time clock, and some video terminals are the I/O devices connected to a computer. All devices are serviced via interrupts. The real-time clock interrupts the processor at regular time intervals (for example, every $\frac{1}{60}$ second) to keep time, and the disk interrupts the processor when it has completed an operation and is ready to receive a new command. Servicing of disk interrupts should take priority over terminal interrupts, with the real-time clock having the highest priority. Suggest suitable numerical values for the priorities of these devices.

4.5. In most computers, interrupts are not acknowledged until the current machine instruction completes execution. Consider the possibility of suspending operation of the processor in the middle of executing an instruction in order to acknowledge an interrupt. Discuss the difficulties that may arise.

4.6. Three devices, A, B, and C, are connected to the bus of a computer. I/O transfers for all three devices use interrupt control. Interrupt nesting for devices A and B is not allowed, but interrupt requests from C may be accepted while either A or B is being serviced. Suggest different ways in which this can be accomplished in each of the following cases:

(*a*) The computer has one interrupt-request line.

(*b*) Two interrupt-request lines, INTR1 and INTR2, are available, with INTR1 having higher priority.

Specify when and how interrupts are enabled and disabled in each case.

4.7. Consider a computer in which several devices are connected to a common interrupt-request line, as in Figure 4.8*a*. Explain how you would arrange for interrupts from device *j* to be accepted before the execution of the interrupt-service routine for device *i* is completed. Comment in particular on the times at which interrupts must be enabled and disabled at various points in the system.

4.8. Consider the daisy chain arrangement in Figure 4.8*a*. Assume that after a device generates an interrupt request, it turns off that request as soon as it receives the interrupt-acknowledge signal. Is it still necessary to disable interrupts in the processor before entering the interrupt-service routine? Why?

4.9. Successive data blocks of *N* bytes each are to be read from a character-oriented input device, and program PROG is to perform some computation on each block of data. Write a control program, CNTRL, for the 68000 or the PowerPC that will perform the following functions.

(*a*) Read data block 1.

(*b*) Activate PROG and point it to the location of block 1 in the main memory.

(*c*) Read block 2 using interrupts while PROG is performing computations on block 1.

(*d*) Start PROG on block 2, and meanwhile start reading block 3, and so on.

Note that CNTRL must maintain correct buffer pointers, keep track of the character count, and correctly transfer control to PROG, whether PROG takes more or less time than block input.

4.10. A computer is required to accept characters from 20 video terminals. The main memory area to be used for storing data for each terminal is pointed to by a pointer PNTR*n*, where *n* = 1 through 20. Input data must be collected from the terminals while another program PROG is being executed. This may be accomplished in one of two ways:

(*a*) Every *T* seconds, program PROG calls a subroutine DEVSUB. This subroutine checks the status of each of the 20 terminals in sequence and transfers any input characters to the memory. Then it returns to PROG.

(*b*) Whenever a character is ready in any of the interface buffers of the terminals, an interrupt request is generated. This causes the interrupt routine DEVINT to be executed. After polling the status registers, DEVINT transfers the input character and then returns to PROG.

Write the routines DEVSUB and DEVINT using either pseudo code or the assembler language of the processor of your choice. Let the maximum character rate for any terminal be *c* characters per second, with an average rate equal to *rc*, where $r \leq 1$. In method (*a*), what is the maximum value of *T* for which it is still possible to guarantee that no input characters will be lost? What is the equivalent value for method (*b*)? Estimate, on the average, the percentage of time spent in servicing the terminals for methods (*a*) and (*b*), for $c = 100$ characters per second and $r = 0.01, 0.1, 0.5,$ and 1. Assume that DEVSUB takes 20 μs (microseconds) to poll all 20 devices and that an interrupt from one device requires 5 μs to process.

4.11. Consider an I/O device that uses the vectored-interrupt capability of the 68000 processor.

(a) Describe the sequence of steps that take place when the processor receives an interrupt request, and give the number of bus transfers required during each of these steps. (Do not give details of bus signals or the microprogram.)

(b) When an interrupt request is received, the processor completes execution of the current instruction before accepting the interrupt. Examine the instruction table in Appendix C, and estimate the maximum possible number of memory transfers that can take place during that period.

(c) Estimate the number of bus transfers that can occur from the instant a device requests an interrupt until the first instruction of the interrupt-service routine is fetched for execution.

4.12. A processor with vectored-interrupt capability has one interrupt-request line and one interrupt-acknowledge line. It inspects the interrupt-request line at the end of the execution phase of each instruction. If an I/O device requests an interrupt, the processor performs all the necessary functions for accepting the interrupt-vector address, storing the processor status register and program counter on a memory stack, and branching to the interrupt-service routine. Assume that the sequence of these actions is identical to that in the 68000, and that the processor has the internal structure given in Figure 3.1. Give the control steps required for accepting an interrupt request, as in Figure 3.5. Make any necessary additions to Figure 3.1.

4.13. A logic circuit is needed to implement the priority network shown in Figure 4.8b. The network handles three interrupt request lines. When a request is received on line INTRi, the network generates an acknowledgment on line INTAi. If more than one request is received, only the highest-priority request is acknowledged, where the ordering of priorities is

$$\text{Priority of INTR1} > \text{priority of INTR2} > \text{priority of INTR3}$$

(a) Give a truth table for each of the outputs, INTA1, INTA2, and INTA3.

(b) Give a logic circuit for implementing this priority network.

(c) Can your design be easily extended for more interrupt-request lines?

(d) By adding inputs DECIDE and RESET, modify your design such that INTAi is set to 1 when a pulse is received on the input DECIDE and is reset to 0 when a pulse is received on the input RESET.

4.14. Interrupts and bus arbitration require means for selecting one of several requests based on their priority. Design a circuit that implements a rotating-priority scheme for four input lines, REQ1 through REQ4. Initially, REQ1 has the highest and REQ4 the lowest priority. After some line receives service, it becomes the lowest priority line, and the next line receives highest priority. For example, after REQ2 has been serviced, the priority order, starting with the highest, becomes REQ3, REQ4, REQ1, REQ2. Your circuit should generate four output grant signals, GR1 through GR4, one for each input request line. One of these outputs should be asserted when a pulse is received on a line called DECIDE.

4.15. The 68000 processor has a set of three lines called IPL2-0 that are used to signal interrupt requests. The 3-bit binary number on these lines is interpreted by the processor as representing the highest-priority device requesting an interrupt. Design a priority encoder circuit that accepts interrupt requests from as many as seven devices and generates a 3-bit code representing the request with the highest priority.

4.16. (This problem is suitable for use as a laboratory experiment.)

Given a video terminal connected to the computer in your laboratory, complete the following two assignments.

(*a*) Write an I/O routine A that prints letters in alphabetical order. It prints two lines as follows, and then stops:

$$ABC\ldots YZ$$
$$ABC\ldots YZ$$

(*b*) Write an I/O routine B that prints the numeric characters 0 through 9 in increasing order three times. Its output should have the following format:

$$012\ldots 9012\ldots 9102\ldots 9$$

Use program A as the main program and program B as an interrupt-service routine whose execution is initiated by entering any character on the keyboard. Execution of program B can also be interrupted by entering another character on the keyboard. When program B is completed, execution of the most recently interrupted program should be resumed at the point of interruption. Thus, the printed output may appear as follows:

$$ABC$$
$$012\ldots 901$$
$$012\ldots 9012\ldots 9012\ldots 9$$
$$2\ldots 9102\ldots 9$$
$$DE\ldots YZ$$

Show how you can use the processor priority either to enable or to inhibit interrupt nesting.

4.17. (This problem is suitable for use as a laboratory experiment.)

Write a program C in addition to programs A and B for Problem 4.16. Program C should perform the carriage control functions required to put the printed output in the following format:

$$ABC$$
$$012\ldots 901$$
$$012\ldots 9012\ldots 9012\ldots 9$$
$$2\ldots 9012\ldots 9$$
$$DE\ldots YZ$$

4.18. Consider the breakpoint scheme described in Section 4.2.4. A software-interrupt instruction replaces a program instruction where the breakpoint is inserted. Before it returns to the original program, the debugging software puts the original program instruction back in its place, thus removing the breakpoint. Explain how the debugger can put the original program instruction in its place, execute it, then install the breakpoint again before any other program instruction is executed.

4.19. The interrupt-request line, which uses the open-collector scheme, carries a signal that is the logical OR of the requests from all the devices connected to it. In a different application, it is required to generate a signal that indicates that all devices connected to the bus are ready. Explain how you can use the open-collector scheme for this purpose.

4.20. In some computers, the processor responds only to the leading edge of the interrupt-request signal on one of its interrupt-request lines. What happens if two independent devices are connected to this line?

4.21. In the arrangement in Figure 4.16, a device becomes the bus master only when it receives a low-to-high transition on its bus grant input. Assume that device 1 requests the bus and receives a grant. While it is still using the bus, device 3 asserts its BR output. Draw a timing diagram showing how device 3 becomes the bus master after device 1 releases the bus.

4.22. Assume that in the bus arbitration arrangement in Figure 4.16, the processor keeps asserting BG1 as long as $\overline{BR}$ is asserted. When device i is requesting the bus, it becomes the bus master only when it receives a low-to-high transition on its BGi input.

   (*a*) Assume that devices are allowed to assert the BR signal at any time. Give a sequence of events to show that the system can enter a deadlock situation, in which one or more devices are requesting the bus, the bus is free, and no device can become the bus master.
   (*b*) Suggest a rule for the devices to observe in order to prevent this deadlock situation from occurring.

4.23. Consider the daisy-chain arrangement shown in Figure P4.1, in which the bus-request signal is fed back directly as the bus grant. Assume that device 3 requests the bus and begins using it. When finished, it deactivates BR3. Assume that the delay from BGi to BG($i + 1$) in any device is d. Show that a spurious bus grant pulse will travel downstream from device 3 (spurious, because it is not a response to any request). Estimate the width of this pulse.

4.24. Shortly after device 3 in Problem 4.23 releases the bus, devices 1 and 5 request the bus simultaneously. Show that they can both receive a bus grant.

4.25. Consider the bus arbitration scheme shown in Figure 4.16. Assume that a local signal called BUSREQ in the device interface circuit is equal to 1 whenever the device needs to use the bus. Design the part of the interface circuit that has BUSREQ, BGi, and $\overline{BBSY}$ as inputs and that generates $\overline{BR}$, BG($i + 1$), and $\overline{BBSY}$ as outputs.

4.26. Consider the arbitration circuit shown in Figure 4.18. Assume that the priority code for a device is stored in a register in the interface circuit. Design a circuit to implement this arbitration scheme. Arbitration should begin when a signal called Compete is asserted. A little later, the arbitration circuit should activate an output called Winner if it wins the arbitration cycle.

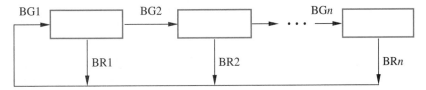

FIGURE P4.1
A decentralized bus assignment scheme.

4.27. How would the timing diagram in Figure 4.20 be affected if the distance between the processor and the I/O device is increased? How can this increased distance be accommodated in the case of Figure 4.19?

4.28. An industrial plant uses several limit sensors for monitoring temperature, pressure, and other factors. The output of each sensor consists of an ON/OFF switch, and eight such sensors must be connected to the bus of a small computer. Design an appropriate interface so that the state of all eight switches can be read simultaneously as a single byte at address $FE10_{16}$. Assume the bus is synchronous and it uses the timing sequence of Figure 4.19.

4.29. Design an appropriate interface for connecting a seven-segment display as an output device on a synchronous bus. (See Figure A.33 for a description of a seven-segment display.)

4.30. The address bus of a computer has 16 address lines, A_{15-0}. If the address assigned to one device is $7CA4_{16}$ and the address decoder for that device ignores lines A_8 and A_9, what are all the addresses to which this device will respond?

4.31. Add interrupt capability to the interface in Figure 4.23. Show how you can introduce an interrupt-enable bit, which can be set or cleared by the processor as bit 6 of the status register of the interface. The interface should assert an interrupt request line, $\overline{INTR}$, when interrupts are enabled and the input data are available to be read by the processor.

4.32. The bus of a processor uses the mixed synchronous/asynchronous approach described in Section 4.5.1. Draw a timing diagram for a read operation in which the entire bus transaction takes four clock cycles.

4.33. Consider a write operation on a bus that uses the mixed synchronous/asynchronous approach described in Section 4.5.1. Assume that the processor can send both addresses and data in the first clock cycle of a bus transaction. But the memory requires two clock cycles after that to store the data.

(*a*) Can the bus be used for other transactions during that period?

(*b*) Can we do away with the memory's response in this case? (*Hint:* Examine carefully the case in which the processor attempts another write operation to the same memory module while that module is still busy completing a previous request. Explain how this situation can be handled.)

REFERENCES

1. *Small Computer System Interface (SCSI)*. ANSI Standard X3.131, 1985.
2. *IEEE Standard for a Versatile Backplane Bus: VMEbus,* ANSI/IEEE Standard 1014, 1987.
3. Z. G. Vranesic and S. G. Zaky, *Microcomputer Structures*, Saunders College Publishing, a Division of HRW, Inc., 1989, Chapter 11.

CHAPTER 5

The Memory

Programs and the data they operate on are held in the main memory of the computer during execution. In this chapter, we discuss how this vital part of the computer operates. By now, the reader appreciates that the execution speed of programs is highly dependent on the speed with which instructions and data can be transferred between the CPU and the main memory. It is also important to have a large memory, to facilitate execution of programs that are large and deal with huge amounts of data.

Ideally, the memory would be fast, large, and inexpensive. Unfortunately, it is impossible to meet all three of these requirements simultaneously. Increased speed and size are achieved at increased cost. To solve this problem, much work has gone into developing clever structures that improve the apparent speed and size of the memory, yet keep the cost reasonable.

First we describe the most common components and organizations used to implement the main memory. Then we examine memory speed and discuss how the apparent speed of the main memory can be increased by means of caches. Next, we present the virtual memory concept, which increases the apparent size of the memory. We also show how these concepts have been implemented in the 68040 and PowerPC processors.

5.1
SOME BASIC CONCEPTS

The maximum size of the memory that can be used in any computer is determined by the addressing scheme. For example, a 16-bit computer that generates 16-bit addresses is capable of addressing up to $2^{16} = 64$K memory locations. Similarly, machines whose instructions generate 32-bit addresses can utilize a memory that contains up to $2^{32} = 4$G (giga) memory locations, whereas machines with 40-bit addresses can access up to $2^{40} = 1$T (tera) locations. The number of locations represents the size of the address space of the computer.

Most modern computers are byte-addressable. Figure 5.1 shows a possible address assignment for a byte-addressable 32-bit computer. The figure depicts the big-endian arrangement, which is explained in Section 2.1. This arrangement is used in both processors that served as examples in Chapter 2, namely, the PowerPC and 68000. The little-endian arrangement, where the byte-address assignment within a word is opposite to that shown in Figure 5.1, is also used in some commercial machines. As far as the memory structure is concerned, there is no substantial difference between the two schemes.

The main memory is usually designed to store and retrieve data in word-length quantities. In fact, the number of bits actually stored or retrieved in one main memory access is the most common definition of the word length of a computer. Consider, for example, a byte-addressable computer with the addressing structure of Figure 5.1, whose instructions generate 32-bit addresses. When a 32-bit address is sent from the CPU to the memory unit, the high-order 30 bits determine which word will be accessed. If a byte quantity is specified, the low-order 2 bits of the address specify which byte location is involved. In a Read operation, other bytes may be fetched from the memory, but they are ignored by the CPU. If the byte operation is a Write, however, the control circuitry of the memory must ensure that the contents of other bytes of the same word are not changed.

From the system standpoint, we can view the memory unit as a "black box." Data transfer between the memory and the CPU takes place through the use of two CPU registers, usually called MAR (memory address register) and MDR (memory data register). If MAR is k bits long and MDR is n bits long, then the memory unit may contain up to 2^k addressable locations. During a "memory cycle," n bits of data are transferred between the memory and the CPU. This transfer takes place over the processor bus, which has k address lines and n data lines. The bus also includes the control lines Read, Write, and Memory Function Completed (MFC) for coordinating data transfers. In byte-addressable computers, another control line may be added to indicate when only a byte, rather than a full word of n bits, is to be transferred. The connection between the CPU and the main memory is shown schematically in Figure 5.2. As Chapter 3 describes, the CPU initiates a memory operation by loading the appropriate data into registers MDR and MAR, and then setting either the Read or Write memory control line to 1. When the required operation is completed, the memory control circuitry indicates this to the CPU by setting MFC to 1. The details of bus operation are presented in Chapter 4.

Word address   Byte address

0	0	1	2	3
4	4	5	6	7
8	8	9	10	11

FIGURE 5.1
Organization of the main memory in a 32-bit byte-addressable computer.

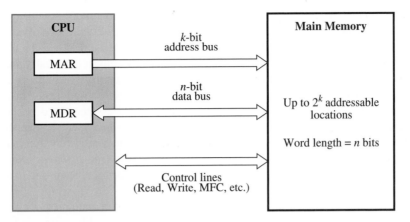

FIGURE 5.2
Connection of the main memory to the CPU.

A useful measure of the speed of memory units is the time that elapses between the initiation of an operation and the completion of that operation, for example, the time between the Read and the MFC signals. This is referred to as the *memory access time.* Another important measure is the *memory cycle time,* which is the minimum time delay required between the initiation of two successive memory operations, for example, the time between two successive Read operations. The cycle time is usually slightly longer than the access time, depending on the implementation details of the memory unit.

Recall that a memory unit is called *random-access memory* (RAM) if any location can be accessed for a Read or Write operation in some fixed amount of time that is independent of the location's address. Main memory units are of this type. This distinguishes them from serial, or partly serial, access storage devices such as magnetic tapes and disks, which we discuss in Chapter 9. Access time on the latter devices depends on the address or position of the data.

The basic technology for implementing main memories uses semiconductor integrated circuits. The sections that follow present some basic facts about the internal structure and operation of such memories. We then discuss some of the techniques used to increase the effective speed and size of the main memory.

The CPU of a computer can usually process instructions and data faster than they can be fetched from a reasonably priced main memory unit. The memory cycle time, then, is the bottleneck in the system. One way to reduce the memory access time is to use a *cache memory.* This is a small, fast memory that is inserted between the larger, slower main memory and the CPU. It holds the currently active segments of a program and their data. Another technique, called *memory interleaving,* divides the system into a number of memory modules and arranges addressing so that successive words in the address space are placed in different modules. If requests for memory access tend to involve consecutive addresses, as when the CPU executes straight-line program segments, then the accesses will be to different modules. Since parallel access to these modules is possible, the average rate of fetching words from the main memory can be increased.

Virtual memory is another important concept related to memory organization. So far, we have assumed that the addresses generated by the CPU directly specify physical locations in the main memory. This may not always be the case. For reasons that will become apparent later in this chapter, data may be stored in physical memory locations that have addresses different from those specified by the program. The memory control circuitry translates the address specified by the program into an address that can be used to access the physical memory. In such a case, an address generated by the CPU is referred to as a *virtual* or *logical address*. The virtual address space is mapped onto the physical memory where data are actually stored. The mapping function is implemented by a special memory control circuit, often called the *memory management unit.* This mapping function can be changed during program execution according to system requirements.

Virtual memory is used to increase the apparent size of the main memory. Data are addressed in a virtual address space that can be as large as the addressing capability of the CPU. But at any given time, only the active portion of this space is mapped onto locations in the physical main memory. The remaining virtual addresses are mapped onto the bulk storage devices used, which are usually magnetic disks. As the active portion of the virtual address space changes during program execution, the memory management unit changes the mapping function and transfers data between the bulk storage and the main memory. Thus, during every memory cycle, an address-processing mechanism determines whether the addressed information is in the physical main memory unit. If it is, then the proper word is accessed and execution proceeds. If it is not, a page of words containing the desired word is transferred from the bulk storage to the main memory, as Section 5.7.1 explains. This page displaces some page in the main memory that is currently inactive. Because of the time required to move pages between bulk storage and the main memory, there is a speed degradation in this type of a system. By judiciously choosing which page to replace in the memory, however, there may be reasonably long periods when the probability is high that the words accessed by the CPU are in the physical main memory unit.

This section has briefly introduced several organizational features of memory systems. These features have been developed to help provide a computer system with as large and as fast a memory as can be afforded in relation to the overall cost of the system. We do not expect the reader to grasp all the ideas or their implications now; more detail is given later. We introduce these terms together to establish that they are related; a study of their interrelationships is as important as a detailed study of their individual features.

5.2
SEMICONDUCTOR RAM MEMORIES

Semiconductor memories are available in a wide range of speeds. Their cycle times range from a few hundred nanoseconds (ns) to less than 10 nanoseconds. When first introduced in the late 1960s, they were much more expensive than the magnetic-core memories they replaced. Because of rapid advances in VLSI (very large scale integration) technology, the cost of semiconductor memories has dropped dramatically. As a result, they are now used almost exclusively in implementing main memories. In this section, we discuss the main characteristics of semiconductor memories. We start by introducing the way that a number of memory cells are organized inside a chip.

5.2.1 Internal Organization of Memory Chips

Memory cells are usually organized in the form of an array, in which each cell is capable of storing one bit of information. One such organization is shown in Figure 5.3. Each row of cells constitutes a memory word, and all cells of a row are connected to a common line referred to as the *word line,* which is driven by the address decoder on the chip. The cells in each column are connected to a Sense/Write circuit by two *bit lines.* The Sense/Write circuits are connected to the data input/output lines of the chip. During a Read operation, these circuits sense, or read, the information stored in the cells selected by a word line and transmit this information to the output data lines. During a Write operation, the Sense/Write circuits receive input information and store it in the cells of the selected word.

Figure 5.3 is an example of a very small memory chip consisting of 16 words of 8 bits each. This is referred to as a 16×8 organization. The data input and the data output of each Sense/Write circuit are connected to a single bidirectional data line in order to

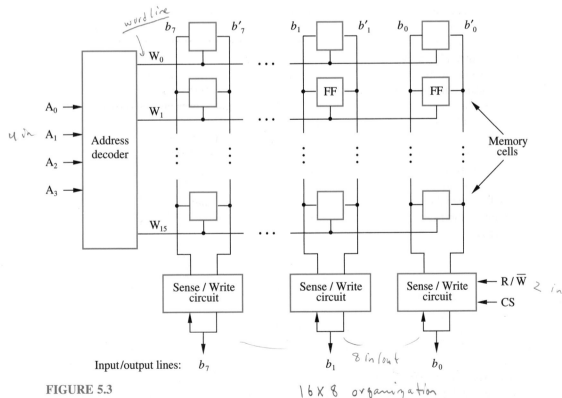

FIGURE 5.3
Organization of bit cells in a memory chip.

reduce the number of pins required. Two control lines, R/W and CS, are provided in addition to address and data lines. The R/W (Read/Write) input specifies the required operation, and the CS (Chip Select) input selects a given chip in a multichip memory system. This will be discussed in Section 5.2.4.

The memory circuit in Figure 5.3 stores 128 bits and requires 14 external connections. Thus, it can be manufactured in the form of a 16-pin chip, allowing 2 pins for power supply and ground connections. Consider now a slightly larger memory circuit, one that has 1K (1024) memory cells. This circuit can be organized as a 128×8 memory chip, requiring a total of 19 external connections. Alternatively, the same number of cells can be organized into a $1K \times 1$ format. This makes it possible to use a 16-pin chip, even if separate pins are provided for the data input and data output lines. Figure 5.4 shows such an organization. The required 10-bit address is divided into two groups of 5 bits each to form the row and column addresses for the cell array. A row address selects a row of 32 cells, all of which are accessed in parallel. However, according to the column address, only one of these cells is connected to the external data lines by the input and output multiplexers.

Commercially available chips contain a much larger number of memory cells than those shown in Figures 5.3 and 5.4. We use small examples here to make the figures easy to understand. Larger chips have essentially the same organization but use a larger memory cell array, more address inputs, and more pins. For example, a 4M-bit chip may have a $1M \times 4$ organization, in which case 20 address and 4 data input/output pins are needed. Chips with a capacity of tens of megabits are now available.

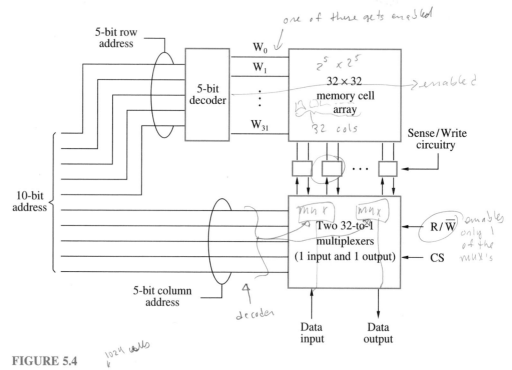

FIGURE 5.4
Organization of a $1K \times 1$ memory chip.

5.2.2 Static Memories

Memories that consist of circuits that are capable of retaining their state as long as power is applied are known as *static memories*. Figure 5.5 illustrates how a *static RAM (SRAM)* cell may be implemented. Two inverters are cross-connected to form a latch. The latch is connected to two bit lines by transistors T_1 and T_2. These transistors act as switches that can be opened or closed under control of the word line. When the word line is at ground level, the transistors are turned off, and the latch retains its state. For example, let us assume that the cell is in state 1 if the logic value at point X is 1 and at point Y is 0. This state is maintained as long as the signal on the word line is at ground level.

Read Operation

In order to read the state of the SRAM cell, the word line is activated to close switches T_1 and T_2. If the cell is in state 1, the signal on bit line b is high and the signal on bit line b' is low. The opposite is true if the cell is in state 0. Thus, b and b' are complements of each other. Sense/Write circuits at the end of the bit lines monitor the state of b and b' and set the output accordingly.

Write Operation

The state of the cell is set by placing the appropriate value on bit line b and its complement on b', and then activating the word line. This forces the cell into the corresponding state. The required signals on the bit lines are generated by the Sense/Write circuit.

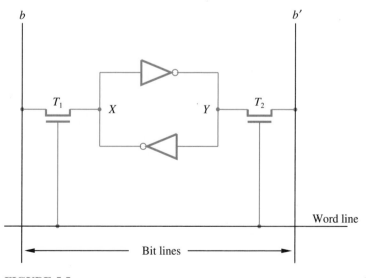

FIGURE 5.5
A static RAM cell.

CMOS Cell

A CMOS realization of the cell in Figure 5.5 is given in Figure 5.6. Transistor pairs (T_3, T_5) and (T_4, T_6) form the inverters in the latch (see Appendix A). The state of the cell is read or written as just explained. For example, in state 1, the voltage at point X is maintained high by having transistors T_3 and T_6 on, while T_4 and T_5 are off. Thus, if T_1 and T_2 are turned on (closed), bit lines b and b' will have high and low signals, respectively.

The power supply voltage, V_{supply}, is 5 volts in standard CMOS SRAMs, or 3.3 volts in low-voltage versions. Note that continuous power is needed for the cell to retain its state. If the power is interrupted, the cell's contents will be lost. When the power is restored, the latch will settle into a stable state, but it will not necessarily be the same state the cell was in before the interruption. SRAMs are said to be *volatile* memories, because their contents can be lost when power is interrupted.

A major advantage of CMOS SRAMs is their very low power consumption, because current flows in the cell only when the cell is being accessed. Otherwise, T_1, T_2, and one transistor in each inverter are turned off, ensuring that there is no active path between V_{supply} and ground.

Static RAMs can be accessed very quickly. Access times under 10 ns are now found in commercially available chips. SRAMs are used in applications where speed is of critical concern.

5.2.3 Dynamic Memories

Static RAMs are fast, but they come at a high cost because their cells require several transistors. Less expensive RAMs can be implemented if simpler cells are used.

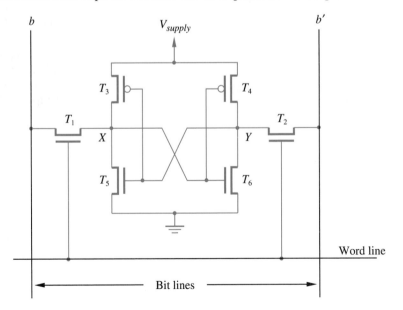

FIGURE 5.6
An example of a CMOS memory cell.

However, such cells do not retain their state indefinitely; hence, they are called *dynamic RAMs (DRAMs)*.

In *dynamic memory*, information is stored in the form of a charge on a capacitor. A DRAM is capable of storing information for only a few milliseconds. Since each cell is usually required to store information for a much longer time, its contents must be periodically refreshed by restoring the capacitor charge to its full value.

An example of a dynamic memory cell that consists of a capacitor, C, and a transistor, T, is shown in Figure 5.7. In order to store information in this cell, transistor T is turned on and an appropriate voltage is applied to the bit line. This causes a known amount of charge to be stored on the capacitor.

After the transistor is turned off, the capacitor begins to discharge. This is caused by the capacitor's own leakage resistance and by the fact that the transistor continues to conduct a tiny amount of current, measured in picoamperes, after it is turned off. Hence, the information stored in the cell can be retrieved correctly only if it is read before the charge on the capacitor drops below some threshold value. During a Read operation, the bit line is placed in a high-impedance state, and the transistor is turned on. A sense circuit connected to the bit line determines whether the charge on the capacitor is above or below the threshold value. Because this charge is so small, the Read operation is an intricate process whose details are beyond the scope of this text. The Read operation discharges the capacitor in the cell that is being accessed. In order to retain the information stored in the cell, DRAM includes special circuitry that writes back the value that has been read. A memory cell is therefore refreshed every time its contents are read. In fact, all cells connected to a given word line are refreshed whenever this word line is activated.

A typical 1-megabit DRAM chip, configured as $1M \times 1$, is shown in Figure 5.8. The cells are organized in the form of a $1K \times 1K$ array such that the high- and low-order 10 bits of the 20-bit address constitute the row and column addresses of a cell, respectively. To reduce the number of pins needed for external connections, the row and column addresses are multiplexed on 10 pins. During a Read or a Write operation, the row address is applied first. It is loaded into the row address latch in response to a signal pulse on the Row Address Strobe (RAS) input of the chip. Then a Read operation is initiated, in which all cells on the selected row are read and refreshed. Shortly after the

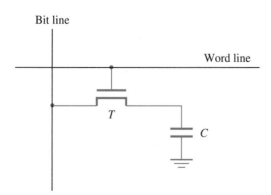

FIGURE 5.7
A single-transistor dynamic memory cell.

row address is loaded, the column address is applied to the address pins and loaded into the column address latch under control of the Column Address Strobe (CAS) signal. The information in this latch is decoded and the appropriate Sense/Write circuit is selected. If the R/$\overline{\text{W}}$ control signal indicates a Read operation, the output of the selected circuit is transferred to the data output, DO. For a Write operation, the information at the data input DI is transferred to the selected circuit. This information is then used to overwrite the contents of the selected cell in the corresponding column.

Applying a row address causes all cells on the corresponding row to be read and refreshed during both Read and Write operations. To ensure that the contents of a DRAM are maintained, each row of cells must be accessed periodically, typically once every 2 to 16 milliseconds. A *refresh circuit* usually performs this function automatically. Some dynamic memory chips incorporate a Refresh facility within the chips themselves. In this case, the dynamic nature of these memory chips is almost completely invisible to the user. Such chips are often referred to as pseudostatic.

Because of their high density and low cost, dynamic memories are widely used in the main memory units of computers. Available chips range in size from 1K to 16M bits, and even larger chips are being developed. To provide flexibility in designing memory systems, these chips are manufactured in different organizations: For example, a 4M chip may be organized as 4M $\times$ 1, 1M $\times$ 4, 512K $\times$ 8, or 256K $\times$ 16. When more than one data bit is involved, it is prudent to combine input and output data lines into single lines to reduce the number of pins, as Figure 5.3 suggests.

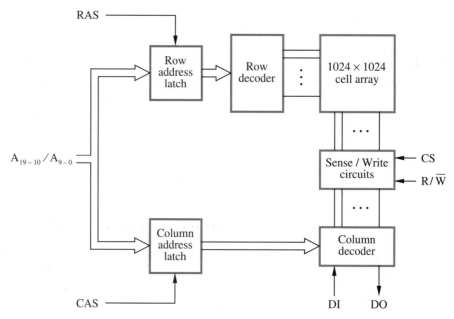

FIGURE 5.8
Internal organization of a 1M $\times$ 1 dynamic memory chip.

We now describe a useful feature that is available on many dynamic memory chips. Consider an application in which a number of memory locations at successive addresses are to be accessed, and assume that the cells involved are all on the same row inside a memory chip. Because row and column addresses are loaded separately into their respective latches, it is only necessary to load the row address once. Different column addresses can then be loaded during successive memory cycles. The rate at which such block transfers can be carried out is typically double that for transfers involving random addresses. The faster rate attainable in block transfers can be exploited in specialized machines in which memory accesses follow regular patterns, such as in graphics terminals. This feature is also beneficial in general-purpose computers for transferring data blocks between the main memory and a cache, as we explain later.

5.2.4 Memory System Considerations

The choice of a RAM chip for a given application depends on several factors. Foremost among these factors are the speed, power dissipation, and size of the chip. In certain situations, other features such as the availability of block transfers may be important.

Static RAMs are generally used only when very fast operation is the primary requirement. Their cost and size are adversely affected by the complexity of the circuit that realizes the basic cell. Dynamic RAMs are the predominant choice for implementing computer main memories. The high densities achievable in these chips make large memories economically feasible.

We now discuss the design of memory subsystems using static and dynamic chips. First, consider a small memory consisting of 64K (65,536) words of 8 bits each. Figure 5.9 gives an example of the organization of this memory using 16K × 1 static memory chips. Each column in the figure consists of four chips, which implement one bit position. Eight of these sets provide the required 64K × 8 memory. Each chip has a control input called Chip Select. When this input is set to 1, it enables the chip to accept data input or to place data on its output line. The data output for each chip is of the three-state type (see Section 3.1.5). Only the selected chip places data on the output line, while all other outputs are in the high-impedance state. The address bus for this 64K memory is 16 bits wide. The high-order 2 bits of the address are decoded to obtain the four Chip Select control signals, and the remaining 14 address bits are used to access specific bit locations inside each chip of the selected row. The R/$\overline{\text{W}}$ inputs of all chips are also tied together to provide a common Read/$\overline{\text{Write}}$ control (not shown in the figure).

Next, let us consider a large dynamic memory. The organization of this type of memory is essentially the same as the memory shown in Figure 5.9. However, the control circuitry differs in three respects. First, the row and column parts of the address for each chip usually have to be multiplexed. Second, a refresh circuit is needed. Third, the timing of various steps of a memory cycle must be carefully controlled.

Figure 5.10 depicts an array of DRAM chips and the required control circuitry for a 16M-byte dynamic memory unit. The DRAM chips are arranged in a 4 × 8 array in a format similar to that shown in Figure 5.9. The individual chips have a 1M × 4

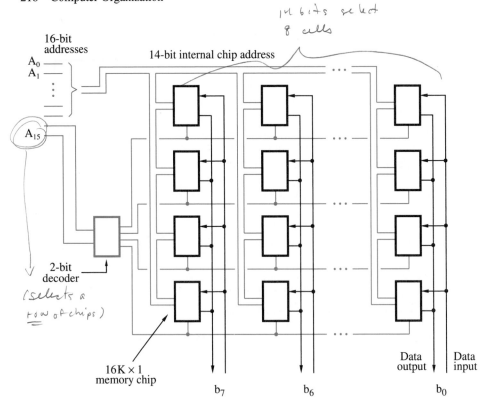

16-bit
addresses

14-bit internal chip address

A_0
A_1
⋮

A_{15}

14 bits select
8 cells

2-bit
decoder

(selects a
row of chips)

16K × 1
memory chip

Data
output   Data
input

b_7 b_6 b_0

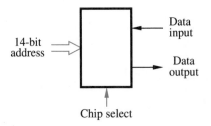

16K × 1 memory chip

Data
input

14-bit
address

Data
output

Chip select

FIGURE 5.9
Organization of a 64K × 8 memory module using 16K × 1 static memory chips.

32 chips of size (16K ×1)

organization; hence, the array has a total storage capacity of 4M words of 32 bits each. The control circuitry provides the multiplexed address and Chip Select inputs and sends the Row and Column Address Strobe signals (RAS and CAS) to the memory chip array. This circuitry also generates refresh cycles as needed. The memory unit is assumed to be connected to an asynchronous memory bus that has 22 address lines ($ADRS_{21-0}$), 32 data lines ($DATA_{31-0}$), two handshake signals (Memory Request and MFC), and a $Read/\overline{Write}$ line to indicate the type of memory cycle requested.

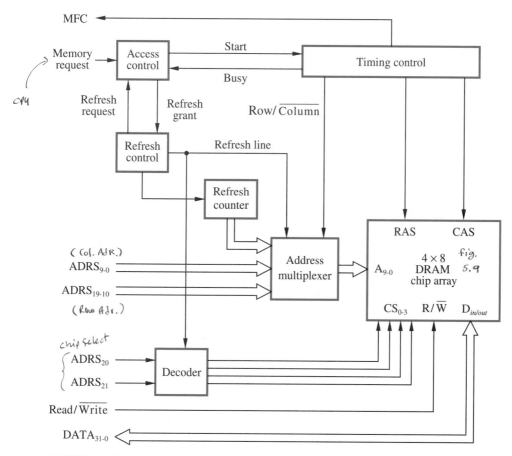

FIGURE 5.10

A block diagram of a 4M × 32 memory unit using 1M × 4 DRAM chips.

- 4m × 32 ≡ 16m×8 or 16 m- byte memory
- (4×8) organization (1m×4) chips ≡ 4m×32 memory

To understand the operation of the control circuitry displayed in Figure 5.10, let us examine a normal memory read cycle. The cycle begins when the CPU activates the address, the Read/Write, and the Memory Request lines. The access control block recognizes the request when the Memory Request signal becomes active, and it sets the Start signal to 1. The timing control block responds immediately by activating the Busy signal, to prevent the access control block from accepting new requests before the cycle ends. The timing control block then loads the row and column addresses into the memory chips by activating the RAS and CAS lines. During this time, it uses the Row/Column line to select first the row address, $ADRS_{19-10}$, followed by the column address, $ADRS_{9-0}$. The decoder block performs exactly the same function as the decoder in Figure 5.9. It decodes the two most significant bits of the address, $ADRS_{21-20}$, and activates one of the Chip Select lines, CS_{3-0}.

After obtaining the row and column parts of the address, the selected memory chips place the contents of the requested bit cells on their data outputs. This information is transferred to the data lines of the memory bus via appropriate drivers. The timing control block then activates the MFC line, indicating that the requested data are available on the memory bus. At the end of the memory cycle, the Busy signal is deactivated, and the access unit becomes free to accept new requests. Throughout the process, the timing unit is responsible for ensuring that various signals are activated and deactivated according to the specifications of the particular type of memory chips used.

Now consider a Refresh operation. The Refresh control block periodically generates Refresh requests, causing the access control block to start a memory cycle in the normal way. The access control block indicates to the Refresh control block that it may proceed with a Refresh operation by activating the Refresh Grant line. The access control block arbitrates between Memory Access requests and Refresh requests. If these requests arrive simultaneously, Refresh requests are given priority to ensure that no stored information is lost.

As soon as the Refresh control block receives the Refresh Grant signal, it activates the Refresh line. This causes the address multiplexer to select the Refresh counter as the source for the row address, instead of the external address lines $ADRS_{19-10}$. Hence, the contents of the counter are loaded into the row address latches of all memory chips when the RAS signal is activated. During this time, the R/$\overline{W}$ line of the memory bus may indicate a Write operation. We must ensure that this does not inadvertently cause new information to be loaded into some of the cells that are being refreshed. We can prevent this in several ways. One way is to have the decoder block deactivate all CS lines to prevent the memory chips from responding to the R/$\overline{W}$ line. The remainder of the refresh cycle is then the same as a normal cycle. At the end, the Refresh control block increments the Refresh counter in preparation for the next refresh cycle.

The main purpose of the refresh circuit is to maintain the integrity of the stored information. Ideally, its existence should be invisible to the remainder of the computer system. That is, other parts of the system, such as the CPU, should not be affected by the operation of the refresh circuit. In effect, however, the CPU and the refresh circuit compete for access to the memory. The refresh circuit must be given priority over the CPU to ensure that no information is lost. Thus, the response of the memory to a request from the CPU, or from a direct memory access (DMA) device, may be delayed if a refresh operation is in progress. The amount of delay caused by refresh cycles depends on the mode of operation of the refresh circuit. During a refresh operation, all memory rows may be refreshed in succession before the memory is returned to normal use. A more common scheme, however, interleaves refresh operations on successive rows with accesses from the memory bus. This results in shorter, but more frequent, refresh periods.

Refreshing detracts from the performance of DRAM memories; hence, we must minimize the total time used for this purpose. Let us consider the refresh overhead for the example in Figure 5.10. The memory array consists of 1M × 4 chips. Each chip contains a cell array organized as 1024 × 1024 × 4, which means that there are 1024 rows, with 4096 bits per row. It takes 130 ns to refresh one row, and each row must be refreshed once every 16 ms. Thus, the time needed to refresh all rows in the chip is 133 μs. Since all chips are refreshed simultaneously, the refresh overhead for the entire memory is 130/16,000 = 0.0081. Therefore, less than 1 percent of the available memory cycles in Figure 5.10 are used for refresh operations. Several schemes have been devised to hide the refresh operations as much as possible. Manufacturers' literature on DRAM products always describes the various possibilities that can be used with a given chip.

At this point, we should recall the discussion of synchronous and asynchronous buses in Chapter 4. There is an apparent increase in the access time of the memory when a request arrives while a refresh operation is in progress. The resulting variability in access time is naturally accommodated on an asynchronous bus, provided that the maximum access time does not exceed the time-out period that usually exists in such systems. This constraint is easily met when the interleaved refresh scheme is used. In the case of a synchronous bus, it may be possible to hide a refresh cycle within the early part of a bus cycle if sufficient time remains after the refresh cycle to carry out a Read or Write access. Alternatively, the refresh circuit may request bus cycles in the same manner as any device with DMA capability.

We have considered the key aspects of DRAM chips and the larger memories that can be constructed using these chips. There is another issue that should be mentioned. Modern computers use very large memories; even a small personal computer is likely to have at least 4M bytes of memory. Typical workstations have at least 16M bytes of memory. A large memory leads to better performance, because more of the programs and data used in processing can be held in the memory, thus reducing the frequency of accessing the information in secondary storage. However, if a large memory is built by placing DRAM chips directly on the main system printed-circuit board that contains the processor and the off-chip cache, it will occupy an unacceptably large amount of space on the board. Also, it is awkward to provide for future expansion of the memory, because space must be allocated and wiring provided for the maximum expected size. These packaging considerations have led to the development of larger memory units known as *SIMM*s (Single In-line Memory Modules). A SIMM is an assembly of several DRAM chips on a separate small board that plugs vertically into a single socket on the main system board. SIMMs of different sizes are designed to use the same size socket. For example, $1M \times 8$, $4M \times 8$, and $16M \times 8$ bit SIMMs all use the same 30-pin socket. Similarly, $1M \times 32$, $2M \times 32$, $4M \times 32$, and $8M \times 32$ SIMMs use a 72-pin socket. Such SIMMs occupy a smaller amount of space on a printed-circuit board, and they allow easy expansion if a larger SIMM uses the same socket as the smaller one.

5.3
READ-ONLY MEMORIES

Chapter 3 discussed the use of read-only memory (ROM) units as the control store component in a microprogrammed CPU. Semiconductor ROMs are well suited for this application. They can also be used to implement parts of the main memory of a computer that contain fixed programs or data.

Figure 5.11 shows a possible configuration for a ROM cell. A logic value 0 is stored in the cell if the transistor is connected to ground at point P; otherwise, a 1 is stored. The bit line is connected through a resistor to the power supply. To read the state of the cell, the word line is activated. Thus, the transistor switch is closed and the voltage on the bit line drops to near zero if there is a connection between the transistor and ground. If there is no connection to ground, the bit line remains at the high voltage, indicating a 1. A sense circuit at the end of the bit line generates the proper output value.

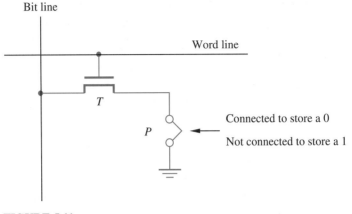

FIGURE 5.11
A ROM cell.

Data are written into a ROM when it is manufactured. However, some ROM designs allow the data to be loaded by the user, thus providing a *programmable ROM (PROM)*. Programmability is achieved by inserting a fuse at point P in Figure 5.11. Before it is programmed, the memory contains all 0s. The user can insert 1s at the required locations by burning out the fuses at these locations using high-current pulses. Of course, this process is irreversible.

PROMs provide flexibility and convenience not available with ROMs. The latter are economically attractive for storing fixed programs and data when high volumes of ROMs are produced. However, the cost of preparing the masks needed for storing a particular information pattern in ROMs makes them very expensive when only a small number are required. In this case, PROMs provide a faster and considerably less expensive approach, because they can be programmed directly by the user.

Another type of ROM chip allows the stored data to be erased and new data to be loaded. Such a chip is an erasable, reprogrammable ROM, usually called an *EPROM*. It provides considerable flexibility during the development phase of digital systems. Since EPROMs are capable of retaining stored information for a long time, they can be used in place of ROMs while software is being developed. In this way, memory changes and updates can be easily made.

An EPROM cell has a structure similar to the ROM cell in Figure 5.11. In an EPROM cell, however, the connection to ground is always made at point P, and a special transistor is used, which has the ability to function either as a normal transistor or as a disabled transistor that is always turned off. This transistor can be programmed to behave as a permanently open switch, by injecting into it a charge that becomes trapped inside. Thus, an EPROM cell can be used to construct a memory in the same way as the previously discussed ROM cell.

An important advantage of EPROM chips is that their contents can be erased and reprogrammed. Erasure requires dissipating the charges trapped in the transistors of memory cells; this can be done by exposing the chip to ultraviolet light. For this reason, EPROM chips are mounted in packages that have transparent windows.

A significant disadvantage of EPROMs is that a chip must be physically removed from the circuit for reprogramming and that its entire contents are erased by the ultraviolet light. It is possible to implement another version of erasable PROMs that can be both programmed and erased electrically. Such chips, called EEPROMs or E^2PROMs, do not have to be removed for erasure. Moreover, it is possible to erase the cell contents selectively. The only disadvantage of EEPROMs is that different voltages are needed for erasing, writing, and reading the stored data.

5.4
SPEED, SIZE, AND COST

We have already stated that an ideal main memory would be fast, large, and inexpensive. From the discussion in Section 5.2, it is clear that a very fast memory can be achieved if SRAM chips are used. But these chips are expensive because their basic cells have six transistors, which precludes packing a very large number of cells onto a single chip. Thus, for cost reasons, it is impractical to build a large memory using SRAM chips. The only alternative is to use DRAM chips, which have much simpler basic cells and thus are much less expensive. But such memories are significantly slower.

Although DRAMs allow main memories in the range of tens of megabytes to be implemented at a reasonable cost, the affordable size is still small compared to the demands of large programs with voluminous data. A solution is provided by using secondary storage, mainly magnetic disks, to implement large memory spaces. Very large disks are available at a reasonable price, and they are used extensively in computer systems. However, they are much slower than the main memory unit. So we conclude the following: A huge amount of cost-effective storage can be provided by magnetic disks. A large, yet affordable, main memory can be built with DRAM technology. This leaves SRAMs to be used in smaller units where speed is of the essence, such as in cache memories.

All of these different types of memory units are employed effectively in a computer. The entire computer memory can be viewed as the hierarchy depicted in Figure 5.12. The figure shows two types of cache memory. A primary cache is located on the CPU chip, as introduced in Figure 1.6. This cache is small, because it competes for space on the CPU chip, which must implement many other functions. A larger, secondary cache is placed between the primary cache and the main memory. Information is transferred between the adjacent units in the figure, but this does not mean that separate paths exist for these transfers. The familiar single-bus structure can be used as the interconnection medium.

Including a primary cache on the processor chip and using a larger, off-chip, secondary cache is the most common way of designing computers in the 1990s. However, other arrangements can be found in practice. It is possible not to have a cache on the processor chip at all. Also, it is possible to have two levels of cache on the processor chip, as in the Alpha 21164 processor (see Table 8.1).

During program execution, the speed of memory access is of utmost importance. The key to managing the operation of the hierarchical memory system in Figure 5.12

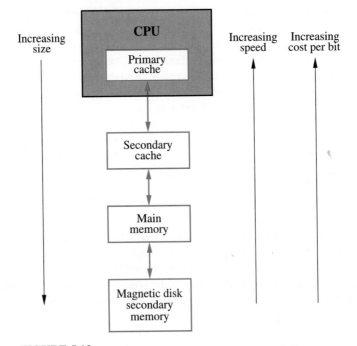

FIGURE 5.12
Memory hierarchy.

is to bring the instructions and data that will be used in the near future as close to the CPU as possible. This can be done by using the mechanisms presented in the sections that follow. We begin with a detailed discussion of cache memories.

5.5
CACHE MEMORIES

The effectiveness of the cache mechanism is based on a property of computer programs called the locality of reference. Analysis of programs shows that most of their execution time is spent on routines in which many instructions are executed repeatedly. These instructions may constitute a simple loop, nested loops, or a few procedures that repeatedly call each other. The actual detailed pattern of instruction sequencing is not important—the point is that many instructions in localized areas of the program are executed repeatedly during some time period, and the remainder of the program is accessed relatively infrequently. This is referred to as *locality of reference*. It manifests itself in two ways—temporal and spatial. The first means that a recently executed instruction is likely to be executed again very soon. The spatial aspect means that instructions in close proximity to a recently executed instruction (with respect to the instructions' addresses) are also likely to be executed soon.

If the active segments of a program can be placed in a fast cache memory, then the total execution time can be reduced significantly. Conceptually, operation of a cache memory is very simple. The memory control circuitry is designed to take advantage of the property of locality of reference. The temporal aspect of the locality of reference suggests that whenever an information item (instruction or data) is first needed, this item should be brought into the cache where it will hopefully remain until it is needed again. The spatial aspect suggests that instead of bringing just one item from the main memory to the cache, it is wise to bring several items that reside at adjacent addresses as well. We will use the term *block* to refer to a set of contiguous addresses of some size. Another term that is often used to refer to a cache block is *cache line*.

Consider the simple arrangement in Figure 5.13. When a Read request is received from the CPU, the contents of a block of memory words containing the location specified are transferred into the cache one word at a time. Subsequently, when the program references any of the locations in this block, the desired contents are read directly from the cache. Usually, the cache memory can store a reasonable number of blocks at any given time, but this number is small compared to the total number of blocks in the main memory. The correspondence between the main memory blocks and those in the cache is specified by a *mapping function*. When the cache is full and a memory word (instruction or data) that is not in the cache is referenced, the cache control hardware must decide which block should be removed to create space for the new block that contains the referenced word. The collection of rules for making this decision constitutes the *replacement algorithm*.

The CPU does not need to know explicitly about the existence of the cache. It simply issues Read and Write requests using addresses that refer to locations in the main memory. The cache control circuitry determines whether the requested word currently exists in the cache. If it does, the Read or Write operation is performed on the appropriate cache location. In this case, a *read* or *write hit* is said to have occurred. In a Read operation, the main memory is not involved. For a Write operation, the system can proceed in two ways. In the first technique, called *write-through* protocol, the cache location and the main memory location are updated simultaneously. The second technique is to update only the cache location and to mark it as updated with an associated flag bit, often called the *dirty* or *modified* bit. The main memory location of the word is updated later, when the block containing this marked word is to be removed from the cache to make room for a new block. This technique is known as the *write-back*, or *copy-back*, protocol. The write-through protocol is simpler, but it results in unnecessary Write operations in the main memory when a given cache word is updated several times during its cache residency. Note that the write-back protocol may also result in unnecessary Write operations, because when a cache block is written back to the memory all words

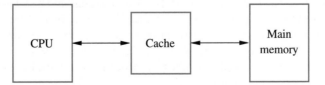

FIGURE 5.13
Use of a cache memory.

of the block are written back, even if only a single word has been changed while the block was in the cache.

When the addressed word in a Read operation is not in the cache, a *read miss* occurs. The block of words that contains the requested word is copied from the main memory into the cache. After the entire block is loaded into the cache, the particular word requested is forwarded to the CPU. Alternatively, this word may be sent to the CPU as soon as it is read from the main memory. The latter approach, which is called *load-through* (or *early restart*), reduces the CPU's waiting period somewhat, but at the expense of more complex circuitry.

During a Write operation, if the addressed word is not in the cache, a *write miss* occurs. Then, if the write-through protocol is used, the information is written directly into the main memory. In the case of the write-back protocol, the block containing the addressed word is first brought into the cache, and then the desired word in the cache is overwritten with the new information.

5.5.1 Mapping Functions

To discuss possible methods for specifying where memory blocks are placed in the cache, we use a specific small example. Consider a cache consisting of 128 blocks of 16 words each, for a total of 2048 (2K) words, and assume that the main memory is addressable by a 16-bit address. The main memory has 64K words, which we will view as 4K blocks of 16 words each.

The simplest way to determine cache locations in which to store memory blocks is the *direct-mapping* technique. In this technique, block j of the main memory maps onto block j modulo 128 of the cache, as depicted in Figure 5.14. Thus, whenever one of the main memory blocks 0, 128, 256, . . . is loaded in the cache, it is stored in cache block 0. Blocks 1, 129, 257, . . . are stored in cache block 1, and so on. Since more than one memory block is mapped onto a given cache block position, contention may arise for that position even when the cache is not full. For example, instructions of a program may start in block 1 and continue in block 129, possibly after a branch. As this program is executed, both of these blocks must be transferred to the block-1 position in the cache. Contention is resolved by allowing the new block to overwrite the currently resident block. In this case, the replacement algorithm is trivial.

Placement of a block in the cache is determined from the memory address. The memory address can be divided into three fields, as shown in Figure 5.14. The low-order 4 bits select one of 16 words in a block. When a new block enters the cache, the 7-bit cache block field determines the cache position in which this block must be stored. The high-order 5 bits of the memory address of the block are stored in 5 *tag* bits associated with its location in the cache. They identify which of the 32 blocks that are mapped into this cache position are currently resident in the cache. As execution proceeds, the 7-bit cache block field of each address generated by the CPU points to a particular block location in the cache. The high-order 5 bits of the address are compared with the tag bits associated with that cache location. If they match, then the desired word is in that block of the cache. If there is no match, then the block containing the required word must first be read from the main memory and loaded into the cache. The direct-mapping technique is easy to implement, but it is not very flexible.

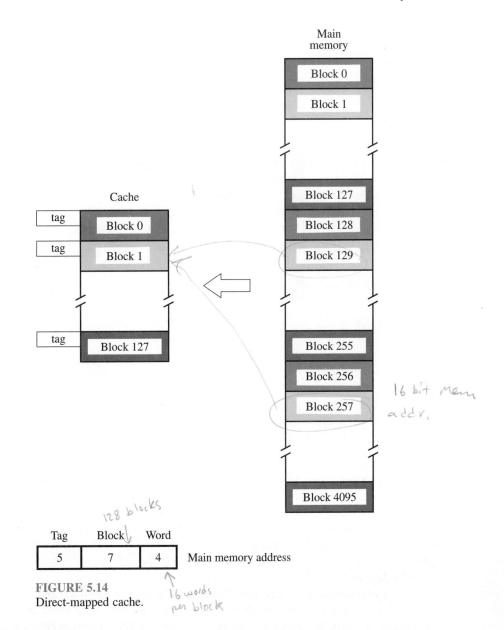

Tag   Block   Word

5	7	4

Main memory address

FIGURE 5.14
Direct-mapped cache.

Figure 5.15 shows a much more flexible mapping method, in which a main memory block can be placed into any cache block position. In this case, 12 tag bits are required to identify a memory block when it is resident in the cache. The tag bits of an address received from the CPU are compared to the tag bits of each block of the cache to see if the desired block is present. This is called the *associative-mapping* technique. It gives complete freedom in choosing the cache location in which to place the memory block. Thus, the space in the cache can be used more efficiently. A new block that has to be brought into the cache has to replace (eject) an existing block only if the cache is full. In this case, we need an algorithm to select the block to be replaced. Many replacement

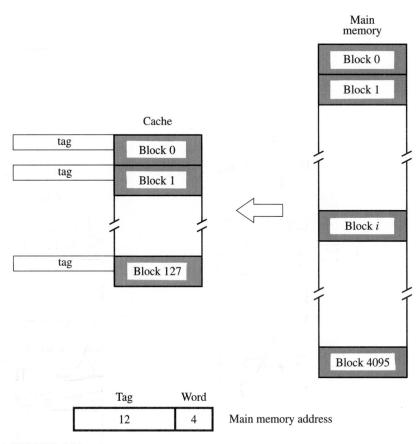

Tag   Word

12	4

Main memory address

FIGURE 5.15
Associative-mapped cache.

algorithms are possible, as we discuss in the next section. The cost of an associative cache is higher than the cost of a direct-mapped cache because of the need to search all 128 tag patterns to determine whether a given block is in the cache. A search of this kind is called an *associative search*. For performance reasons, the tags must be searched in parallel.

A combination of the direct- and associative-mapping techniques can be used. Blocks of the cache are grouped into sets, and the mapping allows a block of the main memory to reside in any block of a specific set. Hence, the contention problem of the direct method is eased by having a few choices for block placement. At the same time, the hardware cost is reduced by decreasing the size of the associative search. An example of this *set-associative-mapping* technique is shown in Figure 5.16 for a cache with two blocks per set. In this case, memory blocks 0, 64, 128, ..., 4032 map into cache set 0, and they can occupy either of the two block positions within this set. Having 64 sets means that the 6-bit set field of the address determines which set of the cache might contain the desired block. The tag field of the address must then be associatively compared to the tags of the two blocks of the set to check if the desired block is present. This two-way associative search is simple to implement.

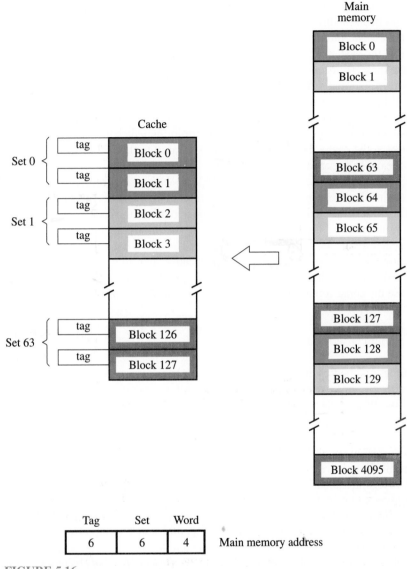

FIGURE 5.16
Set-associative-mapped cache with two blocks per set.

The number of blocks per set is a parameter that can be selected to suit the requirements of a particular computer. For the main memory and cache sizes in Figure 5.16, four blocks per set can be accommodated by a 5-bit set field, eight blocks per set by a 4-bit set field, and so on. The extreme condition of 128 blocks per set requires no set bits and corresponds to the fully associative technique, with 12 tag bits. The other extreme of one block per set is the direct-mapping method.

One more control bit, called the *valid bit*, must be provided for each block. This bit indicates whether the block contains valid data. It should not be confused with the modified, or dirty, bit mentioned earlier. The dirty bit, which indicates whether the block has been modified during its cache residency, is needed only in systems that do not use the write-through method. The valid bits are all set to 0 when power is initially applied to the system or when the main memory is loaded with new programs and data from the disk. Transfers from the disk to the main memory are carried out by a DMA mechanism. Normally, they bypass the cache for both cost and performance reasons. The valid bit of a particular cache block is set to 1 the first time this block is loaded from the main memory. Whenever a main memory block is updated by a source that bypasses the cache, a check is made to determine whether the block being loaded is currently in the cache. If it is, its valid bit is cleared to 0. This ensures that *stale* data will not exist in the cache.

A similar difficulty arises when a DMA transfer is made from the main memory to the disk, and the cache uses the write-back protocol. In this case, the data in the memory might not reflect the changes that may have been made in the cached copy. One solution to this problem is to *flush* the cache by forcing the dirty data to be written back to the memory before the DMA transfer takes place. The operating system can do this easily, and it does not affect performance greatly, because such I/O writes do not occur often. This need to ensure that two different entities (the CPU and DMA subsystems in this case) use the same copies of data is referred to as a *cache-coherence* problem.

5.5.2 Replacement Algorithms

In a direct-mapped cache, the position of each block is predetermined; hence, no re-placement strategy exists. In associative and set-associative caches there exists some flexibility. When a new block is to be brought into the cache and all the positions that it may occupy are full, the cache controller must decide which of the old blocks to overwrite. This is an important issue, because the decision can be a strong determining factor in system performance. In general, the objective is to keep blocks in the cache that are likely to be referenced in the near future. However, it is not easy to determine which blocks are about to be referenced. The property of locality of reference in pro-grams gives a clue to a reasonable strategy. Because programs usually stay in localized areas for reasonable periods of time, there is a high probability that the blocks that have been referenced recently will be referenced again soon. Therefore, when a block is to be overwritten, it is sensible to overwrite the one that has gone the longest time with-out being referenced. This block is called the *least recently used (LRU)* block, and the technique is called the *LRU replacement algorithm.*

To use the LRU algorithm, the cache controller must track references to all blocks as computation proceeds. Suppose it is required to track the LRU block of a four-block set in a set-associative cache. A 2-bit counter can be used for each block. When a hit occurs, the counter of the block that is referenced is set to 0. Counters with values originally lower than the referenced one are incremented by one, and all others remain unchanged. When a *miss* occurs and the set is not full, the counter associated with the new block loaded from the main memory is set to 0, and the values of all other counters are increased by one. When a miss occurs and the set is full, the block with the counter value 3 is removed, the new block is put in its place, and its counter is set to 0. The other three block counters are incremented by one. It can be easily verified that the counter values of occupied blocks are always distinct.

The LRU algorithm has been used extensively. Although it performs well for many access patterns, it can lead to poor performance in some cases. For example, it produces disappointing results when accesses are made to sequential elements of an array that is slightly too large to fit into the cache (see Section 5.5.3 and Problem 5.12). Performance of the LRU algorithm can be improved by introducing a small amount of randomness in deciding which block to replace.

Several other replacement algorithms are also used in practice. An intuitively reasonable rule would be to remove the "oldest" block from a full set when a new block must be brought in. However, because this algorithm does not take into account the recent pattern of access to blocks in the cache, it is generally not as effective as the LRU algorithm in choosing the best blocks to remove. The simplest algorithm is to randomly choose the block to be overwritten. Interestingly enough, this simple algorithm has been found to be quite effective in practice.

5.5.3 Example of Mapping Techniques

We now consider a detailed example to illustrate the effects of different cache mapping techniques. Assume that a processor has separate instruction and data caches. To keep the example simple, assume the data cache has space for only eight blocks of data. Also assume that each block consists of only one 16-bit word of data and the memory is word-addressable with 16-bit addresses. (These parameters are not realistic for actual computers, but they allow us to illustrate mapping techniques clearly.) Finally, assume the LRU replacement algorithm is used for block replacement in the cache.

Let us examine changes in the data cache entries caused by running the following application: A 4×10 array of numbers, each occupying one word, is stored in main memory locations 7A00 through 7A27 (hex). The elements of this array, A, are stored in column order, as shown in Figure 5.17. The figure also indicates how tags for different cache mapping techniques are derived from the memory address. Note that no bits are needed to identify a word within a block, as was done in Figures 5.14 through 5.16, because we have assumed that each block contains only one word. The application normalizes the elements of the first row of A, with respect to the average value of the elements in the row. Hence, we need to compute the average of the elements in the row and divide each element by that average. The required task can be expressed as

$$a_{0,i} \leftarrow \frac{a_{0,i}}{\left(\sum_{j=0}^{9} a_{0,j}\right)/10} \qquad for\ i = 0, 1, \ldots, 9$$

Figure 5.18 gives the structure of a program that corresponds to this task. In a machine language implementation of this program, the array elements will be addressed as memory locations. We use the variables SUM and AVE to hold the sum and average values, respectively. These variables, as well as index variables i and j, will be held in processor registers during the computation.

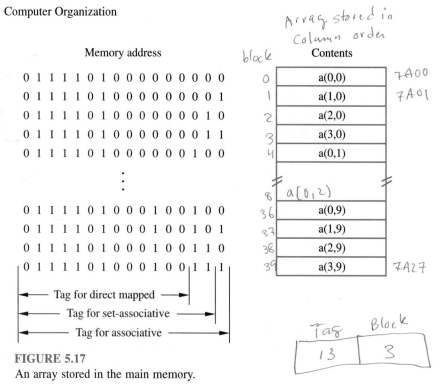

Array stored in Column order *(handwritten)*

Memory address	block	Contents	
0 1 1 1 1 0 1 0 0 0 0 0 0 0 0 0	0	a(0,0)	7A00
0 1 1 1 1 0 1 0 0 0 0 0 0 0 0 1	1	a(1,0)	7A01
0 1 1 1 1 0 1 0 0 0 0 0 0 0 1 0	2	a(2,0)	
0 1 1 1 1 0 1 0 0 0 0 0 0 0 1 1	3	a(3,0)	
0 1 1 1 1 0 1 0 0 0 0 0 0 1 0 0	4	a(0,1)	
⋮	8	a(0,2)	
0 1 1 1 1 0 1 0 0 0 1 0 0 1 0 0	36	a(0,9)	
0 1 1 1 1 0 1 0 0 0 1 0 0 1 0 1	37	a(1,9)	
0 1 1 1 1 0 1 0 0 0 1 0 0 1 1 0	38	a(2,9)	
0 1 1 1 1 0 1 0 0 0 1 0 0 1 1 1	39	a(3,9)	7A27

◄─── Tag for direct mapped ───►
◄─── Tag for set-associative ───►
◄─── Tag for associative ───►

(handwritten table)

Tag	Block
13	3

FIGURE 5.17
An array stored in the main memory.

Direct-mapped cache

In a direct-mapped data cache, the contents of the cache change as shown in Figure 5.19. The columns in the table indicate the cache contents after various passes through the two program loops in Figure 5.18 are completed. For example, after the second pass through the first loop ($j = 1$), the cache holds the elements $a_{0,0}$ and $a_{0,1}$. These elements are in block positions 0 and 4, as determined by the three least-significant bits of the address. During the next pass, the $a_{0,0}$ element is replaced by $a_{0,2}$, which maps into the same block position. Note that the desired elements map into only two positions in the cache, thus leaving the contents of the other six positions unchanged from whatever they were before the normalization task was executed.

```
SUM := 0
for j:= 0 to 9 do
        SUM := SUM + A(0, j)
end
AVE := SUM / 10
for i:= 9 downto 0 do
        A(0, i) := A(0, i) / AVE
end
```

0,9 / 0,8 no replacement here *(handwritten)*
0,7 must replace *(handwritten)*

FIGURE 5.18
Task for the example in Section 5.5.3.

X = replacing (handwritten)

Block position	Contents of data cache after pass:								
	$j = 1$	$j = 3$	$j = 5$	$j = 7$	$j = 9$	$i = 6$	$i = 4$	$i = 2$	$i = 0$
0	a(0,0)	a(0,2)	a(0,4)	a(0,6)	a(0,8)	a(0,6)	a(0,4)	a(0,2)	a(0,0)
1									
2									
3									
4	a(0,1)	a(0,3)	a(0,5)	a(0,7)	a(0,9)	a(0,7)	a(0,5)	a(0,3)	a(0,1)
5									
6									
7									

(handwritten: ← 1st loop → ← 2nd loop →)

FIGURE 5.19
Contents of a direct-mapped data cache in the example in Section 5.5.3.

After the tenth pass through the first loop ($j = 9$), the elements $a_{0,8}$ and $a_{0,9}$ are found in the cache. Since the second loop reverses the order in which the elements are handled, the first two passes through this loop ($i = 9, 8$) will find the required data in the cache. When $i = 7$, the element $a_{0,9}$ is replaced with $a_{0,7}$. When $i = 6$, element $a_{0,8}$ is replaced with $a_{0,6}$, and so on. Thus, eight elements are replaced while the second loop is executed.

The reader should keep in mind that the tags must be kept in the cache for each block; we have not shown them in the figure for space reasons.

Associative-mapped cache

Figure 5.20 presents the changes if the cache is associative-mapped. During the first eight passes through the first loop, the elements are brought into consecutive block positions, assuming that the cache was initially empty. During the ninth pass ($j = 8$), the LRU algorithm chooses $a_{0,0}$ to be overwritten by $a_{0,8}$. The next and last pass through

least recently used (handwritten)

Block position	Contents of data cache after pass:				
	$j = 7$	$j = 8$	$j = 9$	$i = 1$	$i = 0$
0	a(0,0)	a(0,8)	a(0,8)	a(0,8)	a(0,0)
1	a(0,1)	a(0,1)	a(0,9)	a(0,1)	a(0,1)
2	a(0,2)	a(0,2)	a(0,2)	a(0,2)	a(0,2)
3	a(0,3)	a(0,3)	a(0,3)	a(0,3)	a(0,3)
4	a(0,4)	a(0,4)	a(0,4)	a(0,4)	a(0,4)
5	a(0,5)	a(0,5)	a(0,5)	a(0,5)	a(0,5)
6	a(0,6)	a(0,6)	a(0,6)	a(0,6)	a(0,6)
7	a(0,7)	a(0,7)	a(0,7)	a(0,7)	a(0,7)

LRU (handwritten)

FIGURE 5.20
Contents of an associative-mapped data cache in the example in Section 5.5.3.

(handwritten: a(0,9) not in cache → LRU is a(0,1), most rec. used there is a(0,8)) the j loop sees $a_{0,1}$ replaced by $a_{0,9}$. Now, for the first eight passes through the second loop ($i = 9, 8, \ldots, 2$) all required elements are found in the cache. When $i = 1$, the element needed is $a_{0,1}$, so it replaces the least recently used element, $a_{0,9}$. During the last pass, $a_{0,0}$ replaces $a_{0,8}$.

In this case, when the second loop is executed, only two elements are not found in the cache. In the direct-mapped case, eight of the elements had to be reloaded during the second loop. Obviously, the associative-mapped cache benefits from the complete freedom in mapping a memory block into any position in the cache. Good utilization of this cache is also due to the fact that we chose to reverse the order in which the elements are handled in the second loop of the program. It is interesting to consider what would happen if the second loop dealt with the elements in the same order as in the first loop (see Problem 5.12). Using the LRU algorithm, all elements would be overwritten before they are used in the second loop. This degradation in performance would not occur if a random replacement algorithm were used.

Set-associative-mapped cache

For this example, we assume that a set-associative data cache is organized into two sets, each capable of holding four blocks. Thus, the least-significant bit of an address determines which set the corresponding memory block maps into. The high-order 15 bits constitute the tag.

Changes in the cache contents are depicted in Figure 5.21. Since all the desired blocks have even addresses, they map into set 0. Note that, in this case, six elements must be reloaded during execution of the second loop.

Even though this is a simplified example, it illustrates that in general, associative mapping performs best, set-associative mapping is next best, and direct mapping is the worst. However, fully associative mapping is expensive to implement, so set-associative mapping is a good practical compromise.

	Contents of data cache after pass:					
	$j = 3$	$j = 7$	$j = 9$	$i = 4$	$i = 2$	$i = 0$
Set 0	a(0,0)	a(0,4)	a(0,8)	a(0,4)	a(0,4)	a(0,0)
	a(0,1)	a(0,5)	a(0,9)	a(0,5)	a(0,5)	a(0,1)
	a(0,2)	a(0,6)	a(0,6)	a(0,6)	a(0,2)	a(0,2)
	a(0,3)	a(0,7)	a(0,7)	a(0,7)	a(0,3)	a(0,3)
Set 1						

FIGURE 5.21
Contents of a set-associative-mapped data cache in the example in Section 5.5.3.

5.5.4 Examples of On-Chip Caches

We now consider the implementation of primary caches in the 68040 and PowerPC 604 processors.

68040 Caches

Motorola's 68040 has two caches included on the processor chip—one used for instructions and the other for data. Each cache has a capacity of 4K bytes and uses a four-way set-associative organization illustrated in Figure 5.22. The cache has 64 sets, each of which can hold 4 blocks. Each block has 4 long words, and each long word has 4 bytes. For mapping purposes, an address is interpreted as shown in the blue box in the figure. The least-significant 4 bits specify a byte position within a block. The next 6 bits identify one of 64 sets. The high-order 22 bits constitute the tag. To keep the notation in the figure compact, the contents of each of these fields are shown in hex coding.

The cache control mechanism includes one *valid* bit per block and one *dirty* bit for each long word in the block. These bits are explained in Section 5.5.1. The valid bit is set to 1 when a corresponding block is first loaded into the cache. An individual dirty bit is associated with each long word, and it is set to 1 when the long-word data are changed during a write operation. The dirty bit remains set until the contents of the block are written back into the main memory.

When the cache is accessed, the tag bits of the address are compared with the 4 tags in the specified set. If one of the tags matches the desired address, and if the valid bit for the corresponding block is equal to 1, then a hit has occurred. Figure 5.22 gives an example in which the addressed data are found in the third long word of the fourth block in set 0.

The data cache can use either the write-back or the write-through protocol, under control of the operating system software. The contents of the instruction cache are changed only when new instructions are loaded as a result of a read miss. When a new block must be brought into a cache set that is already full, the replacement algorithm chooses at random the block to be ejected. Of course, if one or more of the dirty bits in this block are equal to 1, then a write-back must be performed first.

PowerPC 604 Caches

The PowerPC 604 processor also has separate caches for instructions and data. Each cache has a capacity of 16K bytes and uses a four-way set-associative organization. Figure 5.23 depicts the cache structure. The cache has 128 sets, each with space for four blocks, and each block has 8 words of 32 bits. The mapping scheme appears in blue in the figure. The least-significant 5 bits of an address specify a byte within a block. The next 7 bits identify one of 128 sets, and the high-order 20 bits constitute the tag.

The cache control mechanism includes two bits per cache block. These bits, denoted by *st* in the figure, indicate the state of the block. A block has four possible states. Two of the states have essentially the same meaning as the valid and dirty states in our previous discussion. The other two states are needed when the PowerPC 604 processor is used in a multiprocessor system, where it is necessary to know if data in the cache

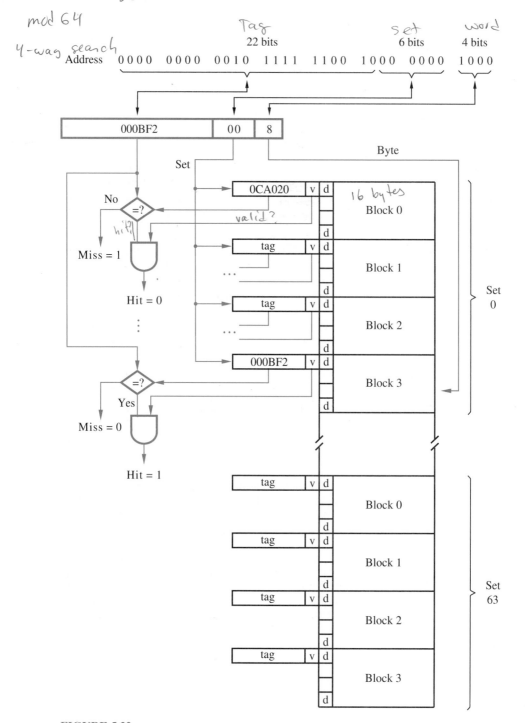

FIGURE 5.22
Data cache organization in the 68040 microprocessor.

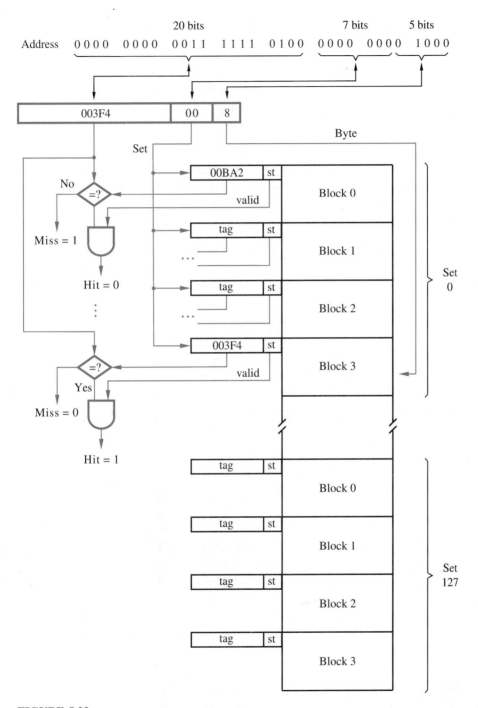

FIGURE 5.23
Cache organization in the PowerPC 604 processor.

are shared by other processors. We discuss the use of such states in Chapter 10, which deals with multiprocessor systems.

A read or write access to the cache involves comparing the tag portion of the address with the tags of the four blocks in the selected set. A hit occurs if there is a match with one of the tags and if the corresponding block is in a valid state. Figure 5.23 shows a memory access request at address 003F4008. The addressed information is found in the third word (containing byte addresses 8 through 11) of block 3 in set 0, which has the tag 003F4.

The data cache is intended primarily for use with the write-back protocol, but it can also support the write-through protocol. When a new block is to be brought into a full set of the cache, the LRU replacement algorithm is used to choose which block will be ejected. If the ejected block is in the dirty state, then the contents of the block are written into the main memory before ejection.

To keep up with the high speed of the functional units of the CPU, the instruction unit can read all 4 words of the selected block in the instruction cache simultaneously. Also, for performance reasons, the load-through approach is used for read misses.

5.6
PERFORMANCE CONSIDERATIONS

Two key factors in the commercial success of a computer are performance and cost; the best possible performance at the lowest cost is the objective. The challenge in considering design alternatives is to improve the performance without increasing the cost. A common measure of success is the *price/performance ratio*. In this section, we discuss some specific features of memory design that lead to superior performance.

Performance depends on how fast machine instructions can be brought into the CPU for execution and how fast they can be executed. We discussed the speed of execution in Chapter 3, and showed how additional circuitry can be used to speed up the execution phase of instruction processing. In this chapter, we focus on the memory subsystem.

The memory hierarchy described in Section 5.4 results from the quest for the best price/performance ratio. The main purpose of this hierarchy is to create a memory that the CPU sees as having a short access time and a large capacity. Each level of the hierarchy plays an important role. The speed and efficiency of data transfer between various levels of the hierarchy are also of great significance. It is beneficial if transfers to and from the faster units can be done at a rate equal to that of the faster unit. This is not possible if both the slow and the fast units are accessed in the same manner, but it can be achieved when parallelism is used in the organization of the slower unit. An effective way to introduce parallelism is to use an interleaved organization.

5.6.1 Interleaving

If the main memory of a computer is structured as a collection of physically separate modules, each with its own address buffer register (ABR) and data buffer register

(DBR), memory access operations may proceed in more than one module at the same time. Thus, the aggregate rate of transmission of words to and from the main memory system can be increased.

How individual addresses are distributed over the modules is critical in determining the average number of modules that can be kept busy as computations proceed. Two methods of address layout are indicated in Figure 5.24. In the first case, the memory address generated by the CPU is decoded as shown in part *a* of the figure. The high-order *k* bits name one of *n* modules, and the low-order *m* bits name a particular word in that module. When consecutive locations are accessed, as happens when a block of data is transferred to a cache, only one module is involved. At the same time, however,

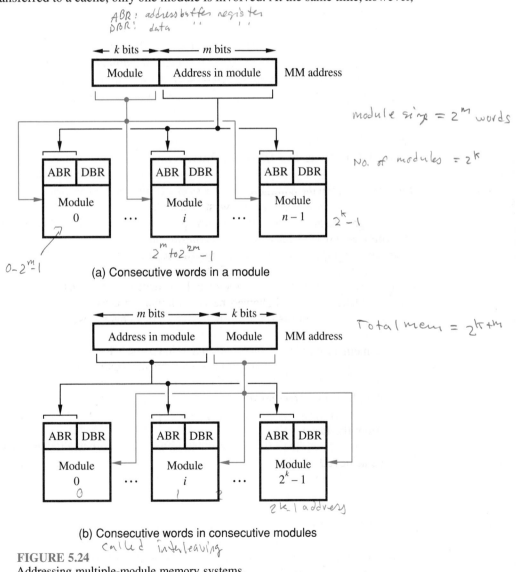

ABR: address buffer register
DBR: data " "

module size $= 2^m$ words

No. of modules $= 2^k$

$0-2^m-1$

2^m to $2^{2m}-1$

2^k-1

(a) Consecutive words in a module

Total mem $= 2^{k+m}$

2^k-1 address

(b) Consecutive words in consecutive modules

called interleaving

FIGURE 5.24
Addressing multiple-module memory systems.

devices with direct memory access (DMA) ability may be accessing information in other memory modules.

The second and more effective way to address the modules is shown in Figure 5.24b. It is called *memory interleaving*. The low-order k bits of the memory address select a module, and the high-order m bits name a location within that module. In this way, consecutive addresses are located in successive modules. Thus, any component of the system that generates requests for access to consecutive memory locations can keep several modules busy at any one time. This results in both faster access to a block of data and higher average utilization of the memory system as a whole. To implement the interleaved structure, there must be 2^k modules; otherwise, there will be gaps of nonexistent locations in the memory address space.

The effect of interleaving is substantial. Consider the time needed to transfer a block of data from the main memory to the cache when a read miss occurs. Suppose that a cache with 8-word blocks is used, similar to our examples in Section 5.5. On a read miss, the block that contains the desired word must be copied from the memory into the cache. Assume that the hardware has the following properties. It takes one clock cycle to send an address to the main memory. The memory is built with DRAM chips that allow the first word to be accessed in 8 cycles, but subsequent words of the block are accessed in 4 clock cycles per word. (Recall from Section 5.2.3 that, when consecutive locations in a DRAM are read from a given row of cells, the row address is decoded only once. Addresses of consecutive columns of the array are then applied to access the desired words, which takes only half the time per access.) Also, one clock cycle is needed to send one word to the cache.

If a single memory module is used, then the time needed to load the desired block into the cache is

$$1 + 8 + (7 \times 4) + 1 = 38 \text{ cycles}$$

Suppose now that the memory is constructed as four interleaved modules, using the scheme in Figure 5.24b. When the starting address of the block arrives at the memory, all four modules begin accessing the required data, using the high-order bits of the address. After 8 clock cycles, each module has one word of data in its DBR. These words are transferred to the cache, one word at a time, during the next 4 clock cycles. During this time, the next word in each module is accessed. Then it takes another 4 cycles to transfer these words to the cache. Therefore, the total time needed to load the block from the interleaved memory is

$$1 + 8 + 4 + 4 = 17 \text{ cycles}$$

Thus, interleaving reduces the block transfer time by more than a factor of 2.

5.6.2 Hit Rate and Miss Penalty

An excellent indicator of the effectiveness of a particular implementation of the memory hierarchy is the success rate in accessing information at various levels of the hierarchy. Recall that a successful access to data in a cache is called a hit. The number of hits stated as a fraction of all attempted accesses is called the *hit rate*, and the *miss rate* is the number of misses stated as a fraction of attempted accesses.

Ideally, the entire memory hierarchy would appear to the CPU as a single memory unit that has the access time of a cache on the CPU chip and the size of a magnetic disk. How close we get to this ideal depends largely on the hit rate at different levels of the hierarchy. High hit rates, well over 0.9, are essential for high-performance computers.

Performance is adversely affected by the actions that must be taken after a miss. The extra time needed to bring the desired information into the cache is called the *miss penalty.* This penalty is ultimately reflected in the time that the CPU is stalled because the required instructions or data are not available for execution. In general, the miss penalty is the time needed to bring a block of data from a slower unit in the memory hierarchy to a faster unit. The miss penalty is reduced if efficient mechanisms for transferring data between the various units of the hierarchy are implemented. The previous section shows how an interleaved memory can reduce the miss penalty substantially.

Consider now the impact of the cache on the overall performance of the computer. Let h be the hit rate, M the miss penalty, that is, the time to access information in the main memory, and C the time to access information in the cache. The average access time experienced by the CPU is

$$t_{ave} = hC + (1 - h)M$$

We use the same parameters as in the example in Section 5.6.1. If the computer has no cache, then, using a fast processor and a typical DRAM main memory, it takes 10 clock cycles for each memory read access. Suppose the computer has a cache that holds 8-word blocks and an interleaved main memory. Then, as we show in Section 5.6.1, 17 cycles are needed to load a block into the cache. Assume that 30 percent of the instructions in a typical program perform a read or a write operation, and assume that the hit rates in the cache are 0.95 for instructions and 0.9 for data. Let us further assume that the miss penalty is the same for both read and write accesses. Then, a rough estimate of the improvement in performance that results from using the cache can be obtained as follows:

$$\frac{Time\ without\ cache}{Time\ with\ cache} = \frac{130 \times 10}{100(0.95 \times 1 + 0.05 \times 17) + 30(0.9 \times 1 + 0.1 \times 17)} = 5.04$$

This result suggests that the computer with the cache performs five times better.

It is also interesting to consider how effective this cache is compared to an ideal cache that has a hit rate of 100 percent (in which case, all memory references take one cycle). Our rough estimate of relative performance for these caches is

$$\frac{100(0.95 \times 1 + 0.05 \times 17) + 30(0.9 \times 1 + 0.1 \times 17)}{130} = 1.98$$

This means that the actual cache provides an environment in which the CPU effectively works with a large DRAM-based main memory that is only half as fast as the circuits in the cache.

In the preceding example, we distinguish between instructions and data as far as the hit rate is concerned. Although hit rates above 0.9 are achievable for both, the hit rate for instructions is usually higher than that for data. The hit rates depend on the design of the cache and on the instruction and data access patterns of the programs being executed.

How can the hit rate be improved? An obvious possibility is to make the cache larger, but this entails increased cost. Another possibility is to increase the block size while keeping the total cache size constant, to take advantage of spatial locality. If all items in a larger block are needed in a computation, then it is better to load these items into the cache as a consequence of a single miss, rather than loading several smaller blocks as a result of several misses. The efficiency of parallel access to blocks in an interleaved memory is the basic reason for this advantage. Larger blocks are effective up to a certain size, but eventually any further improvement in the hit rate tends to be offset by the fact that, in a larger block, some items may not be referenced before the block is ejected (replaced). The miss penalty increases as the block size increases. Since the performance of a computer is affected positively by increased hit rate and negatively by increased miss penalty, the block sizes that are neither very small nor very large give the best results. In practice, block sizes in the range of 16 to 128 bytes have been the most popular choices.

Finally, we note that the miss penalty can be reduced if the load-through approach is used when loading new blocks into the cache. Then, instead of waiting for the completion of the block transfer, the CPU can continue as soon as the required word is loaded in the cache. This approach is used in the PowerPC processor.

5.6.3 Caches on the CPU Chip

When information is transferred between different chips, considerable delays are introduced in driver and receiver gates on the chips. Thus, from the speed point of view, the optimal place for a cache is on the CPU chip. Unfortunately, space on the CPU chip is needed for many other functions; this limits the size of the cache that can be accommodated.

All high-performance processor chips include some form of a cache. Some manufacturers have chosen to implement two separate caches, one for instructions and another for data, as in the 68040 and PowerPC 604 processors. Others have implemented a single cache for both instructions and data, as in the PowerPC 601 processor.

A combined cache for instructions and data is likely to have a somewhat better hit rate, because it offers greater flexibility in mapping new information into the cache. However, if separate caches are used, it is possible to access both caches at the same time, which leads to increased parallelism and, hence, better performance. The disadvantage of separate caches is that the increased parallelism comes at the expense of more complex circuitry.

Since the size of a cache on the CPU chip is limited by space constraints, a good strategy for designing a high-performance system is to use such a cache as a primary cache. An external secondary cache, constructed with SRAM chips, is then added to provide the desired capacity, as we have already discussed in Section 5.4. If both primary and secondary caches are used, the primary cache should be designed to allow very fast access by the CPU, because its access time will have a large effect on the clock rate of the CPU. A cache cannot be accessed at the same speed as a register file, because the cache is much bigger and, hence, more complex. A practical way to speed up access to the cache is to access more than one word simultaneously and then let the CPU use them one at a time. This technique is used in both the 68040 and the PowerPC processors. The 68040 cache is read 8 bytes at a time, whereas the PowerPC cache is read 16 bytes at a time.

The secondary cache can be considerably slower, but it should be much larger to ensure a high hit rate. Its speed is less critical, because it only affects the miss penalty of the primary cache. A workstation computer may include a primary cache with the capacity of tens of kilobytes and a secondary cache of several megabytes.

Including a secondary cache further reduces the impact of the main memory speed on the performance of a computer. The average access time experienced by the CPU in a system with two levels of caches is

$$t_{ave} = h_1 C_1 + (1 - h_1) h_2 C_2 + (1 - h_1)(1 - h_2) M$$

where the parameters are defined as follows:

h_1 is the hit rate in the primary cache.
h_2 is the hit rate in the secondary cache.
C_1 is the time to access information in the primary cache.
C_2 is the time to access information in the secondary cache.
M is the time to access information in the main memory.

The number of misses in the secondary cache, given by the term $(1 - h_1)(1 - h_2)$, should be low. If both h_1 and h_2 are in the 90 percent range, then the number of misses will be less than 1 percent of the CPU's memory accesses. Thus, the miss penalty M will be less critical from a performance point of view. See Problem 5.18 for a quantitative examination of this issue.

5.6.4 Other Enhancements

In addition to the main design issues just discussed, several other possibilities exist for enhancing performance. We discuss three of them in this section.

Write Buffer

When the write-through protocol is used, each write operation results in writing a new value into the main memory. If the CPU must wait for the memory function to be completed, as we have assumed until now, then the CPU is slowed down by all write requests. Yet the CPU typically does not immediately depend on the result of a write operation, so it is not necessary for the CPU to wait for the write request to be completed. To improve performance, a *write buffer* can be included for temporary storage of write requests. The CPU places each write request into this buffer and continues execution of the next instruction. The write requests stored in the write buffer are sent to the main memory whenever the memory is not responding to read requests. Note that it is important that the read requests be serviced immediately, because the CPU usually cannot proceed without the data that is to be read from the memory. Hence, these requests are given priority over write requests.

The write buffer may hold a number of write requests. Thus, it is possible that a subsequent read request may refer to data that are still in the write buffer. To ensure correct operation, the addresses of data to be read from the memory are compared with the addresses of the data in the write buffer. In case of a match, the data in the write buffer are used. This need for address comparison entails considerable cost, but the cost is justified by improved performance.

A different situation occurs with the write-back protocol. In this case, the write operations are simply performed on the corresponding word in the cache. But consider what happens when a new block of data is to be brought into the cache as a result of a read miss, which replaces an existing block that has some dirty data. The dirty block has to be written into the main memory. If the required write-back is performed first, then the CPU will have to wait longer for the new block to be read into the cache. It is more prudent to read the new block first. This can be arranged by providing a fast write buffer for temporary storage of the dirty block that is ejected from the cache while the new block is being read. Afterward, the contents of the buffer are written into the main memory. Thus, the write buffer also works well for the write-back protocol.

Prefetching

In the previous discussion of the cache mechanism, we assumed that new data are brought into the cache when they are first needed. A read miss occurs, and the desired data are loaded from the main memory. The CPU has to pause until the new data arrive, which is the effect of the miss penalty.

To avoid stalling the CPU, it is possible to prefetch the data into the cache before they are needed. The simplest way to do this is through software. A special prefetch instruction may be provided in the instruction set of the processor. Executing this instruction causes the addressed data to be loaded into the cache, as in the case of a read miss. However, the processor does not wait for the referenced data. A prefetch instruction is inserted in a program to cause the data to be loaded in the cache by the time they are needed in the program. The hope is that prefetching will take place while the CPU is busy executing instructions that do not result in a read miss, thus allowing accesses to the main memory to be overlapped with computation in the CPU.

Prefetch instructions can be inserted into a program either by the programmer or by the compiler. It is obviously preferable to have the compiler insert these instructions, which can be done with good success for many applications. Note that software prefetching entails a certain overhead, because inclusion of prefetch instructions increases the length of programs. Moreover, some prefetches may load into the cache data that will not be used by the instructions that follow. This can happen if the prefetched data are ejected from the cache by a read miss involving other data. However, the overall effect of software prefetching on performance is positive, and many processors (including the PowerPC) have machine instructions to support this feature. See reference 1 for a thorough discussion of software prefetching.

Prefetching can also be done through hardware. This involves adding circuitry that attempts to discover a pattern in memory references, and then prefetches data according to this pattern. A number of schemes have been proposed for this purpose, but they are beyond the scope of this book. A description of these schemes is found in references 2 and 3.

Lockup-Free Cache

The software prefetching scheme just discussed does not work well if it interferes significantly with the normal execution of instructions. This is the case if the action of prefetching stops other accesses to the cache until the prefetch is completed. A cache of this type is said to be locked while it services a miss. We can solve this problem by modifying the basic cache structure to allow the CPU to access the cache while a miss is being serviced. In fact, it is desirable that more than one outstanding miss can be supported.

A cache that can support multiple outstanding misses is called *lockup-free*. Since it can service only one miss at a time, it must include circuitry that keeps track of all outstanding misses. This may be done with special registers that hold the pertinent information about these misses. Lockup-free caches were first used in the early 1980s in the Cyber series of computers manufactured by Control Data company.[4]

We have used software prefetching as an obvious motivation for a cache that is not locked by a read miss. A much more important reason is that, in a processor that uses a pipelined organization, which overlaps the execution of several instructions, a read miss caused by one instruction could stall the execution of other instructions. A lockup-free cache reduces the likelihood of such stalling. We return to this topic in Chapter 7, where the pipeplined organization is examined in detail.

5.7
VIRTUAL MEMORIES

In most modern computer systems, the physical main memory is not as large as the address space spanned by an address issued by the processor. When a program does not completely fit into the main memory, the parts of it not currently being executed are stored on secondary storage devices, such as magnetic disks. Of course, all parts of a program that are eventually executed are first brought into the main memory. When a new segment of a program is to be moved into a full memory, it must replace another segment already in the memory. In modern computers, the operating system moves programs and data automatically between the main memory and secondary storage. Thus, the application programmer does not need to be aware of limitations imposed by the available main memory.

Techniques that automatically move program and data blocks into the physical main memory when they are required for execution are called *virtual-memory* techniques. Programs, and hence the processor, reference an instruction and data space that is independent of the available physical main memory space. The binary addresses that the processor issues for either instructions or data are called *virtual* or *logical addresses*. These addresses are translated into physical addresses by a combination of hardware and software components. If a virtual address refers to a part of the program or data space that is currently in the physical memory, then the contents of the appropriate location in the main memory are accessed immediately. On the other hand, if the referenced address is not in the main memory, its contents must be brought into a suitable location in the memory before they can be used.

Figure 5.25 shows a typical organization that implements virtual memory. A special hardware unit, called the *Memory Management Unit* (MMU), translates virtual addresses into physical addresses. When the desired data (or instructions) are in the main memory, these data are fetched as described in our presentation of the cache mechanism. If the data are not in the main memory, the MMU causes the operating system to

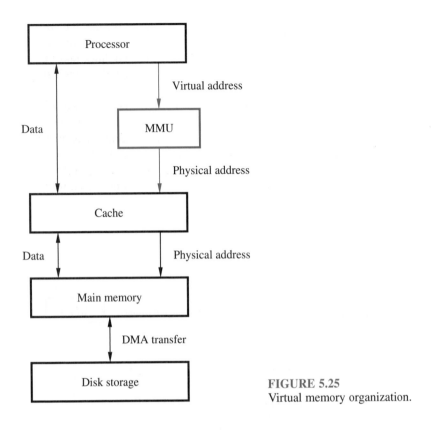

FIGURE 5.25
Virtual memory organization.

bring the data into the memory from the disk. Transfer of data between the disk and the main memory is performed using the DMA scheme discussed in Chapter 4.

5.7.1 Address Translation

A simple method for translating virtual addresses into physical addresses is to assume that all programs and data are composed of fixed-length units called *pages*, each of which consists of a block of words that occupy contiguous locations in the main memory. Pages commonly range from 2K to 16K bytes in length. They constitute the basic unit of information that is moved between the main memory and the disk whenever the translation mechanism determines that a move is required. Pages should not be too small, because the access time of a magnetic disk is much longer (10 to 20 milliseconds) than the access time of the main memory. The reason for this is that it takes a considerable amount of time to locate the data on the disk, but once located, the data can be transferred at a rate of several megabytes per second. On the other hand, if pages are too large it is possible that a substantial portion of a page may not be used, yet this unnecessary data will occupy valuable space in the main memory.

This discussion clearly parallels the concepts introduced in Section 5.5 on cache memory. The cache bridges the speed gap between the processor and the main memory and is implemented in hardware. The virtual-memory mechanism bridges the size and speed gaps between the main memory and secondary storage and is usually implemented in part by software techniques. Conceptually, cache techniques and virtual-memory techniques are very similar. They differ mainly in the details of their implementation.

A virtual-memory address translation method based on the concept of fixed-length pages is shown schematically in Figure 5.26. Each virtual address generated by the processor, whether it is for an instruction fetch or an operand fetch/store operation, is interpreted as a *virtual page number* (high-order bits) followed by an *offset* (low-order bits) that specifies the location of a particular byte (or word) within a page. Information about the main memory location of each page is kept in a *page table*. This information

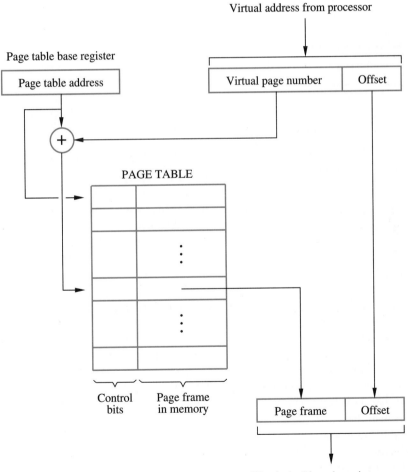

FIGURE 5.26
Virtual-memory address translation.

includes the main memory address where the page is stored and the current status of the page. An area in the main memory that can hold one page is called a *page frame*. The starting address of the page table is kept in a *page table base register*. By adding the virtual page number to the contents of this register, the address of the corresponding entry in the page table is obtained. The contents of this location give the starting address of the page if that page currently resides in the main memory.

Each entry in the page table also includes some control bits that describe the status of the page while it is in the main memory. One bit indicates the validity of the page, that is, whether the page is actually loaded in the main memory. This bit allows the operating system to invalidate the page without actually removing it. Another bit indicates whether the page has been modified during its residency in the memory. As in cache memories, this information is needed to determine whether the page should be written back to the disk before it is removed from the main memory to make room for another page. Other control bits indicate various restrictions that may be imposed on accessing the page. For example, a program may be given full read and write permission, or it may be restricted to read accesses only.

The page table information is used by the MMU for every read and write access, so ideally, the page table should be situated within the MMU. Unfortunately, the page table may be rather large, and since the MMU is normally implemented as part of the CPU chip (along with the primary cache), it is impossible to include a complete page table on this chip. Therefore, the page table is kept in the main memory. However, a copy of a small portion of the page table can be accommodated within the MMU. Tnis portion consists of the page table entries that correspond to the most recently accessed pages. A small cache, usually called the *Translation Lookaside Buffer (TLB)*, is incorporated into the MMU for this purpose. The operation of the TLB with respect to the page table in the main memory is essentially the same as the operation we have discussed in conjunction with the cache memory. In addition to the information that constitutes a page table entry, the TLB must also include the virtual address of the entry. Figure 5.27 shows a possible organization of a TLB where the associative-mapping technique is used. Set-associative mapped TLBs are also found in commercial products.

An essential requirement is that the contents of the TLB be coherent with the contents of page tables in the memory. When the operating system changes the contents of page tables, it must simultaneously invalidate the corresponding entries in the TLB. One of the control bits in the TLB is provided for this purpose. When an entry is invalidated, the TLB will acquire the new information as part of the MMU's normal response to access misses.

Address translation proceeds as follows. Given a virtual address, the MMU looks in the TLB for the referenced page. If the page table entry for this page is found in the TLB, the physical address is obtained immediately. If there is a miss in the TLB, then the required entry is obtained from the page table in the main memory, and the TLB is updated.

When a program generates an access request to a page that is not in the main memory, a *page fault* is said to have occurred. The whole page must be brought from the disk into the memory before access can proceed. When it detects a page fault, the MMU asks the operating system to intervene by raising an exception (interrupt). Processing of the active task is interrupted, and control is transferred to the operating system. The

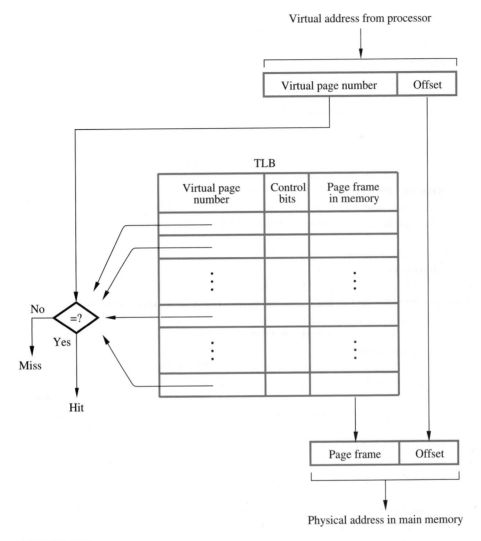

Virtual address from processor

Virtual page number | Offset

TLB

| Virtual page number | Control bits | Page frame in memory |

No

=?

Yes

Miss

Hit

Page frame | Offset

Physical address in main memory

FIGURE 5.27
Use of an associative-mapped TLB.

operating system then copies the requested page from the disk into the main memory and returns control to the interrupted task. Because a long delay occurs while the page transfer takes place, the operating system may suspend execution of the task that caused the page fault and begin execution of another task whose pages are in the main memory.

It is essential to ensure that the interrupted task can continue correctly when it resumes execution. A page fault occurs when some instruction accesses a memory operand that is not in the main memory, resulting in an interruption before the execution of this instruction is completed. Hence, when the task resumes, either the execution of the interrupted instruction must continue from the point of interruption, or the instruction must be restarted. The design of a particular processor dictates which of these options should be used.

If a new page is brought from the disk when the main memory is full, it must replace one of the resident pages. The problem of choosing which page to remove is just as critical here as it is in a cache, and the idea that programs spend most of their time in a few localized areas also applies. Because main memories are considerably larger than cache memories, it should be possible to keep relatively larger portions of a program in the main memory. This will reduce the frequency of transfers to and from the disk. Concepts similar to the LRU replacement algorithm can be applied to page replacement, and the control bits in the page table entries can indicate usage. One simple scheme is based on a control bit that is set to 1 whenever the corresponding page is referenced (accessed). The operating system occasionally clears this bit in all page table entries, thus providing a simple way of determining which pages have not been used recently.

A modified page has to be written back to the disk before it is removed from the main memory. It is important to note that the write-through protocol, which is useful in the framework of cache memories, is not suitable for virtual memory. The access time of the disk is so long that it does not make sense to access it frequently to write small amounts of data.

The address translation process in the MMU requires some time to perform, mostly dependent on the time needed to look up entries in the TLB. Because of locality of reference, it is likely that many successive translations involve addresses on the same page. This is particularly evident in fetching instructions. Thus, we can reduce the average translation time by including one or more special registers that retain the virtual page number and the physical page frame of the most recently performed translations. The information in these registers can be accessed more quickly than the TLB.

5.8
MEMORY MANAGEMENT REQUIREMENTS

In our discussion of virtual-memory concepts, we have tacitly assumed that only one large program is being executed. If all of the program does not fit into the available physical memory, parts of it (pages) are moved from the disk into the main memory when they are to be executed. Although we have alluded to software routines that are needed to manage this movement of program segments, we have not been specific about the details.

Management routines are part of the operating system of the computer. It is convenient to assemble the operating system routines into a virtual address space, called the *system space*, that is separate from the virtual space in which user application programs reside. The latter space is called the *user space*. In fact, there may be a number of user spaces, one for each user. This is arranged by providing a separate page table for each user program. The MMU uses a page table base register to determine the address of the table to be used in the translation process. Hence, by changing the contents of this register, the operating system can switch from one space to another. The physical main memory is thus shared by the active pages of the system space and several user spaces. However, only the pages that belong to one of these spaces are accessible at any given time.

In any computer system in which independent user programs coexist in the main memory, the notion of *protection* must be addressed. No program should be allowed to destroy either the data or instructions of other programs in the memory. Such protection can be provided in several ways. Let us first consider the most basic form of protection. Recall that in the simplest case, the processor has two states, the *supervisor state* and the *user state*. As the names suggest, the processor is usually placed in the supervisor state when operating system routines are being executed, and in the user state to execute user programs. In the user state, some machine instructions cannot be executed. These *privileged instructions*, which include such operations as modifying the page table base register, can only be executed while the processor is in the supervisor state. Hence, a user program is prevented from accessing the page tables of other user spaces or of the system space.

It is sometimes desirable for one application program to have access to certain pages belonging to another program. The operating system can arrange this by causing these pages to appear in both spaces. The shared pages will therefore have entries in two different page tables. The control bits in each table entry can be set to control the access privileges granted to each program. For example, one program may be allowed to read and write a given page, while the other program may be given only read access.

5.9
CONCLUDING REMARKS

The memory is a major component in any computer. Its size and speed characteristics are important in determining the performance of a computer. In this chapter, we presented the most important technological and organizational details of memory design.

Developments in technology have led to spectacular improvements in the speed and size of memory chips, accompanied by a large decrease in the cost per bit. But processor chips have evolved even more spectacularly. In particular, the improvement in the operating speed of processor chips has outpaced that of memory chips. To exploit fully the capability of a modern processor, the computer must have a large and fast memory. Since cost is also important, the memory cannot be designed simply by using fast SRAM components. As we saw in this chapter, the solution lies in the memory hierarchy.

Today, an affordable large memory is implemented with DRAM components. Such a memory may be an order of magnitude slower than a fast processor, in terms of clock cycles, which makes it imperative to use a cache memory to reduce the effective memory access time seen by the processor. The term *memory latency* is often used to refer to the amount of time it takes to transfer data to or from the main memory. Recently, much research effort has focused on developing schemes that minimize the effect of memory latency. We described how write buffers and prefetching can reduce the impact of latency by performing less urgent memory accesses at times when no higher-priority memory accesses (caused by read misses) are required. The effect of memory latency can also be reduced if blocks of consecutive words are accessed at one time; new memory chips are being developed to exploit this fact. As VLSI chips become larger, other interesting possibilities arise in the design of memory components. One possibility is to include a small SRAM and a much larger DRAM on one chip. The advantage of having both a fast SRAM and a much slower DRAM on the same chip is that wider and faster data paths can be used between these units than is possible through external connections via the bus. Such memory chips are called cache DRAMs.

Secondary storage, in the form of magnetic disks, provides the largest capacity in the memory hierarchy. The virtual memory mechanism makes interaction between the disk and the main memory transparent to the user. Hardware support for virtual memory has become a standard feature of modern processors.

PROBLEMS

5.1. Give a block diagram similar to the one in Figure 5.9 for a $4M \times 8$ memory using $256K \times 1$ memory chips.

5.2. Consider the dynamic memory cell of Figure 5.7. Assume that $C = 50$ femtofarads and that leakage current through the transistor is about 9 picoamperes. The voltage across the capacitor when it is fully charged is equal to 4.5 V. The cell must be refreshed before this voltage drops below 3 V. Estimate the minimum refresh rate.

5.3. A dynamic memory is connected to a synchronous bus, on which data transfers take place according to the timing diagram in Figure 4.19. The memory is controlled by a circuit similar to that in Figure 5.10. The processor asserts Memory-request at the beginning of a clock period in which it wishes to read data. If the memory control circuit accepts the request, it asserts MFC and the data transfer is completed in the normal manner. However, if a refresh request is generated during the same cycle, the refresh operation proceeds and MFC remains inactive. In this case, the processor waits for the next clock period, maintaining Memory-request in the active state. Give a suitable design for the Refresh Control and Access Control blocks.

5.4. Criticize the following statement: "Using a faster processor chip results in a corresponding increase in performance of a computer, even if the main memory speed remains the same."

5.5. Figure 5.10 shows a block diagram of a $4M \times 32$ DRAM, where a 22-bit address is used to access a 32-bit word. What has to be done to make this DRAM byte-addressable?

 (*a*) Show the circuit needed if a single byte that is to be read/written is in its normal position on the data bus.
 (*b*) Show the circuit needed if the byte is always transferred in the low-order bit positions on the data bus—that is, no matter which of the four bytes is addressed, the 8 bits of data are transmitted on data lines d_0 to d_7.

5.6. A program consists of two nested loops—a small inner loop and a much larger outer loop. The general structure of the program is given in Figure P5.1. The decimal memory addresses shown delineate the location of the two loops and the beginning and end of the total program. All memory locations in the various sections, 17–22, 23–164, 165–239, and so on, contain instructions to be executed in straight-line sequencing. The program is to be run on a computer that has an instruction cache organized in the direct-mapped

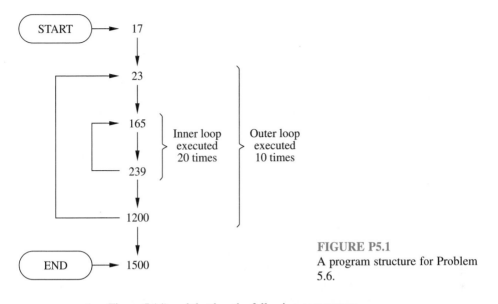

FIGURE P5.1
A program structure for Problem 5.6.

manner (see Figure 5.14) and that has the following parameters:

Main memory size	64K words
Cache size	1K words
Block size	128 words

The cycle time of the main memory is 10τ s, and the cycle time of the cache is 1τ s.

(a) Specify the number of bits in the TAG, BLOCK, and WORD fields in main memory addresses.

(b) Compute the total time needed for instruction fetching during execution of the program in Figure P5.1.

5.7. A computer uses a small direct-mapped cache between the main memory and the CPU. The cache has four 16-bit words, and each word has an associated 13-bit tag, as shown in Figure P5.2a. When a miss occurs during a read operation, the requested word is read from the main memory and sent to the CPU. At the same time, it is copied into the cache, and its block number is stored in the associated tag. Consider the following loop in a program where all instructions and operands are 16 bits long:

```
LOOP    Add         (R1)+,R0
        Decrement   R2
        BNE         LOOP
```

Assume that, before this loop is entered, registers R0, R1, and R2 contain 0, 054E, and 3, respectively. Also assume that the main memory contains the data shown in Figure P5.2b, where all entries are given in hexadecimal notation. The loop starts at location LOOP = 02EC.

(a) Show the contents of the cache at the end of each pass through the loop.

(b) Assume that the access time of the main memory is 10τ and that of the cache is 1τ. Calculate the execution time for each pass. Ignore the time taken by the CPU between memory cycles.

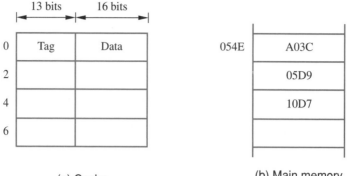

(a) Cache   (b) Main memory

FIGURE P5.2
Cache and main memory contents in Problem 5.7.

5.8. Repeat Problem 5.7, assuming only instructions are stored in the cache. Data operands are fetched directly from the main memory and not copied into the cache. Why does this choice lead to faster execution than when both instructions and data are written into the cache?

5.9. A block-set-associative cache consists of a total of 64 blocks divided into four-block sets. The main memory contains 4096 blocks, each consisting of 128 words.

(*a*) How many bits are there in a main memory address?
(*b*) How many bits are there in each of the TAG, SET, and WORD fields?

5.10. A computer system has a main memory consisting of 1M 16-bit words. It also has a 4K-word cache organized in the block-set-associative manner, with four blocks per set and 64 words per block.

(*a*) Calculate the number of bits in each of the TAG, SET, and WORD fields of the main memory address format.
(*b*) Assume that the cache is initially empty. Suppose that the CPU fetches 4352 words from locations 0, 1, 2, . . . , 4351, in that order. It then repeats this fetch sequence nine more times. If the cache is 10 times faster than the main memory, estimate the improvement factor resulting from the use of the cache. Assume that the LRU algorithm is used for block replacement.

5.11. Repeat Problem 5.10, assuming that whenever a block is to be brought from the main memory and the corresponding set in the cache is full, the new block replaces the most recently used block of this set.

5.12. Section 5.5.3 illustrates the effect of different cache-mapping techniques, using the program in Figure 5.18. Suppose that this program is changed so that in the second loop the elements are handled in the same order as in the first loop; that is, the control for the second loop is specified as

$$\text{for } i := 0 \text{ to } 9 \text{ do}$$

Derive the equivalents of Figures 5.19 through 5.21 for this program. What conclusions can be drawn from this exercise?

5.13. A byte-addressable computer has a small data cache capable of holding eight 32-bit words. Each cache block consists of one 32-bit word. When a given program is executed, the processor reads data from the following sequence of hex addresses:

200, 204, 208, 20C, 2F4, 2F0, 200, 204, 218, 21C, 24C, 2F4

This pattern is repeated four times.

- (a) Show the contents of the cache at the end of each pass through this loop if a direct-mapped cache is used. Compute the hit rate for this example. Assume that the cache is initially empty.
- (b) Repeat part (a) for an associative-mapped cache that uses the LRU replacement algorithm.
- (c) Repeat part (a) for a four-way set-associative cache.

5.14. Repeat Problem 5.13, assuming that each cache block consists of two 32-bit words. For part (c), use a two-way set-associative cache.

5.15. How might the value of k in the interleaved memory system of Figure 5.24b influence block size in the design of a cache memory to be used with the system?

5.16. In the bus transfers in Figures 4.19 and 4.20, the CPU requests a data transfer and maintains the address on the bus until the transfer is completed. This arrangement cannot realize the increase in speed made possible by the interleaved memory of Figure 5.24b. Suggest how to modify the way data transfers take place so several memory modules can be accessed simultaneously.

5.17. Consider the effectiveness of interleaving with respect to the size of cache blocks. Using calculations similar to those in Section 5.6.2, estimate the performance improvement for block sizes of 16, 8, and 4 words. Assume that all words loaded into the cache are accessed by the CPU at least once.

5.18. Assume a computer has a primary and secondary cache, as discussed in Section 5.6.3. The cache blocks consist of 8 words. Assume that the hit rate is the same for both caches, and that it is equal to 0.95 for instructions and 0.90 for data. Assume also that the times needed to access an 8-word block in these caches are $C_1 = 1$ cycle and $C_2 = 10$ cycles.

- (a) What is the average access time experienced by the CPU if the main memory uses interleaving? Assume that the memory access parameters are as described in Section 5.6.1.
- (b) What is the average access time if the main memory is not interleaved?
- (c) What is the improvement obtained with interleaving?

5.19. Repeat Problem 5.18, assuming that a cache block consists of 4 words. Estimate an appropriate value for C_2, assuming that the secondary cache is implemented with SRAM chips.

5.20. A 1024×1024 array of 32-bit numbers is to be "normalized" as follows. For each column, the largest element is found and all elements of the column are divided by this maximum value. Assume that each page in the virtual memory consists of 4K bytes, and that 1M bytes of the main memory are allocated for storing data during this computation. Suppose that it takes 40 ms to load a page from the disk into the main memory when a page fault occurs.

(*a*) How many page faults would occur if the elements of the array are stored in column order in the virtual memory?

(*b*) How many page faults would occur if the elements are stored in row order?

(*c*) Estimate the total time needed to perform this normalization for both arrangements *a* and *b*.

5.21. Consider a computer system in which the available pages in the physical memory are divided among several application programs. When all pages allocated to a program are full and a new page is needed, the new page must replace one of the resident pages. The operating system monitors the page transfer activity and dynamically adjusts the page allocation to various programs. Suggest a suitable strategy that the operating system can use to minimize the overall rate of page transfers.

5.22. In a computer with a virtual-memory system, the execution of an instruction may be interrupted by a page fault. What state information has to be saved so that this instruction can be resumed later? Note that bringing a new page into the main memory involves a DMA transfer, which requires execution of other instructions. Is it simpler to abandon the interrupted instruction and completely reexecute it later? Can this be done?

5.23. When a program generates a reference to a page that does not reside in the physical main memory, execution of the program is suspended until the requested page is loaded into the main memory. What difficulties might arise when an instruction in one page has an operand in a different page? What capabilities must the CPU have to handle this situation?

REFERENCES

1. T. C. Mowry, "Tolerating Latency through Software-Controlled Data Prefetching," *Tech. Report CSL-TR-94-628,* Stanford University, Calif., 1994.

2. J. L. Baer and T. F. Chen, "An Effective On-Chip Preloading Scheme to Reduce Data Access Penalty," *Proceedings of Supercomputing '91*, 1991, pp. 176–186.

3. J. W. C. Fu and J. H. Patel, "Stride Directed Prefetching in Scalar Processors," *Proceedings of the 24th International Symposium on Microarchitecture*, 1992, pp. 102–110.

4. D. Kroft, " Lockup-Free Instruction Fetch/Prefetch Cache Organization," *Proceedings of the 8th Annual International Symposium on Computer Architecture,* 1981, pp. 81–85.

CHAPTER 6

Arithmetic

A basic operation in all digital computers is the addition or subtraction of two numbers. Arithmetic operations occur at the machine instruction level. They are implemented, along with basic logic functions such as AND, OR, NOT, and EXCLUSIVE-OR, in the arithmetic and logic unit (ALU) subsystem of the processor, as Chapters 1 and 3 discuss. In this chapter, we present the circuits used to implement arithmetic operations. The time needed to perform an addition operation affects the processor's performance. Multiply and divide operations, which require more complex circuitry than either addition or subtraction operations, also affect performance. We present some of the techniques used in modern computers to perform arithmetic operations at high speed.

Compared with arithmetic operations, logic operations are simple to implement using combinational circuitry. They require only independent Boolean operations on individual bit positions of the operands, whereas carry/borrow lateral signals are required in arithmetic operations.

Before discussing details of implementing computer arithmetic, we first need to discuss number representation schemes.

6.1
NUMBER REPRESENTATIONS

The binary number system is used in virtually all modern computers. Consider an n-bit vector

$$B = b_{n-1} \ldots b_1 b_0$$

where $b_i = 0$ or 1 for $0 \le i \le n-1$. This vector can represent positive integer values V in the range 0 to $2^n - 1$, where

$$V(B) = b_{n-1} \times 2^{n-1} + \cdots + b_1 \times 2^1 + b_0 \times 2^0$$

Three systems are widely used for representing both positive and negative numbers:

- Sign-and-magnitude
- 1's-complement
- 2's-complement

In all three systems, the leftmost bit is 0 for positive numbers and 1 for negative numbers. Figure 6.1 illustrates all three representations using 4-bit numbers. Positive values have identical representations in all systems, but negative values have different representations. In the *sign-and-magnitude* system, negative values are represented by changing the most significant bit (b_3, in Figure 6.1), to 1 in the B vector of the corresponding positive value. For example, $+5$ is represented by 0101, and -5 is represented by 1101. In the *1's-complement* representation, negative values are obtained by complementing each bit of the corresponding positive number. Thus, the representation for -3 is obtained by complementing each bit in the vector 0011 to yield 1100. The operation of obtaining the 1's complement of a number is equivalent to subtracting that number from $2^n - 1$, that is, from 1111, in the case of the 4-bit numbers in Figure 6.1. Finally, in the *2's-complement* system, a negative number is obtained by subtracting

B	Values represented		
$b_3 b_2 b_1 b_0$	Sign and magnitude	1's complement	2's complement
0 1 1 1	+ 7	+ 7	+ 7
0 1 1 0	+ 6	+ 6	+ 6
0 1 0 1	+ 5	+ 5	+ 5
0 1 0 0	+ 4	+ 4	+ 4
0 0 1 1	+ 3	+ 3	+ 3
0 0 1 0	+ 2	+ 2	+ 2
0 0 0 1	+ 1	+ 1	+ 1
0 0 0 0	+ 0	+ 0	+ 0
1 0 0 0	− 0	− 7	− 8
1 0 0 1	− 1	− 6	− 7
1 0 1 0	− 2	− 5	− 6
1 0 1 1	− 3	− 4	− 5
1 1 0 0	− 4	− 3	− 4
1 1 0 1	− 5	− 2	− 3
1 1 1 0	− 6	− 1	− 2
1 1 1 1	− 7	− 0	− 1

FIGURE 6.1
Binary, signed, integer representations.

the corresponding positive number from 2^n. Hence, the 2's-complement representation is obtained by adding 1 to the 1's-complement representation.

Note that there are distinct $+0$ and -0 representations in both the sign-and-magnitude and 1's-complement systems, but the 2's-complement system has only a $+0$ representation. For 4-bit numbers, the value -8 is representable in the 2's-complement system but not in the other systems. The sign-and-magnitude system seems the most natural, because we deal with sign-and-magnitude decimal values in manual computations. The 1's-complement system is easily related to this system, but the 2's-complement system seems unnatural. However, we show in Section 6.4 that the 2's-complement system yields the most efficient logic circuit implementation, and the one most often used in computers, for addition and subtraction operations.

6.2
ADDITION OF POSITIVE NUMBERS

In this section and the next, we are concerned with only unsigned numbers. Consider adding two 1-bit numbers. The results are shown in Figure 6.2. The sum of 1 and 1 requires the 2-bit vector 10 to represent the value 2. We say that the *sum* is 0 and the *carry-out* is 1. In order to add multiple-bit numbers, we use a method analogous to that used for manual computation with decimal numbers. We add bit pairs starting from the low-order (right) end of the bit vectors, propagating carries toward the high-order (left) end. The truth table for the sum and carry-out functions for adding two equally weighted bits x_i and y_i in vectors X and Y is shown in Figure 6.3. The figure also shows two-level AND-OR logic expressions for these functions, along with an example of addition. Note that each stage of the addition process must accommodate a *carry-in* bit. We use c_i to represent the carry-in to the ith stage, which is the same as the carry-out from the $(i-1)$st stage.

A straightforward, 2-level, combinational logic circuit implementation of the truth table for addition is shown in Figure 6.4a, along with a convenient symbol for the circuit, called an *adder*, A, or sometimes called a *full-adder*, FA. This implementation follows directly from the logic expressions in Figure 6.3. More compact implementations that share some logic gates in generating s_i and c_{i+1} are possible, but they may involve somewhat longer delays. (See Problem 6.11.) Different logic circuits, for example using NAND or NOR gates, can also be used to realize these functions. A cascaded connection of n adder blocks, as shown in Figure 6.4b, can be used to add two

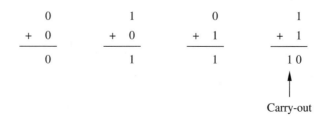

FIGURE 6.2
Addition of 1-bit numbers.

x_i	y_i	Carry-in c_i	Sum s_i	Carry-out c_{i+1}
0	0	0	0	0
0	0	1	1	0
0	1	0	1	0
0	1	1	0	1
1	0	0	1	0
1	0	1	0	1
1	1	0	0	1
1	1	1	1	1

$$s_i = \bar{x}_i \bar{y}_i c_i + \bar{x}_i y_i \bar{c}_i + x_i \bar{y}_i \bar{c}_i + x_i y_i c_i$$
$$c_{i+1} = y_i c_i + x_i c_i + x_i y_i$$

Example:

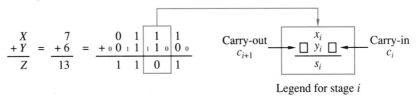

Legend for stage i

FIGURE 6.3
Logic specification for a stage of binary addition.

n-bit numbers. Since the carries must propagate, or ripple, through this cascade, the configuration is called an *n-bit ripple-carry adder*. When the carry-out, c_n, from the *most-significant-bit* (MSB) position equals 1, an *overflow* from the operation occurs; this means that the result cannot be represented in n bits.

The carry-in, c_0, into the *least-significant-bit* (LSB) position provides a convenient means of adding 1 to a number. For instance, in the previous section, we state that forming the 2's-complement of a number involves adding 1 to the 1's-complement of the number. The carry signals are also useful for interconnecting k adders to form an adder capable of handling input numbers that are kn bits long, as shown in Figure 6.4c.

6.3
DESIGN OF FAST ADDERS

The n-bit ripple-carry adder shown in Figure 6.4b may have too much delay in developing its outputs, s_0 through s_{n-1} and c_n. Whether the delay incurred with any particular implementation technology is acceptable can be decided only in the context of the speed of other processor components and the data transfer times of registers and cache

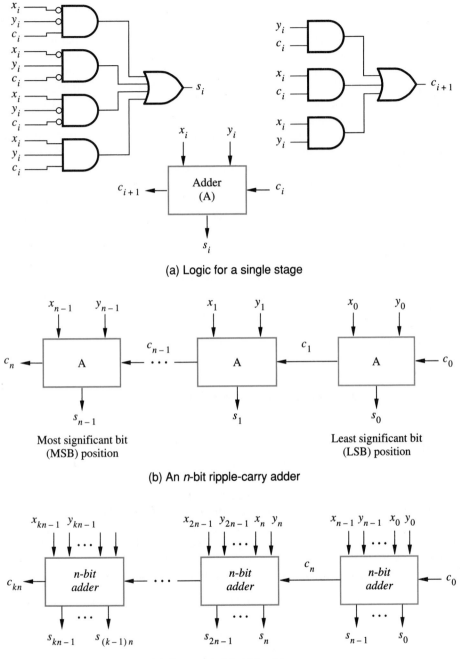

(a) Logic for a single stage

(b) An n-bit ripple-carry adder

Most significant bit
(MSB) position

Least significant bit
(LSB) position

(c) Cascade of k n-bit adders

FIGURE 6.4
Logic circuits for addition of binary vectors.

memories. The length of delay through a network of logic gates depends on the integrated circuit electronic technology (see Appendix A) used in fabricating the network and on the number of gates in the paths from inputs to outputs. After a particular technology is chosen, the delay incurred with any combinational logic network constructed from gates in that technology can be determined by adding up the number of logic-gate delays along the longest path through the network. In the case of the ripple-carry adder, the longest signal propagation is from inputs x_0, y_0, and c_0 at the LSB position to outputs c_n and s_{n-1} at the MSB position.

In Chapter 3, we assume that an arithmetic operation can be performed in the ALU in one clock cycle. This means that, for a processor operating at a clock rate of 100 MHz, an addition operation must be completed within 10 nanoseconds. The delay of the n-bit ripple-carry adder of Figure 6.4b can be estimated as follows. Suppose that the delay from c_i to c_{i+1} of any Adder block is 1 ns in the integrated circuit technology proposed for implementing the processor. An n-bit addition can be performed in the time it takes the carry signal to reach the c_{n-1} position plus the time it takes to develop s_{n-1}. Assuming this last delay is 1.5 ns, a 32-bit addition takes $(31 \times 1) + 1.5 = 32.5$ ns.

Two approaches can be taken to reduce this delay to the desired 10-ns range. The first approach is to use faster electronic circuit technology in implementing the ripple-carry logic design. The second approach is to use a logic network structure different from that shown in Figure 6.4b.

Logic structures for fast adder design must speed up the generation of the carry signals. The logic expressions for s_i (sum) and c_{i+1} (carry-out) of stage i (see Figure 6.3) are

$$s_i = \overline{x}_i\overline{y}_ic_i + \overline{x}_iy_i\overline{c}_i + x_i\overline{y}_i\overline{c}_i + x_iy_ic_i$$

and

$$c_{i+1} = y_ic_i + x_ic_i + x_iy_i$$

Factoring the second equation into

$$c_{i+1} = x_iy_i + (x_i + y_i)c_i$$

we can write

$$c_{i+1} = G_i + P_ic_i$$

where

$$G_i = x_iy_i \qquad \text{and} \qquad P_i = x_i + y_i$$

The expressions G_i and P_i are called the *generate* and *propagate* functions for stage i. The generate function for stage i is equal to 1 if $c_{i+1} = 1$, independent of the input carry, c_i. This occurs when both x_i and y_i are 1. The propagate function means that an input carry will produce an output carry when either x_i is 1 or y_i is 1. All G_i and P_i functions can be formed independently and in parallel in one logic-gate delay after the X and Y vectors are applied to the inputs of an n-bit adder. Expanding c_i in terms of $i - 1$ subscripted variables and substituting into the c_{i+1} equation, we obtain

$$c_{i+1} = G_i + P_iG_{i-1} + P_iP_{i-1}c_{i-1}$$

Continuing this type of expansion, the final expression for any carry variable is

$$c_{i+1} = G_i + P_i G_{i-1} + P_i P_{i-1} G_{i-2} + \cdots + P_i P_{i-1} \cdots P_1 G_0 + P_i P_{i-1} \cdots P_0 c_0$$

Thus, all carries can be obtained three logic-gate delays after the input operands X, Y, and c_0 are available, because only one gate delay is needed to develop all P_i and G_i signals, followed by two gate delays in the AND-OR circuit for c_{i+1}. After another three gate delays (one delay to invert each carry and two further delays to form each sum bit as shown earlier), all sum bits are available. Therefore, independent of n, the n-bit addition process requires only six levels of logic.

A practical problem with this approach is the gate fan-in constraints. The expression for c_{i+1} requires $i + 2$ inputs to the largest AND term and $i + 2$ inputs to the OR term. Because of electronic circuit considerations, logic gate fan-in is restricted in practice. Let us consider the design of a 4-bit adder as a basic unit. The function

$$c_4 = G_3 + P_3 G_2 + P_3 P_2 G_1 + P_3 P_2 P_1 G_0 + P_3 P_2 P_1 P_0 c_0$$

requires a fan-in of five for the basic gates and needs two gate delays after the G_i and P_i functions are available. Using eight of these connected as in Figure 6.4c (with $n = 4$), a 32-bit adder is obtained that requires an amount of time equal to 20 gate delays. This total is composed of one delay for all G_i and P_i information, two delays each for $c_4, c_8, c_{12}, \ldots, c_{28}, c_{31}$, and a final three delays for s_{31}. All other sum bits and c_{32} are available at or before the time for s_{31}. The earlier discussion involving absolute time values used an implied gate delay of 0.5 ns. With this value, the preceding 32-bit adder requires 10 ns to develop all outputs, rather than the 32.5 ns required by the original design in Figure 6.4b. This meets the 10-ns objective for the addition operation. Fast adders that form carry functions, as in this simple example, are called *carry-lookahead adders*. Note that, in the preceding 32-bit adder example, we have assumed that the carries inside each block are formed by lookahead circuits. However, they still ripple between blocks.

For longer word lengths, it may be necessary to speed up the addition operation even further. This can be done by applying the lookahead technique to the carry signals between blocks; thus, a second level of lookahead is employed. We can design a 16-bit adder as follows: Suppose that each of the 4-bit adder blocks provides two new output functions defined as G_k^I and P_k^I, where $k = 0$ for the first 4-bit block, $k = 1$ for the second 4-bit block, and so on. In the first block,

$$P_0^I = P_3 P_2 P_1 P_0$$

and

$$G_0^I = G_3 + P_3 G_2 + P_3 P_2 G_1 + P_3 P_2 P_1 G_0$$

In words, if we say that G_i and P_i determine whether bit stage i generates or propagates a carry, then G_k^I and P_k^I determine whether block k generates or propagates a carry. With these new functions available, it is not necessary to wait for carries to ripple between all of the 4-bit blocks. For example, c_{16} can be formed as

$$c_{16} = G_3^I + P_3^I G_2^I + P_3^I P_2^I G_1^I + P_3^I P_2^I P_1^I G_0^I + P_3^I P_2^I P_1^I P_0^I c_0$$

The delay in developing c_{16} is two gate delays more than the time needed to develop the G_k^I and P_k^I functions. The latter require two gate delays and one gate delay, respectively, after the generation of G_i and P_i. Therefore, c_{16} is available five gate delays after X, Y, and c_0 are applied as inputs. Earlier, using only G_i and P_i functions, c_{16} required nine gate delays.

Longer adders can be constructed by cascading 16-bit basic blocks built using G_k^I and P_k^I functions as well as G_i and P_i functions. The total adder delay is about half what it would be if the longer adders are built by cascading 4-bit basic blocks using only G_i and P_i functions.

6.4
SIGNED ADDITION AND SUBTRACTION

In Section 6.1, we discuss three systems for representing positive and negative numbers, or, simply, signed numbers. These systems differ only in the way they represent negative values. Their relative merits from the standpoint of ease of implementation of arithmetic operations can be determined through a few simple examples. The sign-and-magnitude system is the simplest representation, but it is also the most awkward for addition and subtraction operations. The 1's-complement method is somewhat better. The 2's-complement system is the best method in terms of efficiently implementing addition and subtraction operations.

Why is the 2's-complement representation the best choice? First, consider addition modulo N (mod N). A helpful graphical device for the description of addition mod N of positive integers is a circle with the N values 0 through $N - 1$ marked along its perimeter, as shown in Figure 6.5a. To treat some specific examples, we choose $N = 16$. The operation $(7 + 4)$ mod 16 yields the value 11. To perform this operation graphically, locate 7 mod $16 = 7$ on the circle and then move 4 units in the clockwise direction to arrive at the answer 11. As a second example, consider $(9 + 14)$ mod $16 = 7$; this is modeled on the circle by locating 9 mod $16 = 9$ and moving 14 units in the clockwise direction to arrive at the answer 7. This graphical technique works for the computation of $(a + b)$ mod 16 for any positive numbers a and b; that is, locate a mod 16 and move b units in the clockwise direction to arrive at $(a + b)$ mod 16.

Now consider a different interpretation of the mod 16 circle. Let the values 0 through 15 be represented by the 4-bit binary vectors $0000, 0001, \ldots, 1111$, according to the binary number system. Then reinterpret these binary vectors to represent the signed numbers from -8 through $+7$ in the 2's-complement method (see Figure 6.1), as shown in Figure 6.5b.

Let us apply the mod 16 addition technique to the simple example of adding $+7$ to -3. The 2's-complement representation for these numbers is 0111 and 1101, respectively. To add these numbers, locate 0111 on the circle in Figure 6.5b. Then move 1101 (13 steps) in the clockwise direction to arrive at 0100, which yields the correct answer of $+4$. If we use one of the adder circuits discussed earlier, we obtain

$$
\begin{array}{r}
0\ 1\ 1\ 1 \\
+\ \ 1\ 1\ 0\ 1 \\
\hline
1\ \ 0\ 1\ 0\ 0
\end{array}
$$

↑
Carry-out

Note that if we ignore the carry-out from the fourth bit position in this addition, we obtain the correct answer. In fact, this is always the case.

We now state the rules governing the addition and subtraction of n-bit signed numbers using the 2's-complement representation system.

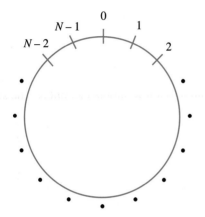

(a) Circle representation of integers mod N

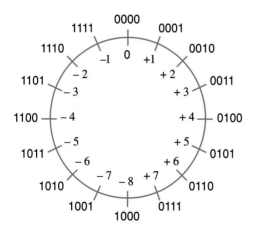

(b) Mod 16 system for 2's-complement numbers

FIGURE 6.5
Modular number systems and the 2's-complement system.

1. To *add* two numbers, add their representations in an *n*-bit adder, ignoring the carry-out signal from the MSB position. The sum will be the algebraically correct value in the 2's-complement representation as long as the answer is in the range -2^{n-1} through $+2^{n-1} - 1$.
2. To *subtract* two numbers X and Y, that is, to perform $X - Y$, form the 2's complement of Y and then add it to X, as in rule 1. Again, the result will be the algebraically correct value in the 2's-complement representation system if the answer is in the range -2^{n-1} through $+2^{n-1} - 1$.

Figure 6.6 shows some examples of addition and subtraction. In all these 4-bit examples, the answers fall into the representable range of -8 through $+7$. When answers

(a)	0 0 1 0	(+2)		(b)	0 1 0 0	(+4)
	+ 0 0 1 1	(+3)			+ 1 0 1 0	(−6)
	0 1 0 1	(+5)			1 1 1 0	(−2)

(c)	1 0 1 1	(−5)		(d)	0 1 1 1	(+7)
	+ 1 1 1 0	(−2)			+ 1 1 0 1	(−3)
	1 0 0 1	(−7)			0 1 0 0	(+4)

(e)   1 1 0 1   (−3)   ⟹   1 1 0 1
    − 1 0 0 1   (−7)   + 0 1 1 1
                                  0 1 0 0   (+4)

(f)   0 0 1 0   (+2)   ⟹   0 0 1 0
    − 0 1 0 0   (+4)   + 1 1 0 0
                                  1 1 1 0   (−2)

(g)   0 1 1 0   (+6)   ⟹   0 1 1 0
    − 0 0 1 1   (+3)   + 1 1 0 1
                                  0 0 1 1   (+3)

(h)   1 0 0 1   (−7)   ⟹   1 0 0 1
    − 1 0 1 1   (−5)   + 0 1 0 1
                                  1 1 1 0   (−2)

(i)   1 0 0 1   (−7)   ⟹   1 0 0 1
    − 0 0 0 1   (+1)   + 1 1 1 1
                                  1 0 0 0   (−8)

(j)   0 0 1 0   (+2)   ⟹   0 0 1 0
    − 1 1 0 1   (−3)   + 0 0 1 1
                                  0 1 0 1   (+5)

FIGURE 6.6
2's-complement Add and Subtract operations.

do not fall within the representable range, we say that an *arithmetic overflow* has occurred. Section 6.4.1 discusses such situations. The four addition operations (*a*) through (*d*) in Figure 6.6 follow rule 1, and the six subtraction operations (*e*) through (*j*) follow rule 2. Note that the subtraction operation requires the subtrahend, that is, the bottom value, to be 2's complemented before the addition is performed. When subtraction is implemented in a logic circuit the 2's complementing can be combined with the addition operation, as shown in Figure 6.7. The Add/Sub control wire is set to 0 for addition. This allows the Y vector to be applied unchanged to one of the adder inputs along with a carry-in signal, c_0, of 0. When the Add/Sub control wire is set to 1 for subtraction, the Y vector is 1's complemented (that is, bit complemented) by the EX-OR gates, and c_0 is set to 1 to complete the 2's complementation of Y. Note that 2's complementing a negative value, as in Figure 6.6*e*, is done in exactly the same manner as for a positive value.

We often need to represent a given number in the 2's-complement system by using a larger number of bits. For a positive number, this is achieved by adding 0s to the left. For a negative number, the leftmost bit, which is the sign bit, is a 1, and a longer number with the same value is obtained by replicating the sign bit to the left as many times as desired. To see why this is correct, scan around the mod 16 circle of Figure 6.5*b* in the counterclockwise direction, starting from the code for 0. If negative numbers of more than 4 bits are written out, they can be derived correctly by extending the 4-bit codes by 1s to the left. In summary, to represent a signed number in 2's-complement form using a larger number of bits, repeat the sign bit as many times as needed to the left. This operation is called *sign extension*.

The logical simplicity and speed of either adding or subtracting signed numbers in 2's-complement representation is the reason why this number representation is used in the ALU subsystems of modern computers. It might seem that the 1's-complement representation would be just as good as the 2's-complement system for use in a combined addition-subtraction logic network. However, although the complementation is easy, the result obtained after the add operation is not always correct. In fact, the carry-out, c_n, cannot be ignored. If $c_n = 1$, then 1 must be added to the result to make it correct. If $c_n = 0$, the result obtained is correct. The need for this correction cycle, which is conditional on the carry-out from the add operation, means that addition and subtraction cannot be implemented as conveniently in the 1's-complement system as in the 2's-complement system.

6.4.1 Overflow in Integer Arithmetic

When adding unsigned numbers, the carry-out, c_n, serves as the overflow indicator. However, this doesn't work for adding signed numbers. If we try to add the numbers +7 and +4 in a 4-bit adder, the output vector, S, is 1011, which is the code for −5, a wrong result. The carry-out signal from the MSB position is 0. Similarly, if we try to add −4 and −6, we get $S = +6$, another error, and in this case, the carry-out signal is 1. Clearly, the addition of numbers with different signs cannot cause overflow, because the absolute value of the sum is always smaller than the absolute value of one of the two summands. This leads to the following conclusions:

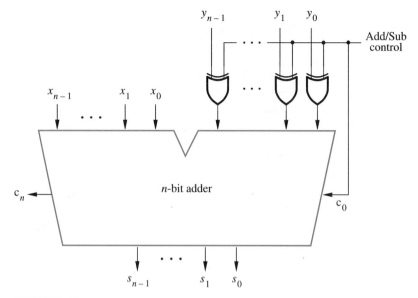

FIGURE 6.7
Binary addition-subtraction logic network.

1. Overflow can occur only when adding two numbers that have the same sign.
2. The carry-out signal from the sign-bit position is not a sufficient indicator of overflow when adding signed numbers.

When both operands X and Y have the same sign, an overflow occurs when the sign of S does not agree with the signs of X and Y. In an n-bit adder, we can define a signal, *Overflow*, by the logical expression

$$\text{Overflow} = x_{n-1}y_{n-1}\bar{s}_{n-1} + \bar{x}_{n-1}\bar{y}_{n-1}s_{n-1}$$

For a combined addition-subtraction unit, such as in Figure 6.7, the variable y_{n-1} in the Overflow expression should be taken from the output of the leftmost EX-OR gate. This leads to the correct indication of overflow from either addition or subtraction.

A computer must be able to detect an overflow. It is customary to dedicate a condition code flag as the indicator, and it is possible to have this flag cause an interrupt when an Add or Subtract instruction results in an overflow. Then the programmer must decide how to correct the problem.

6.5
ARITHMETIC AND BRANCHING CONDITIONS

In the preceding sections, we discussed adding unsigned numbers as well as adding and subtracting signed numbers in the 2's-complement representation. At this point, we return to the discussion of condition codes and conditional branches presented in Chapter 2.

In the 68000 processor, the four condition code flags N, Z, V, and C are set and cleared by arithmetic operations as follows:

N   Set to 1 if the result is negative; otherwise, cleared to 0.
Z   Set to 1 if the result is 0; otherwise, cleared to 0.
V   Set to 1 if arithmetic overflow occurs; otherwise, cleared to 0.
C   For an add operation, set to 1 if a carry-out results; otherwise, cleared to 0.
     For a subtract operation, the C flag indicates a borrow. Set to 1 if no carry-out results; otherwise, cleared to 0.

For purposes of this discussion, assume that addition and subtraction are performed as indicated by the logic unit in Figure 6.7. The carry-out signal referred to in the definition of the C flag is synonymous with the signal c_n in that figure. The V flag is set according to the Overflow expression given in Section 6.4.1.

Let us now consider how conditional branch instructions use the condition code flags. In some branch instructions, the branch condition is determined by the value of a single flag. For example, the instructions BNE (Branch if Not Equal to 0) and BEQ (Branch if EQual to 0) test the Z flag. Other instructions involve testing two or more flags. Consider the BLS (Branch-if-Lower-or-Same) instruction. It is normally used after a Compare instruction, which compares two unsigned integers. The branch is taken if the destination operand is less than or equal to the source operand. The comparison is done by subtracting the source operand from the destination operand. The C flag is set to 1 if no carry occurs in the subtraction operation. A few examples demonstrate that the carry is equal to 0 when the source operand is larger than the destination operand and equal to 1 when the source operand is smaller than the destination operand. When both operands are the same, the carry is 1; thus, the C flag is cleared to 0. However, the Z flag is set to 1, because the result is 0. Therefore, the required branch condition is $C + Z = 1$.

Consider a similar comparison of signed numbers. In this case, the BLE (Branch-if-Less-than-or-Equal) instruction should be used instead of BLS. The result of the comparison is negative if the destination operand is less than the source operand. This is one of the conditions for which the branch should occur. Therefore, it would seem that $N + Z = 1$ is the branch condition for the BLE instruction. This is sufficient if arithmetic overflow does not occur when the subtraction operation is performed. If overflow occurs, however, the sign of the result is opposite to what it should be. To obtain the proper branch condition in this case, the complement of the N flag should be tested. Therefore, the complete branch condition for the BLE instruction is $(N \oplus V) + Z = 1$.

Another important aspect of condition code flags is the role of the C flag in performing multiple-precision arithmetic. Consider the task of adding two operands, each occupying several words in memory. The required addition can be done by a program loop that adds individual words in successive iterations. The C flag must be preserved from one iteration to the next in order to propagate the carries through the complete addition operation. A problem arises if the C flag is altered by instructions other than the Add instruction in the loop. The 68000 processor has a fifth condition code flag, X, that is set in the same way as the C flag but is not affected by as many instructions. Therefore, the X flag serves the role of preserving the value of the carry flag for use in multiple-precision arithmetic routines.

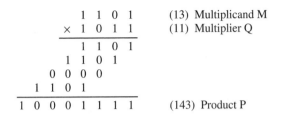

```
        1  1  0  1        (13)  Multiplicand M
    ×   1  0  1  1        (11)  Multiplier Q
        1  1  0  1
     1  1  0  1
  0  0  0  0
1  1  0  1
1  0  0  0  1  1  1  1    (143)  Product P
```

(a) Manual multiplication algorithm

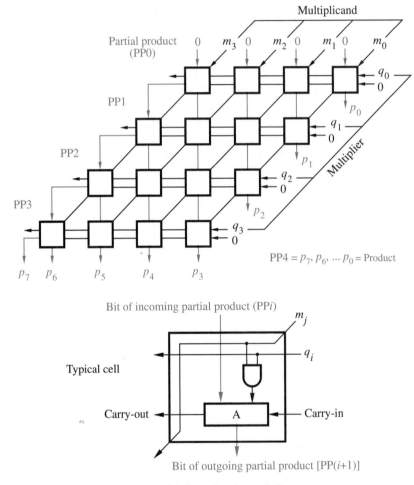

(b) Array implementation

FIGURE 6.8
Array multiplication of positive binary operands.

6.6
MULTIPLICATION OF POSITIVE NUMBERS

The usual algorithm for multiplying integers by hand is illustrated in Figure 6.8*a* for the binary system. This algorithm applies to unsigned numbers and to positive numbers. The product of two *n*-digit numbers can be accommodated in 2*n* digits, so the product of the two 4-bit numbers in this example fits into 8 bits, as shown. In the binary system, multiplication of the multiplicand by one bit of the multiplier is easy. If the multiplier bit is 1, the multiplicand is entered in the appropriate position to be added to the partial product. If the multiplier is 0, then 0s are entered, as in the third row of the example.

Binary multiplication of positive operands can be implemented in a purely combinational, two-dimensional logic array, as shown in Figure 6.8*b*. The main component in each cell is an adder circuit. The AND gate in any cell determines whether a multiplicand bit, m_j, is added to the incoming partial-product bit, based on the value of the multiplier bit, q_i. Each row *i*, where $0 \leq i \leq 3$, adds the multiplicand (appropriately shifted) to the incoming partial product, PP*i*, to generate the outgoing partial product, PP($i + 1$), if $q_i = 1$. If $q_i = 0$, PP*i* is passed vertically downward unchanged. PP0 is all 0s, and PP4 is the desired product. The multiplicand is shifted left one position per row by the diagonal signal path.

Almost all modern computers provide multiplication in the basic machine instruction set. The most recent high-performance processor chips use an appreciable area of the chip to perform arithmetic functions on both integer and floating-point operands. (Floating-point operations are discussed later in this chapter.) Although the preceding combinational multiplier is easy to understand, it may be impractical for long numbers, because it uses many gates. Multiplication can be performed using a mixture of combinational array techniques, similar to those shown in Figure 6.8, and sequential techniques that require less combinational logic.

In early computers, because of logic costs, the adder circuitry in the ALU was used to perform multiplication sequentially. The block diagram in Figure 6.9*a* shows the simplest hardware arrangement for sequential multiplication. This circuit performs multiplication by using a single adder *n* times to implement the spatial addition performed by the *n* rows of ripple-carry adders of Figure 6.8*b*. Registers A and Q combined hold PP*i* while multiplier bit q_i generates the signal Add/Noadd. This signal controls the addition of the multiplicand, M, to PP*i* to generate PP($i + 1$). The product is computed in *n* cycles. The partial product grows in length by 1 bit per cycle from the initial vector, PP0, of *n* 0s in register A. The carry-out from the adder is stored in flip-flop C, shown at the left end of register A. At the start, the multiplier is loaded into register Q, the multiplicand into register M, and C and A are cleared to 0. At the end of each cycle, C, A, and Q are shifted right one bit position to allow for growth of the partial product as the multiplier is shifted out of register Q. Because of this shifting, multiplier bit q_i appears at the LSB position of Q to generate the Add/Noadd signal at the correct time, starting with q_0 during the first cycle, q_1 during the second cycle, and so on. After they are used, the multiplier bits are discarded by the right-shift operation. Note that the carry-out from the adder is the leftmost bit of PP($i + 1$), and it must be held in the C flip-flop to be shifted right with the contents of A and Q. After *n* cycles, the high-order

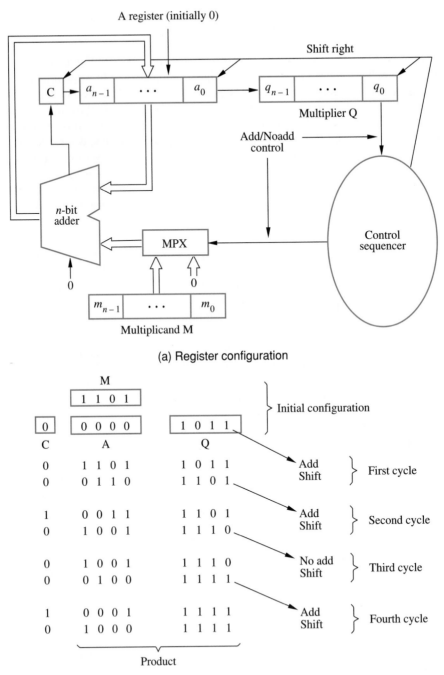

(a) Register configuration

(b) Multiplication example

FIGURE 6.9
Sequential circuit binary multiplier.

half of the product is held in register A and the low-order half is in register Q. The multiplication example of Figure 6.8*a* is shown in Figure 6.9*b* as it would be performed by this hardware arrangement.

Because we are assuming that the Multiply operation is hardwired, the Control sequencer component in Figure 6.9*a* is implemented by the general instruction execution sequencer discussed in Chapter 3. This results in a relatively long execution time for the Multiply instruction. If the adder has a delay of 10 ns and the control settings and shift operations in each cycle take another 10 ns, then a hardwired Multiply operation in a 32-bit word-length computer would take about 640 ns. For this reason, Multiply instructions took much longer to execute than Add instructions in early computers. Several techniques have been used to speed up multiplication in modern processors; we discuss some of them in the next few sections.

6.7
SIGNED-OPERAND MULTIPLICATION

We now discuss multiplication of signed operands, which generates a double-length product in the 2's-complement number system. The general strategy is still to accumulate partial products by adding versions of the multiplicand as selected by the multiplier bits.

First, consider the case of a positive multiplier and a negative multiplicand. When we add a negative multiplicand to a partial product, we must extend the sign-bit value of the multiplicand to the left as far as the product will extend. In Figure 6.10, for example, the 5-bit signed operand, -13, is the multiplicand, and it is multiplied by $+11$, the multiplier, to get the 10-bit product, -143. The sign extension of the multiplicand is shown in blue. Thus, the hardware discussed earlier can be used for negative multiplicands if it provides for sign extension of the partial products.

					1	0	0	1	1	(-13)
				× 0	1	0	1	1	($+11$)
1	1	1	1	1	1	0	0	1	1
1	1	1	1	1	0	0	1	1
0	0	0	0	0	0	0	0
1	1	1	0	0	1	1
0	0	0	0	0	0
1	1	0	1	1	1	0	0	0	1	(-143)

Sign extension is shown in blue

FIGURE 6.10
Sign extension of negative multiplicand.

For a negative multiplier, a straightforward solution is to form the 2's complement of both the multiplier and the multiplicand and proceed as in the case of a positive multiplier. This is possible because complementation of both operands does not change the value or the sign of the product. A technique that works equally well for both negative and positive multipliers, called the Booth algorithm, is described next.

6.7.1 Booth Algorithm

A powerful algorithm for signed-number multiplication, the Booth algorithm generates a $2n$-bit product and treats both positive and negative numbers uniformly. Consider a multiplication operation in which the multiplier is positive and has a single block of 1s, for example, 0011110. To derive the product, we could add four appropriately shifted versions of the multiplicand, as in the standard procedure. However, we can reduce the number of required operations by regarding this multiplier as the difference between two numbers:

$$
\begin{array}{rl}
 0100000 & (32) \\
-0000010 & (2) \\
\hline
 0011110 & (30)
\end{array}
$$

This suggests that the product can be generated by adding 2^5 times the multiplicand to the 2's complement of 2^1 times the multiplicand. For convenience, we can describe the sequence of required operations by recoding the preceding multiplier as $0 +1\,0\,0\,0 -1\,0$.

In general, in the Booth scheme, -1 times the shifted multiplicand is selected when moving from 0 to 1, and $+1$ times the shifted multiplicand is selected when moving from 1 to 0, as the multiplier is scanned from right to left. Figure 6.11 illustrates the normal and the Booth algorithms for the example just discussed. The Booth algorithm clearly extends to any number of blocks of 1s in a multiplier, including the situation in which a single 1 is considered a block. See Figure 6.12 for another example of recoding a multiplier. In this example, the least significant bit is 1. This situation is uniformly handled by assuming that an implied 0 lies to its right.

The Booth algorithm can also be used for negative multipliers, as Figure 6.13 shows. To see the correctness of this technique in general, we use a property of negative-number representations in the 2's-complement system. Let the leftmost zero of a negative number, X, be at bit position k, that is,

$$
X = 11 \dots 10 x_{k-1} \dots x_0
$$

The value of X is given by

$$
V(X) = -2^{k+1} + x_{k-1} \times 2^{k-1} + \cdots + x_0 \times 2^0
$$

This is supported by observing that

$$
\begin{array}{rl}
 11 \dots 100 & \dots 0 \\
+00 \dots 00 x_{k-1} & \dots x_0 \\
\hline
X = \quad 11 \dots 10 x_{k-1} & \dots x_0
\end{array}
$$

```
                  0  1  0  1  1  0  1
                  0  0 +1 +1 +1 +1  0
                  ─────────────────────
                  0  0  0  0  0  0  0
               0  1  0  1  1  0  1
            0  1  0  1  1  0  1
         0  1  0  1  1  0  1
      0  1  0  1  1  0  1
   0  0  0  0  0  0  0
0  0  0  0  0  0  0
─────────────────────────────────────
0  0  0  1  0  1  0  1  0  0  0  1  1  0


                  0  1  0  1  1  0  1
                  0 +1  0  0  0 -1  0
0  0  0  0  0  0  0  0  0  0  0  0  0  0
1  1  1  1  1  1  1  0  1  0  0  1  1  ◄──── 2's complement of
0  0  0  0  0  0  0  0  0  0  0  0             the multiplicand
0  0  0  0  0  0  0  0  0  0  0
0  0  0  0  0  0  0  0  0  0
0  0  0  1  0  1  1  0  1
0  0  0  0  0  0  0  0
─────────────────────────────────────
0  0  0  1  0  1  0  1  0  0  0  1  1  0
```

FIGURE 6.11
Normal and Booth multiplication algorithms.

```
0   0   1   0   1   1   0   0   1   1   1   0   1   0   1   1   0   0

                            ⇓

0  +1  -1  +1   0  -1   0  +1   0   0  -1  +1  -1  +1   0  -1   0   0
```

FIGURE 6.12
Booth recoding of a multiplier.

```
   0 1 1 0 1   (+13)                   0 1 1 0 1
 × 1 1 0 1 0   (−6)                    0 −1 +1 −1 0
 ─────────                  0 0 0 0 0 0 0 0 0 0
                            1 1 1 1 1 0 0 1 1
                            0 0 0 0 1 1 0 1
                            1 1 1 0 0 1 1
                            0 0 0 0 0 0
                            ─────────────────
                            1 1 1 0 1 1 0 0 1 0   (−78)
```

FIGURE 6.13
Booth multiplication with a negative multiplier.

Multiplier		Version of multiplicand selected by bit i
Bit i	Bit $i-1$	
0	0	$0 \times M$
0	1	$+1 \times M$
1	0	$-1 \times M$
1	1	$0 \times M$

FIGURE 6.14
Booth multiplier recoding table.

The top number is the 2's-complement representation of -2^{k+1}. The recoded multiplier now consists of the part corresponding to the second number, with -1 added in position $k + 1$. For example, the multiplier 110110 becomes $0 -1 +1 0 -1 0$.

The Booth technique for recoding multipliers is summarized in Figure 6.14. The transformation $011 \ldots 110 \Rightarrow +100 \ldots 0 -10$ is called *skipping over 1s*. This term is derived from the case in which the multiplier has its 1s grouped into a few contiguous blocks; only a few versions of the multiplicand, that is, the summands, must be added to generate the product, thus speeding up the multiplication operation. However, in the worst case—that of alternating 1s and 0s in the multiplier— each bit of the multiplier selects a summand. In fact, this results in more summands than if the Booth algorithm were not used. A 16-bit, worst-case multiplier, an ordinary multiplier, and a good multiplier are shown in Figure 6.15.

Worst-case multiplier

0 1 0 1 0 1 0 1 0 1 0 1 0 1 0 1

⇓

+1 −1 +1 −1 +1 −1 +1 −1 +1 −1 +1 −1 +1 −1 +1 −1

Ordinary multiplier

1 1 0 0 0 1 0 1 1 0 1 1 1 1 0 0

⇓

0 −1 0 0 +1 −1 +1 0 −1 +1 0 0 0 −1 0 0

Good multiplier

0 0 0 0 1 1 1 1 1 1 0 0 0 0 1 1 1

⇓

0 0 0 +1 0 0 0 0 −1 0 0 0 +1 0 0 −1

FIGURE 6.15
Booth recoded multipliers.

The Booth algorithm has two attractive features. First, it handles both positive and negative multipliers uniformly. Second, it achieves some efficiency in the number of additions required when the multiplier has a few large blocks of 1s. The speed gained by skipping over 1s depends on the data. On average, the speed of doing multiplication with the Booth algorithm is the same as with the normal algorithm.

6.8
FAST MULTIPLICATION

We now describe two techniques for speeding up the multiplication operation. The first technique guarantees that the maximum number of summands (versions of the multiplicand) that must be added is reduced by half. The second technique reduces the time needed to add the summands.

6.8.1 Bit-Pair Recoding of Multipliers

A technique called *bit-pair recoding* halves the maximum number of summands. This technique can be derived directly from the Booth algorithm. Group the Booth-recoded multiplier bits in pairs, and observe the following: The pair $(+1 \ -1)$ is equivalent to the pair $(0 \ +1)$. That is, instead of adding -1 times the multiplicand M at shift position i to $+1 \times$ M at position $i + 1$, the same result is obtained by adding $+1 \times$ M at position i. Other examples follow: $(+1 \ 0)$ is equivalent to $(0 \ +2)$, $(-1 \ +1)$ is equivalent to $(0 \ -1)$, and so on. Thus, if the Booth-recoded multiplier is examined two bits at a time, starting from the right, it can be rewritten in a form that requires at most one version of the multiplicand to be added to the partial product for each pair of multiplier bits. Figure 6.16a shows an example of bit-pair recoding of the multiplier in Figure 6.13, and Figure 6.16b shows a table of the multiplicand selection decisions for all possibilities. The multiplication example in Figure 6.13 is shown again in Figure 6.17 as it would be computed using bit-pair recoding of the multiplier.

6.8.2 Carry-Save Addition of Summands

Multiplication requires the addition of several summands. A technique called *carry-save addition* speeds up the addition process. Consider the addition of three n-bit numbers, W, X, and Y, to produce a sum, Z. We can first add W to X to generate a number A, and then we can add A to Y to produce Z. This can be done by using two ripple-carry adders, as shown in Figure 6.18a.

A different way of using the n full-adder units of the upper ripple-carry adder is shown in Figure 6.18b. Instead of adding W and X to produce A in the upper ripple-carry adder, we introduce the bits of Y into the carry inputs. This generates the vectors S and the "saved" carries C as the outputs of the upper row. In the second row, S and C are added in a ripple-carry adder to produce the desired sum, Z. An example illustrating both alternatives is given in part c of the figure. Note that the intermediate sum, A, from

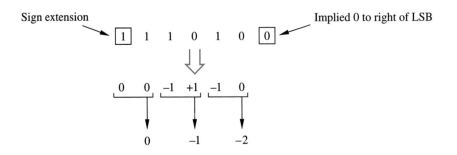

(a) Example of bit-pair recoding derived from Booth recoding

Multiplier bit-pair		Multiplier bit on the right	Multiplicand
$i+1$	i	$i-1$	selected at position i
0	0	0	$0 \times M$
0	0	1	$+1 \times M$
0	1	0	$+1 \times M$
0	1	1	$+2 \times M$
1	0	0	$-2 \times M$
1	0	1	$-1 \times M$
1	1	0	$-1 \times M$
1	1	1	$0 \times M$

(b) Table of multiplicand selection decisions

FIGURE 6.16
Multiplier bit-pair recoding.

the first method, is not explicitly generated in the second method. Carry-save addition transforms W, X, and Y into S and C. Its advantage is that all bits of the S and C vectors are produced in a short, fixed amount of time after W, X, and Y are applied. Carry propagation takes place only in the second row. Note that a carry-lookahead adder could be used effectively to add the S and C vectors in part b, because all bits of S and C are available in parallel. A carry-lookahead adder cannot be used effectively in part a, because the high-order bits a_i of the intermediate sum, A, are not available soon enough.

Now consider the addition of many summands, as is required in multiplication. We can group the summands in threes and perform carry-save addition on each of these groups in parallel to generate a set of S and C vectors. Next, we group all of the S and C vectors into threes, and perform carry-save addition on them. We continue with this process until there are only two vectors remaining. They can then be added in a

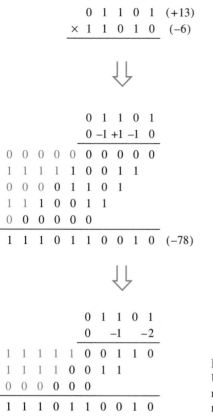

```
    0  1  1  0  1   (+13)
 ×  1  1  0  1  0   (−6)
```

```
             0  1  1  0  1
             0 −1 +1 −1  0
 0  0  0  0  0  0  0  0  0  0
 1  1  1  1  1  0  0  1  1
 0  0  0  0  1  1  0  1
 1  1  1  0  0  1  1
 0  0  0  0  0  0
 ──────────────────────────
 1  1  1  0  1  1  0  0  1  0   (−78)
```

```
             0  1  1  0  1
             0    −1    −2
 1  1  1  1  1  0  0  1  1  0
 1  1  1  1  0  0  1  1
 0  0  0  0  0  0
 ──────────────────────────
 1  1  1  0  1  1  0  0  1  0
```

FIGURE 6.17
Using multiplier bit-pair recoding, multiplication requires only half the number of summands as a normal algorithm.

ripple-carry or a carry-lookahead adder to produce the desired sum. Note that each of the carry-save additions, reducing three vectors to two, is done in only one full adder unit delay, independent of the length of the numbers.

Consider the example of adding 9 numbers using this method. The initial three groups of 3 numbers each is reduced to a total of 6 numbers, the S and C vectors, in the first carry-save addition operation. These 6 numbers are successively reduced to 4, then 3, then 2 numbers in three more carry-save addition operations. The final 2 numbers are added to produce the desired sum. The complete operation requires four full-adder unit delays to do the carry-save additions, followed by a full addition operation on the final 2 vectors.

When the number of summands is large, the time saved is proportionally greater. For example, the addition of 32 numbers using the carry-save addition method requires only 7 full-adder unit delays before the final Add operation. In general, it can be shown that about $1.7 \log_2 k$ full-adder unit delays (that is, carry-save addition steps) are needed to reduce k summands to 2 vectors, which, when added, produce the desired sum. Again, note that a carry-lookahead adder can be used effectively to add the final 2 vectors, because all bits of these vectors are produced in parallel as the result of the carry-save addition operations.

Many ripple-carry adders could be used in parallel to reduce k summands to 2 vectors in a tree-like structure, analogous to the way we reduce the number of summands

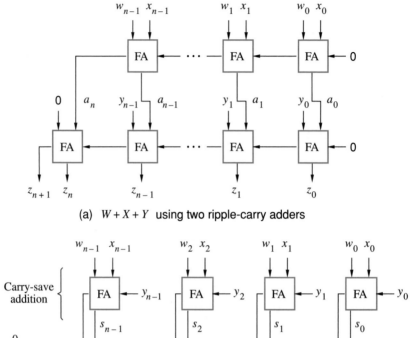

(a) $W + X + Y$ using two ripple-carry adders

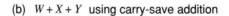

(b) $W + X + Y$ using carry-save addition

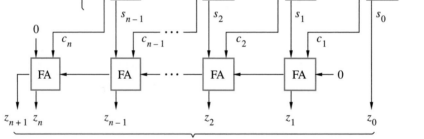

(c) An example

FIGURE 6.18
Carry-save addition.

using carry-save addition. The low-order bits of the final 2 vectors would also be generated quickly, faster than in the linear array in Figure 6.8b. However, because of the ripple-carry effect, the high-order bits of the final 2 vectors would take significantly longer to produce than in the carry-save method. Hence, a fast carry-lookahead adder cannot be used as effectively in adding the final 2 vectors. Because of cost, it is not feasible to use carry-lookahead adders in the earlier stages of the summand-reduction process.

Some details have been omitted in this discussion of ways to reduce a large number of summands to 2 vectors, which are then added to produce the sum. For example, the summands to be added in the multiplication operation are actually shifted, or skewed, relative to each other, as Figure 6.8 shows. Also, in comparing summand reduction by using either carry-save additions or ripple-carry additions, note that the final 2 vectors to be added are not identical in length. And the cost comparisons, although similar, have not been discussed in detail. Problems 6.25, 6.26, 6.35, 6.36, and 6.37 explore some of these issues. Our main purpose is to indicate that using carry-save additions followed by a lookahead-adder operation in implementing multiplication saves time and, thus, enhances performance.

We now summarize the application of these techniques in high-speed multiplication. Bit-pair recoding of the multiplier, derived from the Booth algorithm, reduces the number of summands by up to a factor of 2. These summands can then be reduced to only 2 by using a relatively small number of carry-save addition steps. The final product can be generated by one addition operation, and this last operation can be speeded up by using a lookahead adder. All three of these basic techniques—bit-pair recoding of the multiplier, carry-save addition of the summands, and lookahead addition—have been used in various ways by the designers of high-performance processors to reduce the time needed to perform multiplication.

6.9
INTEGER DIVISION

In Section 6.6, we discuss positive-number multiplication by relating the way the multiplication operation is done manually to the way it is done in a logic circuit. We follow the same strategy here, in discussing integer division. We discuss only positive-number division in detail, and make some general comments on the signed-operand case later.

Figure 6.19 shows examples of decimal division and the binary-coded division of the same values. Consider the decimal version first. The 2 in the quotient is determined

```
          21                        10101
      _____                 _____
  13 ) 274               1101 ) 100010010
        26                       1101
      ____                      _____
        14                       10000
        13                        1101
      ____                      _____
         1                        1110
                                  1101
                                 _____
                                     1
```

FIGURE 6.19
Longhand division examples.

by the following reasoning: First, we try to divide 13 into 2, and it doesn't work. Next, we try to divide 13 into 27. We go through the trial exercise of multiplying 13 by 2 to get 26, and, knowing that $27 - 26 = 1$ is less than 13, we enter 2 as the quotient and perform the required subtraction. The next digit of the dividend, 4, is brought down, and we finish by deciding that 13 goes into 14 once, and the remainder is 1. We can discuss binary division in a similar way, with the simplification that the only possibilities for the quotient bits are 0 and 1.

A circuit that implements division by this longhand method operates as follows: It positions the divisor appropriately with respect to the dividend and performs a subtraction. If the remainder is zero or positive, a quotient bit of 1 is determined, the remainder is extended by another bit of the dividend, the divisor is repositioned, and another subtraction is performed. On the other hand, if the remainder is negative, a quotient bit of 0 is determined, the dividend is restored by adding back the divisor, and the divisor is repositioned for another subtraction.

Figure 6.20 shows a logic circuit arrangement that implements this *restoring-division* technique. Note its similarity to the structure for multiplication that was shown in Figure 6.9. An n-bit positive divisor is loaded into register M and an n-bit positive dividend is loaded into register Q at the start of the operation. Register A is set to 0. After the division is complete, the n-bit quotient is in register Q and the remainder

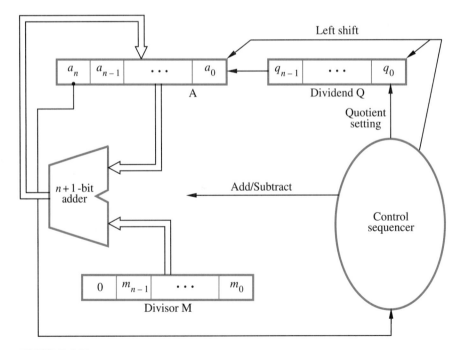

FIGURE 6.20
Circuit arrangement for binary division.

is in register A. The required subtractions are facilitated by using 2's-complement arithmetic. The extra bit position at the left end of both A and M accommodates the sign bit
during subtractions. The algorithm that follows performs the division.

Do the following n times:
Shift A and Q left one binary position.
Subtract M from A, and place the answer back in A.
If the sign of A is 1, set q_0 to 0 and add M back to A (that is, restore A);
  otherwise, set q_0 to 1.

Figure 6.21 shows a 4-bit example as it would be processed by the circuit in Figure 6.20.

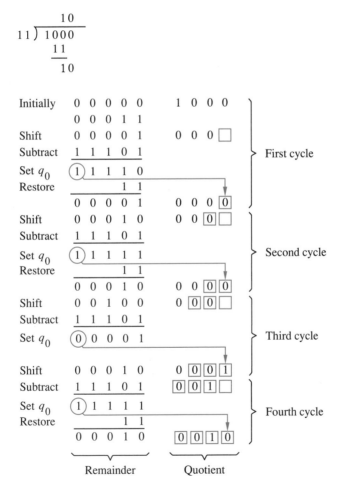

FIGURE 6.21
A restoring-division example.

This algorithm can be improved by avoiding the need for restoring A after an unsuccessful subtraction. (Subtraction is said to be unsuccessful if the result is negative.) Consider the sequence of operations that takes place after the subtraction operation in the preceding algorithm. If A is positive, we shift left and subtract M; that is, we perform $2A - M$. If A is negative, we restore it by performing $A + M$, and then we shift it left and subtract M. This is equivalent to performing $2A + M$. The q_0 bit is appropriately set to 0 or 1 after the correct operation has been performed. We can summarize this in the following *nonrestoring-division* algorithm:

Step 1: Do the following *n* times:
        If the sign of A is 0, shift A and Q left one bit position and subtract M from
           A; otherwise, shift A and Q left and add M to A.
        If the sign of A is 0, set q_0 to 1; otherwise, set q_0 to 0.
Step 2: If the sign of A is 1, add M to A.

Step 2 is needed to leave the proper positive remainder in A at the end of *n* cycles. The logic circuitry in Figure 6.20 can also be used to perform this algorithm. Note that the

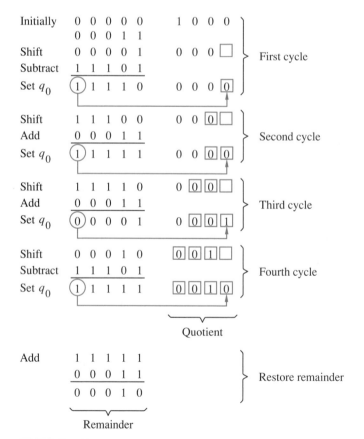

FIGURE 6.22
A nonrestoring-division example.

Restore operations are no longer needed, and that exactly one Add or Subtract operation is performed per cycle. Figure 6.22 shows how the division example in Figure 6.21 is executed by the nonrestoring-division algorithm.

There are no simple algorithms for performing signed division that are comparable to the algorithms for signed multiplication. In division, the operands can be preprocessed to transform them into positive values. After using one of the algorithms just discussed, the results are transformed to the correct signed values, as necessary.

6.10
FLOATING-POINT NUMBERS AND OPERATIONS

Until now, we have dealt exclusively with signed, fixed-point numbers and have conveniently considered them integers, that is, having an implied binary point at the right end of each number. It is also possible to assume that the binary point is just to the right of the sign bit, thus representing a fraction. In the 2's-complement system, the signed value F, represented by the n-bit binary fraction

$$B = b_0.b_{-1}b_{-2}\ldots b_{-(n-1)}$$

is given by

$$F(B) = -b_0 \times 2^0 + b_{-1} \times 2^{-1} + b_{-2} \times 2^{-2} + \cdots + b_{-(n-1)} \times 2^{-(n-1)}$$

where the range of F is

$$-1 \leq F \leq 1 - 2^{-(n-1)}$$

Consider the range of values representable in a 32-bit, signed, fixed-point format. Interpreted as integers, the value range is approximately 0 to $\pm 2.15 \times 10^9$. If we consider them to be fractions, the range is approximately $\pm 4.55 \times 10^{-10}$ to ± 1. Neither of these ranges is sufficient for scientific calculations, which might involve parameters like Avogadro's number (6.0247×10^{23} mole^{-1}) or Planck's constant (6.6254×10^{-27} erg·s). Hence, we need to easily accommodate both very large integers and very small fractions. This means a computer must be able to represent numbers and operate on them in such a way that the position of the binary point is variable and is automatically adjusted as computation proceeds. In such a case, the binary point is said to float, and the numbers are called *floating-point numbers*. This distinguishes them from fixed-point numbers, whose binary point is always in the same position.

Because the position of the binary point in a floating-point number is variable, it must be given explicitly in the floating-point representation. For example, in the familiar decimal scientific notation, numbers may be written as 6.0247×10^{23}, 6.6254×10^{-27}, -1.0341×10^2, -7.3000×10^{-14}, and so on. These numbers are said to be given to five *significant digits*. The *scale factors* (10^{23}, 10^{-27}, and so on) indicate the position of the decimal point with respect to the significant digits. By convention, when the decimal point is placed to the right of the first (nonzero) significant digit, the number is said to be *normalized*. Note that the base, 10, in the scale factor is fixed and does not need to appear explicitly in the machine representation of a floating-point number. The sign, the significant digits, and the exponent in the scale factor constitute the representation.

We are thus motivated to define a floating-point number representation as one in which a number is represented by its sign, a string of significant digits, commonly called the *mantissa*, and an exponent to an implied base for the scale factor.

Let us state a general form and size for such numbers in the decimal system and then relate the form to a comparable binary representation. A useful form is

$$\pm X_1.X_2X_3X_4X_5X_6X_7 \times 10^{\pm Y_1Y_2}$$

where X_i and Y_i are decimal digits. Both the number of significant digits (7) and the exponent range (±99) are sufficient for a wide range of scientific calculations. It is possible to approximate this mantissa precision and scale factor range in a binary representation that occupies 32 bits, which is a standard computer word length. A 24-bit mantissa can approximately represent a 7-digit decimal number, and an 8-bit exponent to an implied base of 2 provides a scale factor with a reasonable range. One bit is needed for the sign of the number. Since the leading nonzero bit of a normalized binary mantissa must be a 1, it does not have to be included explicitly in the representation. Therefore, a total of 32 bits is needed.

This standard for representing floating-point numbers in 32 bits has been developed and specified in detail by the Institute of Electrical and Electronic Engineers (IEEE).[1] The standard describes both the representation and the way in which the four basic arithmetic operations are to be performed. The 32-bit representation is given in Figure 6.23a. The sign of the number is given in the first bit, followed by a representation for the exponent (to the base 2) of the scale factor. Instead of the signed exponent, E, the value actually stored in the exponent field is an unsigned integer $E' = E + 127$. This is called the excess-127 format. Thus, E' is in the range $0 \leq E' \leq 255$.

The end values of E', namely, 0 and 255, are used to indicate the floating-point values of exact 0 and infinity, respectively. Thus, the range of E' for normal values is $0 < E' < 255$. This means that the actual exponent, E, is in the range $-126 \leq E \leq 127$. The *excess-x* representation for exponents enables efficient comparison of the relative sizes of two floating-point numbers. (See Problem 6.14.)

The last 23 bits represent the mantissa. Since binary normalization is used, the most significant bit of the mantissa is always equal to 1. This bit is not explicitly represented; it is assumed to be to the immediate left of the binary point. The 23 bits stored in the M field represent the fractional part of the mantissa, that is, the bits to the right of the binary point. An example of a single-precision floating-point number is shown in Figure 6.23b.

The 32-bit standard representation in Figure 6.23a is called a *single-precision* representation because it occupies a single 32-bit word. The scale factor has a range of 2^{-126} to 2^{+127}, which is approximately equal to $10^{\pm38}$. The 24-bit mantissa provides approximately the same precision as a 7-digit decimal value. Recall that the mantissa consists of the 23-bit fraction given explicitly, as indicated in the figure, and the implied 1 to the left of the binary point. To provide more precision and range for floating-point numbers, the IEEE standard also specifies a *double-precision* format, as shown in Figure 6.23c. The double-precision format has increased exponent and mantissa ranges. The 11-bit excess-1023 exponent E' has the range $0 < E' < 2047$ for normal values, with 0 and 2047 used to indicate the special values 0 and infinity, as before. Thus, the

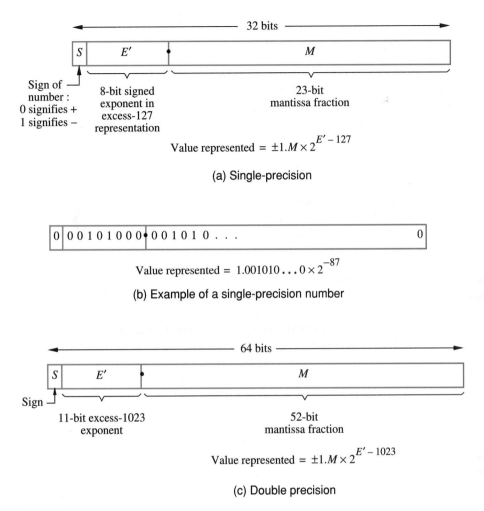

FIGURE 6.23
IEEE standard floating-point formats.

actual exponent E is in the range $-1022 \leq E \leq 1023$, providing scale factors of 2^{-1022} to 2^{1023} (approximately $10^{\pm 308}$). The 53-bit mantissa provides a precision equivalent to about 16 decimal digits.

Any commercial computer implementation must provide at least single-precision representation to conform to the IEEE standard. Double-precision representation is optional. The standard also specifies certain optional extended versions of both of these formats. The extended versions are intended to provide increased precision and increased exponent range for the representation of intermediate values in a sequence of calculations. For example, the dot product of two vectors of numbers can be computed by accumulating the sum of products in extended precision. The inputs are given in a standard precision, either single or double, and the answer is truncated to the same precision. The use of extended formats helps to reduce the size of the accumulated round-off error in a sequence of calculations. Extended formats also enhance the accuracy of evaluation of elementary functions such as sin, cos, and so on.

In addition to requiring the four basic arithmetic operations, the standard requires that the operations of remainder, square root, and conversion between binary and decimal representations be provided. It also specifies what should be done when operations produce results that fall outside the range of normalized floating-point numbers. These are *exceptions*, which cause a trap, that is, a software interrupt, whose action is under user control. Five exceptions must be detected: invalid operation, division by 0, overflow, underflow, and inexact. For example, an invalid operation occurs when the user attempts to take the square root of a negative number. A division by 0 exception occurs when the divisor is 0 and the numerator is a finite, nonzero number; the result is infinity, whose representation is mentioned earlier.

We now consider a few basic aspects of operating with floating-point numbers. First, note that if a number is not normalized, it can always be put in normalized form by shifting the fraction and adjusting the exponent. Figure 6.24 shows an unnormalized value, $0.0010110\ldots \times 2^9$, and its normalized version, $1.0110\ldots \times 2^6$. Since the scale factor is in the form 2^i, shifting the mantissa right or left by one bit position is compensated by an increase or a decrease of 1 in the exponent, respectively.

As computations proceed, a number that does not fall in the representable range might be generated. In single precision, this means that its normalized representation requires an exponent less than -126 or greater than $+127$. In the first case, we say that *underflow* has occurred, and in the second case, we say that *overflow* has occurred.

excess-127 exponent

0	1 0 0 0 1 0 0 0	0 0 1 0 1 1 0 ...

(There is no implicit 1 to the left of the binary point.)

Value represented $= +0.0010110\ldots \times 2^9$

(a) Unnormalized value

0	1 0 0 0 0 1 0 1	0 1 1 0 ...

Value represented $= +1.0110\ldots \times 2^6$

(b) Normalized version

FIGURE 6.24
Floating-point normalization in IEEE single-precision format.

Both underflow and overflow are arithmetic exceptions. The interrupt-service routine can then take actions specified by the user or by a system convention. If underflow occurs, for example, the decision might be to set the value to 0 and proceed.

6.10.1 Arithmetic Operations on Floating-Point Numbers

In this section, we outline the general procedures for addition, subtraction, multiplication, and division of floating-point numbers. The rules we give apply to the single-precision IEEE standard format. The rules here specify only the major steps needed to perform the four operations; for example, the possibility that overflow or underflow might occur is not discussed. Furthermore, intermediate results for both mantissas and exponents might require more than 24 and 8 bits, respectively. These and other aspects of the operations must be carefully considered in designing an arithmetic processor that meets the standard. Although we do not provide full detail in specifying the rules, we consider some aspects of implementation, including rounding, in later sections.

If their exponents differ, mantissas must be shifted with respect to each other before they are added or subtracted. Consider a decimal example in which we wish to add 2.9400×10^2 to 4.3100×10^4. We rewrite 2.9400×10^2 as 0.0294×10^4 and then perform addition of the mantissas to get 4.3394×10^4. A general rule for addition and subtraction can be stated as follows:

Add/Subtract Rule

1. Choose the number with the smaller exponent and shift its mantissa right a number of steps equal to the difference in exponents.
2. Set the exponent of the result equal to the larger exponent.
3. Perform addition/subtraction on the mantissas and determine the sign of the result.
4. Normalize the resulting value, if necessary.

Multiplication and division are somewhat easier than addition and subtraction, in that no alignment of mantissas is needed.

Multiply Rule

1. Add the exponents and subtract 127.
2. Multiply the mantissas and determine the sign of the result.
3. Normalize the resulting value if necessary.

Divide Rule

1. Subtract the exponents and add 127.
2. Divide the mantissas and determine the sign of the result.
3. Normalize the resulting value, if necessary.

The addition or subtraction of 127 in the Multiply and Divide rules results from using the excess-127 notation for exponents.

6.10.2 Guard Bits and Truncation

Let us consider some important details of the steps in the preceding algorithms. Although the mantissas of initial operands and final results are limited to 24 bits, including the implicit leading 1, it is important to retain extra bits, often called *guard* bits, during the intermediate steps. This yields maximum accuracy in the results.

Removing guard bits in generating the final results raises an important issue, however—a binary fraction must be *truncated* to create a fraction that is a shorter approximation of the longer value. This problem also arises in other situations, for instance, in converting from decimal to binary fractions.

There are several ways to truncate. The simplest way is to remove the guard bits and make no changes in the retained bits. This is called *chopping*. Suppose we want to truncate a fraction from six to three bits by this method. All fractions in the range $0.b_{-1}b_{-2}b_{-3}000$ to $0.b_{-1}b_{-2}b_{-3}111$ are truncated to $0.b_{-1}b_{-2}b_{-3}$. The error in the 3-bit result ranges from 0 to 0.000111. In other words, the error in chopping ranges from 0 to almost 1 in the least significant position of the retained bits. In our example, this is the b_{-3} position. The result of chopping is a *biased* approximation, because the error range is not symmetrical about 0.

The next simplest method of truncation is *Von Neumann rounding*. If the bits to be removed are all 0s, they are simply dropped, with no changes to the retained bits. However, if any of the bits to be removed are 1, the least significant bit of the retained bits is set to 1. In our 6-bit to 3-bit truncation example, all 6-bit fractions with $b_{-4}b_{-5}b_{-6}$ not equal to 000 are truncated to $0.b_{-1}b_{-2}1$. The error in this truncation method ranges between -1 and $+1$ in the LSB position of the retained bits. Although the range of error is larger with this technique than it is with chopping, the maximum magnitude is the same, and the approximation is *unbiased* because the error range is symmetrical about 0.

Unbiased approximations are advantageous if many operands and operations are involved in generating a result, because positive errors tend to offset negative errors as the computation proceeds. Statistically, we can expect the results of a complex computation to have a high probability of accuracy.

The third truncation method is a *rounding* procedure. Rounding achieves the closest approximation to the number being truncated and is an unbiased technique. The procedure is as follows: A 1 is added to the LSB position of the bits to be retained if there is a 1 in the MSB position of the bits being removed. Thus, $0.b_{-1}b_{-2}b_{-3}1\ldots$ is rounded to $0.b_{-1}b_{-2}b_{-3} + 0.001$, and $0.b_{-1}b_{-2}b_{-3}0\ldots$ is rounded to $0.b_{-1}b_{-2}b_{-3}$. This provides the desired approximation, except for the case in which the bits to be removed are $10\ldots0$. This is a tie situation; the longer value is halfway between the two closest truncated representations. To break the tie in an unbiased way, one possibility is to choose the retained bits to be the nearest even number. In terms of our 6-bit example, the value $0.b_{-1}b_{-2}0100$ is truncated to the value $0.b_{-1}b_{-2}0$, and $0.b_{-1}b_{-2}1100$ is truncated to $0.b_{-1}b_{-2}1 + 0.001$. The descriptive phrase "round to the nearest number, or nearest even number in case of a tie" is sometimes used to refer to this truncation technique. The error range is approximately $-\frac{1}{2}$ to $+\frac{1}{2}$ in the LSB position of the retained bits. Clearly, this is the best method. However, it is also the most expensive to implement, because it requires an addition operation and a possible renormalization. This rounding technique is the one specified in the IEEE floating-point standard.

This discussion of errors that are introduced when guard bits are removed by truncation has treated the case of a single truncation operation. When a long series of calculations involving floating-point numbers is performed, the analysis that determines error ranges or bounds for the final results can be a complicated study. We do not discuss this aspect of numerical computation further, except to make a few comments on the way that guard bits and rounding are handled in the IEEE floating-point standard.

Results of single operations must be computed to be accurate within half a unit in the LSB position. In general, this requires that rounding be used as the truncation method. Implementing this rounding scheme requires only three guard bits to be carried along during the intermediate steps in performing the operations described. The first two of these bits are the two most significant bits of the section of the mantissa to be removed. The third bit is the logical OR of all bits beyond these first two bits in the full representation of the mantissa. This bit is relatively easy to maintain during the intermediate steps of the operations to be performed. It should be initialized to 0. If a 1 is shifted out through this position, the bit becomes 1 and retains that value; hence, it is usually called the *sticky bit*.

6.10.3 Implementing Floating-Point Operations

The hardware implementation of floating-point operations involves considerable circuitry. These operations can also be implemented by software routines. In either case, the computer must be able to convert input and output to and from the user's decimal representation of numbers. In most modern computers, floating-point operations are available at the machine-instruction level and are implemented in hardware.

An example of the implementation of floating-point operations is shown in Figure 6.25. This is a block diagram of a hardware implementation for the addition and subtraction of 32-bit floating-point operands that have the format shown in Figure 6.23a. Following the Add/Subtract rule given in Section 6.10.1, we see that the first step is to compare exponents to determine how far to shift the mantissa of the number with the smaller exponent. This shift-count value, n, is determined by the 8-bit subtractor circuit in the upper left corner of the figure. The magnitude of the difference $E_A' - E_B'$, or n, is sent to the SHIFTER unit. If n is larger than the number of significant bits of the operands, then the answer is essentially the larger operand (except for guard and sticky-bit considerations in rounding), and shortcuts can be taken in deriving the result. We do not explore this in detail.

The sign of the difference that results from comparing exponents determines which mantissa is to be shifted. Therefore, the sign is sent to the SWAP network in the upper right corner of Figure 6.25. If the sign is 0, then $E_A' \geq E_B'$, and the mantissas M_A and M_B are sent straight through the SWAP network. This results in M_B being sent to the SHIFTER, to be shifted n positions to the right. The other mantissa, M_A, is sent directly to the mantissa adder/subtractor. If the sign is 1, then $E_A' < E_B'$, and the mantissas are swapped before they are sent to the SHIFTER.

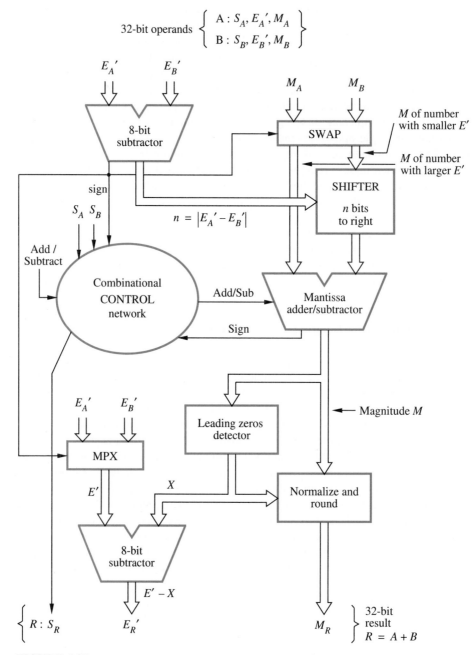

FIGURE 6.25
Floating-point addition-subtraction unit.

292

Step 2 is performed by the two-way multiplexer, MPX, near the bottom left corner of the figure. The exponent of the result, E', is tentatively determined as E'_A if $E'_A \geq E'_B$, or E'_B if $E'_A < E'_B$, based on the sign of the difference resulting from comparing exponents in step 1.

Step 3 involves the major component, the mantissa adder-subtractor in the middle of the figure. The CONTROL logic determines whether the mantissas are to be added or subtracted. This is decided by the signs of the operands (S_A and S_B) and the operation (Add or Subtract) that is to be performed on the operands. The CONTROL logic also determines the sign of the result, S_R. For example, if A is negative ($S_A = 1$), B is positive ($S_B = 0$), and the operation is $A - B$, then the mantissas are added and the sign of the result is negative ($S_R = 1$). On the other hand, if A and B are both positive and the operation is $A - B$, then the mantissas are subtracted. The sign of the result, S_R, now depends on the mantissa subtraction operation. For instance, if $E_A > E_B$, then $M_A -$ (shifted M_B) is positive and the result is positive. But if $E_B > E_A$, then $M_B -$ (shifted M_A) is positive and the result is negative. This example shows that the sign from the exponent comparison is also required as an input to the CONTROL network. When $E_A = E_B$ and the mantissas are subtracted, the sign of the mantissa adder-subtractor output determines the sign of the result. The reader should now be able to construct the complete truth table for the CONTROL network.

Step 4 of the Add/Subtract rule consists of normalizing the result of step 3, mantissa M. The number of leading zeros in M determines the number of bit shifts, X, to be applied to M. The normalized value is truncated to generate the 24-bit mantissa, M_R, of the result. The value X is also subtracted from the tentative result exponent E' to generate the true result exponent, E'_R. Note that only a single right shift might be needed to normalize the result. This would be the case if two mantissas of the form $1.xx\ldots$ were added. The vector M would then have the form $1x.xx\ldots$. This would correspond to an X value of -1 in the figure.

We have not given any details on the guard bits that must be carried along with intermediate mantissa values. In the IEEE standard, only a few bits are needed, as discussed earlier, to generate the 24-bit normalized mantissa of the result.

Let us consider the actual hardware that is needed to implement the blocks in Figure 6.25. The two 8-bit subtractors and the mantissa adder-subtractor can be implemented by combinational logic, as discussed earlier in this chapter. Because their outputs must be in sign-and-magnitude form, we must modify some of our earlier discussions— a combination of 1's-complement arithmetic and sign-and-magnitude representation is often used. Considerable flexibility is allowed in implementing the SHIFTER and the output normalization operation. To make these parts inexpensive, they can be constructed as shift registers. However, they can also be built as a combinational unit for high-performance.

In high-performance processors, a significant portion of the chip area is assigned to the floating-point execution unit. Before it was possible to implement this capability on the processor chip, earlier computers employed a special *floating-point coprocessor* chip. Such chips, of the same complexity as the main processor chip, were dedicated to executing floating-point instructions.

6.11
CONCLUDING REMARKS

Computer arithmetic poses several interesting logic design problems. This chapter discussed some of the techniques that have proven useful in designing binary arithmetic units. Carry-lookahead techniques are the major idea in high-performance adder design. In the design of fast multipliers, the Booth algorithm and the method of bit pairing in the multiplier reduce the number of summands that must be added to generate the product. Carry-save addition substantially reduces the time needed to add the summands.

The IEEE floating-point number representation standard was described, and a set of rules for performing the four standard operations was given. As an example of the circuit complexity required to implement floating-point units, the block diagram of an addition-subtraction unit was described.

PROBLEMS

6.1 Represent the decimal values 26, -37, 497, and -123 as signed, 10-bit numbers in the following binary formats:

(*a*) sign-and-magnitude
(*b*) 1's-complement
(*c*) 2's-complement
(See Appendix D for decimal-to-binary integer conversion.)

6.2 Binary fractions are discussed briefly in Section 6.10.

(*a*) Express the decimal values 0.5, -0.123, -0.75, and -0.1 as signed 6-bit numbers in the binary formats of Problem 6.1. (See Appendix D for decimal-to-binary fraction conversion.)
(*b*) What is the maximum representation error, e, involved in using only 5 significant bits after the binary point?
(*c*) Calculate the number of bits needed after the binary point so that

(*a*) $e < \frac{1}{10}$

(*b*) $e < \frac{1}{100}$

(*c*) $e < \frac{1}{1000}$

(*d*) $e < \frac{1}{10^6}$

6.3. The 1's-complement and 2's-complement binary representation methods are special cases of the $(b-1)$'s-complement and b's-complement representation techniques in base b number systems. For example, consider the decimal system. The sign-and-magnitude values $+527$, $+3219$, -382, and -1999 have 4-digit, signed-number representations in each of the complement systems, as shown in Table P6.1. The 9's-complement is formed by taking the complement of each digit position with respect to 9. The 10's-complement is formed by adding 1 to the 9's-complement. In each of the latter two representations, the leftmost digit is less than 5 for a positive number and greater than or equal to 5 for a negative number.

Representation	Examples			
Sign and magnitude	+0527	−0382	+3219	−1999
9's complement	0527	9617	3219	8000
10's complement	0527	9618	3219	8001

TABLE P6.1
Signed numbers in base 10.

Now consider the base 3 (ternary) system, in which the unsigned, 5-digit number $t_4t_3t_2t_1t_0$ has the value $t_4 \times 3^4 + t_3 \times 3^3 + t_2 \times 3^2 + t_1 \times 3^1 + t_0 \times 3^0$, with $0 \leq t_i \leq 2$. Express the ternary sign-and-magnitude numbers $+11011$, -10222, $+2120$, -1212, $+10$, and -201 as 5-digit, signed, ternary numbers in the 3's-complement system. Note that the largest positive number representable in this system is 11111.

6.4 Represent each of the decimal values 26, -37, 222, and -123 as signed, 6-digit numbers in the following ternary formats:

(*a*) sign-and-magnitude
(*b*) 3's-complement
See Problem 6.3 for a definition of the ternary number system, and use a technique analogous to that given in Appendix D for decimal-to-ternary integer conversion.

6.5 Consider the binary numbers in the following addition and subtraction problems to be signed, 6-bit values in the 2's-complement representation. Perform the operations indicated, specify whether overflow occurs, and check your answers by converting operands and results to decimal sign-and-magnitude representation.

$$
\begin{array}{ccc}
010110 & 101011 & 111111 \\
+001001 & +100101 & +000111
\end{array}
$$

$$
\begin{array}{ccc}
011001 & 110111 & 010101 \\
+010000 & +111001 & +101011
\end{array}
$$

$$
\begin{array}{ccc}
010110 & 111110 & 100001 \\
-011111 & -100101 & -011101
\end{array}
$$

$$
\begin{array}{ccc}
111111 & 000111 & 011010 \\
-000111 & -111000 & -100010
\end{array}
$$

6.6 Using manual methods, perform the operations $A \times B$ and $A \div B$ on the 5-bit unsigned numbers $A = 10101$ and $B = 00101$.

6.7 Show how the multiplication and division operations in Problem 6.6 would be performed by the hardware in Figures 6.9*a* and 6.20, respectively, by constructing charts similar to those in Figures 6.9*b* and 6.22.

6.8 Multiply each of the following pairs of signed, 2's-complement numbers using the Booth algorithm. In each case, assume that A is the multiplicand and B is the multiplier.

(*a*) $A = 010111$
 $B = 110110$
(*b*) $A = 110011$
 $B = 101100$
(*c*) $A = 110101$
 $B = 011011$
(*d*) $A = 1111$
 $B = 1111$

6.9 Repeat Problem 6.8 using bit-pairing of the multipliers.

6.10 Derive logic equations that specify the Add/Sub and S_R outputs of the combinational CONTROL network in Figure 6.25.

6.11 A half-adder is a combinational logic circuit that has two inputs, x and y, and two outputs, s and c, that are the sum and carry-out, respectively, resulting from the binary addition of x and y.

(*a*) Design a half-adder as a two-level AND-OR circuit.
(*b*) Show how to implement a full-adder, as shown in Figure 6.4*a*, by using two half-adders and external logic gates, as necessary.
(*c*) Compare the longest path logic delay through the network derived in part *b* to that of the logic delay of the adder network shown in Figure 6.4*a*.

6.12 Write either a PowerPC or 68000 program for integer division based on the nonrestoring-division algorithm. Assume that both operands are positive; that is, the leftmost bit is zero for both the dividend and the divisor. Do not use the Divide instruction that is available.

6.13 In Section 6.10, we used the practical-sized 32-bit IEEE standard format for floating-point numbers. Here, we use a shortened format that retains all the pertinent concepts but is manageable for working through numerical exercises. Consider that floating-point numbers are represented in a 12-bit format as shown in Figure P6.1. The scale factor has an implied base of 2 and a 5-bit, excess-15 exponent, with the two end values of 0 and 31 used to signify exact 0 and infinity, respectively. The 6-bit mantissa is normalized as in the IEEE format, with an implied 1 to the left of the binary point.

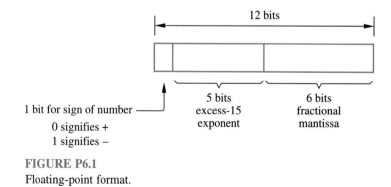

FIGURE P6.1
Floating-point format.

(a) Represent the numbers $+1.7$, -0.012, $+19$, and $\frac{1}{8}$ in this format.

(b) What are the smallest and largest numbers representable in this format?

(c) How does the range calculated in part b compare to the ranges of a 12-bit signed integer and a 12-bit signed fraction?

(d) Perform Add, Subtract, Multiply, and Divide operations on the operands

$$A = \boxed{0}\ \boxed{10001}\ \boxed{011011}$$
$$B = \boxed{1}\ \boxed{01111}\ \boxed{101010}$$

6.14 How does the excess-x representation for exponents of the scale factor in the floating-point number representation of Figure 6.23a facilitate the comparison of the relative sizes of two floating-point numbers? Assume that all bits of E' and M are zero for exact 0 and one for infinity. (*Hint:* Assume that a combinational logic network that compares the relative sizes of two, 32-bit, unsigned integers is available. Use this network, along with external logic gates, as necessary, to design the required network for the comparison of floating-point numbers.)

6.15 Consider the representation of the decimal number 0.1 as a signed, 8-bit, binary fraction in the representation discussed at the beginning of Section 6.10. If the number does not convert exactly into this 8-bit format, approximate the number using all three of the truncation methods discussed in Section 6.10.2.

6.16 Write a PowerPC or 68000 program to transform a 16-bit positive binary number into a 5-digit decimal number in which each digit of the number is coded in the binary-coded decimal (BCD) code. These BCD digit codes are to occupy the low-order 4 bits of five successive byte locations in the main memory. Use the conversion technique based on successive division by 10. This method is analogous to successive division by 2 when converting decimal-to-binary, as discussed in Appendix D. Consult Appendix B or C for the format and operation of the Divide instruction.

6.17 A modulo 10 adder must be built for adding BCD digits. Modulo 10 addition of two BCD digits, $A = A_3A_2A_1A_0$ and $B = B_3B_2B_1B_0$, can be achieved as follows: Add A to B (binary addition). Then, if the result is an illegal code that is greater than or equal to 10_{10}, add 6_{10}. (Ignore overflow from this addition.)

(a) When is the output carry equal to 1?

(b) Show that this algorithm gives correct results for

   (1) $A = 0101$ $B = 0110$

   (2) $A = 0011$ $B = 0100$

(c) Design a BCD digit adder using logic gates and a 4-bit version of the binary adder in Figure 6.7. The inputs are $A_3A_2A_1A_0$, $B_3B_2B_1B_0$, and a carry-in. The outputs are the sum digit $S_3S_2S_1S_0$ and the carry-out. A cascade of such blocks can form a ripple-carry BCD adder.

6.18 If gate fan-in is limited to four, how can the SHIFTER in Figure 6.25 be implemented combinationally?

6.19 (a) Sketch a logic-gate network that implements the multiplexer MPX in Figure 6.25.

(b) Relate the structure of the SWAP network in Figure 6.25 to your solution to part a.

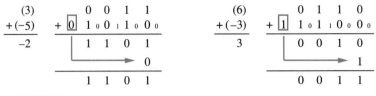

FIGURE P6.2
1's-complement addition.

6.20 How can the leading zeros detector in Figure 6.25 be implemented combinationally?

6.21 The mantissa adder-subtractor in Figure 6.25 operates on positive, unsigned binary fractions and must produce a sign-and-magnitude result. In the discussion accompanying Figure 6.25, we state that 1's-complement arithmetic is convenient because of the required format for input and output operands. When adding two signed numbers in 1's-complement notation, the carry-out from the sign position must be added to the result to obtain the correct signed answer. This is called *end-around carry correction*. Consider the two examples in Figure P6.2, which illustrate addition using signed, 4-bit encodings of operands and answers in the 1's-complement system.

The 1's-complement arithmetic system is convenient when a sign-and-magnitude result is to be generated, because a negative number in 1's-complement notation can be converted to sign-and-magnitude form by complementing the bits to the right of the sign-bit position. Using 2's-complement arithmetic, addition of $+1$ is needed to convert a negative value into sign-and-magnitude notation. If a carry-lookahead adder is used, it is possible to incorporate the end-around carry operation required by 1's-complement arithmetic into the lookahead logic. With this discussion as a guide, give the complete design of the 1's-complement adder-subtractor required in Figure 6.25.

6.22 Give a complete design for the adder shown in Figure 6.7 for $n = 4$. Carry-lookahead logic is to be used for all the internal carries, c_1, c_2, and c_3, as well as for the block output, c_4. Your answer can be in the form of a sketch of the logic-gate network required or a listing of logic equations that describe the network.

6.23 Four of the 4-bit adder circuits shown in Figure 6.7 can be cascaded to form a 16-bit adder. In this cascade, the output, c_4, from the low-order circuit is connected as the carry-in to the next circuit. Its carry-out, c_8, is connected as the carry-in to the third circuit, and so on.

(*a*) A faster adder can be constructed by using external logic to generate the carry-in variables for the three high-order circuits. Give the logic design for a carry-lookahead circuit that has outputs c_4, c_8, and c_{12}. Its inputs are c_0, P_0^I, G_0^I, P_1^I, G_1^I, P_2^I, and G_2^I, as Section 6.3 discusses. Assume that the network in Figure 6.7 produces the variables P^I and G^I. Estimate the possible increase in adder speed by using this circuit in conjunction with the four 4-bit adder circuits—as opposed to using a cascade of the adder circuits—to build a 16-bit adder.

(*b*) Extend your design by assuming that the carry-lookahead chip has P_3^I and G_3^I as additional inputs and that it provides additional outputs P_0^{II} and G_0^{II}. These higher-level propagate-and-generate functions are defined by

$$P_0^{II} = P_3^I P_2^I P_1^I P_0^I$$
$$G_0^{II} = G_3^I + P_3^I G_2^I + P_3^I P_2^I G_1^I + P_3^I P_2^I P_1^I G_0^I$$

(c) Design a 64-bit adder that uses sixteen 4-bit adder circuits, carry-lookahead circuits as defined in part b, and additional logic to generate c_{16}, c_{32}, and c_{48} from c_0 and the P_i^{II} and G_i^{II} variables. What is the relationship of the additional logic to the logic inside each lookahead circuit?

(d) Can this tree-like structure of lookahead circuits be extended further for even longer adders? Comment.

6.24 Assume that each output from each full adder circuit (FA) in parts a and b of Figure 6.18 is available one delay unit after all inputs are fixed. How many delay units are required to develop z_{n+1} in parts a and b of the figure after the W, X, and Y input vectors are fixed?

6.25 The end of Section 6.8.2 mentions that a carry-lookahead adder could be used instead of a ripple-carry adder to speed up the final addition operation in a high-speed multiplier. Suppose two 32-bit numbers are to be multiplied in a high-speed multiplier, generating a 64-bit product. Assume that the final addition operation after all carry-save additions are done requires a 64-bit adder. (The actual length of this adder is somewhat shorter, because the process of reducing shifted summands by carry-save addition produces some of the low-order bits of the product directly.) Estimate the percentage reduction in the overall Multiply operation delay achieved by using a carry-lookahead adder instead of a ripple-carry adder for the final addition. Assume that three levels of lookahead functions, P_i, G_i, P_i^I, G_i^I, and P_i^{II}, G_i^{II}, are used, as discussed in Section 6.3 and Problem 6.23. Also assume that bit-pair recoding of the multiplier is done.

6.26 Develop the derivation for the formula $1.7 \log_2 k$ for the number of carry-save addition steps needed to reduce k summands to two vectors. (This formula is stated without derivation in Section 6.8.2.)

6.27 Assume that four BCD digits, representing a decimal integer in the range 0 to 9999, are packed into the word at main memory location DECIMAL. Write a PowerPC or 68000 subroutine to convert the decimal integer stored at DECIMAL into binary representation and to store it in main memory location BINARY.

6.28 Construct an example to show that three guard bits are needed to produce the correct answer when two positive numbers are subtracted.

6.29 In Problem 6.13a, conversion of the simple decimal numbers into binary floating-point format is straightforward. However, if the decimal numbers are given in floating-point format, conversion is not straightforward because we can't separately convert the mantissa and the exponent of the scale factor. This can't be done because $10^x = 2^y$ does not, in general, allow both x and y to be integers. Suppose a table of binary, floating-point numbers t_i, such that $t_i = 10^{x_i}$ for x_i in the representable range, is stored in a computer. Give a procedure in general terms for converting a given decimal floating-point number into binary floating-point format. You may use both the integer and floating-point instructions available in the computer.

6.30 Consider a 16-bit, floating-point number in a format similar to that discussed in Problem 6.13, with a 6-bit exponent and a 9-bit normalized fractional mantissa. The base of the scale factor is 2 and the exponent is represented in excess-31 format.

(a) Add the numbers A and B, formatted as follows:

$$A = 0 \quad 100001 \quad 111111110$$
$$B = 0 \quad 011111 \quad 001010101$$

Give the answer in normalized form. Remember that an implicit 1 is to the left of the binary point but is not included in the A and B formats. Use rounding when producing the final normalized 9-bit mantissa.

(b) Using decimal numbers w, x, y, and z, express the magnitude of the largest and smallest (nonzero) values representable in the preceding normalized floating-point format. Use the following form:

$$\text{Largest} = w \times 2^x$$
$$\text{Smallest} = y \times 2^{-z}$$

6.31 Indicate generally how to modify the circuit diagram in Figure 6.9a to implement multiplication of signed, 2's-complement, n-bit numbers using the Booth algorithm, by clearly specifying inputs and outputs for the Control sequencer and any other changes needed around the adder and A register.

6.32 Which of the four 6-bit answers to Problem 6.2a are not exact? For each of these cases, give the three 6-bit values that correspond to the three types of truncation defined in Section 6.10.2.

6.33 Write either a PowerPC or 68000 program for the multiplication of two 32-bit unsigned numbers that is patterned after the technique used in Figure 6.9. Do not use the Multiply instruction. Assume that the multiplier and multiplicand are in registers R_2 and R_3, respectively. The product is to be developed in registers R_1 (high-order half) and R_2 (low-order half). (*Hint:* Use a combination of Shift and Rotate operations for a double-register shift.)

6.34 If the product of two n-bit signed numbers in the 2's-complement representation can be represented in n bits, the manual multiplication algorithm shown in Figure 6.8a can be used directly, treating the sign bits the same as the other bits. Try this on the following 4-bit signed numbers:

$$A = 1110 \text{ (multiplicand)}$$
$$B = 1101 \text{ (multiplier)}$$
$$C = 0010$$
$$D = 1110$$

Why does this work correctly?

6.35 Suppose the network of Figure 6.8 is used to multiply two 32-bit numbers. Compare the time needed by this array with the time needed by the scheme described in Problem 6.25, which involves a carry-lookahead adder for the final addition.

6.36 The carry-save addition of summands, used in implementing high-speed multiplication, is described in Section 6.8.2. Each carry-save addition reduces three summands to two. The alternative of using regular ripple-carry adders to reduce the number of summands is also mentioned. Each ripple-carry addition reduces two summands to one. Investigate the logic-cost differences in using these two methods. Let the basic unit of logic cost be a full-adder circuit with 3 inputs and 2 outputs, as shown in Figure 6.18. Assume that the lengths of all additions are the same in either case, even though this is not exactly true. Work with a couple of examples, say, reduce 16 summands to 2 and reduce 32 summands to 2, and then try to generalize your conclusions about logic-cost differences.

6.37 (The concept of pipelining is explained in Chapter 7, in the context of increasing the rate of executing instructions in a processor. Read through the first part of that chapter to understand the basic ideas of pipelining, and then try this question.)

A high-speed combinational multiplier, as described in Section 6.8, is to be pipelined in two stages. The first stage is to consist of bit-pair recoding of the multiplier, summand selection, and summand reduction by carry-save addition to a final two vectors. The second stage consists of a carry-lookahead adder that produces the final product from these two vectors. Suppose that a 32×32 multiplier, producing a 64-bit product, is to be pipelined in this way.

(*a*) Estimate the propagation delay in the first stage, assuming that the delay through a full-adder circuit (3 inputs and 2 outputs) is 3 gate delays.

(*b*) Assume that a 64-bit carry-lookahead adder is used in the second stage and that the circuits used have a logic gate fan-in of 5. Specify the number of levels of functions P_i, G_i, P_i^I, G_i^I, and so on, needed so that the adder is fast enough to have a delay no longer than the answer in part *a*.

REFERENCE

1. Institute of Electrical and Electronic Engineers, "A Proposed Standard for Floating-Point Arithmetic," *Computer,* vol. 14, no. 3, March 1981, pp. 51–62.

CHAPTER 7

Pipelining

The basic building blocks of a computer are introduced in preceding chapters. In this chapter, we discuss in detail the concept of pipelining, which is used in modern computers to achieve high performance.

We begin by explaining the basics of pipelining and how it can lead to improved performance. Then we examine machine instruction features that are compatible with pipelined execution, and we show that the choice of instructions and instruction sequencing can have a significant effect on performance. This means sophisticated compilation techniques are required, and *optimizing compilers* have been developed for this purpose. Among other things, such compilers rearrange the sequence in which some operations are performed to maximize the benefits of pipelined execution.

7.1
BASIC CONCEPTS

The speed of execution of programs is influenced by many factors. One way to improve performance is to use faster circuit technology to build the processor and the main memory. Another possibility is to arrange the hardware so that more than one operation can be performed at the same time. In this way, the number of operations performed per second is increased, even though the elapsed time needed to perform any one operation is not changed.

We have encountered parallel activities several times before. Chapter 1 introduced the concept of multiprogramming and explained how it is possible for I/O transfers and computational activities to proceed simultaneously. DMA devices make this possible because they can perform I/O transfers independently once these transfers are initiated by the processor. Chapter 3 suggested that performance can be improved if multiple functional units operate in parallel within a processor.

Pipelining is a particularly effective way of organizing parallel activity in a computer system—or any other system, for that matter. The basic idea is very simple. It is frequently encountered in manufacturing plants, where pipelining is commonly known as an assembly-line operation. Readers are undoubtedly familiar with the assembly line used in car manufacturing. The first station in an assembly line may prepare the chassis of a car, the next station adds the body, the next one installs the engine, and so on. While one group of workers is installing the engine on one car, another group is fitting a car body on the chassis of another car, and yet another group is preparing a new chassis for a third car. It may take days to complete work on a given car, but it is possible to have a new car rolling off the end of the assembly line every few minutes.

Consider how the idea of pipelining can be used in a computer. The processor executes a program by fetching and executing instructions, one after the other. Let F_i and E_i refer to the fetch and execute steps for instruction I_i. Execution of a program consists of a sequence of fetch and execute steps, as shown in Figure 7.1a.

Now consider a computer that has two separate hardware units, one for fetching instructions and another for executing them, as shown in Figure 7.1b. The instruction fetched by the fetch unit is deposited in an intermediate storage buffer, B1. The results of execution are deposited in the destination location specified by the instruction. For the purposes of this discussion, we assume that both the source and the destination of the data operated on by the instructions are inside the block labeled "Execution unit." The computer is controlled by a clock whose period is such that the fetch and execute steps of any instruction can each be completed in one clock cycle. Operation of the computer proceeds as in Figure 7.1c. In the first clock cycle, the fetch unit fetches an instruction I_1 (step F_1) and stores it in buffer B1 at the end of the clock cycle. In the second clock cycle, the instruction fetch unit proceeds with the fetch operation for instruction I_2 (step F_2). Meanwhile, the execution unit performs the operation specified by instruction I_1, which is available to it in buffer B1 (step E_1). By the end of the second clock cycle, the execution of instruction I_1 is completed and instruction I_2 is available. Instruction I_2 is stored in B1, replacing I_1, which is no longer needed. Step E_2 is performed by the execution unit during the third clock cycle, while instruction I_3 is being fetched by the fetch unit. In this manner, both the fetch and execute units are kept busy all the time. If the pattern in Figure 7.1c can be sustained for a long time, the completion rate of instruction execution will be twice that achievable by the sequential operation depicted in Figure 7.1a.

In summary, the fetch and execute units in Figure 7.1b constitute a two-stage pipeline, in which each stage performs one step in processing an instruction. An interstage storage buffer, B1, is needed to hold the information being passed from one stage to the next. New information is loaded into this buffer at the end of each clock cycle.

The processing of an instruction need not be divided into only two steps. For example, a pipelined processor may process each instruction in four steps, as follows:

F   Fetch: read the instruction from the memory.
D   Decode: decode the instruction and fetch the source operand(s).
O   Operate: perform the operation.
W   Write: store the result in the destination location.

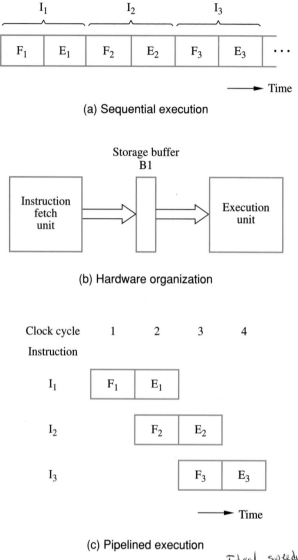

(a) Sequential execution

(b) Hardware organization

(c) Pipelined execution

FIGURE 7.1
Basic idea of instruction pipelining.

The sequence of events for this case is shown in Figure 7.2a. Four instructions are in progress at any given time. This means that four distinct hardware units are needed, as Figure 7.2b shows. These units must be capable of operating in parallel. Each unit operates on different data, and the result is passed to the next unit downstream through a storage buffer. Each buffer holds the information needed by the units downstream to complete execution of an instruction. For example, during clock cycle 4, the information in the buffers is as follows:

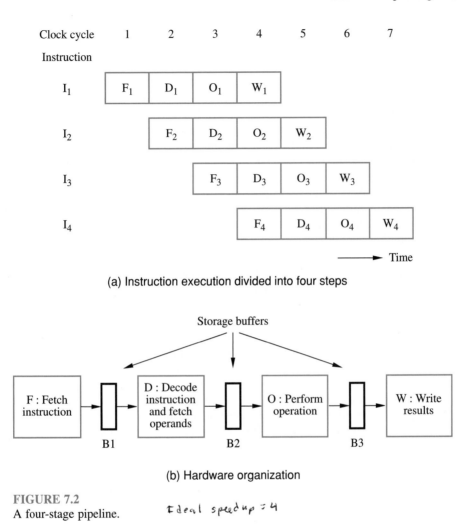

Clock cycle   1   2   3   4   5   6   7

Instruction

I_1 | F_1 | D_1 | O_1 | W_1 |

I_2 | F_2 | D_2 | O_2 | W_2 |

I_3 | F_3 | D_3 | O_3 | W_3 |

I_4 | F_4 | D_4 | O_4 | W_4 |

→ Time

(a) Instruction execution divided into four steps

Storage buffers

| F : Fetch instruction | B1 | D : Decode instruction and fetch operands | B2 | O : Perform operation | B3 | W : Write results |

(b) Hardware organization

FIGURE 7.2
A four-stage pipeline.   *Ideal speedup = 4*

- Buffer B1 holds instruction I_3, which was fetched in cycle 3 and is being decoded by the instruction-decoding unit.
- Buffer B2 holds both the source operands for instruction I_2 and the specification of the operation to be performed, which were produced by the decoding hardware in cycle 3. It also holds the information needed for the write step of instruction I_2 (step W_2). This information is not needed by stage 3 of the pipeline, but it must be passed on to stage 4 in the following clock cycle to enable that stage to perform the required Write operation.
- Buffer B3 holds the results produced by the operation unit and the destination information for instruction I_1.

With a four-stage pipeline, the rate at which instructions are executed is four times that of sequential operation. It is important to understand that pipelining does not result in individual instructions being executed faster; rather, it is the throughput that increases, where throughput is measured by the number of instructions per second whose execution is completed.

Based on this discussion, the increase in performance resulting from pipelining appears to be proportional to the number of pipeline stages. This would be true if pipelined operation as depicted in Figure 7.2a could be sustained throughout program execution. Unfortunately, this is not the case. For a variety of reasons, one of the pipeline stages may not be able to complete its processing task for a given instruction in the time allotted. For example, stage 3 in the four-stage pipeline of Figure 7.2b is responsible for arithmetic and logic operations, and one clock cycle is assigned for this task. Although this may be sufficient for most operations, some operations, such as divide, may require more time to complete. Figure 7.3 shows an example in which the operation specified in instruction I_2 requires three cycles to complete, from cycle 4 through cycle 6. Thus, in cycles 5 and 6, the Write stage must be told to do nothing, because it has no data to work with. Meanwhile, the information in buffer B2 must remain intact until the Operate stage has completed its operation. This means that stage 2 and, in turn, stage 1 are blocked from accepting new instructions because the information in B1 cannot be overwritten by a new fetch operation. The contents of B1, B2, and B3 must always change at the same clock edge. Thus, steps D_3 and F_4 cannot be completed until the end of cycle 6. During that period, the Fetch and Decode stages are holding information relating to instructions 3 and 4, respectively. Pipelined operation is said to have been *stalled* for two clock cycles. Normal pipelined operation resumes in cycle 7.

Any time one of the stages in the pipeline cannot complete its operation in one clock cycle, the pipeline stalls. This can be caused by a time-consuming arithmetic operation, as in the preceding example, or by having to access the main memory following a cache miss. Whenever the pipeline is stalled, some degradation in performance occurs. An important goal in designing a pipelined processor is to identify all such situations and

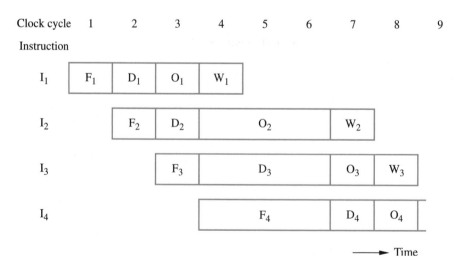

FIGURE 7.3   Two cycle stalls
Effect of an operation that takes more than one clock cycle to complete.

find ways to minimize their impact on performance. We discuss these issues in the following sections.

7.1.1 Role of Cache Memory

The operation of a pipeline can be compared to that of a shift register. At the end of each clock cycle, the information in all pipeline stages moves forward by one stage. We have seen that whenever any stage requires more time to complete its task, the entire pipeline is stalled until that unit is again ready to accept a new instruction.

To avoid stalling the pipeline, the length of the clock cycle should be sufficient to complete the task being performed in any stage. If different units require different amounts of time, the clock period must allow the longest task to be completed. A unit that completes its task early is idle for the remainder of the clock period. Hence, pipelining is most effective in improving performance if the tasks being performed in different stages require about the same amount of time.

This consideration is particularly important for the instruction fetch step, which is assigned one clock period in Figure 7.2a. This arrangement means that the clock cycle has to be equal to or greater than the time needed to complete a fetch operation. However, the access time of the main memory may be as much as ten times greater than the time needed to perform basic pipeline stage operations inside the processor, such as adding two numbers. Thus, if each instruction fetch required access to the main memory, pipelining would be of little value.

The use of cache memories solves the memory access problem. In particular, when a primary cache is included on the same chip as the processor, access time to the cache is the same as the time needed to perform any other operation inside the processor. This makes it possible to divide instruction fetch and execution into steps that are more or less equal in duration. Each of these steps is performed by a different pipeline stage, and the clock period is chosen to correspond to the longest one.

Occasionally, a memory request results in a cache miss. This causes the pipeline stage that issued the memory request to take much longer to complete its task. In this event, the pipeline stalls, as illustrated in Figure 7.4a. Instruction I_1 is fetched from the cache in cycle 1, and its execution proceeds normally. However, the fetch operation for instruction I_2, which is started in cycle 2, results in a cache miss. The instruction fetch unit must now suspend any further fetch requests and wait for I_2 to arrive. We assume that instruction I_2 is received and loaded into buffer B1 at the end of cycle 5. The pipeline resumes its normal operation at that point

Note that, in the sequence in Figure 7.4a, the Decode unit is idle in cycles 3 through 5, the Operate unit is idle in cycles 4 through 6 and the Write unit is idle in cycles 5 through 7. Such idle periods are sometimes referred to as *bubbles* in the pipeline. Once created as a result of a delay in one of the pipeline stages, a bubble moves downstream until it reaches the last unit.

An alternative representation of the operation of a pipeline is shown in Figure 7.4b. This figure gives the function performed by each pipeline stage in each clock cycle. The three-cycle idle period, or bubble, created by the cache miss is shown moving downstream.

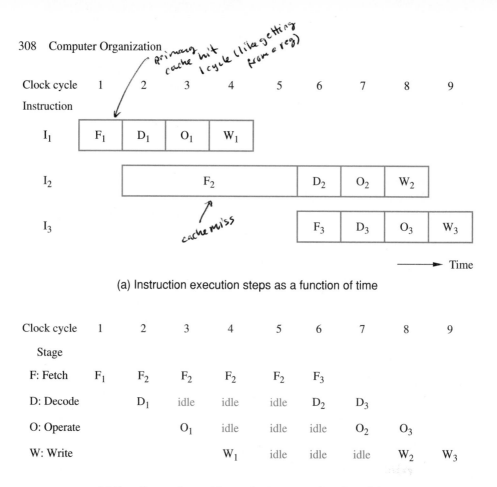

(a) Instruction execution steps as a function of time

Clock cycle	1	2	3	4	5	6	7	8	9
Stage									
F: Fetch	F_1	F_2	F_2	F_2	F_2	F_3			
D: Decode		D_1	idle	idle	idle	D_2	D_3		
O: Operate			O_1	idle	idle	idle	O_2	O_3	
W: Write				W_1	idle	idle	idle	W_2	W_3

(b) Function performed by each stage as a function of time

FIGURE 7.4
Pipeline stall caused by a cache miss in F_2.

Memory read and write operations are needed to provide access to program instructions and data. The data transfer capability of the cache should be such that the pipeline cannot stall as long as the instructions and data being accessed reside in the cache. This is facilitated by providing separate on-chip instruction and data caches. In addition to increasing the data transfer capability of the cache, having separate caches eliminates the possibility of an instruction fetch operation being delayed by an operand access in progress.

7.1.2 Dependency Constraints

Consider a program that contains two instructions, I_1 followed by I_2. When this program is executed in a pipeline, the execution of I_2 can begin before the execution of I_1 is completed. This means that the results generated by I_1 may not be available for use by I_2. We must ensure that the results obtained when instructions are executed in a pipelined processor are identical to those obtained when the same instructions are executed sequentially. The potential for obtaining incorrect results when operations are performed in parallel can be demonstrated with a simple example. Assume that A = 5, and consider the following two operations:

$$A \leftarrow 3 + A$$
$$B \leftarrow 4 \times A$$

When these operations are performed in the order given, the result is B = 32. But if they are performed in parallel, the value of A used in computing B is the original value 5; this leads to an incorrect result. If these two operations are performed by instructions in a program, then the instructions must be executed one after the other, because the data used in the second instruction depend on the result of the first instruction. On the other hand, the two operations

$$A \leftarrow 5 \times C$$
$$B \leftarrow 20 + C$$

can be performed in parallel, because these operations are independent.

This example illustrates a basic constraint that must be enforced to guarantee correct results. No two operations that depend on each other can be performed in parallel. This rather obvious condition has far-reaching consequences. Understanding the implications of this condition is the key to understanding the variety of design alternatives and trade-offs encountered in pipelined computers.

Consider the two-stage pipeline in Figure 7.1b. The operation of the Fetch stage must not depend on the operation performed during the same clock cycle by the Execute stage. This means that step F_2 in Figure 7.1c must not depend on E_1, and F_3 must not depend on E_2. In other words, the operation of fetching an instruction must be independent of the execution results of the previous instruction. This condition is met when the processor fetches instructions from successive address locations, but it is not necessarily met in the presence of branch instructions. The address from which the next instruction is to be fetched depends on the result of executing the branch instruction. Without some special provision, the pipeline would stall for one clock cycle, as shown in Figure 7.5.

In a longer pipeline, such as that in Figure 7.2, the execution phases of successive instructions overlap. (We use the term "execution phase" to refer to all the operations performed after an instruction is fetched.) Hence, the dependency just described arises when the destination of one instruction is used as a source in a subsequent instruction. Such dependency is illustrated by the following sequence of instructions:

```
Mul     R2,R3,R4
Add     R5,R4,R6
```

The result of the multiply instruction is placed into register R4. Assuming that the multiply operation takes one clock cycle to complete, execution of the Mul instruction would proceed as shown in Figure 7.6. As the Decode unit begins decoding the Add instruction in cycle 3, it realizes that R4 is used as a source operand. Hence, the D step of that instruction cannot be completed until the W step of the multiply instruction has been completed. As a result, pipelined execution stalls as shown.

Instruction

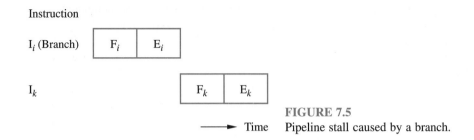

FIGURE 7.5
Pipeline stall caused by a branch.

Instruction I_3 is fetched in cycle 3 as I_2 is being decoded. If I_3 is independent of I_1 and I_2, there is no reason to delay its execution. However, this would lead to D_3 preceding D_2, which is physically impossible for the hardware organization of Figure 7.2b. While the D stage is stalled during clock cycles 3 and 4 in Figure 7.6, this stage and the interstage buffer preceding it are occupied with data related to instruction I_2. Therefore, I_3 cannot proceed until D_2 is completed. High-performance processors often have multiple execution units to avoid blocking an instruction that is able to proceed, such as I_3 in this example. We discuss this possibility in Section 7.6.

7.2
INSTRUCTION QUEUE

The purpose of the instruction fetch unit is to supply the execution units with a steady stream of instructions. Whenever this stream is interrupted, the pipeline stalls, as Figure 7.4 illustrates for the case of a cache miss. A branch instruction may also cause the pipeline to stall. The instruction following an unconditional branch cannot be fetched

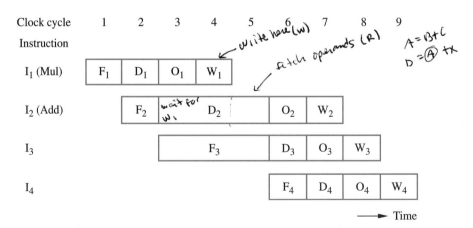

FIGURE 7.6
Pipeline stalled by data dependency between D_2 and W_1.

until the branch instruction has been decoded and its target address computed. In the case of a conditional branch, the branch condition must also be evaluated.

Such situations mean that the instruction stream generated by the fetch unit may be frequently interrupted. To reduce the effect of these interruptions, most processors employ sophisticated fetch units that can fetch instructions before they are needed and put them in a queue. Typically, the instruction queue can store several instructions. A separate unit, which we call the *dispatch unit*, takes instructions from the front of the queue and sends them to the execution units as these units become free. This leads to the organization shown in Figure 7.7.

To be effective, the fetch unit must have sufficient decoding and processing capability to recognize and execute branch instructions. Thus, an unconditional branch does not lead to much delay, because the fetch unit computes the branch target address and continues to fetch instructions starting at that address. The same is true for a conditional branch instruction for which the branch condition has already been computed by other units.

The fetch unit attempts to keep the instruction queue filled at all times. This reduces the impact of occasional delays when fetching instructions. For example, after a cache miss, the dispatch unit continues to send instructions for execution as long as the instruction queue is not empty. Meanwhile, the appropriate cache block is read from the main memory or from a secondary cache. When fetch operations are resumed, the instruction queue is refilled. If the queue does not become empty, a miss in the cache has no effect on the rate of instruction execution. The rate at which instructions can be read from the cache must be sufficiently high to enable the fetch unit to refill the queue. The objective is to keep the instruction queue full most of the time.

An instruction queue is particularly effective when multiple execution units are used, and instructions may be executed out of order. These possibilities are discussed in Section 7.6.

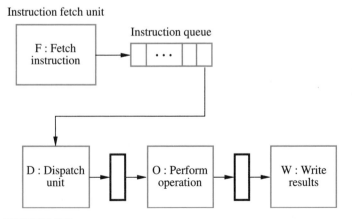

FIGURE 7.7
Use of an instruction queue in the hardware organization of Figure 7.2*b*.

7.3
BRANCHING

Branch instructions require special handling in a pipelined processor. First, let us consider a case in which the instruction queue is not used and instruction execution proceeds strictly as shown in Figure 7.1c. Figure 7.8 shows a sequence of instructions in which instructions I_j and I_{j+1} are stored at successive locations in the main memory and I_j is a branch instruction. Let the branch target be instruction I_k. The fetch operation for instruction I_{j+1} is in progress when the branch address is computed. But the processor must discard I_{j+1} and begin fetching instruction I_k, as shown. The hardware unit responsible for the Execute (E) step must be told to do nothing during the clock period in which it was to perform step E_{j+1}. The time lost as a result of a branch instruction is often referred to as the *branch penalty*. In Figure 7.8, the branch penalty is equal to one clock cycle.

This example illustrates the basic problem caused by branch instructions. The use of an instruction queue and a fast cache is a very effective way of handling unconditional branches because instruction fetches are performed before the instructions are actually needed. This is illustrated in Figure 7.9. We have assumed that four instructions can be fetched at a time from the instruction cache. Instructions I_1 through I_4 are fetched and placed in the instruction queue. Of these, instruction I_3 is an unconditional branch. As soon as the fetch unit sees this instruction, it executes it immediately (step E3). In the following cycle, it fetches four more instructions, I_k through I_{k+3}, starting at the branch target address. Instruction I_4 is discarded. Meanwhile, instruction I_1 proceeds to the execution phase, followed by I_2. As I_2 moves through the pipeline, it is followed immediately by I_k. Thus, the branch instruction contributes no delay at all because it is executed by the fetch unit in parallel with the execution of I_1 and I_2. This technique is referred to as *branch folding*.

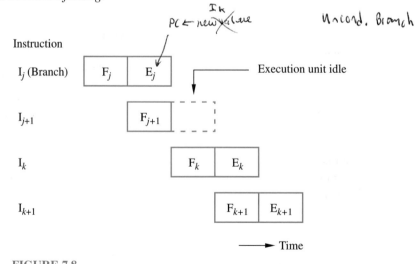

FIGURE 7.8
An idle cycle caused by a branch instruction.

One cycle of branch penalty

Assumption: Ex. of uncond branch takes 1 cycle

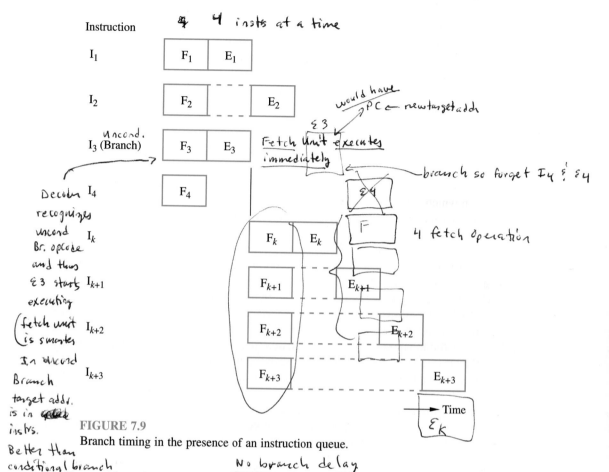

FIGURE 7.9

Branch timing in the presence of an instruction queue.

(handwritten annotations throughout the figure:)
Cycle 1 2 3
4 insts at a time
would have
gPC ← new target addr
E3 Fetch Unit executes immediately
branch so forget I4 & E4
4 fetch operation
Time
Ek

uncond.
I3 (Branch)
Decode I4 recognizes uncond Br. opcode and thus E3 starts executing (fetch unit is smarter)
In uncond Branch target addr. is in Branch instrs.
Better than conditional branch
No branch delay

Even with an instruction queue, conditional branches incur a branch penalty because the branch condition often depends on the result of a preceding instruction. The decision to branch cannot be made until the execution of that instruction has been completed.

Branch instructions occur frequently. In fact, they represent about 20 percent of the dynamic instruction count of most programs. (The dynamic count is the number of instruction executions, taking into account the fact that some program instructions are executed many times because of loops.) Because of the branch penalty, this large percentage would reduce the gain in performance expected from pipelining. Fortunately, branch instructions can be handled in several ways to reduce their negative impact on the rate of execution of instructions.

7.3.1 Delayed Branch

In Figure 7.8, the processor begins fetching instruction I_{j+1} before it determines whether the current instruction, I_j, is a branch instruction. When execution of I_j is completed and a branch must be made, the processor must discard the instruction that was fetched and now fetch the instruction at the branch target. The location following a branch instruction is called a *branch delay slot*. There may be more than one branch delay slot, depending on the time it takes to execute a branch instruction. For example, if the execution phase of a branch instruction occupies two steps in the pipeline, the processor has two delay slots. The instructions in the delay slots are always fetched and at least partially executed before the branch decision is made and the branch target address is computed.

A technique called *delayed branching* can minimize the penalty incurred as a result of conditional branch instructions. The idea is simple. Because the instructions in the delay slots are always fetched, we can arrange for them to be fully executed whether or not the branch is taken. The objective is to be able to place useful instructions in these slots. If no useful instructions can be placed in the delay slots, these slots must be filled with NOP (no-operation) instructions.

Consider, for example, the instruction sequence given in Figure 7.10a. Register R2 is used as a counter to determine the number of times the contents of register R1 are shifted left. For a processor with a two-stage pipeline and one delay slot, the instructions can be reordered as shown in Figure 7.10b. In this case, the shift instruction is fetched while the branch instruction is being executed. After evaluating the branch condition, the processor fetches the instruction at LOOP or at NEXT, depending on whether the branch condition is true or false, respectively. In either case, it completes execution of the shift instruction. The sequence of events during the last two passes in the loop is illustrated in Figure 7.11. Pipelined operation is not interrupted at any time, and there are no idle cycles. Logically, the program is executed as if the branch instruction were placed after the shift instruction. That is, branching takes place one instruction later than where the branch instruction appears in the instruction sequence in the memory, hence the name "delayed branch." The instruction that appears sequentially after the branch instruction is always executed.

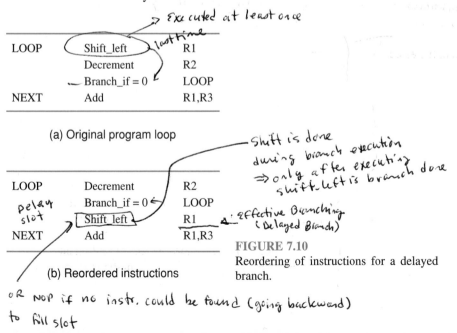

→ Executed at least once

LOOP	Shift_left	R1	*last time*
	Decrement	R2
	Branch_if = 0	LOOP
NEXT	Add	R1,R3

(a) Original program loop

Shift is done during branch execution ⇒ only after executing shift_left is branch done

LOOP	Decrement	R2
delay slot	Branch_if = 0	LOOP
	Shift_left	R1	*← Effective Branching (Delayed Branch)*
NEXT	Add	R1,R3

(b) Reordered instructions

FIGURE 7.10
Reordering of instructions for a delayed branch.

OR NOP if no instr. could be found (going backward) to fill slot

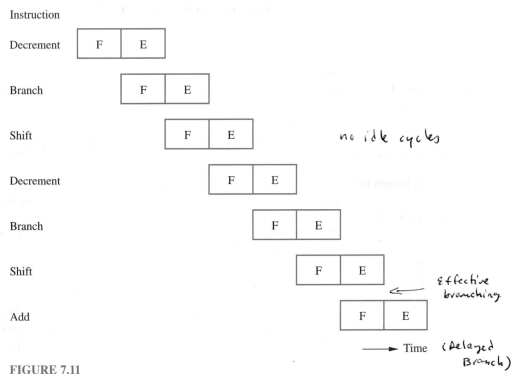

Instruction

Decrement

Branch

Shift

Decrement

Branch

Shift

Add

no idle cycles

effective
branching

Time   (Delayed
       Branch)

FIGURE 7.11

Execution timing for the last two passes through the loop in Figure 7.10*b*.

· Logically, the program is executed as if the branch instr.
were placed after the shift instr.

In a machine that uses the delayed-branch approach, the compiler should place appropriate instructions in the branch delay slots. If nothing useful is to be done in these slots, NOP instructions must be used. Note that some processors, such as the 68000, have explicit NOP instructions. Others, such as the PowerPC, do not. In this case, the effect of a NOP can be achieved by an instruction such as

OR   R1,R1,R1

which does not change the contents of any processor register except the program counter. Its execution introduces only one instruction delay in the instruction execution pipeline.

The effectiveness of the delayed branch approach depends on how often it is possible to reorder instructions as in Figure 7.10. Experimental data collected from many programs indicate that sophisticated compilation techniques can use one branch delay slot in as many as 85 percent of the cases. For a machine with two branch delay slots, the compiler attempts to find two instructions preceding the branch instruction that it can move into the delay slots without introducing a logical error. The chances of finding two such instructions are considerably less than the chances of finding one. Thus, if increasing the number of pipeline stages involves an increase in the number of branch delay slots, the potential gain in performance may not be fully realized.

7.3.2 Branch Prediction

Another technique for reducing the branch penalty is to attempt to predict whether or not a particular branch will be taken. For example, a branch instruction at the end of a loop causes a branch to the start of the loop for every pass through the loop except the last one. Only after the last pass through the loop does branching not occur. Hence, when the branch instruction is encountered, it is advantageous for the processor to assume that the branch will be taken. Based on this assumption, the instruction fetch unit fetches instructions starting at the branch target address and loads them into the instruction queue. If, after the branch condition is computed, it turns out that the branch should indeed have been taken, execution continues normally. In this case, the branch instruction has introduced no delay at all. On the other hand, if the branch should not have been taken, the fetched instructions must be discarded and the correct instructions must be fetched. A similar argument can be made for a branch instruction at the beginning of a program loop. In this case, it is advantageous to assume that the branch will not be taken.

To take full advantage of branch prediction, we can have the instructions following the branch not only fetched but also begin execution. However, this must be done on a speculative basis. *Speculative execution* means that instructions are executed before the processor is certain that they are in the correct execution path. Hence, care must be taken that no processor registers or memory locations are updated until it is confirmed that these instructions should indeed be executed. If the branch decision indicates otherwise, the instructions and all their associated data in the execution units must be purged, and the correct instructions must be fetched and executed.

An incorrectly predicted branch is illustrated in Figure 7.12. To show instruction timing in more detail, we consider a four-stage pipeline similar to the one in Figure 7.2.

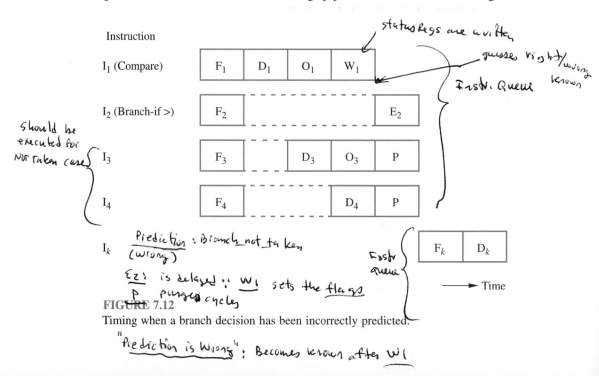

FIGURE 7.12
Timing when a branch decision has been incorrectly predicted.

Furthermore, we assume that the branch condition and target address are computed in one cycle and that instructions are fetched four at a time from the instruction cache. Instruction I_1 compares two operands, and instruction I_2 is a conditional branch based on the result of the comparison. Assume that the fetch unit predicts that the branch will not be taken and leaves instructions I_3 and I_4 in the instruction queue. Thus, instruction I_3 begins execution after I_1, followed by I_4. The final decision on the branch cannot be made until after the condition code flags have been updated at the end of the compare instruction. (Later, we will see that the decision can sometimes be made a little earlier.) Hence, after step W_1, the instruction fetch unit realizes that the prediction was incorrect and that the instructions in the execution pipe must be purged. Purge cycles are marked "P" in the figure. Four new instructions, I_k through I_{k+3}, are fetched, starting at the address computed in step E_2 (only I_k is shown in the figure).

Note that write steps, in which results are stored in the destination registers, cannot be allowed to proceed until the branch condition has been resolved. Had instruction I_1 taken longer to complete, step W_3 and any subsequent W steps would have had to be delayed. We return to this issue in Section 7.6.

Branch prediction can be done in one of two ways. It can be done by the compiler, in which case it is encoded in the branch instruction. The OP-code word of the instruction indicates to the instruction fetch unit whether this branch should be predicted as taken or not taken. The prediction result is the same every time a given branch instruction is encountered; hence, this approach is called *static branch prediction*.

Another approach is to have the processor hardware assess the likelihood of a branch being taken every time a branch instruction is encountered. This can be done by keeping track of the result of the branch decision the last time that instruction was executed and assuming that the decision in the current instance is likely to be the same. Clearly, the prediction result may be different for different instances of execution of the same branch instruction. This approach is called *dynamic branch prediction*. Both static and dynamic prediction lead to significant improvement in performance.

7.4
DATA DEPENDENCY

Section 7.1.2 introduced the idea of data dependency, which arises when a source operand for an instruction depends on the results of execution of a preceding instruction. If the results of the execution of the preceding instruction have not yet been recorded in their respective registers, the pipeline is stalled.

Consider a processor that uses the four-stage pipeline in Figure 7.2b. The first stage fetches an instruction from the cache. The second stage decodes the instruction and reads the source operands from the register file. The third stage performs an ALU operation and stores the result in the destination location. Assume that some processor instructions have three operands—two source operands and one destination operand. A hardware organization that supports these features is shown in Figure 7.13. Part a of the figure shows the connection between the ALU and the register file. The register file allows three different locations to be accessed simultaneously during each clock period; two locations provide the two source operands, SRC1 and SRC2, which are transferred

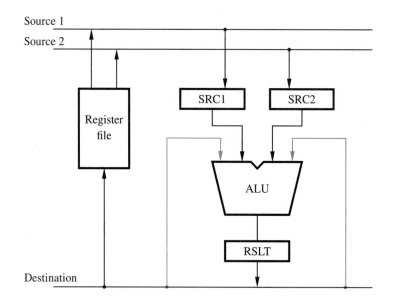

(a) Part of the data paths of a CPU

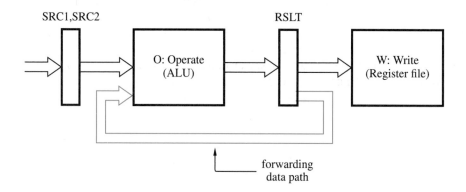

(b) Position of the source and result registers in the processor pipeline

FIGURE 7.13
Operand forwarding in a pipelined processor.

in parallel to the input registers of the ALU. At the same time, the contents of RSLT, the result register, are stored in a third location in the register file. Thus, at the end of each clock period, two new source operands are loaded in SRC1 and SRC2, and a new result at the output of the ALU is stored in the RSLT register. That result will be transferred to the register file in the following clock cycle.

Figure 7.13b shows the positions of the three registers, SRC1, SRC2, and RSLT, in the pipeline, assuming the overall structure is similar to that in Figure 7.2b. The three registers are part of the interstage buffers used to pass data from one stage to the next during pipelined operation.

Consider the following two instructions:

$$I_1: \quad \text{Add} \qquad \text{R1,R2,R3}$$
$$I_2: \quad \text{Shift\_left} \qquad \text{R3}$$

The timing of the execution of these two instructions is depicted in Figure 7.14. The Add instruction, which is fetched in the first clock cycle, performs the operation $R3 \leftarrow [R1] + [R2]$. The contents of the two source registers, R1 and R2, are read during the second clock cycle and are clocked into registers SRC1 and SRC2. Their sum is generated by the ALU and loaded into the ALU output register, RSLT, during clock cycle 3. From there, it is transferred into register R3 in the register file in cycle 4. What happens to the source operand of instruction I_2? The processor hardware must detect that the source operand for this instruction is the same as the destination operand of the previous instruction, and it must ensure that the updated value is used. Hence, the decode stage, which is responsible for getting the source operand from R3, cannot complete this task until cycle 5; so the pipeline is stalled for two cycles. Subsequent instructions proceed as shown, for the same reasons as Section 7.1.2 explains for Figure 7.6.

To avoid the delay, the hardware can be organized to allow the result of one ALU operation to be available for another ALU operation in the cycle that immediately follows. This technique is called *operand forwarding*, and the blue connection lines shown in Figure 7.13 can be added for this purpose. After decoding instruction I_2, the control circuitry determines that the source operand of I_2 is the same as the destination operand of I_1. Hence, the Operand Fetch operation, which would have taken place in the Decode stage, is inhibited. In the next clock cycle, the control hardware in the Operate stage arranges for the source operand to come directly from register RSLT, as indicated by the word "fwd" in Figure 7.15a. Thus, execution of I_2 proceeds without interruption.

In the case of a longer pipeline, operation may be stalled for a few cycles, even with operand forwarding. An example of a six-stage pipeline is shown in Figure 7.15b. In

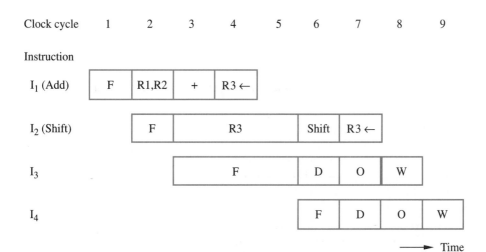

FIGURE 7.14
Interruption of pipelined operation because of data dependency.

Instruction

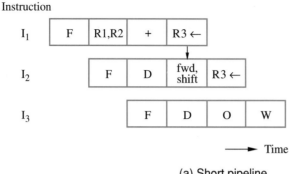

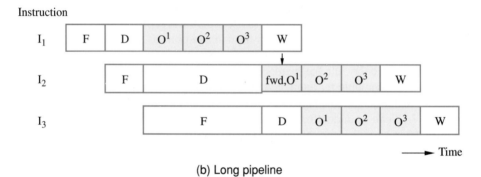

(a) Short pipeline

Instruction

(b) Long pipeline

FIGURE 7.15
Instruction execution using operand forwarding.

this case, the Operate phase of instruction execution consists of three pipeline steps, O^1, O^2, and O^3 (see blue shading). When needed, operand forwarding takes place after all three steps have been completed. In this case, the O^1 phase of instruction I_2 is delayed by two cycles.

Data dependency also occurs when operands are read from the memory. Consider, for example, the two instructions:

$$
\begin{array}{lll}
I_1: & \text{Load} & \text{(R1),R2} \\
I_2: & \text{Add} & \text{R2,R3,R4}
\end{array}
$$

One possible sequence of events during execution of these instructions is shown in Figure 7.16. The processor uses one clock cycle to obtain the contents of R1 and one cycle to read the source operand of instruction I_1 from the data cache. Because the destination register, R2, appears as a source register in I_2, the memory data are forwarded to the ALU directly as soon as they are received. For example, because of the path shown in blue in Figure 7.13a, when the memory data are available at the input of the register file, they are also available at the input of the ALU. Thus, operand forwarding makes it possible to continue execution of I_2 without stalling the pipeline. Of course, in the case of a cache miss, the pipeline is stalled and execution of both I_1 and I_2 is delayed until the requested data are read from the main memory or a secondary cache.

Instruction

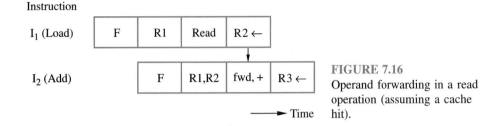

FIGURE 7.16
Operand forwarding in a read operation (assuming a cache hit).

In Figure 7.14, the data dependency is discovered by the hardware while the instruction is being decoded in cycle 3. The dependency involves the contents of R3, which would normally have been read during the same cycle. Since this value is not yet available, the control hardware delays reading it until cycle 5. Such dependencies can also be dealt with in software. In this case, the task of detecting the dependency and introducing the delay needed to resolve it is left to the compiler. For example, the compiler must introduce a two-cycle delay between instructions I_1 and I_2 in Figure 7.14 by inserting NOP instructions, as follows

I_1:   Add   R1,R2,R3
           NOP
           NOP
I_2:   Shift_left   R3

Without the NOP instructions, the processor would use the old contents of R3 in instruction I_2, producing an incorrect result.

The possibility of having the compiler introduce the delay needed for correct operation illustrates the close link between the compiler and the hardware. A particular feature can be either implemented in hardware or left to the compiler. Leaving tasks such as inserting NOP instructions to the compiler has an important advantage. Being aware of the need for a delay, the compiler can attempt to place useful instructions in the NOP slots. This is done by reordering instructions, as in the case of the delayed branch in Figure 7.10.

7.4.1 Side Effects

The data dependencies encountered in the two preceding examples are explicit and easily detected, because the register involved is named as the destination in instruction I_1 and as a source in I_2. Sometimes an instruction changes the contents of a register other than the one named as the destination. An instruction that uses an autoincrement or autodecrement addressing mode is an example. In addition to storing new data in its destination location, the instruction also changes the contents of a source register used to access one of its operands. All the precautions needed to handle data dependencies involving the destination location must also be used for the registers affected by an autoincrement or autodecrement operation. Stack instructions, such as push and pop, produce similar side effects because they implicitly use the autoincrement and autodecrement addressing modes.

Another possible side effect involves the condition code flags, which are used by instructions such as conditional branches and add-with-carry. For example, consider the 68000 instruction sequence

```
MOVE    #50,D3
ADD     D1,D2
ADDX    D3,D4
```

An explicit dependency exists between the ADDX and MOVE instructions through register D3, and an implicit dependency exists between ADDX and ADD through the X flag. (The X flag is a copy of the carry used in extended, or multiple-precision, operations.) In a processor structured like the 68000, the condition code flags are affected by most instructions. Hence, they give rise to frequent data dependencies and must be handled accordingly.

Clearly, instructions that have side effects give rise to multiple data dependencies. These dependencies are more difficult to detect and lead to a substantial increase in the complexity of the hardware or software needed to resolve them. The complexity becomes even greater when interrupts and exceptions are considered. For this reason, instructions designed for execution on pipelined hardware should have no side effects. This means that only the contents of the register or memory location named as the destination should be affected by any given instruction. Most modern processors adhere to this restriction.

The requirement that instructions have no side effects may seem too restrictive; Chapter 2 showed that the autoincrement and autodecrement addressing modes are potentially useful, and condition code flags are needed for recording such information as the generation of a carry or the occurrence of overflow in an arithmetic operation. The following sections show how the functions of these features can be provided by other means that are consistent with a pipelined organization and with the requirements of optimizing compilers.

7.5
INFLUENCE OF PIPELINING ON INSTRUCTION SET DESIGN

In this section, we examine the relationship between pipelined execution and machine instruction features. Some instructions are much better suited to pipelined execution than others. For example, the previous section shows that instruction side effects can lead to undesirable data dependencies. Next, we discuss two key aspects of machine instructions—addressing modes and condition code flags.

7.5.1 Addressing Modes

Addressing modes should provide the means for accessing a variety of data structures simply and efficiently. Useful addressing modes include index, indirect, autoincrement, and autodecrement. Many computers provide various combinations of these modes to increase the flexibility of their instruction sets. Complex addressing modes, such as those involving double indexing, are often encountered.

In choosing the addressing modes to be implemented in a pipelined processor, we must consider how our choice affects the clock period, the instruction execution pipeline, and so on. The extent to which various modes are likely to be used by compilers must be considered. To compare various approaches, we assume a simple model for accessing operands in the memory. The instruction

Load   (R1),R2

reads the contents of the memory location pointed to by R1 and stores the result in R2. The execution of this instruction can be organized to fit a four-stage pipeline, as shown for instruction I_1 in Figure 7.16.

More complex addressing modes may require several accesses to the memory to reach the named operand. For example, consider the following instruction:

Load   (X(R1)),R2

Assume that the index offset, X, is a short value given as part of the instruction word. While executing this instruction, the processor needs to access the memory twice—first to read location X+[R1] and second to read location [X+[R1]]. To accommodate this instruction in the pipeline, the execution phase occupies five clock cycles, as shown in Figure 7.17a, allowing one cycle for computing X+[R1]. If the next instruction requires the contents of R2, it will be stalled for two cycles in its Decode step.

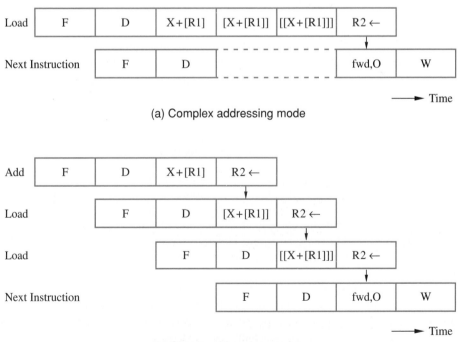

(a) Complex addressing mode

(b) Simple addressing modes

FIGURE 7.17
Equivalent operations using complex and simple addressing modes.

To implement the same Load operation using only simple addressing modes requires several instructions. For example, on a computer that allows three operand addresses, we can use

                    Add   #X,R1,R2
                    Load   (R2),R2
                    Load   (R2),R2

The Add instruction performs the operation R2 ← X+ [R1]. The two Load instructions fetch the address and then the operand from the memory. Because of pipelining, this sequence of instructions takes exactly the same number of clock cycles as the original, single Load instruction. This is shown in Figure 7.17b. We assume that the processor has the operand forwarding capability described earlier. Hence, while it executes the first Load instruction, the processor obtains the value X+[R1] directly from the output of the ALU and sends it to the memory to read [X+[R1]]. The value read from memory is forwarded for use as an address in the second Load instruction, which reads the final data to be deposited in R2.

This example indicates that, in a pipelined processor capable of starting a new instruction in every clock cycle, complex addressing modes that involve several accesses to the memory do not necessarily lead to faster execution. The main advantage of such modes is that they reduce the number of instructions needed to perform a given task and thereby reduce the program space needed in the main memory. Their main disadvantage is that their long execution times cause the pipeline to stall, thus reducing its effectiveness. Instructions that use such modes require more complex hardware to decode and execute them.

The instruction sets of modern processors are designed to take maximum advantage of pipelined hardware. Complex addressing modes are not suitable for pipelined execution and are not convenient for compilers to work with, so they should be avoided. The addressing modes used in modern processors often have the following features:

• Access to an operand does not require more than one access to the memory.
• Only load and store instructions access memory operands.
• The addressing modes used do not have side effects.

Three basic addressing modes that have these features are register, register indirect, and indexed. With indexed addressing, the operand address is the sum of the contents of a processor register and an offset value. The offset can be either the contents of a second register or an immediate value in the instruction word. In either case, only one access to the memory is needed to get the operand. Relative addressing can also be used; this is a special case of indexed addressing in which the program counter is used as the index register.

The three features just listed were first emphasized as part of the concept of RISC processors. However, more recently the distinction between RISC and CISC concepts has been blurred. The design of a processor, like any other design activity, involves many trade-offs. The result is often a combination of features that cannot be labeled as either RISC or CISC.

The PowerPC processor is a case in point. The addressing modes of the PowerPC follow the guidelines mentioned earlier in this section, with one notable exception: The index mode with update causes a change in the contents of the index register, thus producing a side effect. This means that the PowerPC is not a "pure" RISC architecture. We return to this question in Chapter 8, where another architecture, the DEC Alpha, is introduced for comparison. The Alpha architecture adheres strictly to the guidelines for pipelined processors.

7.5.2 Condition Codes

In processors such as the 68000, the condition code flags are stored in the processor status register. They are either set or cleared by many instructions so that they can be tested by subsequent conditional branch instructions to change the flow of program execution. Section 7.3 states that the compiler for a pipelined processor attempts to reorder instructions to avoid stalling the pipeline when branches or data dependencies between successive instructions occur. In doing so, the compiler must ensure that reordering does not cause a change in the outcome of a computation. The dependency introduced by the condition-code flags reduces the flexibility available for the compiler to reorder instructions.

Consider the sequence of instructions in Figure 7.18a. The carry that results from the second instruction is used in the third instruction; the two instructions perform a double-precision addition operation. The data dependency involving the carry flag must be recognized by both the compiler and the hardware. The compiler needs to know about it because it must not reverse the order of the two instructions when it attempts to reorder instructions. Also, it must not put the Increment instruction between the two Add instructions, because the Increment instruction may change the value of the carry. The hardware must know about the data dependency because it may have to delay the second Add instruction until the first one is completed. Although detecting and dealing with such data dependencies is a relatively straightforward task for the compiler, it is a difficult task for the hardware.

Increment	R5
Add	R2,R4
Add-with-carry	R1,R3

(a) A double-precision addition

ADDI	R5,R5,1
ADDC	R4,R2,R4
ADDE	R3,R1,R3

(b) PowerPC instructions

FIGURE 7.18
Explicit specification of condition code changes in the PowerPC instructions.

These observations lead to two important conclusions about the way condition codes should be handled. First, instructions that affect a given condition-code flag should be easy for the instruction-decoding circuits to recognize so that the hardware is able to maintain correct pipelined operation. One possibility is to use a few bits in the instruction word to indicate which flags, if any, are affected by the instruction. In the PowerPC, for example, the suffixes "." and "o" are used in an instruction when we want that instruction to affect the condition code flags. Two bits in the instruction word are used to provide this information in the encoded instruction generated by the assembler (see Appendix B).

The second conclusion is that the condition-code flags should be affected by as few instructions as possible. In the program segment in Figure 7.18a, the Add instruction needs to set or clear one flag only, the carry, to enable a double-precision addition. The Increment instruction should not affect any of the condition-code flags. In other parts of the program, the situation may be different. Thus, the compiler should be able to specify which flags are to be affected by any given instruction when it generates an assembly-language program.

The assembly language of the PowerPC demonstrates this flexibility. The suffixes "." and "o" specify whether an instruction affects the LT, GT, EQ, SO, and OV flags. And separate instructions are provided for operations that use the carry flag. For example, the two instructions ADD and ADDC (Add carrying) perform the same operation, but only the latter changes the value of the carry flag based on the outcome of the addition operation. Part b of Figure 7.18 shows how the example in part a would be written using these instructions. The PowerPC instruction ADDE (Add extended) adds the contents of its two source operands and the carry flag and writes the result into the destination register. The ADDI instruction does not affect the carry flag. Hence, the compiler can reverse the order of the first two instructions to increase the distance between the instruction that sets the carry and the instruction that uses it. This saves some of the time that might be wasted if the pipeline stalls while waiting for the carry to be computed.

7.6
MULTIPLE EXECUTION UNITS

Pipelining makes it possible to execute instructions in parallel. At the same time, it enforces correct sequencing of operations when dependencies are present. So far, we have assumed that the units operating in parallel implement different stages of the pipeline; one unit fetches instructions, another fetches the source operands, another performs arithmetic and logic operations, and so on.

Next, we consider the possibility of having more than one unit perform the operations needed in any one pipeline stage. As long as we can enforce the dependency constraints, there is no reason why multiple units cannot be used in the same pipeline stage. For example, several arithmetic and logic operations can proceed in parallel, provided they do not depend on each other.

One example of multiple execution units in high-performance processors is the use of separate integer and floating-point units. This is illustrated in Figure 7.19. To use

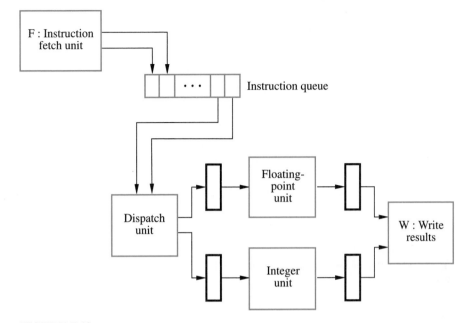

FIGURE 7.19
A processor with two execution units in the Operate stage.

the two units effectively, the dispatch unit must be able to issue two instructions in one clock cycle, one to the integer unit and one to the floating-point unit. The dispatch unit must be able to partially decode the instruction to determine which unit should execute it, and it may also have to fetch the source operands from the register files.

Internally, the execution units themselves may consist of more than one pipeline stage. The integer unit may fetch the source operands and perform an arithmetic or logic operation in one clock cycle. Floating-point operations, on the other hand, are more complex. Let us assume that three clock cycles are needed to complete a floating-point operation. When an operation is completed in either unit, one clock cycle is used to store the results back into the register files.

Using the organization in Figure 7.19 and assuming that the fetch unit reads four instructions at a time from the instruction cache, the pipeline timing would be as shown in Figure 7.20. In clock cycle 1, four instructions are fetched and placed into the instruction queue, and the first two enter the dispatch unit in clock cycle 2. Assuming that both execution units are free at this time, the two instructions are dispatched, one to each unit, and execution proceeds in cycle 3. The blue shading indicates operations in the floating-point unit. The next two instructions enter the dispatch unit in cycle 3, and again, both are dispatched because both execution units can receive new instructions in cycle 4. The integer unit can receive new instructions because instruction I_2 has proceeded to the Write stage. Instruction I_1 is still in execution, but it has moved to the second stage of the internal pipeline in the floating-point unit. Hence, instruction I_3 can enter the first stage.

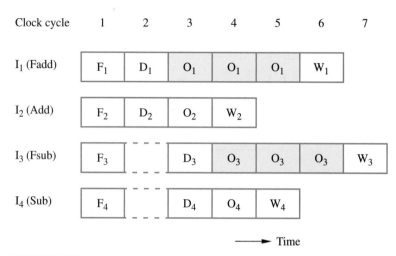

Clock cycle

FIGURE 7.20
An example of instruction execution flow in the processor in Figure 7.19.

Although we have used one floating-point and one integer unit to illustrate a pipeline with multiple execution units, it is possible to have several units of each type. In this case, the instruction dispatcher simply chooses any free unit that is capable of executing the instruction.

Exceptions

In Figure 7.20, instructions are dispatched in the same order as they appear in the program. However, their execution is completed out of order. Does this lead to any problems? We have already discussed the issues arising from dependencies among instructions. For example, if instruction I_2 depends on the result of I_1, the execution of I_2 will be delayed, as Section 7.4 explains. As long as such dependencies are handled correctly, there is no reason to delay the execution of an instruction. However, a new complication arises when we consider the possibility of an instruction causing an exception. Exceptions may be caused by a bus error during an operand fetch or by an illegal operation, such as an attempt to divide by zero. The results of I_2 are written back into the register file in cycle 4. If instruction I_1 causes an exception, program execution is in an inconsistent state. The program counter points to the instruction in which the exception occurred. However, one or more of the succeeding instructions have been executed to completion. If such a situation is permitted, the processor is said to have *imprecise exceptions*.

To guarantee a consistent state when exceptions occur, the results of the execution of instructions must be written into the destination locations strictly in program order. This means we must delay step W_2 in Figure 7.20 until cycle 6, assuming that the hardware allows two results to be written in the register file simultaneously. Similarly, step W_4 must be delayed until cycle 7, as shown in Figure 7.21. If an exception occurs during an instruction, all subsequent instructions that may have been partially executed are discarded. This is called a *precise exception*.

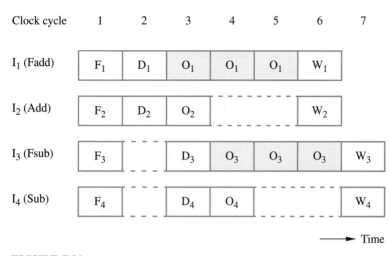

FIGURE 7.21
Instruction completion in program order.

It is somewhat easier to guarantee a consistent state and, hence, precise behavior in the case of external interrupts. When an external interrupt is received, the Dispatch unit stops reading any new instructions from the instruction queue, and the instructions remaining in the queue are discarded. Meanwhile, all instructions whose execution is pending continue to completion. At this point, the processor and all its registers are in a consistent state, and interrupt processing can begin.

Execution Completion

Out-of-order execution creates a situation similar to that with branch prediction and speculative instruction execution. In both situations, an instruction that has been executed may have to be discarded, and we must ensure that no register contents have been changed in the process. The desired behavior can be obtained by allowing instruction execution to proceed as shown in Figure 7.20, but the results must be written into temporary registers. The contents of these registers are later transferred to the permanent register file in the same order as the instructions appear in the program. In this case, an instruction is not regarded as having completed execution until the contents of the temporary registers have been copied into the permanent registers. After this happens, the temporary registers are released to be used for storing the results of other instructions. If an instruction causes an exception, the results of any subsequent instruction that has been executed are still in temporary registers and can be safely discarded.

To guarantee in-order completion, an instruction completion queue is needed. Instructions are entered in the queue buffer strictly in program order as they are dispatched for execution. When an instruction reaches the head of that queue and the execution of that instruction has been completed, the corresponding results are transferred from the temporary registers to the register file, and the instruction is removed from the completion queue. The instruction is said to have been *retired* at this point. An instruction is retired when its results have been written into their permanent destinations and all resources that were assigned to the instruction have been released.

Dispatch Operation

We now return to the dispatch operation. When dispatching decisions are made, the dispatch unit must ensure that all the resources needed for the execution of an instruction are available. For example, since the results of an instruction may have to be written in a temporary register, the required register must be free, and it must be assigned for use by that instruction as a part of the dispatch operation. A location in the completion queue must also be available for the instruction. When all the resources needed are assigned, including an appropriate execution unit, the instruction is dispatched.

Should instructions be dispatched out of order? For example, if instruction I_2 in Figure 7.20 is delayed because of a cache miss for a source operand, the integer unit will be busy in cycle 4, and I_4 cannot be dispatched. Should I_5 be dispatched instead? In principle, this is possible, provided that a place is reserved in the completion queue for instruction I_4, to ensure that all instructions are retired in the correct order. However, dispatching instructions out of order requires considerable care. If I_5 is dispatched while I_4 is still waiting for some resource, we must ensure that there is no possibility of a deadlock occurring. For example, assume that the processor has only one temporary register. When I_5 is dispatched, that register is reserved for it. If instruction I_5 also needs to wait for a result generated by I_4, we have a deadlock. Instruction I_4 cannot be dispatched because it is waiting for the temporary register, which, in turn, will not become free until instruction I_5 is retired.

To prevent deadlocks, the dispatcher must take many factors into account. Hence, issuing instructions out of order is likely to increase the complexity of the Dispatch unit significantly. It may also mean more time is required to make dispatching decisions. For these reasons, many pipelined processors use only in-order dispatching. Thus, the program order of instructions is enforced at the time instructions are dispatched and again at the time instructions are retired. Between these two points, the execution of several instructions can proceed in parallel, subject only to any interdependencies that may exist among instructions.

In Figure 7.19, two instructions can be dispatched in the same clock cycle only if one is a floating-point instruction and the other is an integer instruction. Thus, interleaving floating-point and integer instructions would make it possible for the dispatch unit to keep both the integer and floating-point units busy most of the time. This is another example of the tasks that an optimizing compiler needs to perform. The compiler needs to optimize the choice and ordering of instructions to take maximum advantage of the opportunities for parallel execution.

Superscalar Operation

With multiple execution units, an average of more than one instruction is executed per clock cycle. For this to happen, the processor must be able to fetch and dispatch two or more instructions at a time. The data paths, particularly the register files, must allow multiple registers to be accessed simultaneously to keep data flowing to and from all execution units. Most importantly, the compiler must be able to arrange program instructions to take maximum advantage of the available hardware units. Combined, these features allow several instructions to be completed per clock cycle. Processors that have this capability are called *superscalar* machines.

The PowerPC 603 Pipeline

The PowerPC 603 processor provides an example of multiple execution units in a pipeline. Its pipeline structure is illustrated in Figure 7.22. The instruction fetch unit fetches up to two instructions in one clock cycle from the instruction cache. Branch instructions are forwarded immediately to the branch execution unit. All other

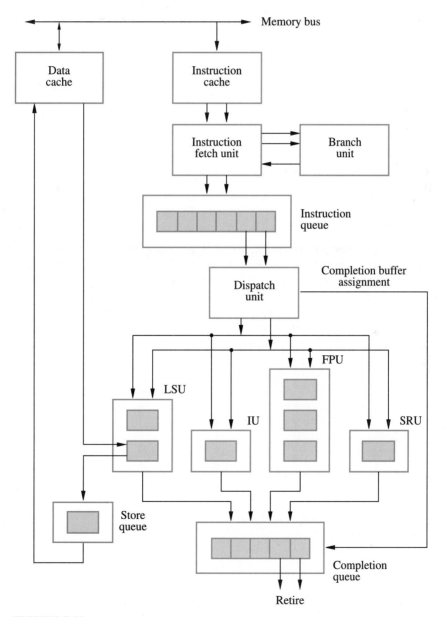

FIGURE 7.22
Flow of instruction execution in the PowerPC 603.

instructions are entered in the instruction queue, which is capable of holding up to six instructions. The branch unit executes branch instructions, using static branch prediction, if necessary, and begins to fetch instructions at the branch target address. When branch prediction is used, the instructions fetched are executed on a speculative basis.

The dispatch unit takes instructions from the end of the instruction queue, two at a time, and sends them to one of four execution units: the Load/Store Unit (LSU), the Integer Unit (IU), the Floating-Point Unit (FPU), or the System Register Unit (SRU). At the same time, it reserves space for these instructions in the Completion Queue.

As part of dispatching an instruction, temporary registers are assigned to hold the results until they can be safely written into the appropriate processor registers. A temporary register is called a *rename* register, because it assumes the name of one of the processor registers when it is assigned for use in a given instruction. An instruction is dispatched only when all the necessary resources are available. These resources include the rename registers and a place in the Completion Queue. Instructions cannot be dispatched out of order.

As their names imply, each of the four execution units is responsible for the execution of a certain type of instruction. Internally, these units consist of one to three pipeline stages. The IU executes all instructions that perform arithmetic or logic operations on integer operands. It reads the specified operands from the general-purpose register file, performs the computation, and stores the result in the assigned rename register or registers in one clock cycle. The FPU performs a similar function for floating-point operations on operands in the floating-point register file. This unit has three pipeline stages. The SRU executes instructions that operate on the system registers. These include instructions that perform logic operations on the condition register (CR) or that move data to or from the special-purpose registers. This unit has only one pipeline stage.

The LSU executes load and store instructions and consists of two pipeline stages. The first stage computes the effective address of the operand, and the second stage transfers the requested operand between the cache and the assigned rename register. Such transfers could be delayed because of a cache miss. To avoid stalling the pipeline during a memory write operation, the operand of a store instruction is placed in a Store Queue and held there until the write operation is completed. A subsequent load instruction that refers to the same memory location reads its operand directly from the Store Queue if the write operation has not yet been completed. The Store Queue performs the function of the write buffer discussed in Section 5.6.4.

The Completion Queue ensures that instructions are retired strictly in program order. Instructions are entered in this queue at the time they are dispatched. When the execution unit handling the instruction in location 0 has completed its execution phase, the instruction is ready to be retired. The process of retiring an instruction involves writing the contents of the corresponding rename registers into the appropriate processor registers and freeing up the rename registers for reuse. The two instructions at the head of the completion queue can be retired in the same clock cycle. However, the instruction in location 1 cannot be retired before the instruction in location 0.

7.7
PERFORMANCE CONSIDERATIONS

In this section, we examine some quantitative aspects of pipelining to demonstrate the performance gains that are possible. We refer to the number of instructions executed per second as the *instruction throughput*. Figure 7.1 shows that a two-stage pipeline may increase the instruction throughput by a factor of two, compared to nonpipelined operation. The four-stage pipeline of Figure 7.2 may increase instruction throughput by a factor of four. In general, an *n*-stage pipeline has the potential to increase throughput *n* times. Hence, it would appear that the higher the value of *n*, the larger the performance gain. This leads to two questions:

- How much of this potential increase in instruction throughput can be realized in practice?
- What is a good value for *n*?

Any time a pipeline is stalled, the instruction throughput is reduced. Hence, the design of a pipeline is highly influenced by factors such as branch and cache miss penalties. First, we discuss the effect of these factors on performance, and then we return to the question of how many pipeline stages should be used.

7.7.1 Effect of Delay Penalties

A major factor limiting the increase in the throughput achievable with pipelining is the delay incurred when the pipeline is stalled as a result of cache misses, data dependencies, and branch instructions. These effects have been examined qualitatively in the previous sections. We now consider their impact in quantitative terms.

Suppose a processor uses the four-stage pipeline of Figure 7.2. The time allocated to each step in the pipeline is determined by the longest step. Let the delay through the ALU be the critical parameter. This is the time needed to add two integers. Thus, if the ALU delay is 10 ns, a processor clock of 100 MHz would be used. Section 7.1.1 argues that it is important to be able to access instructions and data in one clock cycle. This means that the on-chip instruction and data caches for this processor should be designed to have an access time of 10 ns. Ideally, the processor executes one instruction per clock cycle, or 100 million instructions per second.

To evaluate the effect of cache misses, we use the same parameters as in Section 5.6.2. The cache miss penalty in that system is computed to be 17 clock cycles. Let T_I be the time between two successive instruction completions. Without misses, and ignoring the effects of data dependencies and branch instructions, the processor completes the execution of one instruction each clock cycle; thus, $T_I = 1$ cycle. A cache miss delays the instruction in which the miss occurred, and all subsequent instructions, by an amount equal to the cache miss penalty. This means that the value of T_I increases by an amount equal to the cache miss penalty for the instruction in which the miss occurs and is equal to one for all other instructions. Let δ_{miss} be the average increase in the value of T_I as a result of cache misses. Assume that 30 percent of the instructions refer to data operands in the memory. With a 95 percent instruction hit rate and a 90 percent data hit rate, δ_{miss} is given by

$$\delta_{miss} = (0.05 + 0.3 \times 0.1) \times 17 = 1.36 \quad \text{cycles}$$

If this were the only penalty encountered during program execution, the processor's throughput would be

$$\text{Throughput}_{pipelined} = \frac{1}{T_I} = \frac{1}{1 + \delta_{miss}} = 0.42 \quad \text{instructions/cycle}$$

Let us compare this value to the throughput obtainable without pipelining. A processor that uses sequential execution requires four cycles per instruction. Its throughput would be

$$\text{Throughput}_{nonpipelined} = \frac{1}{4 + \delta_{miss}} = 0.19 \quad \text{instructions/cycle}$$

Clearly, pipelining leads to significantly higher throughput. But the performance gain of $\frac{0.42}{0.19} = 2.2$ is only slightly better than one-half the ideal case.

Reducing the cache miss penalty is particularly worthwhile in a pipelined processor. As Chapter 5 explains, this can be achieved by introducing a secondary cache between the primary, on-chip cache and the main memory. Assume that the time needed to transfer an 8-word block from the secondary cache is 50 ns. Hence, a miss in the primary cache for which the required block is found in the secondary cache introduces a penalty of 5 cycles instead of 17. In the case of a miss in the secondary cache, the full 17-cycle penalty is still incurred. Hence, assuming a hit rate of 94 percent in the secondary cache, the average miss penalty is

$$\delta_{miss} = (0.05 + 0.3 \times 0.1) \times (0.94 \times 5 + 0.06 \times 17) = 0.46 \quad \text{cycle}$$

The instruction throughput in this case is 0.68. An equivalent nonpipelined processor would have a throughput of 0.22. Thus, pipelining provides a performance gain of $\frac{0.68}{0.22} = 3.1$.

The penalty values of 1.36 and 0.46 are, in fact, somewhat pessimistic, because we have assumed that every time a data miss occurs, the entire miss penalty is incurred. This is the case only if the instruction immediately following the instruction that references memory is delayed while the processor waits for the memory access to be completed. However, an optimizing compiler attempts to increase the distance between two instructions that create a dependency by placing other instructions between them whenever possible. Thus, there are many situations in which, following a cache miss, at least one or two instructions are executed before the pipeline is stalled.

Let us now estimate the effect of the branch penalty on instruction throughput. The amount of delay incurred following a branch instruction depends on the details of implementation of the pipeline. A processor that uses an instruction queue benefits from branch folding, as discussed in Section 7.3. In this case, the branch instruction is executed by the instruction fetch unit in parallel with other instructions, as shown in Figure 7.9. Therefore, it does not add to the execution time of the program. In effect, program execution proceeds as if the branch instruction is not there. This effect can be modeled by saying that the branch penalty is −1 for unconditional branch instructions and for conditional branch instructions in which the branch condition is already known. Where branch prediction is used, correctly predicted branches also benefit from branch folding.

On the other hand, in the case of an incorrectly predicted branch or in situations where branch prediction is not used, a penalty of several cycles is incurred. For example, instruction I_2 in Figure 7.12 completes execution in cycle 5. The next instruction to complete execution is I_k in cycle 9. There are no execution completions in cycles 6 through 8. Hence, the branch penalty is 3 cycles. With operand forwarding, step E_2, and as a result E_k, would take place one cycle earlier, thus reducing the branch penalty to 2 cycles.

Assume that 20 percent of the dynamic instruction count in a program consists of branch instructions. If no branch prediction is used, only a small fraction of the branch instructions benefit from branch folding, perhaps 30 percent. If the remaining branch instructions incur a penalty of 2 cycles, the average branch penalty is

$$\delta_{branch} = 0.2(0.3 \times (-1) + 0.7 \times 2) = 0.82 \quad \text{cycle}$$

This represents a substantial reduction in throughput, to 0.55 instructions per cycle. Branch prediction can have a very high success rate in loop termination but may not be very successful with other branch instructions. Let us assume that, with branch prediction, 80 percent of all branch instructions benefit from branch folding. In this case,

$$\delta_{branch} = 0.2(0.8 \times (-1) + 0.2 \times 2) = -0.08 \quad \text{cycle}$$

and a throughput of 1.09 instructions per cycle is achieved. The fact that instruction throughput is more than one should not be surprising. Recall that the instruction fetch unit in Figure 7.7 can execute branch instructions completely. Other instructions are placed in the queue and are executed in the rest of the pipeline. Hence, there are two parallel paths for instruction execution.

The combined effect of cache miss and branch penalties on instruction throughput can now be computed as follows. We assume that the computer has primary and secondary caches and uses branch prediction. Using the same parameters as in the preceding discussion, we obtain

$$\text{Throughput} = \frac{1}{1 + \delta_{miss} + \delta_{branch}} = \frac{1}{1 + 0.46 + (-0.08)} = 0.72 \quad \text{instructions/cycle}$$

The effect of data dependencies can be estimated in a similar fashion. Performance clearly varies from one program to another. In all cases, the benefits of pipelining depend greatly on the extent to which the compiler can reduce dependencies or take advantage of branch prediction. For these reasons, performance studies are often done using detailed simulations of program execution from which the frequency of various events can be measured.

7.7.2 Number of Pipeline Stages

The fact that an n-stage pipeline appears to increase instruction throughput by a factor of n suggests that we should use a large number of stages. However, as the number of pipeline stages increases, so does the probability of the pipeline being stalled, because more instructions are being executed in parallel. Thus, dependencies between instructions that are far apart become significant and may cause the pipeline to stall. For these reasons, the gain from increasing the value of n begins to diminish, and the associated cost is not justified.

Another important factor in determining the number of stages is the inherent delay in the basic operations performed by the processor. The most important among these is the ALU delay. In many processors, the cycle time of the processor clock is chosen such that one ALU operation can be completed in one cycle. Other operations, such as cache access and instruction decoding and dispatching, are divided into steps that take about the same time as an add operation. It is also possible to use a pipelined ALU. For example, the ALU of the DEC Alpha 21064 processor consists of a two-stage pipeline, in which each stage completes its operation in 5 ns.

Many pipelined processors use four to six stages. This is the case for the PowerPC 603 processor. Some processors divide instruction execution into smaller steps and use more pipeline stages and a faster clock. For example, the DEC Alpha 21064 uses an eight-stage pipeline for integer instructions and an eleven-stage pipeline for floating-point instructions. Intel's P6 processor uses a twelve-stage pipeline.

7.8
CONCLUDING REMARKS

Pipelining offers significant potential for enhanced performance by allowing several operations to proceed in parallel. However, this potential can only be realized by careful attention to three aspects:

- The instruction set of the processor
- The design of the pipeline hardware
- The design of the associated compiler

It is important to appreciate that there are strong interactions among all three. High performance is critically dependent on the extent to which these interactions are taken into account in the design of a processor. An instruction set that is particularly well suited for pipelined execution is one of the main features of modern processors.

PROBLEMS

7.1. Consider the following sequence of instructions

$$
\begin{array}{ll}
\text{Add} & \#20,\text{R0,R1} \\
\text{Mul} & \#3,\text{R2,R3} \\
\text{And} & \#\$3\text{A,R2,R4} \\
\text{Add} & \text{R0,R2,R5}
\end{array}
$$

In all instructions, the destination operand is given last. Initially, registers R0 and R2 contain 2000 and 50, respectively. These instructions are executed in a computer that has a four-stage pipeline similar to that shown in Figure 7.2b. Assume that the first instruction is fetched in clock cycle 1, and that instruction fetch requires only one clock cycle.

    (*a*) Draw a diagram similar to Figure 7.2*a*. Describe the operation being performed by each pipeline stage during each of clock cycles 1 through 4.

    (*b*) Give the contents of the interstage buffers, B1, B2, and B3, during clock cycles 2, 4, and 5.

7.2. Repeat Problem 7.1 for the following program:

Add	#20,R0,R1
Mul	#3,R2,R3
And	#$3A,R1,R4
Add	R0,R2,R5

7.3. Instruction I_2 in Figure 7.6 is delayed because it depends on the results of I_1. By occupying the Decode stage, instruction I_2 blocks I_3 which, in turn, blocks I_4. Assuming that I_3 and I_4 do not depend on either I_1 or I_2 and that the register file allows two Write steps to proceed in parallel, how would you use additional storage buffers to make it possible for I_3 and I_4 to proceed earlier than in Figure 7.6? Redraw the figure, showing the new order of steps.

7.4. The delay bubble in Figure 7.6 arises because instruction I_2 is delayed in the Decode stage. As a result, instructions I_3 and I_4 are delayed even if they do not depend on either I_1 or I_2. Assume that the Decode stage allows two Decode steps to proceed in parallel. Show that the delay bubble can be completely eliminated if the register file also allows two Write steps to proceed in parallel.

7.5. Figure 7.4 shows an instruction being delayed as a result of a cache miss. Redraw this figure for the hardware organization of Figure 7.7. Assume that the instruction queue can hold up to four instructions and that the instruction fetch unit reads two instructions at a time from the cache.

7.6. A program loop ends with a conditional branch to the beginning of the loop. How would you implement this loop on a pipelined computer that uses delayed branching with one delay slot? Under what conditions would you be able to put a useful instruction in the delay slot?

7.7. With delayed branching, the instructions in the delay slots are always executed. Thus, the instructions placed in the delay slots should be ones that must be executed, whether or not the branch is taken. Consider an alternative strategy: A computer has one delay slot. The instruction in this slot is always executed, but only on a speculative basis. If a branch is to take place, the results of that instruction are discarded, and the instruction at the branch target is fetched and executed instead. Suggest a way to implement program loops efficiently on this computer.

7.8. Rewrite the sort routine shown in Figure 2.46 for the PowerPC assuming that one delay slot follows each branch instruction. Attempt to fill these slots with useful instructions wherever possible.

7.9. The program segment in Figure 2.47*c* illustrates how logic operations on the condition code flags can be used in making branch decisions. Assume a simple two-stage pipeline, and draw a diagram similar to that in Figure 7.8 to show the sequence of steps during the execution of this segment. Then rewrite the same program segment without using the

CRAND instruction, that is, using the approach in Figure 2.47*b*. Draw a diagram showing the execution sequence in this case, and compare the two sequences.

7.10. The feed-forward paths in Figure 7.13 (blue lines) allow the contents of the RSLT register to be used directly in an ALU operation. The result of that operation is stored back in the RSLT register, replacing its previous contents. What type of register is needed to make such an operation possible?

Assume that before instruction I_1 is executed, R1, R2, R3, and RSLT contain the values 30, 100, 45, and 198, respectively. Draw a timing diagram for clock cycles 3 through 5 in Figure 7.15*a*, showing the clock signal and the contents of the RSLT register during each cycle. Use your diagram to show that correct results will be obtained during the forwarding operation in cycle 4. (Recall that I_1 is an Add instruction, and I_2 shifts the contents of its register operand one bit position to the left.)

7.11. Identify all dependencies in the program in Figure 2.44*a*. How would you reorder the instructions in this program to increase the speed of execution?

7.12. Assume that 20 percent of the instructions executed on a computer are branch instructions. Delayed branching is used, with one delay slot. Estimate the gain in performance if the compiler is able to use 85 percent of the delay slots.

7.13. A pipelined processor has two branch delay slots. An optimizing compiler can fill one of these slots 85 percent of the time and can fill the second slot only 20 percent of the time. What is the percentage improvement in performance achieved by this optimization?

7.14. A pipelined processor uses the delayed branch technique. You are asked to recommend one of two possibilities for the design of this processor. In the first possibility, the processor has a four-stage pipeline and one delay slot, and in the second possibility, it has a six-stage pipeline with two delay slots. Compare the performance of these two alternatives, taking only the branch penalty into account. Assume that 20 percent of the instructions are branch instructions and that an optimizing compiler has an 80 percent success rate in filling the single delay slot. For the second alternative, the compiler is able to fill the second slot 25 percent of the time.

CHAPTER 8

Examples of CISC, RISC, and Stack Processors

Chapter 2 shows how basic programming concepts are implemented at the assembly language level and illustrates the need for various machine instructions and addressing modes; the Motorola 68000 and PowerPC instruction sets and addressing modes are used as examples. In this chapter, we complete the discussion of the 68000 and PowerPC architectures, elaborating on features found in the various members of these processor families that span a range of performance levels. We also describe some other commercial processors that provide competitive alternatives to the 68000 and the PowerPC. The Intel 80X86 is considered a complex-instruction-set computer (CISC) alternative to the 68000, and the Digital Equipment Corporation Alpha processor is another example of the reduced-instruction set-computer (RISC) approach that can be compared to the PowerPC. Finally, a very different approach, that of the Hewlett-Packard HP3000, shows how an instruction set can be organized for a machine that has computation facilities heavily influenced by the use of a stack data structure for holding operands.

Chapters 1, 2, 3, and 7 describe various aspects of the RISC and CISC approaches to processor design. We now briefly review some of the salient features of each approach before giving other examples from each class. CISC instruction sets provide many powerful instructions for more direct implementation of high-level language operations and program sequencing control features. The execution of such instructions can become quite complex, and the instructions are usually implemented by microcode. The rationale of the CISC approach is that it leads to fewer machine language instructions for a given high-level language program, thus leading to shorter program execution times. This is true if complex instructions can be executed quickly and efficiently. In practice, however, the microcoded or hardwired implementations of these instructions have not always met high performance expectations, and CISC instruction sets have actually proved to be difficult targets for optimizing compilers.

The RISC approach of using very simple instructions may at first appear to be less effective than the CISC alternative, because more RISC instructions are needed to perform a given computational task. However, RISC instructions are well-suited to pipelined execution, and hardwired implementation of simple instructions leads to fast execution rates. A key advantage of RISC instruction sets is that they can be used effectively by optimizing compilers. Another advantage is related to very-large-scale integration (VLSI) fabrication technology: Because of the smaller chip area needed for instruction handling and sequencing control in RISC processors, more space is available for processor registers and on-chip caches. Higher performance results because off-chip data and instruction accesses are reduced.

Taking all factors into account, the result is that, although both approaches have led to very competitive commercial products, machines that feature RISC design principles have become increasingly dominant in recent years.

8.1
THE MOTOROLA 680X0 FAMILY

In Chapter 2 we introduce the 68000 processor. Here, we discuss the key features of this family's next level of processors. The processors at this level use full 32-bit address and data paths. They are the 68020, 68030, and 68040 processors.

The 68020 is much more powerful than the 68000, mainly because of some significant architectural enhancements. These advances were made possible by improved VLSI technology and larger packages that removed many constraints of pin limitations. Although the 68030 is superior to the 68020, the difference between them is less significant. In fact, as far as the programming model is concerned, they are essentially identical; both have some instructions that are not available in the 68000 instruction set. The 68000 is *upward compatible* with the 68020, 68030, and 68040; in other words, the 68000 code can be executed on the other processors without modification, but not vice versa.

In the following subsection, we first discuss the common features of the 68020, 68030, and 68040 microprocessors. We refer to the 68020 most of the time and assume the reader is aware that the same comments apply to the 68030 and 68040. Later, we describe the additional enhancements found in the 68030 and 68040.

8.1.1 68020 Processor

This section highlights the main differences between the 68020 and the 68000 processors. The features that we describe in the 68020 apply to the 68030 and the 68040 as well.

Address and Data Buses

The 68020 has external connections for 32-bit addresses and 32-bit data. Its address space is 4 gigabytes (2^{32}, or 4,294,967,296 bytes). Although its data bus is 32 bits wide, the 68020 can deal efficiently with devices that transfer 8, 16, or 32 bits at a time. The processor can adjust dynamically to the data bus width requirements of a particular device in a manner that is transparent to the programmer. The 68020 bus includes control lines that are activated by the devices connected to the bus to indicate the required size of their data transfers. Thus, the processor can deal with devices of different data transfer sizes without knowing the actual size before a data transfer is initiated.

The 68000 restriction that word operands must be aligned on even address boundaries has been eliminated in the 68020; operands of any size may start at any address. This means that 16- and 32-bit operands can occupy parts of two adjacent 32-bit locations in the main memory. Two access cycles are therefore needed to reach such operands, and this affects performance. The processor automatically performs these two accesses. From the address, the processor knows which 32-bit locations must be accessed and in what pattern the individual bytes from these locations should be assembled to obtain the desired operand.

Register Set and Data Types

Like the 68000, the 68020 has user and supervisor modes of operation. In the user mode, the registers available are essentially the same as those given in Figure 2.21 for the 68000. In the supervisor mode, however, the 68020 has several additional control registers intended to simplify implementation of operating system software.

The 68000 addressable data units are bit, byte, word, long word, and packed BCD. In addition to these, the 68020 allows quad word, unpacked binary-coded decimal (BCD), and bit-field data types. A quad word consists of 64 bits, and unpacked BCD has one BCD digit per byte. A bit-field consists of a variable number of bits in a 32-bit long word, and it is specified by the location of its leftmost bit and the number of bits in the field.

Addressing Modes

All 68000 addressing modes, shown in Table 2.1, are available in the 68020. Several extra versions of the indexed mode have been added to the 68020 to allow flexible and efficient access to data and address list structures.

The full indexed mode is more powerful because it allows a range of displacements, or offsets, and provides for a scaling factor. Recall that the 68000 syntax for the full indexed mode is

$$\text{disp}(An, Rk.\text{size})$$

where the displacement is a signed, 8-bit number and the size designation indicates whether 32 or 16 bits of the Rk register are to be used in computing the effective address. The 68020 version of this mode allows the displacement to be an 8-, 16-, or 32-bit value. It also introduces a scale factor by which the contents of Rk are multiplied. The value of the scale factor may be 1, 2, 4, or 8. The syntax for the mode is

$$(\text{disp}, An, Rk.\text{size}*\text{scale})$$

Note that the displacement is given within the parentheses in this case. The effective address, EA, is computed as

$$EA = \text{disp} + [An] + ([Rk] \times \text{scale})$$

This mode is useful when dealing with lists of items that are 1, 2, 4, or 8 bytes long. If the scale factor is chosen so that it equals the size of the items, then successive items in the list can be accessed by incrementing the contents of Rk by 1.

Another powerful extension of indexed addressing is the memory indirect indexed modes, in which an address operand is obtained indirectly from the main memory. Two such modes exist. In *memory indirect postindexed* mode, an address is fetched from the memory before the normal indexing process takes place. Its syntax is

$$([basedisp,An],Rk.size*scale,outdisp)$$

and the effective address is computed as

$$EA = [basedisp + [An]] + ([Rk] \times scale) + outdisp$$

Note that two displacements are used. A base displacement of 16 or 32 bits is used to modify the address in An, which is then used to fetch the address operand from the memory. This allows an address to be selected from a list of addresses stored in memory starting at the location given by the contents of An. The second displacement is the normal displacement used in indexed addressing, called outer displacement to distinguish it from the base displacement.

The second version is the *memory indirect preindexed* mode, in which most of the indexing modification is done before the address operand is fetched. The syntax for this mode is

$$([basedisp,An,Rk.size*scale],outdisp)$$

and the effective address is determined as

$$EA = [basedisp + [An] + ([Rk] \times scale)] + outdisp$$

In both of these modes, the values An, Rk, basedisp, and outdisp are optional and are not included in the computation of the effective address unless specified by the user. These addressing modes are useful for dealing with lists in which contiguous memory locations are used to store addresses of data items, rather than the data items themselves. The latter can be anywhere in memory.

A relative version of all indexed modes is available in which the program counter is used in place of the address register, An.

Instruction Set

All 68000 instructions are available in the 68020. Some have extra flexibility. For example, branch instructions can have 32-bit displacements, and several instructions have the option of using longer operands. Some new instructions are also provided, such as instructions that deal with bit-field operands.

On-Chip Cache

The 68020 chip includes a small instruction cache that has 256 bytes organized as 64 long-word blocks. A direct-mapping scheme is used when loading new words into the cache.

8.1.2 Enhancements in the 68030 Processor

The 68030 differs from the 68020 in two significant ways. In addition to the instruction cache, the 68030 has another cache of the same size for data. The data cache organization has 16 blocks of 4 long words each. The 68030 also contains a memory management unit (MMU).

The execution unit in the 68030 generates virtual addresses. The cache access circuitry determines if the desired operand is in the cache, based on virtual addresses. The MMU translates the virtual address into a physical address in parallel with the cache access so that, in the case of a cache access miss, the physical address needed to access the operand in the main memory is immediately available.

8.1.3 Further Enhancements in the 68040 Processor

The 68040 processor has an integer processing unit that is object-code compatible with other processors in the 68000 family. In addition to the integer unit, the 68040 includes a floating-point unit, which implements the IEEE floating-point standard described in Chapter 6. The 68040 has instruction and data caches, as in the 68030 processor. Its memory management unit is improved over that in the 68030; this unit has two independent address translation caches that permit simultaneous translation of addresses for both instructions and data. The 68040 has a pipelined structure that permits fetching of instructions while previous instructions are still being processed. Two internal buses are used to transfer instructions and data from the respective caches. These buses, in conjunction with the two address translation circuits, allow simultaneous access to instruction and data caches.

Finally, the 68040 includes circuits that monitor activity on the external bus. This feature makes the 68040 suitable for use in multiprocessor systems. One of the key requirements in such systems is to maintain consistency of the common data that may temporarily reside in several caches of different processors. The bus-monitoring circuits detect bus transfers that change cached data, as we describe in Chapter 10.

8.2
THE INTEL 80X86 FAMILY

Intel processors have attained strong commercial success because they have been used in IBM personal computers (PCs) and other PC-compatible products. In the 1980s, Intel produced a series of processors based on the 8086 processor, which externally handles 20-bit addresses and 16-bit data. Because it comes in a 40-pin package, the address and data values are time-multiplexed on the same set of pins. Progressively more powerful processors using the same basic architecture have been introduced. These are the 80286, 80386, and 80486. The first is a 16-bit chip, and the others are 32-bit chips whose external addresses and data are handled in 32-bit quantities. The 32-bit chips come in larger packages that obviate the need for address and data line multiplexing. Although they retain the fundamentals of the 8086 architecture, they have features that enhance their computing power. The latest members in the Intel family, called the Pentium and the P6, provide significantly higher instruction execution performance than the 80486. They also have wider external buses to facilitate rapid loading of cache blocks.

We do not discuss the Intel processors in detail. However, we consider some of their features that differ notably from the Motorola 68000 family of processors—in particular, the way they access main memory and I/O devices. Since the 8086 is the basic component of the Intel family and has a relatively simple structure, we use it as a representative example in the discussion that follows.

8.2.1 Memory Segmentation

The 8086 processor views the memory as being organized in segments of 64K bytes each. The processor has four registers that serve as pointers to the segments, and instructions and data are addressed relative to these pointers. One of these registers, called the Code Segment register (CS), is used to access instructions. Another, called the Data Segment register (DS), is used when accessing data. This means that the most natural way to organize programs for the 8086 is to fully separate the instruction space from the data space. Compilers and operating systems, including memory management components, usually do this in any event. In some early computers, the assignment of program and data spaces to physically separate memory units was referred to as the *Harvard architecture.* All modern computers use the *von Neumann architecture,* in which instructions and data share the same physical memory unit.

The 8086 segments may overlap; this happens if the segment registers are loaded with values that are within 64K of each other. In addition to the DS register, there is an Extra Segment register (ES) that is also used for accessing data. The fourth register of this type is the Stack Segment register (SS), which points to a 64K-byte area in which a stack is located. Since the contents of the SS register can be changed by the program, several different stacks can be created.

The concept of memory segmentation as implemented in the 8086 is conducive to modular software development. Individual modules can be independent but also share some common data. Using the CS register to point to the segment that is currently being executed provides an efficient mechanism for relocation; a program module can be relocated to a different segment in the memory without any changes to its code. Then it can be executed by simply changing the contents of the CS register to point to the new location. Data are normally placed in DS segments. By default, most instructions use the DS register when accessing data. If an instruction is to access data in an ES segment, a prefix byte is added to the instruction. The ES segment is convenient for storing data common to two or more program modules.

8.2.2 Register Structure

Figure 8.1 shows the register structure of the 8086 processor. In addition to the segment registers, it has a set of data, pointer, and index registers.

The four data registers are general-purpose registers that can be used for temporary storage of data. However, some instructions implicitly assign a more specific function to these registers. The AX register is normally used as the accumulator. The BX register is used to hold a base address, typically the starting address of a list or an array of data in the main memory. The CX register contains the count for Shift and Rotate instructions, which indicates the number of bit positions that the operand is to be shifted or rotated. The DX register holds the address of an I/O device during some I/O operations. All

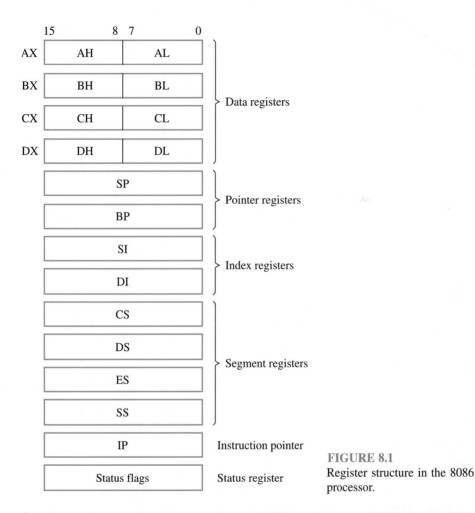

FIGURE 8.1
Register structure in the 8086 processor.

four data registers can be accessed either as 16-bit words or as individual bytes. When a byte is to be accessed, the register name specifies the desired byte. For example, AH and AL refer to the high- and low-order bytes of the accumulator, AX.

Register SP is the processor stack pointer. Its contents are added to the contents of the SS register to obtain the address that defines the top of the stack. Note that the bottom of the stack is not defined by the value in SS alone—it is defined by the value in SS plus the initial contents of SP.

The base pointer register, BP, provides another option in based addressing. It is often used to hold the base address of a list or an array. Recall that this addressing function can also be achieved with the BX register. Index registers SI and DI are used in various versions of the index addressing mode in conjunction with the BP and BX registers. When strings are used as operands, these registers provide the source index and the destination index. The pointer and index registers can also be used to hold general operands. These operands can only be accessed as 16-bit words.

The instruction pointer, IP, has the function of a program counter, but it does not contain the actual address of the current instruction. This address is the sum of the

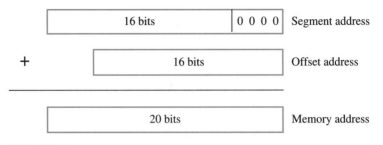

FIGURE 8.2
Generation of a memory address in the 8086 processor.

contents of IP and the code segment register, CS. The status register contains condition code flags and status flags.

We can conclude that the 8086 does not have a general register structure like the 68000. Although most registers in the 8086 can be used as general-purpose data registers, their roles in various instructions are often constrained to specific functions.

8.2.3 Generation of Memory and I/O Addresses

The registers in the 8086 are 16 bits long. In order to generate a 20-bit memory address, the contents of a segment register used in the computation of the address are multiplied by 16 (shifted left 4 bit positions) and then added to a 16-bit offset address, as shown in Figure 8.2. The offset address is the 16-bit value determined from the addressing mode involved. Intel's literature calls this offset the effective address. Note that, as the offset address is continuously incremented, it goes from FFFF to 0000, which means that addresses wrap around from the end of a segment to the beginning of the same segment.

Although I/O devices can be mapped into memory address space, the 8086 also has special I/O instructions that use a separate I/O address space. I/O addresses consist of 16 bits; this allows access to as many as 64K byte I/O locations. If 16-bit I/O registers are used, they should be located at even addresses so that a single operation can transfer a 16-bit quantity between the I/O device and the processor.

Two special instructions, IN and OUT, transfer data between an I/O device and the 8086. These instructions may include an 8-bit address as an immediate value, which can be used to directly access the first 256 I/O locations. The remaining I/O locations are accessed indirectly, using the address in the DX register. The IN and OUT instructions are more compact and faster to execute than the memory reference instructions that are used if I/O devices are memory-mapped. However, memory-mapped addressing is easier, so it is often used.

8.2.4 Intel 80286 and 80386 Processors

The 80286 is a 16-bit microprocessor that enhances the 8086 architecture by including on-chip memory-management circuitry. Its overall capabilities, including memory management, are not as extensive as those found in the 80386 processor. Hence, we proceed directly to the 80386.

The 80386 is a 32-bit processor. Its register structure, from the programmer's viewpoint, is similar to that shown in Figure 8.1. A significant difference is that all registers are 32 bits long, except for the segment registers, which are 16 bits long. Another difference is that the 80386 has six segment registers rather than four; the two extra registers are used to point to data segments.

In addition to memory segmentation, the 80386 provides a virtual-memory paging capability. The segmentation and paging features are not necessarily used at the same time. In fact, the memory can be organized in any of the following ways:

- As a flat, 32-bit address space in which the effective address is used as the physical address
- As one or more variable-length segments (without paging)
- As a 32-bit space divided into one or more 4K-byte pages
- As a structure that combines segmentation and paging

Figure 8.3 shows the most general way to generate a physical address. A 32-bit effective address can be determined in the normal indexed mode; the contents of the index register are multiplied by a scale factor of 1, 2, 4, or 8 and then added to the base and

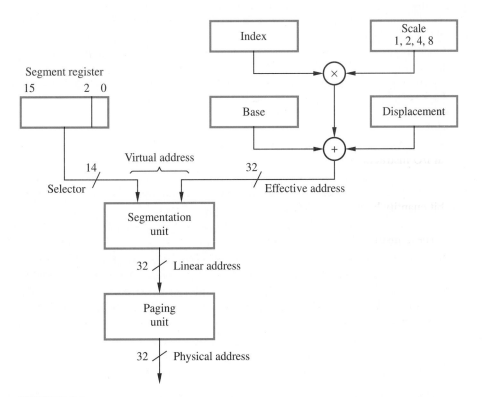

FIGURE 8.3
Address generation in the 80386 processor.

displacement. One of the six segment registers specifies the required segment. Only the most significant 14 bits of the register are used. These bits, called a *selector*, are used as an index to a segment descriptor table from which a 32-bit *linear base address* is obtained. This address is added to the effective address to produce a 32-bit *linear address*. The paging unit translates the linear address into a 32-bit physical address using a page table. Note that together, the 14-bit selector and the 32-bit effective address can be thought of as a 46-bit virtual address, as Figure 8.3 indicates. Therefore, the total address space of the 80386 is 64 terabytes (2^{46} bytes).

The segment descriptor and page tables are large and are therefore kept in the main memory. In order to ensure fast address translation, on-chip caches are included in the 80386 to hold the active parts of these tables. An address translation cache holds the physical addresses of the 32 most recently used pages. A set of *descriptor registers* is provided for the linear base addresses, and one descriptor register is associated with each segment register. Each descriptor register contains three entries: a linear base address, a limit value that defines the maximum size of the segment, and an access rights field. Whenever a new value is loaded into one of the segment registers, the corresponding descriptor register is updated automatically.

This address translation mechanism just described takes place in a *protected mode* of operation. The 80386 can also operate in another mode, called the *real mode,* in which it behaves as an 8086 processor that uses 32-bit registers. In the real mode, memory addressing and segmentation are done as explained in Section 8.2.3.

Segmentation and paging are two key features of the 80386 processor. Segmentation allows the application programmer to organize the main memory in logical modules. Paging provides a convenient mechanism for the system programmer to manage the physical memory.

The 80386 is a complex processor. We have considered in detail only its addressing mechanism, which differs from those we examined in earlier chapters.

8.2.5 Intel 80486 Processor

The Intel 80486 processor was one of the first chips to contain 1 million transistors, roughly the same number as in the 68040. This processor provides significantly improved performance over the 80386 class of chips, an advance made possible by the expanded circuitry. The 80486 includes both integer and floating-point processing units and an 8K-byte cache.

The integer unit is fully compatible with the 80386 processor. The floating-point unit implements the IEEE floating-point standard presented in Chapter 6. In 80386-based computers, the same capability can be achieved by using a coprocessor chip. Paging and memory management support in the 80486 is the same as in the 80386.

A four-way, set-associative cache is included for instructions and data. The loading of new information into the cache is enhanced by a burst data-transfer mechanism, which enables four 32-bit words to be read as a block and loaded into the cache. The cache has a write-through feature, whereby any data written into the cache are also automatically written into the main memory.

To achieve high performance, the 80486 exploits parallelism and pipelining to a considerable extent. Both the integer unit and the floating-point unit can execute instructions in parallel. When one instruction is being executed, subsequent instructions are fetched from the memory. Execution of frequently used instructions requires fewer clock cycles than in the 80386; those that load and store data or perform register-to-register operations require only one cycle. Thus, although the design of the 80486 has performance features similar to those found in RISC processors, the well-established 80386 instructions were retained. Thus, the 80486 is compatibile with the previous processors in the 80X86 family and can use existing software.

8.2.6 Intel Pentium Processor

The Pentium processor is also in the 80X86 family. Introduced in 1993, its performance is a significant improvement over that of the 80486. The Pentium has 3 million transistors, compared to 1 million in the 80486, and its computational power is over twice that of the 80486 on integer-intensive benchmark programs and about five times that of the 80486 on floating-point-intensive benchmark programs. The computational power of the Pentium, averaged over integer and floating-point benchmarks, is about two-thirds that of the PowerPC 601, which was the first chip in the PowerPC family.

The Pentium processor is a CISC architecture that achieves high performance by using many of the organizational features present in RISC processors, as is done in the 80486 to a lesser extent. In particular, split on-chip caches of 8K-bytes each are used for instructions and data. This superscalar processor, supported by multiple, pipelined operation units, can issue two instructions per clock cycle. A 64-bit-wide external data bus allows caches to be rapidly loaded from main memory. The caches are two-way associative, with 32-byte blocks. Three independent, pipelined, operational units are included—two for integer operations and one for floating-point operations. Each integer pipeline is five stages deep, and each floating-point unit has eight stages.

In general, branch instructions interrupt the smooth flow of overlapped and parallel instruction execution in high-performance RISC and CISC processors. The Pentium processor uses dynamic branch prediction to predict which instruction block will be executed following a conditional branch instruction; instructions in that block can be fetched and their execution can begin before the branch decision is made. If the prediction is correct, instruction execution proceeds smoothly; if it is not, the processing of instructions in the predicted direction is abandoned, the state of the processor is reset as necessary, and then execution proceeds along the correct path. Performance degrades when this latter situation occurs; however, performance increases overall if the predicted path is usually the correct direction. The Pentium branch chooses the same direction that it went the last time the branch was executed. This requires a table of last-branch address values to be kept for each branch instruction. The predicted direction is correct for all branches at the end of a program loop after the first branch, until the loop is exited.

8.2.7 Intel P6 Processor

Introduced in 1995, the P6 is the latest processor in the 80X86 family.[1,2] At a clock rate of 133 MHz, it provides about twice the performance of a 100 MHz Pentium. Most of the performance gain results from an increased superscalar factor and the capability to execute instructions out-of-order. The superscalar factor, or the maximum number of instructions that can be completed in a clock cycle, is three in the P6, compared to two in the Pentium. Pipeline depth in the multiple execution units is twelve, compared to five in the Pentium, and datapath width inside the processor is 64 bits, double that of the Pentium. The P6 has split, on-chip instruction and data caches of 8K bytes each, the same size as in the Pentium. These caches are intended to be used in systems that have an off-chip secondary cache.

Superscalar operation is provided by multiple execution units, including two for integer operations and one for floating-point operations. A major performance-enchancing feature of the P6 is its ability to execute instructions in an order different from that specified in the program fetched from memory. This feature allows more instructions to be executed in parallel. Of course, adequate control is provided to ensure that the resulting computations specified by the program are correct. Dynamic branch prediction is implemented in the P6, as in the Pentium. This capability allows the processor to look far enough ahead in the instruction stream to take advantage of parallel execution.

External bus monitoring circuits enable the P6 to be used in multiprocessor systems. These monitoring circuits, and the control actions that they initiate, maintain consistency of common data that may temporarily reside in the caches of different processors.

8.3
THE PowerPC FAMILY

Basic characteristics of the PowerPC instruction set and addressing modes are described in Chapter 2, providing an example of a RISC approach in computer design. The discussion of the Motorola 68000 provided similar insights into a CISC computer design.

The previous section on the Intel family explains how the most advanced processors in the family, the Pentium and the P6, achieve high performance through multiple functional units, pipelining, on-chip instruction and data caches, and the capability for issuing multiple instructions per cycle. The PowerPC has all of these performance-enhancing features. Later, this section details the extent to which different PowerPC processors use these features. Thus, both RISC and CISC design approaches share many performance-enhancing features.

If we consider only instruction sets and addressing modes, the PowerPC architecture has somewhat more complex features than those found in most RISC designs. Consider the following:

The PowerPC has a Multiply-add instruction that performs the operation

$$RD \leftarrow ([RA] \times [RB]) \pm [RC]$$

on floating-point operands in registers RA, RB, and RC.

In the index addressing mode, the index register can be updated to the computed effective address value as a side effect, leaving the displacement value unchanged.

Load/Store Multiple instructions cause a contiguous block of operands to be transferred between the memory and the processor registers.

A class of conditional branch instructions decrement a counter and then branch, based on whether or not the decremented value has reached 0.

Such instructions and addressing mode features exceed the usual RISC style. These four features are useful in performing multiple arithmetic operations required in signal processing tasks, processing lists of operands, saving and restoring processor registers on procedure entry and exit, and efficiently terminating loops, respectively. Using these features yields shorter programs. PowerPC designers have incorporated these features without unduly compromising the efficient, streamlined flow of simple, pipelined instructions that is a basic property of RISC machines.

The PowerPC architecture is a successor to the POWER architecture used in the processors of the IBM Risc System (RS)/6000 line of computers. The first implementation of the PowerPC architecture is the 601 processor, introduced in 1993. The 601 is a transition processor between the two architectures; as such, it implements a superset of POWER and PowerPC instructions. This allows the 601 to run compiled POWER machine programs as well as PowerPC programs. The second processor in the family, the 603, is the first purely PowerPC processor.

8.3.1 PowerPC 601 Processor

The 601 processor chip, containing 2.8 million transistors, was first used in IBM desktop machines in late 1993. The 601 is a 32-bit processor, intended for desktop, portable, and low-end multiprocessor systems. Different versions are available with processor clock rates of 50, 66, 80, and 100 MHz.

The PowerPC 601 has a 32K-byte cache on the processor chip for holding both instructions and data. The cache is organized in eight-way associative sets. Three independent execution units are provided: an integer unit, a floating-point unit, and a branch-processing unit. Up to three instructions can be issued for execution in a clock cycle, for superscaler operation. The 601 has four pipeline stages for integer instructions and six for floating-point instructions.

8.3.2 PowerPC 603 Processor

The 603 processor also has a 32-bit processing width. Intended for desktop and portable machines, it is a low-cost, low-power processor, consuming about 3 watts of electrical power at 80 MHz. The five execution units provided can operate in parallel, so the instruction issuing and control hardware, which can issue up to three instructions per clock cycle, is somewhat more complex than in the 601. The on-chip cache is divided into two 8K-byte sections for separate, temporary storage of instructions and data. The instruction execution pipeline of the 603 is described in Chapter 7.

8.3.3 PowerPC 604 Processor

The 32-bit 604 processor is designed for higher performance than is available in either the 601 or the 603; both integer and floating-point speeds are approximately double those in the 601 and 603 processors. The 604 achieves this performance level with a 100 MHz clock rate and a superscaler capability for issuing up to four instructions per clock cycle. The processor has six independent execution units: three integer units, a floating-point unit, a memory load/store unit, and a branch-processing unit. Personal computers and midrange workstations are the intended market for this processor.

8.3.4 PowerPC 620 Processor

The 620 processor implements the full 64-bit PowerPC architecture and supports super-scalar performance. It is targeted for high-end desktop computers, work-group servers, transaction processing systems, and multiprocessor systems.

   Like the 604, the 620 has six independent execution units, and up to four instructions can be completed in a clock cycle. The actual rate of processing instructions in a particular program is enhanced by the processor's ability to execute instructions out of order, as in the Intel P6 described in Section 8.2.7. The description of out-of-order execution of instructions in this section applies to the 620 as well. The clock rate is 133 MHz in the 620, the same as that in the P6. Dynamic branch prediction is used, and the processor chip contains both instruction and data caches. Each cache holds 32K bytes and is organized in eight-way associative sets.

8.4
THE ALPHA AXP FAMILY

The latest processor architecture developed by Digital Equipment Corporation is the Alpha AXP. This family of processors is the successor to the 32-bit VAX family. The first processor in the new family is the 21064, whose specific features are described here. The Alpha AXP architecture has a 64-bit address and data size. It is a RISC design that adheres more closely to basic RISC principles than does the PowerPC. For instance, none of the four extended features of the PowerPC described in Section 8.3 are present in the Alpha AXP.

   A basic goal of pipelined processor design is to reduce logic depth in any pipeline stage in order to minimize the stage delay for any given implementation technology. This permits a high clock rate—one of the basic processor properties that leads to high performance. An important design characteristic of the Alpha AXP architecture is that it uses only the simplest of instruction formats and addressing modes to achieve short pipeline stage delays.

8.4.1 Alpha 21064 Processor

This first implementation of the Alpha AXP architecture, the Alpha 21064, has a 200-MHz clock rate on a 1.7-million transistor chip. The processor has 32 general-purpose and 32 floating-point registers, and all registers are 64 bits wide. The processor uses an 8K-byte instruction cache and an 8K-byte data cache. A maximum of two instructions can be issued per clock cycle. Four independent processing units are in the Alpha

21064: an integer unit, a floating-point unit, an instruction fetch and branching unit, and a memory load/store unit. The pipeline depths in these four units are seven, ten, six, and seven, respectively; the first four stages are common and can handle two instruction streams in parallel. At a 200-MHz clock rate, each pipeline stage delay is only 5 nanoseconds.

Instruction and Addressing Mode Formats

The Alpha 21064 has only four instruction types, all 32 bits long:

Operate—Integer, floating-point, and byte-manipulation operations are included in this class. These instructions use a three-operand format, with operands contained in processor registers or in an immediate field of the instruction.

Memory—Load/store operations use register plus displacement indexed addressing as the only addressing mode.

Branch—Conditional branch instructions contain a displacement value that specifies the direction and distance of the branch target address relative to the program counter. There is no condition code register; condition codes are optionally written into a general-purpose register by operate instructions. This register is then named by branch instructions that need to test the codes. Unconditional branch instructions use the named register to hold the updated value of the program counter as the return address if the branch is a subroutine call.

Call-PAL—Privileged Architecture Library (PAL) instructions perform operating system functions not available in user mode. These privileged instructions can access hardware resources, that is, processor state registers, that are not accessible by the normal instruction set. PAL routines also contain instructions that do not exist in the defined Alpha AXP instruction set. They service interrupts and manipulate memory management unit registers.

Data Alignment and Byte Operations

Only 32-bit and 64-bit aligned loads and stores are directly handled in the datapath between the cache and the processor. Byte extraction and manipulation is done in the registers by operate instructions. If byte load/store operations or unaligned accesses are permitted in a processor architecture, then shifter and multiplexer logic delays are added to the processor/cache interface; this degrades performance for aligned as well as unaligned data transfers. Therefore, only aligned transfers are supported in the 21064 processor in order to keep this stage of instruction and data transfer operations as fast as possible. In the PowerPC processors, unaligned data access is supported directly in the datapath.

Branch Prediction

Both static and dynamic branch prediction is supported for conditional branch instructions. In static prediction, the sign of the displacement field determines the prediction. For example, choosing the negative, or backward, displacement direction in branch instructions at the end of a loop improves performance. In dynamic prediction, the last direction taken by a branch instruction is recorded so that the processor can make the best prediction the next time that branch is executed. Close attention to branch prediction is warranted because of the large branch penalty in a processor with deep pipelines.

8.5
ARCHITECTURAL AND PERFORMANCE COMPARISONS

Some comparisons of architectural, implementation, and performance features among the 680X0, 80X86, PowerPC, and Alpha processors are scattered throughout this chapter. Table 8.1 gathers some of these features together to make the similarities and differences more evident. The first section of the table displays architectural features, the second section lists implementation features, and the third section shows relative speed performance data. No entries are listed for the number of independent processing units in either the 68040 or the 80486, because this parameter is meaningful only if the processor can issue more than one instruction per clock cycle. Note, however, that each of these processor chips has separate circuitry for integer and floating-point operations because these operations have different processing requirements. The performance values indicate execution speeds on two different types of benchmark programs. These benchmarks have been developed by the System Performance Evaluation Corporation (SPEC). SPECint92 is a benchmark that stresses integer operations, whereas the SPECfp92 benchmark emphasizes floating-point operations. Most of the data in this table are taken from Diep et al.[3] and from Geppert.[4,5] The first five processors listed in Table 8.1 were introduced in the early 1990s, and the last five were introduced in 1995.

8.5.1 Comparison of the PowerPC and Alpha Processors

Section 8.4 states that the Alpha processor adheres more closely to the RISC style of simple instruction sets than the PowerPC does. In particular, the PowerPC has several instructions with more powerful operational features than any Alpha instructions. Here, we compare programs for these two processors for a computational task that can take advantage of the more powerful PowerPC instructions to make the program compact.

Consider a simple signal processing task in which two sequences of numbers, $X(k)$ and $Y(k)$, where $k = 1, 2, \ldots, 100$, represent two input signals. These sequences are to be weighted by numbers R and T, respectively, and added in pairs to produce an output sequence, $Z(k)$, that replaces the $X(k)$ sequence. The required computation is $Z(k) = (R \times X(k)) + (T \times Y(k))$. A program loop that performs the desired task is shown in Figure 8.4a, along with a register assignment for addresses and signal values. Parts b and c of the figure give PowerPC and Alpha programs for the task, respectively. Instead of using the actual assembly language mnemonics, we have used a common word-instruction format for both programs so that they can be easily compared. The operations performed by each instruction are shown as comments. This example and the program loops are taken from Smith and Weiss.[6] The performance observations that follow are derived from that article, based on the 601 and Alpha 21064 processors.

Each instruction in both machines is represented by a single 32-bit word. Therefore, the PowerPC program loop requires 40 percent less memory space for its six instructions than the Alpha program requires for its ten instructions. This task illustrates the utility of the PowerPC instructions Load(Store)FP-update, FPMultAdd, and Branch-Not-Equal. These are examples of the types of instructions in the PowerPC that are somewhat more complex than the instructions usually found in RISC designs. The Alpha requires two

TABLE 8.1

Architectural, implementation, and performance comparisons among ten processors

	68040	80486	Pentium	Alpha 21064	PowerPC 601	PowerPC 604	PowerPC 620	Alpha 21164	Ultra Sparc	MIPS 10000
Architectural features										
Register/datapath width (bits)	32	32	32	64	32	32	64	64	64	64
Number of processor registers (general-purpose/floating-point)	16/8	8/8	8/8	32/32	32/32	32/32	32/32	32/32	Register windows	32/32
On-chip cache (instruction/data in kilobytes)	4/4	8 unified	8/8	8/8	32 unified	16/16	32/32	8/8 prim. + 96 sec.	16/16	32/32
Superscalar factor (maximum instructions issued per processor cycle)	1	1	2	2	3	4	4	4	4	4
Number of independent processing units			3	4	3	6	6	4	9	5
Number of pipeline stages (integer/floating-point)	3/6	5 integer	5/8	7/10	4/6	4/6	4/6	7/9	9/9	5/7
Implementation features										
Clock rate (megahertz)	25	50	66	200	80	100	133	300	167	200
Number of transistors (millions)	1.2	1.2	3.1	1.7	2.8	3.6	7.0	9.3	3.8	6.4
Peak power (watts)	6	5	16	30	9.1	13	30	50	30	30
Performance speeds										
SPECint92	21	27.9	67.4	130	85	160	225*	330*	275*	300*
SPECfp92	15	13.1	63.6	184	105	165	300*	500*	305*	600*

Processors

*Figure is estimated.

For k := 1 **to** 100 **do**

    $X(k) := R \times X(k) + T \times Y(k)$

end

Register assignments:

    R0 points to $X(k)$, initially holds address $X(1) - 4$

    R1 points to $Y(k)$, initially holds address $Y(1) - 4$

    CTR initially holds loop count 100

    FP0 holds $X(k)$

    FP1 holds $Y(k)$

    FP2 holds R

    FP3 holds T

(a) Signal processing task and register assignment

A	LOOP	LoadFP_update	FP1,R1,4	; FP1 ← [[R1] + 4]
				; R1 ← [R1] + 4
		FPMult	FP1,FP1,FP3	; FP1 ← [FP1] × [FP3]
		LoadFP	FP0,R0,4	; FP0 ← [[R0] + 4]
B		FPMultAdd	FP0,FP0,FP2,FP1	; FP0 ← [FP0] × [FP2] + [FP1]
C		StoreFP_update	FP0,R0,4	; [R0] + 4 ← [FP0]
				; R0 ← [R0] + 4
D		Branch_NE	LOOP,CTR	; CTR ← [CTR] − 1
				; Branch LOOP if [CTR] ≠ 0

(b) Program for the PowerPC 601

FIGURE 8.4

Program comparison between the PowerPC 601 and the Alpha 21064 processors.

instructions to emulate each of these PowerPC instructions. The labels A, B, C, and D in Figure 8.4 identify corresponding operations in the two programs.

    It should be possible to estimate the relative execution times of these two programs using the formula developed in Chapter 1, Section 5. Total execution time, T, for a program is estimated by $T = N/R$ for a pipelined processor that has the capability issue a new instruction in each clock cycle, where N is the number of instructions executed and R is the clock rate. The PowerPC and Alpha processors can issue more than one instruction per clock cycle. If M is the average number of instructions issued

Additional register assignments:

R2 holds address of $Y(100)$
R3 is a work register
R0 initially holds address of $X(1)$
R1 initially holds address of $Y(1)$

A	LOOP	LoadFP	FP1,R1,0	; FP1 ← [[R1] + 0]
		FPMult	FP1,FP1,FP3	; FP1 ← [FP1] × [FP3]
		LoadFP	FP0,R0,0	; FP0 ← [[R0] + 0]
B		FPMult	FP0,FP0,FP2	; FP0 ← [FP0] × [FP2]
B		FPAdd	FP0,FP0,FP1	; [FP0] ← [FP0] + [FP1]
C		StoreFP	FP0,R0,0	; [R0] + 0 ← [FP0]
D		Sub	R3,R2,R1	; R3 ← [R2] − [R1]
C		Add	R0,R0,4	; R0 ← [R0] + 4
A		Add	R1,R1,4	; R1 ← [R1] + 4
D		Branch_NE	LOOP,R3	; Branch LOOP if [R3] ≠ 0

(c) Program for the Alpha 21064

FIGURE 8.4 (*continued*)

per clock cycle during program execution, then the formula for execution time becomes $T = N/(MR)$. The shortest possible execution times on the example task for the PowerPC and the Alpha are determined by using the maximum M values from Table 8.1 along with the appropriate R and N values. Let T_{PC} and T_α be the execution times for the PowerPC and the Alpha, respectively. For this example signal processing task, the ratio of PowerPC to Alpha execution times is

$$T_{PC}/T_\alpha = (N_{PC}/N_\alpha) \times (M_\alpha/M_{PC}) \times (R_\alpha/R_{PC})$$

$$= (6/10)(2/3)(200/80)$$

$$= 1$$

Execution times are thus predicted to be the same. (In this comparison, we ignore the possibility of branch folding.)

This result contradicts the SPEC benchmark performance comparisons shown in Table 8.1; the latter imply that the Alpha is about 1.6 times faster than the PowerPC in typical programs. This contradiction is explained by the M parameter. The average number of instructions issued per clock cycle in executing a program may be significantly less than the maximum achievable rate given in Table 8.1. In general, only certain combinations of instruction types can be issued in parallel. These combinations are determined by the issuing rules and resource requirements for the various instructions, as Chapter 7 discusses. If these instruction types do not occur together in a stream of program instructions, the actual issuing rate is reduced. The issuing rate is also reduced by the effects of conditional branch instructions and by the ordering dependencies among the variables used and generated by the instructions. For the short loops of the two example programs, Smith and Weiss[6] have shown that the average instruction issuing rate is 1 for the PowerPC and only 0.63 for the Alpha, even though the maximums are 3 and 2, respectively. This leads to an execution time ratio of $T_{PC}/T_\alpha = 0.94$. However, the short-loop branching situation in the example task is a much more severe performance restriction for the Alpha than for the PowerPC.

The performance disadvantage caused by conditional branching at the end of short loops can be reduced by a technique called *loop unrolling*. Instructions of the loop body are repeated as in-line code that executes several passes of the original loop in one pass through the new, longer loop. The unrolling can be done by an optimizing compiler. In the preceding example, if the loops are unrolled to perform four iterations of the original loop in one pass through the new loop, then the average instruction issuing rate improves significantly in the Alpha, to 1.74, but only marginally in the PowerPC, to 1.26. This leads to an execution time ratio of $T_{PC}/T_\alpha = 2.1$. The improvement in instruction issuing rates caused by loop unrolling results from two factors. First, the reduction in rate caused by conditional branch instructions is decreased because the loop bodies are four times longer, and thus branches occur only 0.25 times as often as in the original programs. Second, with longer loop bodies, the compiler has more opportunities to rearrange the execution order of instructions. This leads to reduced dependencies among the variables referenced in successive or closely adjacent instructions. In this particular example, more opportunities exist for improvement in the Alpha code than in the PowerPC code. The extent to which the potential improvement can be realized also depends on the quality of the compiler.

This example shows that it is difficult to obtain realistic execution performance comparisons among processors by using simple calculations based on architectural and implementation features or on the results of executing simple, short programs. Benchmark program measurements of reasonable scale, such as those used in the SPEC comparisons, are needed. The major factor that cannot be easily determined for a large, practical programming task is the average rate of instruction issuing for that program in a particular processor. Another factor that has not been considered here is the effect of the cache miss rates. Finally, we emphasize that the study by Smith and Weiss used the 601 implementation of the PowerPC and the 21064 implementation of the Alpha. Different implementations of these two architectures, such as the PowerPC 620 and the Alpha 21164, which are also listed in Table 8.1, lead to different comparative performance results.

8.6
A STACK PROCESSOR

All processors discussed in this book use general-purpose registers to hold data operands. Some years ago, the Hewlett-Packard Company designed and manufactured a computer called the HP3000, whose main architectural feature is an instruction set that is keyed to processing operands held in a stack data structure.

As Chapter 2 describes, access to operands in a stack is restricted to only those operands residing at the top of the stack, and results are always returned to the top of the stack. This type of organization is not appropriate for current RISC and CISC processor designs that are highly parallel; in these processors, simultaneous access to several operands in a large register set is required for high performance.

Nevertheless, the HP3000 and the earlier series of B5500, B6500, and B6700 computers from the Burroughs Corporation, which also featured stack-oriented processing, are historically important as commercial implementations of stack computing. The way these machines process arithmetic expressions is both interesting and elegant. We illustrate the main ideas by describing the HP3000 instruction set and addressing modes. Our discussion concentrates on only the features that characterize the stack organization of this computer.

8.6.1 Stack Structure

The HP3000 is a 16-bit computer. Its main memory contains program instructions and data in separate domains; instructions and data cannot be intermixed except for immediate data that can be used in programs. Hardware registers are used as pointers to the program and data segments, as shown in Figure 8.5.

Three registers specify the program segment. The program base (PB) and the program limit (PL) registers indicate the memory area occupied by the program, and the program counter (PC) points to the current instruction. Each of these registers contains the appropriate 16-bit address.

The data segment is divided into two parts—the stack and the data area. Five 16-bit pointers are used to delineate and access these memory locations. The contents of the data base (DB) register denote the starting location of the stack. The stack grows in the higher-address direction. If the top element of the stack is at location i, then the next element pushed onto the stack will be at location $i + 1$. This contrasts with 68000 stacks, which expand in the direction of decreasing addresses, as explained in Section 2.16. The address of the top element in the stack, also called the top of stack (TOS), is stored in the 16-bit stack pointer (SP). The SP is not actually a single hardware register, as we explain shortly, but it can be thought of that way. It is incremented or decremented when data elements are pushed onto or popped off the stack. From the user's point of view, it functions as any other 16-bit pointer register. The upper limit of the stack is defined by the contents of the stack limit (SL) register. Therefore, the stack is allowed to grow until [SP] = [SL]. Any attempt to extend the stack past the limits defined by DB and SL is prevented by the hardware. The data area extends from the location immediately preceding the location pointed to by the DB register to the limit specified in the data limit (DL) register.

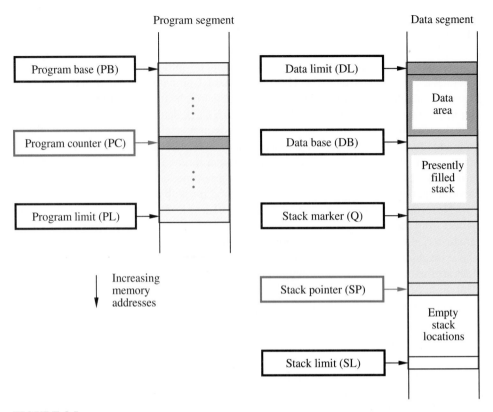

FIGURE 8.5
Program and data segment organization in the HP3000 processor.

The pointer registers specify the stack's current size, maximum size, and location in memory. The stack is thus a dynamic structure that can be easily changed. Figure 8.5 shows one other pointer, the stack marker (Q) register. This register denotes the starting point for the data stack of the current procedure. Actually, Q points to the fourth word of a four-word entry in the stack, called the *stack marker,* that facilitates passing control between procedures. When a procedure must be suspended, for example, as a result of an interrupt, the information needed to allow proper return to the suspended procedure is placed onto the stack in the form of a stack marker.

The first word of the stack marker stores the current contents of an index register, and the second word contains the return address. The return address information is actually stored as the difference between the value in the PC, which points to the next instruction to be executed in the current procedure, and the contents of the PB register. By storing the difference, instead of the absolute value, programs can be moved out of the memory and later returned to a different place in the memory. The new area in memory is pointed to by loading a new value in the PB register. The third word saves the status information contained in the status register, and the fourth word stores the distance between this stack marker and the one immediately preceding it.

Figure 8.6 shows one stack marker, denoted k, that was placed on the stack at the time Procedure$_k$ was initiated, and another stack marker, denoted $k + 1$, that is placed

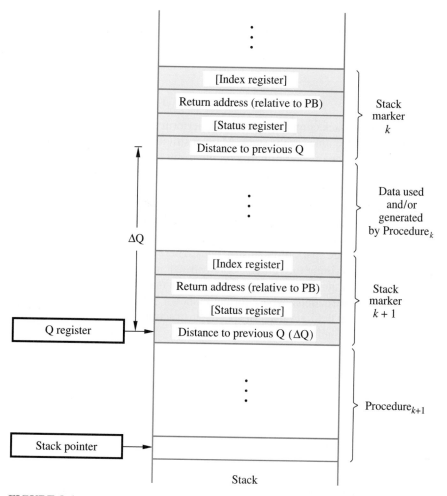

FIGURE 8.6
Stack markers in the HP3000 processor.

onto the stack when a new procedure, Procedure$_{k+1}$, is initiated. When the new procedure is completed, the machine transfers control to the previous procedure using the data in the stack marker $k + 1$. At that time, the Q register must be set to point to the fourth word of stack marker k. This is readily accomplished because the distance between the stack markers is stored as a part of each marker. Also, the SP is set to point to the location immediately preceding stack marker $k + 1$. As a result, SP points to the top of the stack used by Procedure$_k$, thus restoring the situation that existed at the time Procedure$_{k+1}$ was invoked. This technique can be used to nest any number of procedures. Parameter-passing between procedures also uses the stack.

In addition to the pointer registers, HP3000 computers have other hardware registers used in the internal organization of the machine. The only two of these that are visible to the programmer are the index and status registers, which function in essentially the same ways as similarly named registers in most other computers. Note, however, that there are no general-purpose registers available to the programmer. Instead, data are manipulated using the stack as temporary storage, as we show in an example in the next section.

8.6.2 Stack Instructions

As a basic strategy, stack computers attempt to perform most operations on the data that occupy the top few locations of the stack. Many instructions therefore use operands that are already in these locations. Furthermore, the results generated are left on the stack. This assumes that there are instructions that can move data between the stack and other main memory locations.

The HP3000 has a variety of instructions that are all 16 bits long. Most of the instructions involve the stack in some way, and typically either the operands, operand addresses, or other relevant parameters reside in the stack. This allows great flexibility in using the 16-bit code space of the instructions. There are 13 major classes of instructions. Instead of describing the full HP3000 instruction set, we restrict our attention to the classes that illustrate the stack organization of the machine. Let us first consider the Memory Address instructions, whose format is shown in Figure 8.7. Eleven valuations of the 5-bit OP-code field are used to specify instructions in this class. The Memory Address instructions include:

LOAD   Push a specific memory word onto the stack.

STOR   Pop the top word of the stack (TOS) into a specified memory location.

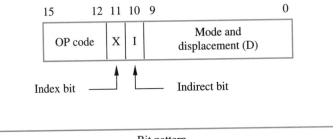

	15	12 11	10	9	0
	OP code	X	I	Mode and displacement (D)	

Index bit ———⌐   ⌐——— Indirect bit

Mode	Bit pattern $b_9 b_8 b_7 b_6 b_5 b_4 b_3 b_2 b_1 b_0$	Effective memory address
PC + relative	0 0 ◄——— D ———►	[PC] + D
PC − relative	0 1 ◄——— D ———►	[PC] − D
DB + relative	1 0 ◄——— D ———►	[DB] + D
Q + relative	1 1 0 ◄——— D ———►	[Q] − D
Q − relative	1 1 1 0 ◄— D ———►	[Q] − D
SP − relative	1 1 1 1 ◄— D ———►	[SP] − D

FIGURE 8.7
Memory Address instruction format in the HP3000 processor.

ADDM   Add a specified memory word to TOS and replace the TOS operand
              with the resultant sum.

MPYM   Multiply a specified memory word with TOS and replace the TOS
              operand with the least significant word of the product.

INCM   Increment a specified memory word.

These instructions specify the memory operand in the relative address mode, in which addresses are given relative to the contents of the PC, DB, Q, or SP registers. The 10-bit mode and displacement field indicate the mode and the magnitude of the displacement, as the figure shows. The displacement is not the same in all modes, because the displacement field varies from 6 to 8 bits. Index and indirect bits specify whether indexed or indirect addressing or both are to be performed. These are the only addressing modes that can be used to address operands in the data area of Figure 8.5.

The second class of instructions is the Move instructions, which reference either one or two memory operands. These instructions can move words or bytes from one memory location to another, compare two strings of bytes in the memory, or scan a byte string until a particular byte value is found. Memory addresses are again computed in the relative mode. The displacement is not given explicitly within the instruction, however, but is included as data in the stack. Moreover, addresses can only be specified relative to the program or data bases, that is, the contents of the PB or DB registers. A good example of this class of instructions is the basic MOVE instruction. It transfers k words from one memory location to another, where

- The first stack element (TOS) specifies k.
- The contents of the second stack element give the address of the first source memory location, relative to either PB or DB.
- The contents of the third stack element give the address of the first destination memory location, relative to DB.

This instruction can be represented within a 16-bit code space, because most of the addressing data and the length parameter are given in implicitly specified stack locations. These data must be loaded onto the stack before the instruction can be executed.

Next, we consider the Stack instructions, whose format is shown in Figure 8.8. This class of instructions is identified by four 0s in the high-order bit positions. The remaining 12 bits are available to specify particular instructions and are split into two 6-bit fields, each of which can be used to specify a distinct operation. The 6 bits allow as many as 64 distinct stack operations to be defined. This number is large enough to accommodate a variety of stack operations. An instruction specifying one stack operation uses 10 bits (the main OP code plus stack OP code A) and disregards the remaining

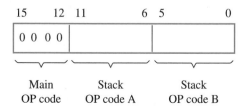

FIGURE 8.8
Format for Stack instructions in the HP3000 processor.

6 bits. When the remaining bits specify a second stack operation (using stack OP code B), that operation is performed after the first operation is completed. In this way, two stack operations can be packed within a single instruction. Such efficient utilization of the instruction code space is possible only because addressing data and operands are not included explicitly as part of an instruction.

Some examples of Stack instructions are

ADD   Add the contents of the top two words on the stack, delete them from the stack, and push the sum onto the stack.

CMP   Compare the contents of the top two words on the stack, set the condition codes accordingly, and delete both words from the stack.

DIV   Divide the integer in the second word of the stack by the integer in TOS. Replace the second word with the quotient and the word in TOS with the remainder.

DEL   Delete the top word of the stack.

Many instructions of this type are provided, although some are more complicated. A Divide Long instruction (DIVL), for example, divides a double-word integer in the second and third elements of the stack by the integer in the first element. Then these three words are deleted, and the remainder and quotient are pushed onto the stack to become the first and second elements, respectively. We use the term "instruction" somewhat loosely in this discussion of stack instructions. It would be more accurate to refer to Add and Divide operations, for example, since these two operations can be specified within a single instruction. However, it is more customary to speak in terms of instructions when describing such actions, and it is appropriate to describe the preceding technique as packing two instructions into one. Such packing is possible only when two consecutive stack operations are to be performed. In other cases, OP code B is left unused.

So far, we have emphasized only one advantage of compressing instructions, that of the low code-space requirements. Another advantage stems from the reduced number of memory accesses, because two instructions are effectively fetched as part of one 16-bit word. We must remember that, during execution of a stack instruction, operands in the stack must be accessed, and this requires memory accesses if the stack resides in the main memory.

To illustrate the role of the stack as temporary storage for intermediate results in arithmetic processing, we consider a simple example. Figure 8.9 shows how the arithmetic expression

$$w = \frac{(a + b)}{c/d + (e \times f)/(g + h)}$$

is evaluated. We assume that the values of the variables a, b, ..., h are not available at the top of the stack. They are stored in memory locations with addresses A, B, ..., H, and can be accessed with the addressing mechanism given in Figure 8.7. Furthermore, let all operands be integers whose ranges are such that only single-length products need to be considered. The figure shows 13 processing steps that must be performed. The required operations follow the order obtained by scanning the numerator and denominator of the expression from left to right. In our notation, the top element of the stack (TOS) is denoted as S. Thus, the operation $S \leftarrow [S] + [B]$ means that the contents of TOS and

Step	Operation performed	Machine instruction	
1	$S \leftarrow [A]$	LOAD	A
2	$S \leftarrow [S] + [B]$	ADDM	B
3	$S \leftarrow [C]$	LOAD	C
4	$S \leftarrow [D]$	LOAD	D
5	$S \leftarrow [S-1]/[S]$	DIV	} combined
		DEL	
6	$S \leftarrow [E]$	LOAD	E
7	$S \leftarrow [S] \times [F]$	MPYM	F
8	$S \leftarrow [G]$	LOAD	G
9	$S \leftarrow [S] + [H]$	ADDM	H
10	$S \leftarrow [S-1]/[S]$	DIV	} combined
		DEL	
11	$S \leftarrow [S-1] + [S]$	ADD	
12	$S \leftarrow [S-1]/[S]$	DIV	} combined
		DEL	
13	$W \leftarrow [S]$	STOR	W

(a) Operations to be performed and the necessary machine instructions

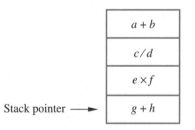

Stack pointer ⟶

(b) Temporary results stored in the stack after step 9

FIGURE 8.9
Stack usage in processing the expression $w = \dfrac{(a + b)}{c/d + (ef)/(g + h)}$

operand B are added, and the sum replaces the value in TOS. The operation $S \leftarrow [S-1]/[S]$ indicates that the contents of the second element in the stack are divided by the contents of TOS. The two operands are deleted from the stack and the quotient and remainder are pushed onto the stack.

The HP3000 machine instructions needed to perform the necessary computation are shown in the figure. Their function is described earlier in this section. Most steps can

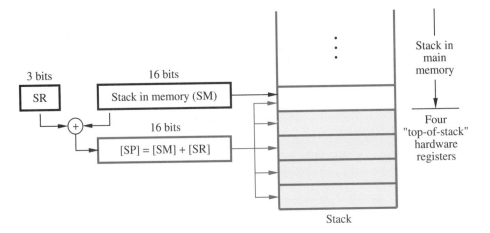

FIGURE 8.10
Top-of-stack structure in the HP3000 processor.

be implemented with a single instruction, except for the division operation. The DIV instruction replaces the dividend and the divisor with the quotient and the remainder, respectively. Because we are only interested in the quotient, we use the DEL instruction to delete the remainder from the stack. Whenever two consecutive Stack instructions are encountered, they can be combined into one 16-bit instruction, as we explain earlier. All intermediate results are stored on the stack. Figure 8.9*b* shows the top elements of the stack after step 9 is completed.

8.6.3 Hardware Registers in the Stack

Accessing main memory locations is one of the most critical time constraints in a computer. The time needed to read an operand from the main memory tends to be longer than the time required to transfer data or perform operations within the processor. This is the main reason for including general-purpose registers in the processor. In the case of stack computers, the temporary storage function of the general-purpose registers is provided through the stack mechanism. If the stack is implemented entirely in the main memory, the processor must make frequent memory accesses, because all temporary storage locations are part of the stack. The time spent on such accesses makes it unlikely that a stack machine of this type compares favorably with a computer that has a set of hardware registers for general-purpose use.

The possibility of implementing the entire stack with hardware registers could be expensive and somewhat inflexible. A compromise between an all-register or an all-memory implementation of the stack is possible, however, if most of the stack is located in the main memory and its top few elements are held in hardware registers in the processor. The time to access the stack is then reduced, because most accesses involve only the top few elements and therefore only require register transfers within the processor. In the HP3000 computer, four registers contain the top four elements of the stack.

Including hardware registers in the stack implies that the true top of the stack (TOS) is often one of the registers. This means that the SP does not necessarily point to a memory location. To keep track of where the top elements of the stack are at any given time, the SP function is implemented by two registers. A 16-bit stack in memory (SM) register contains the address of the highest memory location presently occupied by the stack, and a 3-bit register (SR) indicates whether zero, one, two, three, or four top elements of the stack are presently contained in the hardware registers. Thus, the value [SP] is

$$[SP] = [SM] + [SR]$$

This value is equal to the address in the main memory where the top element of the stack would be if all elements of the stack were in the main memory. This structure is illustrated in Figure 8.10.

The programmer does not have to be aware of the inclusion of hardware registers in the stack. For the programmer's purpose, only one pointer exists—the stack pointer, SP. Hardware stack registers reduce the number of memory references required and thus speed up the operation of the computer.

8.7
CONCLUDING REMARKS

High-performance processors, such as the PowerPC, Alpha, and P6, all employ on-chip caches for both instructions and data. They have multiple, independent, pipelined processing units and have the capability to issue more than one instruction per processor clock cycle to these units. These design features are fundamental to achieving high execution rates for programs, independent of whether the instruction sets and addressing modes follow the RISC or CISC design approaches. Optimizing compilers that translate high-level language programs into efficient machine language code are also critical to achieving high performance. Many factors must be considered when evaluating the performance of a computer, and standardized benchmark programs are commonly used for this purpose. References 7 through 11, in addition to references 1 through 6, which are cited in this chapter, contain interesting material on the architectural and hardware aspects of the processors discussed here.

PROBLEMS

8.1. Discuss the similarities and differences between the Motorola 680X0 family and the Intel 80X86 family of processors.

8.2. The 68030 microprocessor has a 256-byte instruction cache and a 256-byte data cache. Is this better than having a 512-byte instruction cache and no data cache? What are the advantages and disadvantages of these two alternatives?

8.3. What are the advantages and disadvantages of memory-mapped I/O compared to schemes in which a separate I/O space is defined? What I/O arrangements can be used with Motorola and Intel processors?

8.4. Section 8.2.4 explains that the 80386 processor can view the memory as being organized in four different ways, depending on how segmentation and paging are used. Give some examples of applications in which each of the four possibilities is beneficial.

8.5. Discuss the relative merits of addressing modes in the Motorola 680X0 and Intel 80X86 processors. In particular, discuss how the addressing modes in each processor facilitate relocation, implementation of a stack, accessing an operand list, and manipulating character strings.

8.6. Write either a 68000 or a PowerPC program to evaluate the arithmetic expression in Figure 8.9. How does your program compare to the one in the figure with respect to the number of machine instructions required?

8.7. Show how the expression

$$w = a\left[(bc + de) + \frac{fg}{hi}\right]$$

can be evaluated in an HP3000 computer.

8.8. In an HP3000 computer, Procedure$_i$ generates eight words of data, $DI_1, \ldots, DI_8$, which are stored in the stack. After these words are placed in the stack, but before the completion of Procedure$_i$, a new procedure, Procedure$_j$, is called. It generates 10 words of data, $DJ_1, \ldots, DJ_{10}$, which are also stored in the stack. Then another procedure, Procedure$_k$, is called, which places three words of data in the stack. Show the contents of the top words of the stack at this time.

8.9. Show how the expression

$$w = (a + b)(c + d) + (d \times e)$$

can best be evaluated by the HP3000, Motorola 68000, and PowerPC computers. The values of variables w, a, b, c, d, and e are stored in memory locations. The following assumptions are made: The addresses do not reference successive locations. Direct memory addressing in the DB+ relative mode is used in the HP3000. Absolute memory addressing is used in the 68000 and in the Power PC. All products are single length.

8.10. What is the largest number of stack locations occupied during execution of the program in Figure 8.9?

8.11. Repeat Problem 8.10 for the HP3000 programs in Problems 8.7 and 8.9.

8.12. The performance comparison between the PowerPC and Alpha processors described in Section 8.5.1 is for the 601 and 21064 implementations of those processors.

(a) Using the instruction issuing rates of 1.26 for the PowerPC and 1.74 for the Alpha calculated by Smith and Weiss[6] and using data in Table 8.1, calculate the execution time ratio T_{PC}/T_α if the example program with loop unrolling is run on the 620 and 21164 implementations. How does this ratio compare to what might have been expected from the SPECfp92 values in Table 8.1?

(b) The Smith and Weiss study[6] did not take into account the effect of cache misses. In general, execution times should decrease if cache misses decrease. Suppose that cache misses decrease in proportion to increases in the total size of on-chip cache storage. Using the data in Table 8.1, predict whether the T_{PC}/T_α ratio calculated in part (a) would increase or decrease if cache misses are taken into account. Assume that the T_{PC}/T_α ratio of 2.1 calculated by Smith and Weiss would not change if cache misses were taken into account.

8.13. As Section 8.5.1 discusses, instruction issuing rates improve because of loop unrolling. This is partly because the compiler has more opportunities to rearrange instruction order (while preserving correctness of computation) to reduce dependencies among the variables referenced in successive, or closely adjacent, instructions. Unroll the loop of Figure 8.4(*c*) four times and rearrange the instruction order to reduce dependencies, where possible. (See Chapter 7 for a discussion of dependencies.)

8.14. As Section 8.4.1 discusses, only 32-bit and 64-bit aligned loads and stores are directly handled in the datapath between the cache and the processor in Alpha processors. Sketch the combinational logic network that would be required in a 32-bit-wide datapath to permit loading any one of the four bytes of a 32-bit quantity into the low-order byte position at the destination side of the path.

REFERENCES

1. R.P. Colwell and R.L. Steck, "A 0.6-Micron BiCMOS Processor with Dynamic Execution," *Proceedings of the International Solid State Circuits Conference,* February 1995.
2. "A Tour of the P6 Microarchitecture," Intel Corporation, 1995.
3. T.A. Diep, C. Nelson, and J.P. Shen, "Performance Evaluation of the PowerPC 620 Microarchitecture," *Proceedings of the 22nd International Symposium on Computer Architecture,* June 1995, pp. 163–174.
4. L. Geppert, "Not Your Father's CPU," *IEEE Spectrum,* vol. 30, no. 12, December 1993, pp. 20–23.
5. L. Geppert, "Solid State," *IEEE Spectrum,* vol. 32, no. 1, January 1995, pp. 35–39.
6. J.E. Smith and S. Weiss, "PowerPC 601 and Alpha 21064: A Tale of Two RISCs," *IEEE Computer,* vol. 27, no. 6, June 1994, pp. 46–58.
7. Communications of the ACM, vol. 37, no. 6, special section of eight articles on the PowerPC, June 1994.
8. E. McLellan, "The Alpha AXP Architecture and 21064 Processor," *IEEE Micro,* vol. 13, no. 3, June 1993, pp. 36–47.
9. *IEEE Micro,* vol. 14, no. 5, five articles on the PowerPC, October 1994.
10. D. Alpert and D. Avnon, "Architecture of the Pentium Microprocessor," *IEEE Micro,* vol. 13, no. 3, June 1993, pp. 11–21.
11. D. Tabak, *Advanced Microprocessors,* 2d ed., McGraw-Hill, New York, 1995.

CHAPTER 9

Computer Peripherals

In previous chapters, we discussed hardware and software features of processors and main memories. We also discussed the means by which a computer communicates with external devices, including the hardware and software facilities that support program-controlled I/O, interrupts, and direct memory access. This chapter presents the characteristics of commonly used computer peripherals and gives an overview of the effects these devices have on system performance.

Peripheral refers to any external device connected to a computer. In this context, the computer consists only of the processor and the main memory. Computer peripherals can be divided into two categories according to function. The first category contains devices that perform input and output operations; this category includes keyboards, trackballs, mice, printers, and video displays. The second category contains devices intended primarily for secondary storage of data, with primary storage being provided by the main memory of the computer. These are mass storage devices, such as magnetic disks, optical disks, and magnetic tapes, which are capable of storing large amounts of data. These secondary storage devices are mainly used as an *on-line* extension to the main memory; however, they can also be used as *off-line* storage for programs and data files, such as data stored on tape reels or cartridges and disks that can be removed from the drive units when not in use.

9.1
I/O DEVICES

A wide range of devices can be used for I/O purposes. The most commonly used devices are video terminals and printers.

9.1.1 Video Terminals

A video terminal consists of a keyboard as the input device, usually complemented by a trackball or mouse device, and a video display as the output device. It is used for direct human interaction with the computer—entering commands, programs, and data, and receiving results of computations in an interactive environment. A video terminal can also be used to monitor and control the overall operation of the computer system. Most terminals include processors that provide these devices with considerable capability for sophisticated graphics and text manipulation.

First, we consider how such terminals can be connected to a computer system. Since terminals are used for interaction with human operators, very high rates of data transmission are not necessary. Therefore, a simple, inexpensive, serial link, suitable for transmission of characters one bit at a time, is normally used to connect terminals. Standard formats exist for such interconnections.

Serial transmission of data requires that both the transmitting and the receiving devices use the same timing information for interpretation of individual bits; for example, a clock signal may be used to indicate the occurrence of each data bit. There are two basic ways of realizing serial transmission. In a synchronous scheme, the receiver recovers the clock timing used by the transmitter by observing the positions of the transitions in the transmitted data signal. Alternatively, an asynchronous scheme can be used, in which the sender and the receiver generate their clock signals independently. In this case, it is necessary to ensure that the two clocks have similar frequencies and that the start of a sampling period for each multibit unit of data can be identified.

A common scheme known as *start-stop* is used for asynchronous serial transmission to or from terminals. This scheme is used for transmitting alphanumeric characters, usually encoded in 8-bit data units, as shown in Figure 9.1. The line connecting the transmitter and the receiver is normally in the 1 state when idle. Transmission of a character is preceded by a 0 bit, referred to as the Start bit, followed by 8 bits of data and 1 or 2 Stop bits (each with logic value 1). The Start bit alerts the receiver that data transmission is about to begin. Its leading edge is used to synchronize the receiver clock with that of the transmitter. The Stop bits at the end delineate consecutive characters in the case of continuous transmission. If only one character is being transmitted, the line

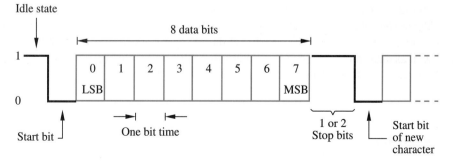

FIGURE 9.1
Asynchronous serial character transmission.

remains in the 1 state after the end of the Stop bits. During an input operation, it is the responsibility of the interface connecting the terminal to the I/O bus of the computer to remove the Start and Stop bits. The interface also assembles the 8 serially transmitted data bits in its input data register in preparation for later parallel transfer to the computer when an input instruction is executed. The reverse sequence takes place for an output operation. An example of this type of interface is given in Figure 4.29.

To ensure proper synchronization at the receiving end, the frequency of the local clock should be substantially higher than the transmission rate. Usually, the clock frequency is chosen to be 16 times the rate of transmission. This means that 16 clock pulses occur during each data bit interval. The receiver clock is used to increment a modulo-16 counter. This counter is reset to 0 when the leading edge of a Start bit is detected. When the count reaches 8, it indicates that the middle of the Start bit has been reached. The value of the Start bit is sampled to confirm that it is a valid Start bit, and the counter is again reset to 0. From this point onward, the incoming data signal is sampled whenever the count reaches 16, which should be close to the middle of each bit transmitted. Therefore, as long as the relative positioning of bits within a transmitted character is not in error by more than eight clock cycles, the receiver correctly interprets the bits of the encoded character.

A range of standard transmission rates is found in commercially available equipment. The most common rates are 1200, 2400, 4800, 9600, 14,400, 19,200, and 28,800 bits per second. A particular rate is chosen based on the characteristics of the transmission link, as well as on the nature of the application. The rate of transmission is often referred to, somewhat incorrectly, as the *baud* rate. A baud is actually a unit of signaling speed and refers to the number of times the state of a signal changes per second. For binary signals, the baud rate is the same as the bit rate. However, more complicated signaling schemes exist in which the baud rate is not the same as the bit rate. (See Problem 9.2 for an example.)

The transmitted characters are represented by the 7-bit ASCII code (see Appendix D) occupying bits 0 through 6 in Figure 9.1. The MSB, bit 7 of the transmitted byte, is usually set to 0. The ASCII character set consists of letters, numbers, and special symbols, such as $, +, and >. A number of nonprinting characters are also provided, for example, EOT (end of transmission) and CR (carriage return). These characters may be used by the programmer to request specific actions, particularly when transmitting or receiving messages to or from a remote computer.

The start-stop scheme defines the format used for transmission of character data. Several techniques can be used to establish the physical connection between the transmitter and the receiver. A popular standard that defines the electrical connections required is the RS-232-C, which we discuss in the next section.

9.1.2 Communication with a Remote Terminal

If a terminal is connected to a computer over standard telephone network facilities, establishing the connection and then transmitting the data bits involves several considerations. To transmit binary data over telephone lines, an encoding scheme is used

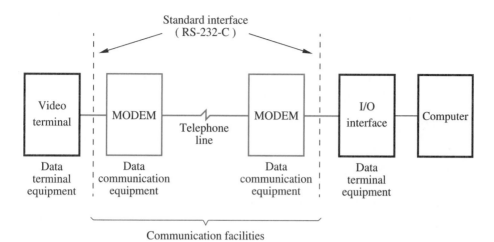

FIGURE 9.2
Remote connection of a video terminal over a telephone line.

to represent the data by signals that are within the transmission band of the line. This function is performed by a *modem* (MOdulator-DEModulator), which is installed at each end of the line. Figure 9.2 shows how a video terminal can be connected to a computer via a telephone line.

Synchronous and Asynchronous Transmission

The asynchronous start-stop format described in the previous section is most commonly used for communication with remote terminals, particularly over the dialed public network. However, for higher-speed devices, the start and stop bits of this transmission format waste the line bandwidth. Line *bandwidth* is the transmission capacity of the line in bits per second. Better use is made of the transmission link through synchronous transmission. In this case, data are transmitted in blocks consisting of several hundreds or thousands of bits each. The beginning and end of each block is marked by an appropriate coding technique, and data within a block are organized according to a known set of rules.

When long blocks of data bits are transmitted, the receiver must be able to synchronize with the successive bit positions in the incoming data stream. This is necessary because the receiver does not have direct access to the clock timing signal used by the transmitter in sending the data bits. Several clock recovery methods can be used to synchronize the receiver with the transmitter. Many modems require a significant start-up time. This time is needed to complete such operations as transmitting and detecting carrier frequencies and establishing synchronization. In some modems, the start-up time is also used to adapt the modem circuits to the current transmission properties of the link.

Modems with data rates up to 28,800 bits per second can be used on regular telephone system lines.

Full-Duplex and Half-Duplex Links

In general, a communication link may be one of the following three types:

Simplex allows transmission in one direction only.
Half duplex (HDX) allows transmission in either direction, but not at the same time.
Full duplex (FDX) allows simultaneous transmission in both directions.

The simplex configuration is useful only if the remote location contains an input or an output device, but not both. Hence, it is seldom used. The choice between half and full duplex is a trade-off between economy and speed of operation.

Using the most straightforward electrical circuit arrangement, a pair of wires enables transmission in one direction only, that is, simplex operation. To obtain a half-duplex link, switches at both ends must connect either the transmitter or the receiver, but not both, to the line. When transmission in one direction is completed, the switches are reversed to enable transmission in the reverse direction. Control of the position of the switches is a part of the function of the devices at each end of the line.

Full-duplex operation can be achieved on a four-wire link that has two wires dedicated to each direction of transmission. Full-duplex operation can also be achieved on a two-wire link by using two nonoverlapping frequency bands, creating two independent transmission channels, one for each direction of transmission. Alternatively, full-duplex operation can be achieved in a common frequency band using a device called a *hybrid* at each end of the line. Providing full-duplex operation on a two-wire link is important because dialed telephone connections use lines of this type.

In the case of synchronous, half-duplex operation, a time delay occurs whenever the direction of transmission is reversed, because the transmitting modem may have to transmit an initializing sequence of signals to allow the receiving end to adapt to the conditions of the channel. The amount of delay encountered depends on the modem and the transmission facilities, and may be anywhere from a few milliseconds to over a hundred milliseconds.

The above discussion relates directly to the characteristics of the transmission link and the modems. Other important factors that influence the choice between half- and full-duplex operation are the nature of the data traffic and the way the system reacts to errors during transmission. We discuss only the first of these factors here.

Many computer applications require the computer to receive input data, perform some processing, and then return output data. This is half-duplex operation. A half-duplex link not only satisfies the requirements for such an application, but also enables data transmission to take place at the maximum possible speed. If the messages exchanged between the two ends are short and frequent, however, the delay encountered in reversing the direction of transmission becomes significant. For that reason alone, many such applications use full-duplex transmission facilities, although actual data transmission never takes place in both directions at the same time.

In some situations, simultaneous transmission in both directions can be used to considerable advantage. Let us again consider the system in Figure 9.2, with the remote terminal being a video terminal. Each character entered at the keyboard should be echoed back to be displayed on the screen. This may be done locally, by the control circuitry of the terminal, or remotely, by the computer or its peripherals. The use of remote echo provides an automatic checking capability to ensure that no errors have been introduced during transmission. If a half-duplex link is used in such a case, transmission of the next character must be delayed until the first character has been echoed back. No such restriction is necessary with full-duplex operation. Another example is high-speed computer communication networks. Messages traveling in opposite directions on any given link often bear no relation to each other; hence, they can be transmitted simultaneously.

Standard Communications Interface

To allow interconnection of equipment made by different manufacturers, it is useful to develop standards that define how these devices can be interconnected. Such standards should define both the physical and functional characteristics of the interface. A standard interface refers to the dividing line, or the collection of points at which two devices are connected together. One such standard that has gained wide acceptance is the EIA (Electronics Industry Association) Standard RS-232-C. Outside North America, this is known as CCITT (Comité Consultatif International Télégraphique et Téléphonique) Recommendation V24. This standard completely specifies the interface between data communication devices, such as modems, and data terminal equipment, such as computers and video terminals. The RS-232-C interface consists of 25 connection points, which are described in Table 9.1.

Let us discuss a simple but common example. Consider the link in Figure 9.2, and assume the remote terminal is a video terminal and the connection is made over the dialed telephone network. The modem on the computer side, modem A, can detect the ringing signal on the telephone line and go on- and off-hook under computer control. A similar modem, called B, is used on the video terminal side.

We assume a simple signaling scheme called *frequency-shift keying* (FSK). In this scheme, different frequencies are used to provide a full-duplex connection. One channel uses the frequencies 1275 and 1075 Hz, and the other uses frequencies 2225 and 2025 Hz to represent logic levels 1 and 0, respectively.

Figure 9.3 gives the sequence of logic signals needed to establish a connection, transmit data, and terminate the connection. The steps involved in this process are described briefly as follows:

1. When the computer is ready to accept a call, it sets the data-terminal-ready signal (CD) to 1.
2. Modem A monitors the telephone line, and when it detects the ringing current that indicates an incoming call, it signals the computer by setting the ringing indicator (CE) to 1. If CD = 1 at the time the ringing current is detected, the modem automatically answers the call by going off-hook. It then sets the modem-ready signal (CC) to 1.
3. The computer instructs modem A to start transmitting the frequency representing a 1 (2225 Hz) by setting request-to-send (CA) to 1. When this is accomplished, modem A responds by setting clear-to-send (CB) to 1. The detection of this frequency at modem B causes it to set the received-line-signal detector (CF) to 1.
4. The terminal sets CA to 1, causing transmission of the 1275-Hz signal. Modem B then sets CB and CC to 1. When modem A detects the 1275-Hz frequency, it sets CF to 1.

5. A full-duplex link is now established between the computer and the remote terminal. The computer can transfer data to and from the remote terminal in the same way it transmits to and from local terminals. Interface pins BA (transmitted data) and BB (received data) are used for this purpose; all other signals in the interface remain unchanged.
6. When the user signs off, the computer sets the request-to-send and data-terminal-ready signals (CA and CD) to 0, causing modem A to drop the 2225-Hz signal and disconnect from the line. Signals CB, CF, and CC are set to 0 by modem A. When modem B senses the disappearance of the signal on the line, it sets the received-line-signal detector (CF) to 0.
7. Modem B responds by removing its 1275-Hz signal from the line and setting CB and CC to 0. The user terminates the connection by going on-hook.
8. The computer sets data-terminal-ready (CD) to 1 in preparation for a new call.

TABLE 9.1
Summary of the EIA Standard RS-232-C signals
(CCITT Recommendation V24)

Name			
EIA	**CCITT**	**Pin* no.**	**Function**
AA	101	1	Protective ground
AB	102	7	Signal ground-common return
BA	103	2	Transmitted data
BB	104	3	Received data
CA	105	4	Request to send
CB	106	5	Clear to send
CC	107	6	Data set ready
CD	108.2	20	Data terminal ready
CE	125	22	Ring indicator
CF	109	8	Received line signal detector
CG	110	21	Signal quality detector
CH	111	23§	Data signal rate selector (from DTE† to DCE‡)
CI	112	23§	Data signal rate selector (from DCE‡ to DTE†)
DA	113	24	Transmitter signal element timing (DTE†)
DB	114	15	Transmitter signal element timing (DCE‡)
DD	115	17	Receiver signal element timing (DCE‡)
SBA	118	14	Secondary transmitted data
SBB	119	16	Secondary received data
SCA	120	19	Secondary request to send
SCB	121	13	Secondary clear to send
SCF	122	12	Secondary received line signal detector

* Pins 9 and 10 are used for testing purposes and pins 11, 18, and 25 are spare.

† Data terminal equipment.

‡ Data communication equipment.

§The name of the signal on this pin depends on the signal's direction.

Step no.	Terminal	Interface signals	Modem B	Modem A	Interface signals	Computer
1				Enable automatic answering	CD	← 1
2	Dialed digits →			1 → Goes off hook 1 →	CE CC	
3		CF	← 1	← 2225 Hz 1 →	CA CB	← 1
4	1 →	CA CB CC	1275 Hz → ← 1 ← 1	1 →	CF	
5	Output data ← Input data →	BB BA	← Data 1275/1075 Hz →	← 2225/2025 Hz Data →	BA BB	← Output data → Input data
6		CF	← 0	Drop 2225 Hz and disconnect 0 → 0 → 0 →	CA CD CF CC CB	← 0 ← 0
7	(0 →)	CA CB CC	Drop 1275 ← 0 ← 0			
8	Terminate connection				CD	← 1

FIGURE 9.3
RS-232-C standard signaling sequence.

This description pertains specifically to a transmission link involving a simple modem. The FSK scheme is suitable only for low data rates; it has been used for rates up to 1200 bits per second. Modern modems use a variety of encoding techniques to enable higher data rates. A scheme known as *quadrature amplitude modulation* (QAM) is commonly used for data transmission rates of up to 28,800 bits per second. QAM is based on a combination of amplitude and phase modulation of the carrier signal.[1]

The initial connection procedure used with modems involves an exchange of messages in which the two sides agree on such parameters as the encoding scheme to be used, the speed of transmission, the size of data blocks, and so on. The RS-232-C interface can provide a serial connection between any two digital devices. Of course, the interpretation of individual signals such as CA and CD depends on the functional capabilities of the devices involved. When these signals are not needed, they are simply ignored by both devices. In most applications, no more than nine of the signals in Table 9.1 are used.

9.1.3 Video Displays

Video displays are used whenever visual representation of computer output is needed but a hard copy of this output is not required. Although a video display is an output device, it can perform limited input functions when used in conjunction with a mouse, joystick, or trackball. We present a brief description of the video display unit to give the reader an appreciation of the hardware involved. Detailed technological and engineering aspects of the design of the video display, however, are beyond the scope of this book.

Let us start by describing how a picture is formed. A focused beam of electrons strikes a fluorescent screen, causing emission of light that is seen as a bright spot against a dark background. The dot thus formed disappears when the beam is turned off or moved to another spot. Thus, in general, three independent variables need to be specified at all times: the position of the beam can be specified in terms of its X and Y coordinates, and the intensity of the beam, usually referred to as the Z-axis control, provides the *gray scale,* that is, the brightness. In color displays, additional information is needed to specify the color. The size of the spot formed on the screen by the electron beam determines the total number of distinct point positions that can be used on the screen. This is usually in the range of 300 to 1500 points along each of the X and Y coordinates. A large amount of information is required to define the status of all these points. Usually, a considerable amount of hardware is provided in the display to convert data from the format generated by the computer to that required to drive the display screen. Both alphanumeric data, in a variety of fonts, and graphical shapes can be displayed.

Many applications require graphical output. Computer-aided design applications provide one important example. The computer may be required to present to the designer a drawing representing the layout of an integrated circuit, a circuit diagram, or the outline of a structural member to be analyzed or modified. Real-time control applications provide another example of graphical output. From the viewpoint of a human user, it is convenient to represent, say, the state of the switchgear in a power-generating station or of the valves in a chemical plant by familiar graphical symbols. In this way, users can assess the overall state of the system much more quickly than if they have to interpret alphanumeric descriptions. Graphics are also used in applications such as video games and computer animation.

Both alphanumeric text and graphical pictures can be constructed using a raster scan technique. A *raster scan* is the sweeping of the electron beam successively across each row from left to right, until all rows have been scanned from the top to the bottom of the screen. A *bit map*, consisting of one bit for each dot position on the screen, represents the picture to be displayed. Hence, a screen with a 1000×1000 dot matrix requires a 1-Mbit *display buffer* memory. To refresh the display at the rate of 60 times per second, the data rate is 60 megabits per second (Mbps). High-quality terminals provide many intensity levels for each display point, thus requiring several bits to provide the gray scale information for each point. The display points are called *pixels*. Color displays also require several bits per pixel to provide color information. This leads to display buffers that require many millions of bits to represent the full screen output image. Modern systems have the capability to overlap multiple distinct screen images, thus requiring several separate display buffers.

9.1.4 Flat-Panel Displays

Although cathode-ray tube technology has dominated display applications, flat-panel displays are thinner and lighter in weight. They provide better linearity and, in some cases, even higher resolution. Several types of flat-panel displays have been developed, including liquid crystal panels, plasma panels, and electroluminescent panels.

Liquid crystal panels are constructed by sandwiching a thin layer of liquid crystal— a liquid that exhibits crystalline properties—between two electrically conducting plates. The top plate has transparent electrodes deposited on it, and the back plate is a mirror. By applying proper electrical signals across the plates, various segments of the liquid crystal can be activated, causing changes in their light-diffusing or polarizing properties. These segments then either transmit or block the light. An image is produced by passing light through selected segments of the liquid crystal and then reflecting it back from the mirror to the viewer. Liquid crystal displays have found extensive use in watches, calculators, notebook computers, and many other devices where small-sized displays are needed.

Plasma panels consist of two glass plates separated by a thin gap filled with a gas such as neon. Each plate has several parallel electrodes running across it. The electrodes on the two plates run at right angles to each other. A voltage pulse applied between two electrodes, one on each plate, causes a small segment of gas at the intersection of the two electrodes to glow. The glow of gas segments is maintained by a lower voltage that is continuously applied to all electrodes. A similar pulsing arrangement can be used to selectively turn points off. Plasma displays can provide high resolution but are rather expensive. They are found in applications where display quality is important and the bulky size of a cathode-ray tube is undesirable.

Electroluminescent panels use a thin layer of phosphor between two electrically conducting panels. The image is created by applying electrical signals to the plates, making the phosphor glow.

The viability of flat-panel displays for different applications is closely linked to developments in the competing cathode-ray tube display technology, which continues to provide a good combination of price and performance and permits easy implementation of color displays.

9.1.5 Graphic Input Devices

Convenient and flexible means are needed for creating and changing display images. In most video terminals, a keyboard is the basic input device. It is used to enter both control commands and characters to be displayed. By controlling the position of the cursor, a user can determine the position on the screen where the next input character will be displayed. This can be done with key commands such as Space, Backspace, Carriage Return, Line Feed, Tab, and four-direction cursor control.

In addition to basic cursor control from a keyboard, we often want a more powerful means of specifying locations on the screen. Simple input devices that can be used for this purpose include the mouse, trackball, and joystick.

The mouse and trackball operate on similar principles. The small, movable device called a *mouse* has a ball fixed to its bottom side. The device is moved over a flat surface, causing the ball to rotate. The rotation of the ball is sensed and translated into the desired displacement of the cursor position on the screen, relative to a starting point. The absolute position of the mouse on the surface is not important; it is the relative movement away from the initial mouse position that determines cursor movement on the screen. Pushbuttons on the top side of the mouse are clicked to initiate input actions when the cursor has reached the desired position on the screen.

The *trackball* is a ball fixed in a shallow well on the keyboard. The user rotates the ball to indicate the desired relative movement of the cursor on the screen.

The *joystick* is a short, pivoted stick that can be moved by hand to define an absolute point, such as a cursor position, in two dimensions. The position of the stick, hence, the coordinates of that point, can be sensed by a suitable linear or angular position transducer, such as the potentiometer arrangement shown in Figure 9.4. The voltage outputs of the X and Y potentiometers are fed to two analog-to-digital (A/D) converters. The outputs of the A/D converters determine the position of the joystick and, thus, the desired position of the cursor.

9.1.6 Printers

Printers are used to produce hard copy of output data or text. They are usually classified as either impact or nonimpact type, depending on the nature of the printing mechanism used. Impact printers use mechanical printing mechanisms, and nonimpact printers rely on optical, ink-jet, or electrostatic techniques. Mechanical printers can be only as fast as their mechanical parts allow, with speeds upwards of 1000 lines per minute being attainable. Considerably higher speeds can be achieved with nonimpact printers, where printing several thousand lines per minute is possible in large, high-speed printers.

We consider two representative examples of mechanical printers—drum and chain printers. If a line contains n characters (132 characters is common), then the drum in

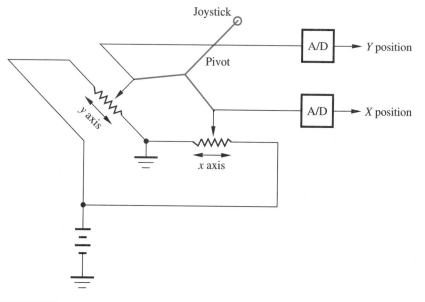

FIGURE 9.4
Joystick, using potentiometers as position transducers.

a drum line printer is divided into n tracks, each track consisting of a complete set of characters. A set of n print hammers, one per track, presses the printing paper and the ink ribbon against the characters on the drum. The line to be printed is held in a buffer, which is loaded by the output circuits of the computer. As the drum rotates, the characters on the drum are compared with those in the buffer. When a desired character passes in front of the hammer, the hammer is activated to print the character. Thus, a complete line is printed within one revolution of the drum.

Chain printers employ a belt that contains a set of characters. As the belt rotates, the characters move along the line past the print hammers. Each hammer is activated when the character to be printed at that position passes in front of it. A complete line is printed within one revolution of the belt. Faster operation can be achieved if the belt contains duplicate copies of the character set. For example, if five full sets of characters are used, a complete line can be printed in one-fifth of one revolution of the belt.

Nonimpact printers use fewer mechanical parts and can be operated at higher speeds. Several different techniques are used in printers of this type. Photocopying technology is used in *laser* printers. A drum coated with positively charged photoconductive material is scanned by a laser beam. The positive charges that are illuminated by the beam are dissipated. Then a negatively charged toner powder is spread over the drum. It adheres to the positive charges, thus creating a page image that is then transferred to the paper. As the last step, the drum is cleaned of any excess toner material to prepare it for printing the next page.

Other types of nonimpact printers use ink jets. In an ink-jet printer, electrically charged droplets of ink are fired from a nozzle. They are deflected by an electric field to trace out the desired character patterns on the paper they strike. Several nozzles with different color inks can be used to generate color output.

Most printers form characters and graphic images in the same way that images are formed on a video screen. Characters are formed by printing dots in matrices. This arrangement can easily accommodate a variety of fonts and can also be used for printing graphical images. Development of printers has been characterized by intense activity. A variety of techniques have been developed and successfully applied.

9.2
ON-LINE STORAGE

Most computer systems require a storage space much larger than the main memory that can be provided economically. The required extra storage space is provided by magnetic disks and tapes.

9.2.1 Magnetic-Disk Systems

As the name implies, the storage medium in a magnetic-disk system consists of one or more disks stacked one on top of another. A thin magnetic film is deposited on each disk, usually on both sides. The disks are mounted on a rotary drive so that the magnetized surfaces move in close proximity to Read/Write heads, as shown in Figure 9.5a. The disks rotate at a uniform speed. Each head consists of a magnetic yoke and a magnetizing coil, as in Figure 9.5b.

Digital information can be stored on the magnetic film by applying current pulses of suitable polarity to the magnetizing coil. This causes the magnetization of the film in the area immediately underneath the head to switch to a direction parallel to the applied field. The same head can be used for reading the stored information. In this case, changes in the magnetic field in the vicinity of the head caused by the movement of the film relative to the yoke induce a voltage in the coil, which now serves as a sense coil. The polarity of this voltage is monitored by the control circuitry to determine the state of magnetization of the film. Only changes in the magnetic field under the head can be sensed during the Read operation. Therefore, if the binary states 0 and 1 are represented by two opposite states of magnetization, a voltage is induced in the head only at 0-to-1 and at 1-to-0 transitions in the bit stream. A long string of 0s or 1s causes an induced voltage only at the beginning and end of the string. To determine the number of consecutive 0s or 1s stored, a clock must provide information for synchronization. The clock can be recorded on a separate track, where a change in magnetization is forced for each bit period. A simple memory circuit that records the direction of the last change in magnetization on the data track, plus the clock signal, allow correct reading of the stored data.

Several different techniques have been developed for encoding data on magnetic disks. As an alternative to storing the clock on a separate track, the clocking information can be combined with the data. One common scheme, depicted in Figure 9.5c, is known as *phase encoding* or *Manchester encoding*. In this scheme, changes in magnetization occur for each data bit, as shown in the figure. Note that a change in magnetization is guaranteed at the midpoint of each bit period, thus providing the clocking information. With this type of encoding, it is not necessary to provide a separate track for clocking,

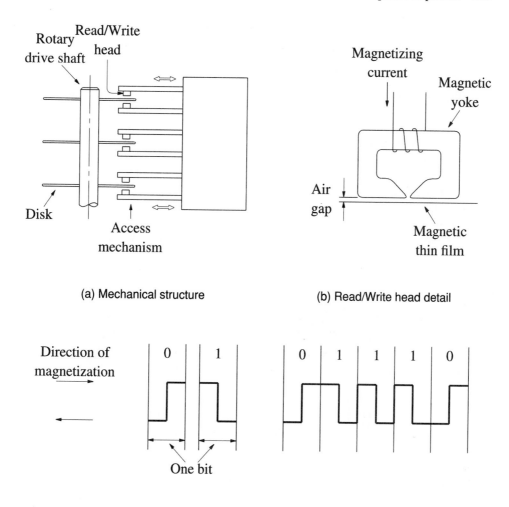

(a) Mechanical structure

(b) Read/Write head detail

(c) Bit representation by phase encoding

FIGURE 9.5
Magnetic disk principles.

because the clock is easily extracted from the encoded data. The drawback of Manchester encoding is its poor bit-storage density. The space required to represent each bit must be large enough to accommodate two changes in magnetization. Other, more compact codes have been developed. These require more complex control circuitry but provide better storage density.

Read/Write heads must be maintained at a very small distance from the moving disk surfaces in order to achieve high bit densities and reliable Read/Write operations. When the disks are moving at their steady rate, air pressure develops between the disk surface and the head and forces the head away from the surface. This force can be counteracted by a spring-loaded mounting arrangement for the head that allows it to be pressed toward the surface. The flexible spring connection between the head and its arm mounting permits the head to fly at the desired distance away from the surface in spite of any small variations in the flatness of the surface.

Organization and Accessing of Data on a Disk

The organization of data on a disk is illustrated in Figure 9.6a. Each surface is divided into concentric *tracks*, and each track is divided into *sectors*. The set of corresponding tracks on all surfaces of a stack of disks forms a logical *cylinder*. Data bits are stored serially on each track. Data on disks are addressed by specifying the surface number, the track number, and the sector number. In most disk systems, Read and Write operations always start at sector boundaries. If the number of words to be written is smaller than that required to fill a sector, the disk controller repeats the last bit of data for the remainder of the sector.

The Read/Write heads of a disk system are either fixed or movable. In the former case, a separate head is provided for each track of each surface. In the latter case, there

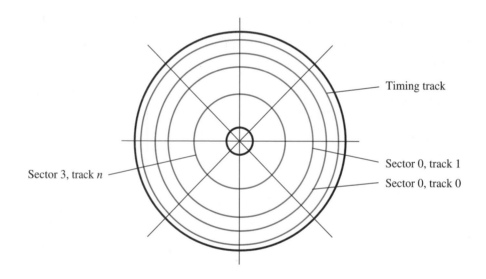

(a) Organization of one surface of a disk

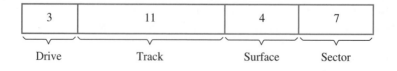

(b) Format of a disk address word

FIGURE 9.6
Addressing of data on magnetic disks.

is one head per surface. All heads are mounted on a comb-like arm that can move radially across the stack of disks to provide access to individual tracks, as shown in Figure 9.5a. The moving-head system is the most common arrangement. Usually, only one head is actively reading or writing data at any time. The fixed-head organization results in faster access to a sector location, because in the moving-head system, the arm holding the Read/Write heads must first be positioned to the correct track. More electronic circuitry is involved in the one-head-per-track scheme than in the movable-head disk system. On the other hand, more mechanical complexity is required in the moving-arm organization.

It is common to have one or more permanently written tracks to provide timing pulses. The pulses, in conjunction with counters in the disk control circuits, can be used to determine sector and track origin positions on the data tracks. Figure 9.6a indicates a timing track at the outer edge of the surface. This is a feasible arrangement in fixed-head systems. The heads that operate on the timing tracks provide positional addressing information for the remainder of the tracks. In multiple-surface moving-head systems, one of the surfaces may be dedicated to providing timing-pulse information that can be used in addressing data on the remainder of the surfaces. In addition to these methods of deriving positional information from timing tracks, there are various ways in which additional timing information can be included in the data-encoding scheme, as we have described.

Let us consider an example of how a disk might be organized, using specific values for the various parameters. We use values typical of the high-capacity, high-data-rate disks available today. Suppose that the disk system has 16 data recording surfaces with 2048 tracks per surface. Tracks are divided into 128 sectors, and each sector of a track contains 512 bytes of data, recorded bit-serially. The total capacity of the disk is $16 \times 2048 \times 128 \times 512 \approx 2 \times 10^9 = 2$ gigabytes. Assume that the diameter of the inner cylinder is 3 inches and that of the outer cylinder is 5 inches. If the bit capacity of all tracks is the same, the maximum bit density occurs along the inner tracks, where it is $(128 \times 512 \times 8)/3\pi \approx 56{,}000$ bits/in. Since there are 2048 tracks per surface and the tracks are spread over one inch of radial distance, the track density is 2048 tracks per inch.

The data transfer rate for this disk is calculated as follows. Assuming a rotational speed of 5400 revolutions per minute, a complete track can be read or written in $60/5400 \approx 0.011$ seconds. This corresponds to a byte transfer rate of $(128 \times 512)/0.011 \approx 6$ MB/s.

For a moving-head system, there are two components involved in the time delay between receiving an address and the beginning of the actual data transfer. The first, called the *seek time*, is the time required to move the Read/Write head to the proper track. This depends on the initial position of the head relative to the track specified in the address. Average values are in the 10-ms range. The second component is the *rotational delay*, also called *latency time*. This is the amount of time that elapses after the head is positioned over the correct track until the starting position of the addressed sector passes under the Read/Write head. On average, this is the time for half a rotation of the disk, that is, $0.5(\frac{60}{5400}) = 5.6$ ms in the preceding example. The sum of these two delays is usually called the disk *access time*. Note that if only a few sectors of data are moved in a single operation, the access time is at least an order of magnitude longer than the actual data transfer period.

Examples

The parameters just used for the physical size, data-storage capacity, access time, and byte-transfer rate of a disk are typical for a 5.25-inch diameter disk with multiple surfaces. A specific commercial example is a Seagate Technology, Inc. 5.25-inch disk product with the following parameters.[2] There are 21 surfaces for data storage, and the platters rotate at 5400 rpm. Average seek time is 11 ms and the average latency, that is, the time for a half-rotation, is 5.6 ms. There are 2627 tracks per surface, and 99 sectors per track, with 512 bytes per sector. Total storage capacity is 2.8 gigabytes, and the transfer rate is 4.6 MB/s. Smaller disks with 3.5-inch diameter platters are also available. These have a higher rotational speed of 7200 rpm, which provides faster access times. Capacities of these disks are in the range of 1 to 2 gigabytes.

Disk operations

Communication between a disk and the main memory is done through DMA, as described in Chapter 4. Here, we concentrate on the logical requirements rather than the method of implementation. The following information must be exchanged between the processor and the disk controller in order to specify a transfer:

Main memory address—The address of the first main memory location of the block of words involved in the transfer.

Disk address—The location of the sector containing the beginning of the desired block of words.

Word count—The number of words in the block to be transferred.

We assume, for convenience, that these three quantities are placed in registers in the disk controller.

The disk address format for our disk example is shown in Figure 9.6*b*. The lengths of the track, surface, and sector fields are consistent with the parameters of 2048 tracks, 16 surfaces, and 128 sectors per track. The fourth field, named the drive field, specifies which of eight disk drives is involved. This applies when several disk drives are controlled by one controller.

Next, we consider an interesting characteristic of the disk address word format of Figure 9.6*b*. The word count may correspond to fewer or more bytes than are contained in a sector. Let us consider a data block that is longer than 128 sectors. The disk address register is incremented as successive sectors are read or written. When the sector count goes from 127 to 0, the surface count increases by 1. Thus, long data blocks are laid out on cylinder surfaces as opposed to being laid out on successive tracks of a single disk surface. This is efficient for moving-head systems, because successive 128-sector areas of data storage on the disk can be accessed by electrically switching from one Read/Write head to the next rather than by mechanically moving the arm from track to track. The track-to-track move is required only at cylinder-to-cylinder boundaries.

The disk controller must be able to accept commands to initiate various functions in the disk drives as well as handle the addressing and block-length information. The major functions of the disk controller are as follows:

Seek—Selects the desired track. In a moving-head system, the disk drive specified in the disk address register moves the Read/Write head arm from its current position to the track specified; in a fixed-head system, the appropriate Read/Write head is selected electronically.

Read—Initiates a Read operation, starting at the address specified in the disk address register. Data read serially from the disk are assembled into words and transferred to the main memory, starting at the location specified in the memory address register in the DMA controller. The number of words transferred to memory is determined by the word count register. The word count is decremented after each word transfer, and the memory address is incremented. The disk address is incremented at the end of each sector.

Write—Transfers data from the main memory to the disk. Data transfers are controlled by a method similar to that described for the Read command.

Write Check—Can be used after a Write operation to ensure that no errors have been introduced during the transfer. The controller starts a Read operation on the disk and compares the contents of the addressed sector to the data read from the corresponding locations in the main memory. If a mismatch is detected, an error message is returned to the processor.

To synchronize the issuing of these commands from the processor, the disk system can be arranged to raise an interrupt at the completion of a Seek operation in a moving-head disk. Interrupts are also normally used to signal the completion of a Read, Write, or Write Check operation. In addition, many disk systems possess a lookahead register, which contains the address of the sector currently passing underneath the Read/Write head. This enables the operating system to check the disk position in order to efficiently schedule a series of input or output operations.

Winchester Disks

In most modern disk units, the disks and the Read/Write heads are placed in a sealed, air-filtered enclosure. This approach is known as *Winchester technology*. In such units, the Read/Write heads can operate closer to the magnetized track surfaces because dust particles, which are a problem in unsealed assemblies, are absent. The closer the heads are to a track surface, the more densely the data can be packed along the track, and the closer the tracks can be to each other. Thus, Winchester disks have a larger capacity for a given physical size compared to unsealed units. Another advantage of Winchester technology is that data integrity tends to be greater in sealed units where the storage medium is not exposed to contaminating elements.

Floppy Disks

The devices previously discussed are known as hard or rigid disk units. *Floppy disks* are smaller, simpler, and cheaper disk units that consist of a flexible, removable, plastic *diskette* coated with magnetic material. The diskette is enclosed in a plastic jacket, which has an opening where the Read/Write head makes contact with the diskette. A hole in the center of the diskette allows a spindle mechanism in the disk drive to position and rotate the diskette.

Information is recorded on floppy disks by combining the clock and data information along each track. One of the simplest schemes used in the first floppy disks is essentially the same as phase or Manchester encoding, mentioned earlier. Disks encoded in this way are said to have *single density*. A more complicated variant of this scheme, called *double density*, is most often used in current standard floppy disks. It increases the storage density by a factor of 2 but also requires more complex circuits in the disk controller.

The main attraction of floppy disks is their low cost and shipping convenience. However, they have much smaller storage capacities and longer access times than hard disks. Current standard floppy disks are 3.25 inches in diameter and store 1.44 or 2 megabytes of data.

Disk Arrays

The magnetic disk systems just described provide a single, serial bit-stream during data transfer. Recent disk-system developments have been directed at decreasing access time and increasing bandwidth during data flow through the use of multiple disks operating in parallel. The concept is simple enough, but the technological problems that had to be solved to provide reliable high performance were not simple. The name RAID (Redundant Arrays of Inexpensive Disks) was coined in the late 1980s by the first researchers to draw attention to this storage architecture.[2] Since it makes use of large numbers of currently available inexpensive disks, the RAID concept has moved quickly into commercial use, with several companies now marketing disk arrays.

In a RAID system, a single large file is stored in several separate disk units by breaking the file up into a number of smaller pieces and storing these pieces on different disks. This is called *data striping*. When the file is accessed for a read, all disks can deliver their data in parallel. The total transfer time of the file is equal to the transfer time that would be required in a single-disk system divided by the number of disks used in the array. However, access time, that is, the seek and rotational delay needed to locate the beginning of the data on each disk, is not reduced. In fact, since each disk operates independently of the others, access times vary, and buffering of the accessed pieces of data is needed so that the complete file can be reassembled and sent to the requesting processor as a single entity. This is the simplest possible disk array operation, in which only data-flow-time performance is improved. Many other organizational and reliability characteristics have been incorporated into the design of RAID systems. We mention a few of them here.

Data striping provides an opportunity to use redundancy as a means for increasing the reliability of the storage system. The data replication and checking in such a system can be made completely transparent to the computer that uses the system. The most basic form of redundancy that can be considered is to duplicate all pieces of the distributed, or striped, file on additional disk units, thus doubling the total number of disks used. For a read access, the disk with the shortest access time for each piece of the file is used. On average, this arrangement reduces the access time for Read operations significantly, at the cost of doubling the number of disks required. For Write operations, since both copies of each piece must be updated, the average access is actually longer. This use of redundancy in disk arrays is expensive relative to the performance gain achieved. There is, however, an obvious reliability enhancement resulting from the duplication of data; if a disk fails, the other copy of various file pieces that it stores can be used.

Enhanced reliability is probably the most important reason for using redundancy in RAID systems. Because of the use of data striping across all disks of the system, a single error on any disk invalidates the access in progress unless some form of redundancy is used so that errors can be detected and corrected. Other approaches to error detection and correction require fewer redundant disks than the doubling just discussed, but these methods are beyond the scope of our presentation.

We have given a brief introduction to the essential concepts of RAID systems. Performance improvement and reliability through the use of redundancy are the attractive features of these parallel disk arrays. However, data striping is not the only organization that provides these features. Computer manufacturers have provided reliability and performance in secondary storage systems consisting of multiple disk units in a variety of ways over the years. What is novel and significant about RAID systems is their cost effectiveness. They achieve performance and reliability through the use of relatively inexpensive commodity disk products.

9.2.2 Magnetic-Tape Systems

Magnetic tapes are particularly suited for off-line storage of large amounts of data and are also used extensively for shipping information when telecommunication facilities are either not available or inappropriate. Magnetic-tape recording uses the same principle as in magnetic-disk recording. The main difference is that the magnetic film is deposited on a very thin $\frac{1}{2}$-inch- or $\frac{1}{4}$-inch-wide plastic tape. Seven or 9 bits (corresponding to one character) are recorded in parallel across the width of the tape, perpendicular to the direction of motion. A separate Read/Write head is provided for each bit position on the tape, so that all bits of a character can be read or written in parallel. One of the character bits is used as a parity bit.

Data on the tape are organized in the form of *records* separated by gaps, as shown in Figure 9.7. Tape motion is stopped only when a record gap is underneath the Read/Write heads. The record gaps are long enough to allow the tape to attain its normal speed before the beginning of the next record is reached. If a coding scheme such as that in Figure 9.5c is used for recording data on the tape, record gaps are identified as areas where there is no change in magnetization. This allows record gaps to be detected independently of the recorded data. To help users organize large amounts of data, a group of related records is called a file. The beginning of a file is identified by a *file mark*, as shown in Figure 9.7. The file mark is a special single- or multiple-character record, usually preceded by a gap longer than the interrecord gap. The first record following a

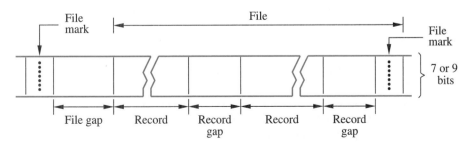

FIGURE 9.7
Organization of data on magnetic tape.

file mark can be used as a *header* or *identifier* for this file. This allows the user to search a tape containing a large number of files for a particular file.

The controller of a magnetic tape drive enables the execution of a number of control commands in addition to read and write commands. Control commands include the following operations:

- Rewind tape
- Rewind and unload tape
- Erase tape
- Write tape mark
- Forward space one record
- Backspace one record
- Forward space one file
- Backspace one file

The tape mark referred to in the operation Write-tape-mark is similar to a file mark except that it is used for identifying the beginning of the tape. The end of the tape is sometimes identified by the EOT (end of tape) character (see Appendix D).

Two methods of formatting and using tapes are available. In the first method, the records are variable in length. This allows efficient use of the tape, but it does not permit updating or overwriting of records in place. The second method is to use fixed-length records. In this case, it is possible to update records in place. Although this may seem to be a significant advantage, in practice it has turned out to be of little importance. The most common uses of tapes are backing up information on magnetic disks and archival storage of data. In these applications, a tape is written from the beginning to the end, so that the size of the records is irrelevant.

Cartridge Tape System

A tape system that has been developed for backup of on-line disk storage uses an 8-mm video format tape housed in a cassette. These units are called cartridge tapes. They have capacities in the range of 2 to 5 gigabytes and handle data transfers at the rate of a few hundred kilobytes per second. Reading and writing is done by a helical scan system operating across the tape, similar to that used in video cassette tape drives. Bit densities of tens of millions of bits per square inch are achievable. Multiple-cartridge systems are available that automate the loading and unloading of cassettes so that tens of gigabytes of on-line storage can be backed up unattended.

9.2.3 CD-ROM Systems

The compact disk (CD) technology used in audio systems has been adapted to the computer system environment to provide high-capacity, read-only storage referred to as CD-ROM technology. This adaptation is possible because audio CDs use a binary-encoded digitized representation of analog sound signals.

To provide high-quality sound recording and reproduction, 16-bit samples of the analog signal are taken at a rate of 44,100 samples per second. This sampling rate is twice the highest frequency in the original sound signal, thus allowing for accurate reconstruction. Up to 75 minutes of music can be recorded on a CD, requiring a total of about 3×10^9 bits (3 gigabits) of storage. A video CD is capable of storing a full-length movie. This requires approximately an order of magnitude more bit-storage capacity than that of audio CDs. Multimedia CDs are also adaptable to storing computer data, providing a correspondingly substantial increase in storage capacity over that of audio CDs.

The optical technology that is used for CD systems is based on a laser light source. A sharply focused laser beam is directed onto the surface of the spinning disk. Physical variations in the surface, called dimples, are arranged along concentric tracks of the disk. The dimples deflect the focused beam toward an optical receiver to signify a 1, or they disperse it away from the receiver to signify a 0. The physical geometry is similar to that of the magnetic disk system. But the dimple arrangements are permanent, unlike the changeable magnetic spots on the magnetic disk, so the CD system is a read-only device. Read/write optical disks are also available, but they have much lower storage density and capacity than ready-only disks.

The importance of CD ROMs for computer systems stems from their immense storage capacity, which can be used for interactive selection and composition of multimedia data for display. CD ROMs are also widely used for the distribution of software.

9.3
SYSTEM PERFORMANCE CONSIDERATIONS

We have described some of the most important peripheral devices, both communication devices and secondary storage devices. We now discuss computer performance issues beyond the processor/memory subsystem performance considerations addressed in Section 7.7. We make only a limited assessment of system-level performance, using a few facts related to disk and communication line speeds, in order to give the reader a perspective on how these components affect overall performance of a computer system.

Many different forms of computer systems are possible, depending on the application. A system meant for large-scale scientific calculations is quite different from a system intended to handle airline reservation requests in real time from travel agents scattered across the globe. We deal with large computer systems in Chapter 10. Here, we limit the discussion to relatively simple computer systems, such as a typical workstation that may be connected to other computers some distance away by means of a communication network. Figure 9.8 gives a block diagram of such a system. It includes a video terminal, processor, memory module, communication transceiver, and disk storage, all interconnected by a single bus. Only one of each type of unit is indicated, but any specific system may contain several units of each type.

9.3.1 Disk Access Considerations

Section 7.7 presents a detailed analysis of the effect of pipelined architecture on performance. That discussion begins with the assumption that a single pipeline stage, say, an integer addition in the ALU, has a delay of 10 nanoseconds. If all stages in the flow of instruction processing have the same delay, and if the flow is never interrupted, instructions would be executed at a rate of 100 million instructions per second (MIPS).

Remote computer system

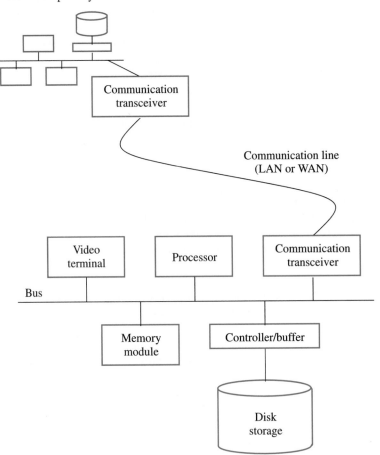

FIGURE 9.8
Generic computer system.

In practice, this ideal maximum rate is reduced, perhaps to 50 MIPS, because of miss penalties in the on-chip and secondary caches, pipeline stalls caused by data dependencies, and branches. In Section 7.7, we assume that programs and data are already loaded in the main memory. Hence, transfers between the main memory and disk storage are not considered.

In practice, the program and its data do not always fit in the main memory; hence, misses may occur in the main memory. A miss in the main memory is referred to as a page fault in Chapter 5. When a page fault occurs, the operating system must initiate a transfer of a page of program or data between the disk and the main memory. Suppose that a page consists of 8K bytes. If the disk has an average access time of 15 ms and if the actual transfer of the 8K-byte page is done at 4 MB/s, then the miss penalty is $15 + 2 = 17$ ms. Since this is a long delay, the discussion in Chapter 5 reasons that the processor should be switched to some other task whenever a page fault occurs in the running task. If the processor is to be kept busy all of the time, then a page fault is only allowed to occur every 17 ms in the running time of any program. If programs execute at 50 MIPS, then the number of instructions executed between page faults should be $50 \times 10^6 \times 17 \times 10^{-3} = 850 \times 10^3$. This represents a hit rate several orders of magnitude higher than those discussed for primary and secondary caches. When computations require more frequent access to a disk, it is inevitable that program execution stalls at some point. In this case, program execution is said to be *I/O-bound*. This means that the capability of a processor, in terms of MIPS and MFLOPS that it can deliver, can be fully used only if a program and its data fit entirely in the main memory.

9.3.2 Communication Line Considerations

We first consider the rates at which data can be moved over communication lines be-tween computer systems that are located some distance from each other. There are striking differences between these data rates and those we have discussed for memory and disks. Communication facilities fall into two major groups—Local Area Networks (LANs) and Wide Area Networks (WANs). LANs are used for intercomputer com-munication for distances up to a few kilometers. WANs allow communication among computers over much larger distances (hundreds or thousands of kilometers) by us-ing local and long-distance telephone company equipment that is designed for much broader classes of traffic.

In systems that use LANs, transfer rates of 100 Mb/s and higher are possible. Thus, workstations can be connected to remote disk file servers over such networks, without the LAN becoming a bottleneck. The communication transceiver performs the neces-sary buffering and assembly/disassembly between the bit-serial communication line and the parallel computer system bus, and it performs the access protocol required for orderly sharing of the communication line by many computers.

When computers are interconnected over telephone lines in WANs, usually much lower data transfer rates are encountered. For example, 28,800 bps communication transceivers, that is, modems, might be used to connect a personal computer to the Internet for access to e-mail or data-bank facilities. This is a 0.0036 MB/s rate, and it is used for a completely different application than the computation-intensive environment we have assumed until now. Travel agents accessing reservation systems might also use similar facilities. In that application, the performance issues are associated with the ca-pacity of a central database system to handle up to hundreds or thousands of agents accessing the system at the same time. The 28,800 bps rate can be supported by normal telephone lines that service homes and businesses. Another rate that is common over the telephone company facilities is a 56,000 bps rate that is provided for packet-switched data transfers between computers.

So far, our discussion of communication facilities has mentioned only the rate of bit transfer. But just as in the case of access delays for disks (seek and rotation), a delay factor arises in considering the performance of communication facilities. This is the propagation delay that occurs from the time data are sent from the source until they are received at the destination. At 360,000 miles per second, a signal can propagate around the earth at the equator, which is 25,000 miles in circumference, in 100 milliseconds, or it can travel between New York and Los Angeles in about 10 milliseconds. This is the best possible free-space propagation delay. The real delay is considerably longer because of the electrical properties of physical communication lines. Actually, long-distance propagation delays are similar to disk access delays.

9.4
CONCLUDING REMARKS

Input/output devices are a fundamental part of a computer system because they constitute the link for feeding information into a computer and for receiving the results. The choice of I/O devices and the way they are connected to the computer is important for both performance and cost. For performance reasons, no particular I/O device should create a bottleneck by forcing the rest of the computer system to idly wait for long periods of time until an input or output function is completed. Cost considerations are particularly important in small computer systems, where the cost of peripherals is often a major portion of the total system cost.

PROBLEMS

9.1. The following components are provided.

- A 6-bit binary counter, with Clock and Clear inputs and six outputs

- A 3-bit serial-input–parallel-output shift register

- A clock running at eight times the input data rate

- Logic gates and JK flip-flops with Preset and Clear controls

Design a circuit using these components to load 3 bits of serial data from an input data line into the shift register. Assume the data to have the format of Figure 9.1, but with only 3 bits of data instead of 8. The circuit you design should have two outputs, A and B, both initially cleared to 0. Output A should be set to 1 if a Stop bit is detected following the data bits. Otherwise, output B should be set to 1. Give an explanation of the operation of your design.

9.2. In Section 9.1.1, we defined the term "baud rate" and pointed out that, in the case of binary signaling, the baud rate is the same as the bit rate. Consider now a communications channel that uses eight-valued signals instead of the two-valued signals used in a binary channel. If the channel is rated at 9600 baud, what is its capacity in bits per second?

9.3. The display on a video screen must be refreshed at least 30 times per second to remain flicker-free. During each full scan of the screen, the total time required to illuminate each point is 1 μs. The beam is then turned off and moved to the next point to be illuminated. On the average, this process takes 3 μs. Because of power-dissipation limitations, the beam cannot be turned on more than 10 percent of the time. Determine the maximum number of points that can be illuminated on the screen.

To illuminate more points than the maximum, the display can be made to flash at the rate of once every 800 ms. In this case, the display is turned on for 500 ms and off for 300 ms. Determine the maximum number of points that can be illuminated under these conditions.

9.4. A disk unit has 15 recording surfaces. The storage area on each surface has an inner diameter of 6 cm and an outer diameter of 12 cm. The maximum storage density along any track is 16,000 bits/cm, and the minimum spacing between tracks is 0.02 mm.

   (*a*) What is the maximum number of bytes that can be stored in this unit?

   (*b*) What is the data transfer rate in bytes per second at a rotational speed of 5400 rpm?

   (*c*) Using a 32-bit word, suggest a suitable scheme for specifying the disk address, assuming that there are 512 bytes per sector.

   (*d*) The main memory of a computer has a 32-bit word length and 0.1-μs cycle time. Assuming that the disk transfers data to or from the memory on a cycle-stealing basis, what percentage of the available memory cycles are stolen during the data-transfer period?

9.5. The seek time plus rotational delay in accessing a particular data block on a disk is usually much longer than the data flow period for most disk transfers. Consider a long sequence of accesses to a Seagate disk (see the example in Section 9.2.1) for either Read or Write operations in which the average block being accessed is 8000 bytes long.

   (*a*) Assuming that the blocks are randomly located on the disk, estimate the average percentage of the total time taken for seek operations and rotational delays.

   (*b*) Repeat part *a* for the situation in which the disk accesses have been arranged so that, in 90 percent of the cases, the next access will be to a data block on the same cylinder.

9.6. The average seek time and rotational delay in a disk system are 11 ms and 5.6 ms, respectively. The rate of data transfer to or from the disk is 4.6 million bytes per second, and all disk accesses are for 8 kilobytes of data. Disk DMA controllers, the CPU, and the main memory are all attached to a single bus. The bus data width is 32 bits, and a bus transfer to or from the main memory takes 100 nanoseconds.

   (*a*) What is the maximum number of disk units that can simultaneously transfer data to or from the main memory?

   (*b*) What percentage of main memory cycles are stolen by a disk unit, on average, over a long period of time during which a sequence of independent 8-kilobyte transfers takes place?

9.7. Magnetic disk technology has densities of 10×10^6 bits per square centimeter of surface.

   (*a*) If the outer diameter of the recording area is 10 cm and the inner diameter is 6 cm, what is the average bit density along a track if there is one track every 0.018 mm in the radial direction?

   (*b*) What is the transfer rate in bytes per second if the disk rotates at 3600 rpm?

   (*c*) If such a disk is attached to a computer with a 32-bit word length, what memory cycle time (including bus delay) is needed if disk transfers are to steal no more than 50 percent of the bus cycles during the actual data flow time?

9.8. A tape drive has the following parameters:

Bit density	2000 bits/cm
Tape speed	800 cm/s

Time to reverse direction of motion   225 ms
Minimum time spent at an interrecord gap   3 ms
Average record length   4000 characters

Estimate the percentage of time gained from the ability to read records both forward and backward. Assume that records are accessed at random and that the average distance between two records accessed in sequence is four records.

9.9. Consider the operation of a line printer. The paper must be stationary during the printing process. Assume that the total time required for printing a line is 10 ms. At the end of this period, the paper is advanced to bring the next line to the printing position. This process takes T seconds. The speed, v, of the paper expressed as a function of time, t, is assumed to be

$$v = V_0\left(1 - \cos\frac{2\pi t}{T}\right)$$

where V_0 is a constant. If the maximum acceleration that the paper can sustain without tearing is 65,000 cm/s^2, what is the maximum possible printing rate in lines per minute? Assume line spacing to be 4.2 mm.

9.10. Given that magnetic disks are used as the secondary storage for program and data files in a virtual-memory system, which disk parameter(s) should influence the choice of page size?

9.11. Consider a communication line modem connected to a computer through an RS-232-C interface. The control signals associated with this interface are accessed by the computer through a 16-bit register, as shown in Figure P9.1. The status change bit, b_{15}, is set to 1 whenever there is a change in the state of bits b_{12} or b_{13}, or when b_{14} is set to 1. Bit b_{15} is cleared whenever this register is accessed by the processor. Write a program for either the 68000 or the PowerPC to implement the control sequence required to establish a telephone connection according to steps 1 through 4 of Figure 9.3.

9.12. Section 9.3.2 states that a Local Area Network (LAN) can transfer data between workstations and remote disk file servers at a rate of 100 Mbits/s. Suppose that each transfer consists of a 16K-byte block and that bits are read off the surface of the disk at a rate of 32 Mbits/s. Also, successive block transfers involving any particular disk reference blocks that are randomly located on the disk with respect to each other, requiring an average access time of 15 ms. Assume that adequate buffering capacity is available to distribute the actual data transfer periods evenly and to facilitate speed matching of the LAN and disk transfer rates. How many disks can be accommodated by a single LAN if the disks are continuously busy either accessing or transferring data, and if no more than 50 percent of the LAN capacity is to be used on average?

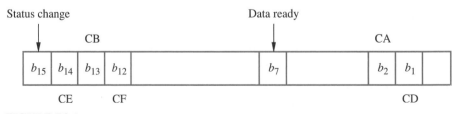

FIGURE P9.1
Organization of an I/O register for a modem interface.

REFERENCES

1. S. Haykin, *Communication Systems,* 3d ed., Wiley, New York, 1994.
2. Peter M. Chen, et al., "RAID: High-Performance, Reliable Secondary Storage," *ACM Computing Surveys*, vol. 26, no. 2, June 1994, pp. 145–185.

CHAPTER 10

Large Computer Systems

When a computer application requires a very large amount of computation to be completed in a reasonable amount of time, we must use machines with correspondingly large computing capacity. Such machines are often called *supercomputers*. Typical applications that require supercomputers include weather forecasting, finite element analysis in structural design, fluid flow analysis, simulation of large complex physical systems, and computer-aided design (CAD). None of the machines discussed in previous chapters are in the supercomputer class.

A high-performance processor can be designed using fast circuit technology and architectural features such as multiple functional units, pipelining, large caches, interleaved main memory, and separate buses for instructions and data. All these possibilities are exploited in ongoing research and development efforts by many manufacturers to produce processors intended primarily for use in workstations. Their quest is to increase performance without substantially increasing cost, and the results have been spectacular—we now have workstations that outperform machines that were considered to be in the supercomputer class only a decade ago.

However, many applications still demand computing power that greatly exceeds the capability of workstations. Thus, the need for supercomputing power remains strong. One approach is to build a supercomputer that has only a few very powerful processing units. This is typically done by using the fastest possible circuits, wide paths for accessing a large main memory, and extensive I/O capability. Such computers dissipate considerable power and require expensive cooling arrangements. In computationally demanding applications, supercomputers are needed to handle vectors of data, where a *vector* is a linear array of numbers (elements), as efficiently as possible. Single operations are often performed on entire vectors. For example, an add operation may generate a vector that is the element-by-element sum of two 64-element vectors. Also, a single memory access operation can cause an entire vector to be transferred between the main memory and processor registers. If an application is conducive to vector processing, then computers that feature a vector architecture provide excellent performance. Supercomputers of this class have been marketed by companies such as

Cray Research (Cray-1, Cray-2, and Y-MP), Fujitsu (VP2000), Hitachi (S820), and NEC (SX/2). The main drawback of such machines has been their high cost—both the purchase price and the operating maintenance cost. Smaller machines of this type have also been developed, for example, Convex's C-2 and Cray's J916.

An attractive alternative for providing supercomputing power is to use a large number of processors designed for the workstation market. This can be done in two basic ways. The first possibility is to build a machine that includes an efficient high-bandwidth medium for communication among the multiple processors, memory modules, and I/O devices. Such machines are usually referred to as *multiprocessors*. The second possibility is to implement a system using many workstations connected by a local area communication network. Systems of this type are often called *distributed computer systems*. Multiprocessors and distributed computer systems have many similarities. The former offer superior performance, but at a higher price. The latter are naturally available in a modern computing environment at low cost. In the remainder of this chapter, we discuss the salient characteristics of each of these types, because they provide large computing capabilities at a reasonable cost.

A system that uses many processors derives its high performance from the fact that many computations can proceed in parallel. The difficulty in using such a system efficiently is that it may not be easy to break an application down into small tasks that can be assigned to individual processors for simultaneous execution. Determining these tasks and then scheduling and coordinating their execution in multiple processors requires sophisticated software and hardware techniques. We consider these issues later in the chapter.

10.1
FORMS OF PARALLEL PROCESSING

Many opportunities are available for parts of a given computational task to be executed in parallel. We have already seen several of them in earlier chapters. For example, in handling I/O operations, most computer systems have hardware that performs direct memory access (DMA) between an I/O device and main memory. The transfer of data in either direction between the main memory and a magnetic disk can be accomplished under the direction of a DMA controller that operates in parallel with the processor.

When a block of data is to be transferred from disk to main memory, the processor initiates the transfer by sending instructions to the DMA controller. While the controller transfers the required data using cycle stealing, the processor continues to perform some computation that is unrelated to the data transfer. When the controller completes the transfer, it sends an interrupt request to the processor to signal that the requested data are available in the main memory. In response, the processor switches to a computation that uses the data.

This simple example illustrates two fundamental aspects of parallel processing. First, the overall task has the property that some of its subtasks can be done in parallel by different hardware components. In this example, a processor computation and an I/O transfer are performed in parallel by the processor and the DMA controller. Second, some means must exist for initiating and coordinating the parallel activity. Initiation occurs when the processor sets up the DMA transfer and then continues with another computation. When the transfer is completed, the coordination is achieved by the interrupt signal sent from the DMA controller to the processor. This allows the processor to begin the computation that operates on the transferred data.

The preceding example illustrates a simple case of parallelism involving only two tasks. In general, large computations can be divided into many parts that can be performed in parallel. Several hardware structures can be used to support such parallel computations.

10.1.1 Classification of Parallel Structures

A general classification of parallel processing has been proposed by Flynn.[1] In this classification, a single-processor computer system is called a *Single Instruction stream, Single Data stream* (SISD) system. A program executed by the processor constitutes the single instruction stream, and the sequence of data items that it operates on constitutes the single data stream. In the second scheme, a single stream of instructions is broadcast to a number of processors. Each processor operates on its own data. This scheme, in which all processors execute the same program but operate on different data, is called a *Single Instruction stream, Multiple Data stream* (SIMD) system. The multiple data streams are the sequences of data items accessed by the individual processors in their own memories. The third scheme involves a number of independent processors, each executing a different program and accessing its own sequence of data items. Such machines are called *Multiple Instruction stream, Multiple Data stream* (MIMD) systems. The fourth possibility is a *Multiple Instruction stream, Single Data stream* (MISD) system. In such a system, a common data structure is manipulated by separate processors, each executing a different program. This form of computation does not occur often in practice, so it is not pursued here.

This chapter concentrates on MIMD structures, because they are most useful for general purposes. However, we first briefly consider the SIMD structure to illustrate the kind of applications for which it is well-suited.

10.2
ARRAY PROCESSORS

The SIMD form of parallel processing, also called *array processing*, was the first form of parallel processing to be studied and implemented. In the early 1970s, a system named ILLIAC-IV[2] was designed at the University of Illinois using this approach and was later built by Burroughs Corporation. Figure 10.1 illustrates the structure of an array processor. A two-dimensional grid of processing elements executes an instruction stream that is *broadcast* from a central control processor. As each instruction is broadcast, all elements execute it simultaneously. Each processing element is connected to its four nearest neighbors for purposes of exchanging data. End-around connections may be provided in both rows and columns, but they are not shown in the figure.

Let us consider a specific computation in order to understand the capabilities of the SIMD architecture. The grid of processing elements can be used to solve two-dimensional problems. For example, if each element of the grid represents a point

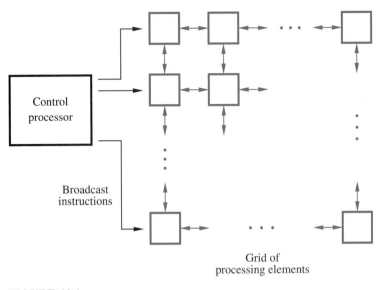

FIGURE 10.1
Array processor.

in space, the array can be used to compute the temperature at points in the interior of a conducting plane. Assume that the edges of the plane are held at some fixed temperatures. An approximate solution at the discrete points represented by the processing elements is derived as follows. The outer edges are initialized to the specified temperatures. All interior points are initialized to arbitrary values, not necessarily the same. Iterations are then executed in parallel at each element. Each iteration consists of calculating an improved estimate of the temperature at a point by averaging the current values of its four nearest neighbors. The process stops when changes in the estimates during successive iterations are less than some predefined small quantity.

The capability needed in the array processor to perform such calculations is quite simple. Each element must be able to exchange values with each of its neighbors over the paths shown in the figure. Each processing element has a few registers and some local memory to store data. It also has a register, which we can call the network register, that facilitates movement of values to and from its neighbors. The central processor can broadcast an instruction to shift the values in the network registers one step up, down, left, or right. Each processing element also contains an ALU to execute arithmetic instructions broadcast by the control processor. Using these basic facilities, a sequence of instructions can be broadcast repeatedly to implement the iterative loop. The control processor must be able to determine when each of the processing elements has developed its component of the temperature to the required accuracy. To do this, each element sets an internal status bit to 1 to indicate this condition. The grid interconnections include a facility that allows the controller to detect when all status bits are set at the end of an iteration.

An interesting question with respect to array processors is whether it is better to use a relatively small number of powerful processors or a large number of very simple processors. ILLIAC-IV is an example of the former choice. Its 64 processors had a 64-bit internal structure. More recent array processors introduced in the late 1980s are examples of the latter choice. The CM-2 machine[3] produced by the Thinking Machines Corporation could accommodate up to 65,536 processors, but each processor is only one bit wide. Maspar's MP-1216 has a maximum of 16,384 processors that are 4 bits wide.[4] These choices reflect the belief that, in the SIMD environment, it is more useful to have a high degree of parallelism rather than to have fewer but more powerful processors.

Array processors are highly specialized machines. They are well-suited to numerical problems that can be expressed in matrix or vector format. Recall that supercomputers with a vector architecture are also suitable for solving such problems. A key difference between vector-based machines and array processors is that the former achieve high performance through heavy use of pipelining, whereas the latter provide extensive parallelism by replication of computing modules. Neither array processors nor vector-based machines are particularly useful in speeding up general computations, and they do not have a large commercial market.

10.3
THE STRUCTURE OF GENERAL-PURPOSE MULTIPROCESSORS

The array processor architecture described in the preceding section is a design for a computer system that corresponds directly to a class of computational problems that exhibit an obvious form of data parallelism. In more general cases in which parallelism is not so obvious, it is useful to have an MIMD architecture, which involves a number of processors capable of independently executing different routines in parallel.

Figures 10.2, 10.3, and 10.4 show three possible ways of implementing a multiprocessor system. The most obvious scheme is given in Figure 10.2. An *interconnection network* permits n processors to access k memories so that any of the processors can access any of the memories. The interconnection network may introduce considerable delay between a processor and a memory. If this delay is the same for all accesses to memory, which is common for this organization, then such a machine is called a Uniform Memory Access (UMA) multiprocessor. Because of the extremely short instruction execution times achievable by processors, the network delay in fetching instructions and data from the memories is unacceptable if it is too long. Unfortunately, interconnection networks with very short delays are costly and complex to implement.

An attractive alternative, which allows a high computation rate to be sustained in all processors, is to attach the memory modules directly to the processors. This organization is shown in Figure 10.3. In addition to accessing its local memory, each processor can also access other memories over the network. Since the remote accesses pass through the network, these accesses take considerably longer than accesses to the local memory. Because of this difference in access times, such multiprocessors are called Non-Uniform Memory Access (NUMA) multiprocessors.

The organizations of Figures 10.2 and 10.3 provide a *global memory*, where any processor can access any memory module without intervention by another processor. A different way of organizing the system is shown in Figure 10.4. Here, all memory modules serve as private memories for the processors that are directly connected to them. A processor cannot access a remote memory without the cooperation of the remote processor. This cooperation takes place in the form of messages exchanged by the

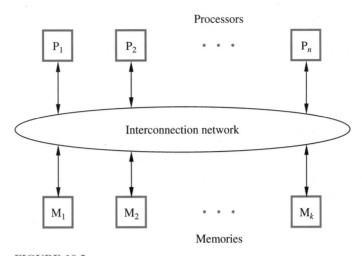

FIGURE 10.2
A UMA multiprocessor.

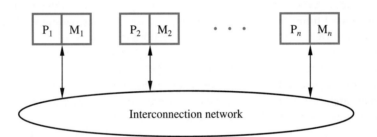

FIGURE 10.3
A NUMA multiprocessor.

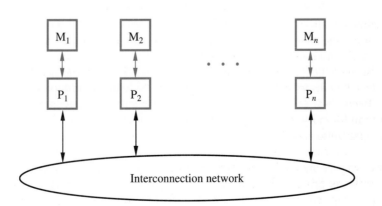

FIGURE 10.4
A distributed memory system.

processors. Such systems are often called *distributed-memory* systems with a *message-passing protocol*.

The preceding discussion uses processors and memory modules as the main functional units in a multiprocessor system. Although we have not discussed I/O modules explicitly, any multiprocessor must provide extensive I/O capability. This capability can be provided in different ways. Separate I/O modules can be connected directly to the network, providing standard I/O interfaces, as discussed in Chapter 4. Some I/O functions can also be incorporated into the processor modules.

Figures 10.2, 10.3, and 10.4 depict a high-level view of possible multiprocessor organizations. The performance and cost of these machines depend greatly on implementation details. In the next two sections, we consider the most popular schemes for realizing the communication network and the structure of the memory hierarchy.

10.4
INTERCONNECTION NETWORKS

In this section, we examine some of the possibilities for implementing the interconnection network in multiprocessor systems. In general, the network must allow information transfer between any pair of modules in the system. The network may also be used to broadcast information from one module to many other modules. The traffic in the network consists of requests (such as read and write), data transfers, and various commands.

The suitability of a particular network is judged in terms of cost, bandwidth, effective throughput, and ease of implementation. The term *bandwidth* refers to the capacity of a transmission link to transfer data and is expressed in bits or bytes per second. The *effective throughput* is the actual rate of data transfer. This rate is less than the available bandwidth, because a given link usually does not carry data all of the time.

Information transfer through the network usually takes place in the form of *packets* of fixed length and specified format. For example, a read request is likely to be a single packet that contains the addresses of the source (the processor module) and destination (the memory module) and a command field that indicates what type of read operation is required. A write request that writes one word in a memory module is also likely to be a single packet that includes the data to be written. On the other hand, a read response that involves an entire cache block requires several packets. Longer messages may require many packets.

Ideally, a complete packet would be handled in parallel in one clock cycle at any node or switch in the network. This implies having wide links, comprising many wires. However, to reduce cost and complexity, the links are often considerably narrower. In such cases, a packet must be divided into smaller pieces, each of which can be transmitted in one clock cycle.

10.4.1 Single Bus

The simplest and most economical means for interconnecting a number of modules is to use a single bus. The detailed aspects of bus design, as discussed in Chapter 4, apply here as well. Since several modules are connected to the bus and any module can request a data transfer at any time, it is essential to have an efficient bus arbitration scheme. Examples of such schemes are given in Chapter 4.

In a simple mode of operation, the bus is dedicated to a particular source-destination pair for the full duration of the requested transfer. For example, when a processor issues a read request on the bus, it holds the bus until it receives the desired data from the memory module. Since the memory module needs a certain amount of time to access the data (as discussed in Chapter 5), the bus will be idle until the memory is ready to respond with the data. Then the data are transferred to the processor. When this transfer is completed, the bus can be assigned to handle another request.

Suppose that a bus transfer takes T time units, and the memory access time is $4T$ units. It then takes $6T$ units to complete a read request. Thus, the bus is idle for two-thirds of the time. A scheme known as the *split-transaction protocol* makes it possible to use the bus during the idle period to serve another request. Consider the following method of handling a series of read requests, possibly from different processors. After transferring the address involved in the first request, the bus may be reassigned to transfer the address for the second request. Assuming that this request is to a different memory module, we now have two modules proceeding with read access cycles in parallel. If neither module has finished with its access, the bus may be reassigned to a third request, and so on. Eventually, the first memory module completes its access cycle and uses the bus to transfer the word to the source that requested it. As other modules complete their cycles, the bus is used to transfer their data to the corresponding sources. Note that the actual length of time between address transfer and word return is not critical. Address and data transfers for different requests represent independent uses of the bus that can be interleaved in any order.

The split-transaction protocol allows the bus and the available bandwidth to be used more efficiently. The performance improvement achieved with this protocol depends on the relationship between the bus transfer time and the memory access time. Performance is improved at the cost of increased bus complexity. There are two reasons why complexity increases. Since a memory module needs to know which source initiated a given read request, a source identification tag must be attached to the request. This tag is later used to send the requested data to the source. Complexity also increases because all modules, not just the processors, must be able to act as bus masters.

A number of multiprocessors that use the split-transaction bus are commercially available. The size of these systems varies from 4 to 32 processors, each with a cache memory, and all these systems have multiple memory modules. The split-transaction protocol allows several processors to initiate accesses to different memory modules at any given time.

The Symmetry multiprocessor,[5] manufactured by Sequent Computer Systems, can have up to 30 processors. It uses a split-transaction bus that has a 100-nanosecond transfer time. Addresses are multiplexed over a 64-bit data bus, and block requests for 16 bytes are provided. The maximum aggregate data transfer rate across the bus is 53.3 megabytes per second.

The bandwidth of a bus can be increased if a wider bus, that is, a bus that has more wires, is used. Most of the data transferred between processors and memory modules consist of cache blocks, where a block consists of a number of words. If the bus is

wide enough to transfer several words at a time, then a complete block can be transferred more quickly than if the words were transferred one at a time. The Challenge
multiprocessor,[6] from Silicon Graphics Corporation, uses a bus that allows parallel
transfer of 256 bits of data. The machine uses MIPS R4400 processors, which have
a 64-bit organization. Thus, the width of the bus is four times that of the processors.

The main limitation of a single bus is that the number of modules that can be connected to the bus is not large. An ordinary bus functions well if no more than 10 to
15 modules are connected to it. Using a wider bus to increase the bandwidth allows
the number of modules to be doubled. The bandwidth of a single bus is limited by
contention for the use of the bus and by the increased propagation delays caused by
electrical loading when many modules are connected. Networks that allow multiple independent transfer operations to proceed in parallel can provide significantly increased
data transfer rates.

10.4.2 Crossbar Networks

A versatile switching arrangement is shown in Figure 10.5. It is known as the *crossbar
switch*, which was originally developed for use in telephone networks. For clarity of
illustration, the switches in the figure are depicted as mechanical switches, although in
practice these are electronic switches. Any module, Q_i, can be connected to any other
module, Q_j, by closing an appropriate switch. Such networks, where there is a direct
link between all pairs of nodes, are called *fully connected* networks. Many simultaneous
transfers are possible. If n sources need to send data to n distinct destinations, then all
of these transfers can take place concurrently. Since no transfer is prevented by the lack
of a communication path, the crossbar is called a *nonblocking switch.*

In Figure 10.5, we show just a single switch at each crosspoint. In an actual multiprocessor, however, the paths through the crossbar network are much wider. This means

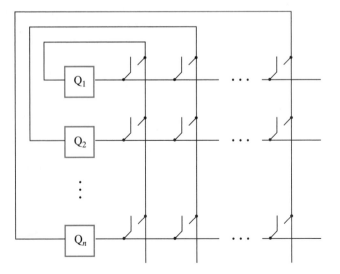

FIGURE 10.5
Crossbar interconnection network.

that many switches are needed at each crosspoint. Since the number of crosspoints is n^2 in a network used to interconnect n modules, the total number of switches becomes large as n increases. This results in high cost and cumbersome implementation. Crossbars are attractive as interconnection networks only in small systems.

10.4.3 Multistage Networks

The bus and crossbar systems just described use a single stage of switching to provide a path from a source to a destination. It is also possible to implement interconnection networks that use multiple stages of switches to set up paths between sources and destinations. Such networks are less costly than the crossbar structure, yet they provide a reasonably large number of parallel paths between sources and destinations. Multistage switching is best illustrated by an example. Figure 10.6 shows a three-stage network

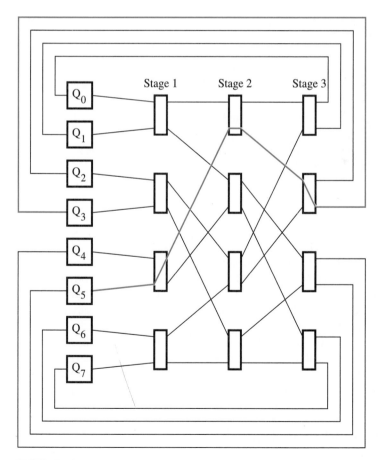

FIGURE 10.6
Multistage shuffle network.

called a *shuffle network* that interconnects eight modules. The term "shuffle" describes the pattern of connections from the outputs of one stage to the inputs of the next stage. This pattern is identical to the repositioning of playing cards in a deck that is shuffled by splitting the deck into two halves and interleaving the cards in each half.

Each switchbox in the figure is a 2×2 switch that can route either input to either output. If the inputs request distinct outputs, then they can both be routed simultaneously in the straight-through or crossed pattern. If both inputs request the same output, only one request can be satisfied. The other one is blocked until the first request finishes using the switch. It can be shown that a network consisting of s stages can be used to interconnect 2^s modules. In this case, there is exactly one path through the network from any module Q_i to any other module Q_j. Therefore, this network provides full connectivity between sources and destinations. Many request patterns, however, cannot be satisfied simultaneously. For example, the connection from Q_0 to Q_4 cannot be provided at the same time as the connection from Q_1 to Q_5.

A multistage network is less expensive to implement than a crossbar network. If n nodes are to be interconnected using the scheme in Figure 10.6, then we must use $s = \log_2 n$ stages with $n/2$ switchboxes per stage. Since each switchbox contains four switches, the total number of switches is

$$4 \times \frac{n}{2} \times \log_2 n = 2n \times \log_2 n$$

which, for large networks, is considerably less than the n^2 switches needed in a crossbar network.

A particular request can be routed through the network using the following scheme. The source sends a binary pattern representing the destination number into the network. As the pattern moves through the network, each stage examines a different bit to determine switch settings. Stage 1 uses the most significant bit, stage 2 the middle bit, and stage 3 the least significant bit. When a request arrives on either input of a switch, it is routed to the upper output if the controlling bit is a 0 and to the lower output if the controlling bit is a 1. For example, a request from source Q_5 for destination Q_3 moves through the network as shown by the blue lines in Figure 10.6. Its route is controlled by the bit pattern 011, which is the destination address.

An example of a multiprocessor based on a multistage network is the BBN Butterfly,[7] manufactured by BBN Advanced Computers. A 64-processor model of this system contains a three-stage network built with 4×4 switches. The routing through each stage of these switches is determined by successive 2-bit fields of the destination address.

Multistage networks are less capable of providing concurrent connections than crossbar switches, but they are also less costly to implement. Interest in these networks peaked in the 1980s and has diminished greatly in the past few years. Other schemes, which we discuss in the remainder of this section, have become more attractive.

10.4.4 Hypercube Networks

In the three schemes discussed previously, the interconnection network imposes the same delay for paths connecting any two modules. Such schemes can be used to

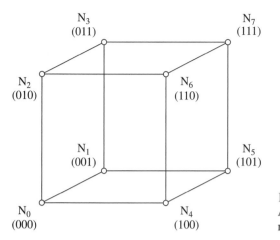

N_3
(011)

N_7
(111)

N_2
(010)

N_6
(110)

N_1
(001)

N_5
(101)

N_0
(000)

N_4
(100)

FIGURE 10.7
A three-dimensional hypercube network.

implement UMA multiprocessors. We now discuss network topologies that are suitable only for NUMA multiprocessors. The first such scheme that gained popularity uses the topology of an n-dimensional cube, called a *hypercube*, to implement a network that interconnects 2^n nodes. In addition to the communication circuits, each node usually includes a processor and a memory module as well as some I/O capability.

Figure 10.7 shows a three-dimensional hypercube. The small circles represent the communication circuits in the nodes. The functional units attached to each node are not shown in the figure. The edges of the cube represent bidirectional communication links between neighboring nodes. In an n-dimensional hypercube, each node is directly connected to n neighbors. A useful way to label the nodes is to assign binary addresses to them in such a way that the addresses of any two neighbors differ in exactly one bit position, as shown in the figure.

Routing messages through the hypercube is particularly easy. If the processor at node N_i wishes to send a message to node N_j, it proceeds as follows. The binary addresses of the source, i, and the destination, j, are compared from least to most significant bits. Suppose that they differ first in position p. Node N_i then sends the message to its neighbor whose address, k, differs from i in bit position p. Node N_k forwards the message to the appropriate neighbor using the same address comparison scheme. The message gets closer to destination node N_j with each of these hops from one node to another. For example, a message from node N_2 to node N_5 requires 3 hops, passing through nodes N_3 and N_1. The maximum distance that any message needs to travel in an n-dimensional hypercube is n hops.

Scanning address patterns from right to left is only one of the methods that can be used to determine message routing. Any other scheme that moves a message closer to its destination on each hop is equally acceptable, as long as the routing decision can be made at each node on the path using only local information. This feature of the hypercube is attractive from the reliability viewpoint. The existence of multiple paths between two nodes means that when faulty links are encountered, they can usually be avoided by simple, local routing decisions. If one of the shortest routes is not available, a message may be sent over a longer path. When this is done, care must be taken to avoid looping, which is the situation in which the message circulates in a closed loop and never reaches its destination.

Hypercube interconnection networks have been used in a number of machines. The better known examples include Intel's iPSC,[8] which uses a 7-dimensional cube to connect up to 128 nodes, and NCUBE's NCUBE/ten, which has up to 1024 nodes in a 10-dimensional cube.[9] The hypercube networks lost much of their popularity in the early 1990s when mesh-based structures emerged as a more attractive alternative.

10.4.5 Mesh Networks

One of the most natural ways of interconnecting a large number of nodes is by means of a *mesh*. An example of a mesh with 16 nodes is given in Figure 10.8. Again, the links between the nodes are bidirectional. Meshes have gained popularity in recent years and have essentially displaced hypercubes as the favorite choice for interconnection networks in large multiprocessors.

Routing in a mesh network can be done in several different ways. One of the simplest and most effective possibilities is to choose the path between a source node N_i and a destination node N_j such that the transfer first takes place in the horizontal direction from N_i toward N_j. When the column in which N_j resides is reached, the transfer proceeds in the vertical direction along this column.

Well-known examples of mesh-based multiprocessors are Intel's Paragon,[10] which uses the i860 XP processors, and the experimental machines Dash[11] and Flash[12] at Stanford University and Alewife[13] at MIT.

If a wraparound connection is made between the nodes at the opposite edges in Figure 10.8, the result is a network that comprises a set of bidirectional rings in the X direction connected by a set of rings in the Y direction. In this network, called a *torus*, the average latency of information transfer is reduced, but at the cost of greater complexity.

Both the regular mesh and the torus schemes can also be implemented as three-dimensional networks, in which the links are between neighbors in the X, Y, and Z directions. An example of a three-dimensional torus is found in the T3D multiprocessor[14] manufactured by Cray Research, Inc., which uses the DEC Alpha processors.

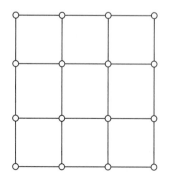

FIGURE 10.8
A two-dimensional mesh network.

10.4.6 Tree Networks

A hierarchically structured network implemented in the form of a tree is another inter-connection topology. Figure 10.9a depicts a four-way tree that interconnects 16 mod-ules. In this tree, each parent node allows communication between two of its children at a time. An intermediate-level node, for example node A in the figure, can provide a connection from one of its child nodes to its parent. This enables two leaf nodes that are any distance apart to communicate. Only one path at a time can be established through a given node in the tree.

A tree network performs well if there is a large amount of locality in communica-tion, that is, if only a small portion of network traffic goes through the single root node. If this is not the case, performance deteriorates rapidly, because the root node becomes a bottleneck.

To reduce the possibility of a bottleneck, the number of links in the upper levels of a tree hierarchy can be increased. This is done in a *fat tree* network, in which each node in the tree (except at the top level) has more than one parent. An example of a fat tree is given in Figure 10.9b. In this case, each node has two parent nodes. A fat tree structure is used in the CM-5 machine[15] by Thinking Machines Corporation.

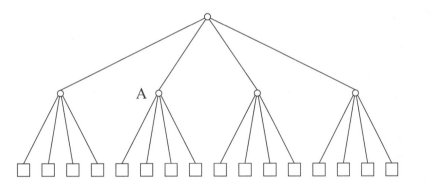

(a) Four-way tree

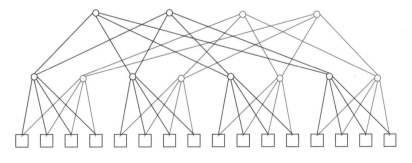

(b) Fat tree

FIGURE 10.9
Tree-based networks.

10.4.7 Ring Networks

One of the simplest network topologies uses a ring to interconnect the nodes in the system, as shown in Figure 10.10a. The main advantage of this arrangement is that the ring is easy to implement. Links in the ring can be wide, usually accommodating a complete packet in parallel, because each node is connected to only two neighbors. However, it is not useful to construct a very long ring to connect many nodes, because the latency of information transfer would be unacceptably large.

Rings can be used as building blocks for the topologies discussed in previous sections, such as meshes, hypercubes, trees, and fat trees. We consider the simple possibility of using rings in a tree structure; this results in a hierarchy of rings as shown in Figure 10.10b. A two-level hierarchy is depicted in the figure, but more levels can be used. Having short rings reduces substantially the latency of transfers that involve nodes on the same ring. Moreover, the latency of transfers between two nodes on different rings is shorter than if a single ring were used. The drawback of this scheme is that the highest-level ring may become a bottleneck for traffic.

Examples of ring networks are found in the commercial multiprocessors KSR-1 by Kendal Square Research[16] and Exemplar by Convex,[17] as well as in the experimental machines Hector[18] and NUMAchine[19] at the University of Toronto.

10.4.8 Practical Considerations

We have seen that several different topologies can be used to implement the interconnection network in a multiprocessor system. It would be difficult to argue that any

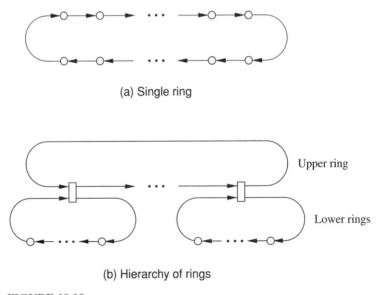

(a) Single ring

(b) Hierarchy of rings

FIGURE 10.10
A ring-based interconnection network.

topology is clearly superior to others. Each has certain advantages and disadvantages. When comparing different approaches, we must take into account several practical considerations.

The most fundamental requirement is that the communication network be fast enough and have sufficient throughput to satisfy the traffic demand in a multiprocessor system. This implies high speed of transfer along the communication path and a simple routing mechanism that allows routing decisions to be made quickly. The network should be easy to implement; the wiring complexity must be reasonable and conducive to simple packaging. Complexity is inevitably reflected in the cost of the network, which is another major consideration.

Multiprocessors of different sizes are needed. The ideal network would be suitable for all sizes, ranging from just a few processors to possibly thousands of processors. The term *scalability* is often used to describe the ability of a multiprocessor architecture (which includes the interconnection network) to provide increased performance as the size of the system increases, while the increase in cost is proportional to the increase in size. It is particularly advantageous if a relatively small multiprocessor system can be acquired at a low cost but can be easily expanded to a large system with a linear increase in cost. Unfortunately, this is not true for many commercial products. Often, the up-front cost for even a small system is large, because much of the communication hardware needed to accommodate a larger system must be provided in one piece.

In addition to providing the basic communication between sources and destinations, it is useful to have broadcasting capability. The ability to send data to only a subset of the network modules is also beneficial. Such transfers are called *multicasting*.

The choice of the interconnection network affects the implementation of schemes used to ensure that any multiple copies of data that may exist in caches of different processors acquire the updates made so that all copies always have the same values. Such schemes are discussed in Section 10.6.2.

Reliability is another important factor. The more complex the network, the more likely it is to fail. Ideally, the machine could continue to function even if some link in the network fails. This is possible in networks that provide at least two different paths between each pair of communicating nodes. In general, simple networks tend to be robust, and they do not fail any more often than the processing and memory modules in the system. Highly reliable networks that include additional hardware can be built at considerable cost. This topic is beyond the scope of this book, however.

To demonstrate how all these characteristics can be evaluated, let us make a brief qualitative comparison of networks based on meshes and rings.

Meshes and Rings

Both mesh and ring networks are characterized by point-to-point links (connecting adjacent nodes), which can be driven at high clock rates. Both are viable in small configurations and can be expanded without difficulty. Incremental expansion is simpler in a ring network than in a mesh network.

In Figures 10.8 and 10.10, we indicate the nodes in the network as small circles and the links as single lines. Consider a more detailed picture; Figure 10.11 shows the communication paths associated with one node that has a processing module attached to it.

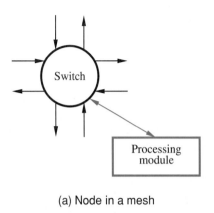

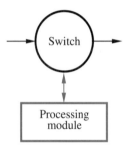

(a) Node in a mesh

(b) Node in a ring

FIGURE 10.11
Nodes in mesh and ring networks.

The switch block includes both the circuitry that selects the path for a transfer and the buffers needed to hold the data being transferred. Data are transferred from the buffer in one node to the buffer in the next node in one clock cycle. Part *a* of the figure depicts a node in a two-dimensional mesh network. Since bidirectional communication is needed in both the X and Y directions, eight distinct network links must be connected to the node. The width of these links is limited by the total number of wires that can be used, taking into account the cost and packaging. Thus, it is unlikely that an individual link could be wide enough to carry an entire packet in parallel. To deal with this constraint, a packet can be divided into smaller portions to correspond to the width of the link. The term *flit* (FLow control digIT) is often used to refer to a portion of the packet that can be accepted by the switching circuitry in the node for forwarding, or delayed because the forward path is blocked by another transfer. In practice, it is convenient if the flit corresponds to the width of the link.

   If a packet must be divided into flits, how should it be routed through the network? A straightforward scheme, known as the *store-and-forward* method, is to provide a large enough buffer in each node to hold all flits of a packet. Thus, an entire packet is transferred from one node to another, where it is stored until it can be forwarded to the next node. (The number of clock cycles required for the transfer depends on the number of flits.) The negative aspects of this scheme are the size of the buffers needed and the increased latency in passing through a node. An alternative that has gained popularity is the *wormhole* routing scheme (which has also been referred to as *pipelining*), in which the sequence of flits that constitute a packet can be viewed as a *worm* that moves through the network. The first flit in a worm contains a *header* that includes the address of the destination node. As this flit moves through the network, it establishes a path along which the remaining flits will pass. The tail of the worm closes the established path. The head of the worm may be temporarily blocked at any node, because another worm may be passing through this node. However, once the head moves, the rest of the worm moves along in subsequent clock cycles. Some control mechanism must stop the transmission of flits from preceding nodes when the head of the worm is blocked; a simple scheme using two buffers per node for each direction of transfer has been developed for this purpose.[20] Wormhole routing has lower latency than store-and-forward routing, because the head flit is sent on its way without waiting for the remaining flits of the packet.

Wormhole routing is an application of a strategy known as circuit switching. *Circuit switching* is a familiar concept from telephone networks, where a path through the network is established when a number is dialed. The conversation takes place along this path, called a *circuit*. The circuit is deactivated when the calling party hangs up. In the case of wormhole routing, it is the head flit that establishes the path. The progression of this flit may be temporarily blocked as explained above. Once a circuit is established, however, the remaining flits of the packet move toward the destination without experiencing any contention. In contrast, strategies in which an entire packet is buffered at each node, as in the store-and-forward method, are called *packet switching*. In this case, no circuit is set up, and the packet moves through the network as the buffer in each node becomes available.

Connections to a node in a ring network are shown in Figure 10.11*b*. Here, transfer occurs in only one direction, in addition to the connection to the processing module. Thus, the width of the link can be four times that in a mesh network for the same wire count. This means that it is feasible for an entire packet to be transferred in parallel from one node to another in one clock cycle. Figure 10.11*b* shows a node in the lowest level ring, to which a processing module is attached. If a ring hierarchy such as that in Figure 10.10*b* is used, then the inter-ring interfaces will have two input and two output links, one of each belonging to the upper- and lower-level rings.

Routing in a hierarchical ring network is very simple. A packet is never blocked, except possibly at an inter-ring interface when incoming packets on both upper- and lower-level rings are destined to continue along just one of the rings. To handle this situation, buffers (queues) must be provided in the interface, one from the lower- to the upper-level ring and another in the opposite direction. A processing module may inject a new packet onto the ring whenever no packet is arriving to the node from its upstream neighbor.

Next we consider the ability of networks to broadcast or multicast data. This ability is naturally available in ring networks. For example, a packet can be broadcast to all nodes by sending it to the top-level ring. As the packet traverses this ring, a copy is made at each inter-ring interface and sent along to the next lower-level ring. This process is repeated at all levels so that the copies of the original packet visit all nodes in the lowest-level rings. Broadcasting in a mesh network is more difficult, because the broadcast packet has to be broken up into flits and the progress of the broadcast worm may be blocked at various nodes by other traffic. Moreover, the completion of a broadcast is not easy to detect.

The main disadvantage of a hierarchical ring network is that the ring at the top of the hierarchy may become a bottleneck if too many packets need to be transferred over it. This will occur if the locality in communication is low. The limited bandwidth of the top-level ring restricts the scalability of systems based on such networks to hundreds of processors. In contrast, mesh-based systems scale well to thousands of processors.

The preceding discussion shows that both meshes and rings are good choices for interconnection networks. Ring-based systems are easier to implement, but do not scale as well as mesh-based systems. Thus, rings merit serious consideration if the maximum size of the system is a few hundred processors. Mesh systems are suitable for use in both small and very large systems. For very small systems, say, up to 16 processors, the most effective choice is still the single bus.

Since the size of a multiprocessor system has important implications, the reader may wonder what range of systems are in practical use. Most multiprocessor systems are relatively small. Many machines are in the range of 4 to 128 processors. Some very large machines with thousands of processors exist. However, the market for such large machines is small.

10.4.9 Mixed Topology Networks

Since various network topologies have certain specific advantages, it is possible to combine different topologies for use in a multiprocessor system. Several attempts to do this can be found in practice.

Single-bus connected clusters of processing modules have been used in Stanford University's Dash[11] and University of Toronto's NUMAchine[19] multiprocessors. In Dash, these clusters are interconnected by means of a mesh network. In NUMAchine, the clusters are interconnected by a hierarchical ring network. The Exemplar multiprocessor from Convex[17] uses a crossbar to interconnect processors in a cluster, and it uses rings to interconnect the clusters.

These mixed topology networks are intended to take advantage of the optimal cost/performance features of the individual component networks.

10.5
MEMORY ORGANIZATION IN MULTIPROCESSORS

In Chapter 5 we saw that the organization of the memory in a uniprocessor system has a large impact on performance. The same is true in multiprocessor systems. To exploit the locality of reference phenomenon, each processor usually includes a primary cache and a secondary cache. If the organization in Figure 10.2 is used, then each processor module can be connected to the communication network as shown in Figure 10.12. Only the secondary cache is shown in the figure, since the primary cache is assumed to be a part of the processor chip. The memory modules are accessed using a single *global address space*, where a range of physical addresses is assigned to each memory

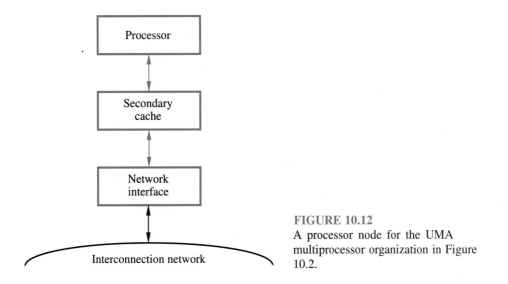

FIGURE 10.12
A processor node for the UMA multiprocessor organization in Figure 10.2.

module. In such a *shared memory* system, the processors access all memory modules in the same way. From the software standpoint, this is the simplest use of the address space.

In NUMA-organized multiprocessors, shown in Figure 10.3, each node contains a processor and a portion of the memory. A natural way of implementing the node is illustrated in Figure 10.13. In this case it is also convenient to use a single global address space. Again, the processor accesses all memory modules in the same way, but the accesses to the local memory component of the global address space take less time to complete than accesses to remote memory modules.

In the organization of Figure 10.4, each processor accesses directly only its own local memory. Thus, each memory module constitutes the *private address space* of one processor; there is no global address space. Any interaction among programs or processes running on different processors is implemented by sending *messages* from one

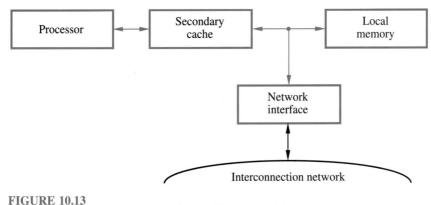

FIGURE 10.13
Node structure for the NUMA multiprocessor organization in Figure 10.3.

processor to another. In this form of communication, each processor views the interconnection network as an I/O device. In effect, each node in such a system behaves as a
computer in the same manner as discussed in previous chapters for uniprocessor machines. For this reason, systems of this type are referred to also as *multicomputers*. This
organization provides the easiest way to connect a number of computers into a large system. Communication between tasks running on different computers is relatively slow,
because the exchange of messages requires software intervention. We consider this type
of system in Section 10.7.

When data are shared among many processors, we must ensure that the processors
observe the same value for a given data item. The presence of many caches in a shared-
memory system creates a problem in this respect. Multiple copies of some data items
may exist in various caches. Whenever a processor changes (writes) a data item in its
own cache, the same change must be made in all caches that have a copy. Alternatively,
the other copies must be invalidated. In other words, shared data must be *coherent* in
all caches in the system. The problem of maintaining cache coherence can be solved in
several different ways. We examine the most popular solutions in Section 10.6.2.

10.6
PROGRAM PARALLELISM AND SHARED VARIABLES

The introduction to this chapter states that it is difficult to break large tasks down into
subtasks that can be executed in parallel on a multiprocessor. In some special cases,
however, this division is easy. If a large task originates as a set of independent programs,
then these programs can simply be executed on different processors. Unless these programs block each other in competing for shared I/O devices, the multiprocessor is fully
used by such a workload.

Another easy case occurs when a high-level source programming language has con-
structs that allow an application programmer to explicitly declare that certain subtasks
of a program can be executed in parallel. Figure 10.14 shows such a construct, often
called a PAR segment. The PARBEGIN and PAREND control statements bracket a list
of procedures, named Proc1 through Proc$K$, that can be executed in parallel. The order
of execution of this program is as follows. When the segment of the program preceding

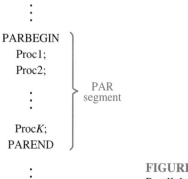

FIGURE 10.14
Parallel programming construct.

the PARBEGIN statement is completed, any or all of the K parallel procedures can be started immediately, depending on the number of idle processors available. They can be started in any order. Execution of the part of the program following PAREND is allowed to begin only after all of the K procedures have completed execution.

If this program is the only one being executed on the multiprocessor, then the burden of using the processors efficiently is placed on the application programmer. The degree of parallelism, K, of the PAR segments and their total size relative to the sequential segments determine the level of utilization achievable by the multiprocessor.

The most challenging task in achieving high utilization of multiprocessor systems is to develop compilers that can automatically detect parallelism in a user program. The usefulness of automatic detection of parallelism is based on the following reasoning. An application programmer naturally visualizes a program as a set of serially performed operations. However, even though the programmer specifies the operations as a serial list of instructions in some high-level language, many opportunities may exist for executing various groups of instructions in parallel. A simple example is that of successive passes through a loop. If no data dependency is involved, then successive passes can be executed in parallel. On the other hand, if the first pass through the loop generates data that are needed in the second pass, and so on, then parallel execution is not possible. Data dependencies must be detected by the compiler to determine which operations can be performed in parallel and which cannot. The design of compilers that can detect parallelism is complex. Even after the parallel parts of a program are identified, their subsequent scheduling for execution on a multiprocessor with a limited number of processors is a nontrivial task. Scheduling may be done either by the compiler or at runtime by the operating system. We do not pursue this topic of determining and scheduling tasks that can be executed in parallel. Instead, we turn to the issue of accessing shared variables that are modified by programs running in parallel on different processors of a multiprocessor system.

10.6.1 Accessing Shared Variables

Assume that we have identified two tasks that can run in parallel on a multiprocessor. The tasks are largely independent, but from time to time they access and modify some common, shared variable in the global memory. For example, let a shared variable SUM represent the balance in an account. Moreover, assume that several tasks running on different processors need to update this account. Each task manipulates SUM in the following way: The task reads the current value from SUM, performs an operation that depends on this value, and writes the result back into SUM. It is easy to see how errors can occur if such *read-modify-write* accesses to SUM are performed by tasks T1 and T2 running in parallel on processors P1 and P2. Suppose that both T1 and T2 read the current value from SUM, say 17, and then proceed to modify it locally. T1 adds 5 for a result of 22, and T2 subtracts 7 for a result of 10. They then proceed to write their individual results back into SUM, with T2 writing first followed by T1. The variable SUM now has the value 22, which is wrong. SUM should contain the value 15 ($= 17 + 5 - 7$), which is the intended result after applying the modifications strictly one after the other, in either order.

To guarantee correct manipulation of the shared variable SUM, each task must have exclusive access to it during the complete read-modify-write sequence. This can be provided by using a global *lock* variable, LOCK, and a machine instruction called Test-and-Set. The variable LOCK has two possible values, 0 or 1. It serves as a guard to ensure that only one task at a time is allowed access to SUM during the time needed to execute the instructions that update the value of this shared variable. Such a sequence of instructions is called a *critical section*. LOCK is manipulated as follows. It is equal to 0 when neither task is in its critical section that operates on SUM. When either task wishes to modify SUM, it first checks the value of LOCK and then sets it to 1, regardless of its original value. If the original value was 0, then the task can safely proceed to work on SUM, because no other task is currently do-ing so. On the other hand, if the original value of LOCK was 1, then the task knows that some other task is operating on SUM. It must wait until that task resets LOCK to 0 before it can proceed. This desired mode of operation on LOCK is made fool-proof by the Test-and-Set instruction. As its name implies, this instruction performs the critical steps of testing and setting LOCK in an indivisible sequence of opera-tions executed as a single machine instruction. While this instruction is executing, the memory module involved must not respond to access requests from any other processor.

As a specific example, consider the Test-and-Set instruction denoted as TAS in the Motorola 68000 microprocessor. This instruction has one operand that is always a byte. Assume that it is stored in the memory at location LOCKBYTE. Bit b_7, the most significant bit of this operand, serves as the variable LOCK just discussed. The TAS instruction performs the uninterruptible test and set operations on bit b_7. Condition code flag N (Negative) is set to the original value of b_7. Thus, after the execution of TAS is completed, the program can continue into its critical section if N equals 0, but it must wait if N equals 1. Figure 10.15 shows how two tasks, T1 and T2, can

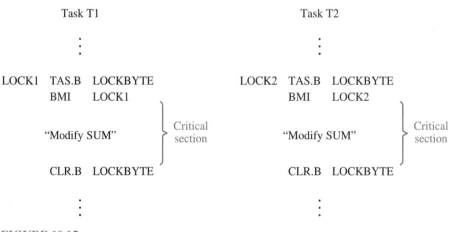

FIGURE 10.15
Mutually exclusive access to critical sections.

manipulate LOCKBYTE to enter critical sections of code in which they update the shared variable SUM. The TAS instruction is followed by a conditional branch instruction. This instruction causes a branch back to TAS if N = 1, resulting in a wait loop that continues to execute TAS on the operand in location LOCKBYTE until it finds b_7 equal to 0. The branch instruction fails if TAS is executed when b_7 is 0, allowing the program to continue into its critical section. When execution of the critical section is completed, LOCKBYTE is cleared. As a result, bit b_7 is reset to 0, allowing any waiting program to proceed into its critical section.

The TAS instruction is an example of a simple machine instruction that can be used to implement a lock. Most computers include an instruction of this type. These instructions may provide additional capabilities, such as incorporating a conditional branch based on the result of the test.

10.6.2 Cache Coherence

Shared data leads to another problem in a multiprocessor machine; the presence of multiple caches means that copies of shared data may reside in several caches. When any processor writes to a shared variable in its own cache, all other caches that contain a copy of that variable will then have the old, incorrect value. They must be informed of the change so that they can either update their copy to the new value or invalidate it. *Cache coherence* is defined as the situation in which all cached copies of shared data have the same value at all times.

In Chapter 5 we discussed two basic approaches for performing write operations on data in a cache. The write-through approach changes the data in both the cache and the main memory. The write-back approach changes the data only in the cache; the main memory copy is updated when a dirty data block in the cache has to be replaced. Similar approaches can also be used in a multiprocessor system.

Write-Through Protocol

A write-through protocol can be implemented in two fundamental versions. One version is based on updating the values in other caches, while the second relies on invalidating the copies in other caches.

Let us consider the *write-through with update* protocol first. When a processor writes a new value into its cache, the new value is also written into the memory module that holds the cache block being changed. Since copies of this block may exist in other caches, these copies must be updated to reflect the change caused by the write operation. Conceptually, the simplest way of doing this is to broadcast the written data to all processor modules in the system. As each processor module receives the broadcast data, it updates the contents of the affected cache block if this block is present in its cache (primary or secondary).

The second version of write-through protocol is based on *invalidation* of copies. When a processor writes a new value into its cache, this value is written into the memory module, and all copies in other caches are invalidated. Again, broadcasting can be used to send the invalidation requests throughout the system.

Write-Back Protocol

In the write-back protocol, multiple copies of a cache block may exist if different processors have loaded (read) the block into their caches. If some processor wants to change this block, it must first become an exclusive owner of this block. When the ownership is granted to this processor by the memory module that is the home location of the block, all other copies, including the one in the memory module, are invalidated. Now the owner of the block may change the contents at will without having to take any other action. When another processor wishes to read this block, the data are sent to this processor by the current owner. The data are also sent to the home memory module, which reacquires ownership and updates the block to contain the latest value.

The write-back protocol causes less traffic than the write-through protocol, because a processor is likely to perform several writes to a cache block before this block is needed by another processor.

So far, we have assumed that update and invalidate requests in these protocols are broadcast through the interconnection network. Whether it is practical to implement such broadcasts depends largely on the structure of the interconnection network. The most natural network for supporting broadcasting is the single bus, discussed in Section 10.4.1. In small multiprocessors that use a single bus, cache coherence can be realized using a scheme known as snooping.

Snoopy Caches

In a single-bus system, all transactions between processors and memory modules occur via the bus. In effect, they are broadcast to all units connected to the bus. Suppose that each cache associated with a processor has a controller circuit that observes the transactions on the bus that involve other processors. Suppose also that the write-back protocol just described is used.

Whenever a processor writes to its cache block for the first time, the cache block is marked as dirty, and the write is broadcast on the bus. The memory module and all other caches invalidate their copies. The processor that performed the write is now the owner of the cache block. It can do further writes in the same block without broadcasting them. If another processor issues a read request for the same block, the memory module cannot respond because it does not have a valid copy. But the present owner also sees this request when it appears on the bus, and it must supply the correct value to the requesting processor. The memory module is informed that an owner is supplying the correct value by a broadcast signal from the owner (which includes the data that the owner places on the bus), and the memory updates its value. Finally, the owner marks its copy as clean. Operation now proceeds with multiple caches and the memory module all having the correct value of the block. In the case in which a dirty value must be replaced to make room for a new block, a write-back operation to the memory module must be performed.

If two processors want to write to the same cache block at the same time, one of the processors will be granted the use of the bus first and will become the owner. As a result, the other processor's copy of the cache block will be invalidated. The second processor can then repeat its write request. This sequential handling of write requests ensures that the two processors can correctly change different words in a given cache block.

The scheme just described is based on the ability of cache controllers to observe the activity on the bus and take appropriate actions. We refer to such schemes as *snoopy-cache* techniques.

For performance reasons, it is important that the snooping function not interfere with the normal operation of a processor and its cache. Such interference would occur if, for each request on the bus, the cache controller had to access the tags of its cache to see if the block in question is present in the cache. And in most cases, the answer would be negative. To eliminate unnecessary interference, each cache can be provided with a set of duplicate tags, which maintain the same status information about the blocks in the cache but can be accessed separately by the snooping circuitry.

While the concept of snoopy caches is effective and simple to implement, it is suitable only for single-bus systems. In larger multiprocessors, more complex arrangements must be used.

Directory-Based Schemes

Enforcing cache coherence using a broadcast mechanism for distribution of invalidation or update requests becomes less attractive as the multiprocessor system grows in size. The main reason is that a large amount of unnecessary traffic may be generated by a full broadcast, because, in practical applications, copies of a given block are usually present in only a few caches.

A useful alternative is to keep a *directory* of the locations, that is, the caches where copies exist at any given time. One way to implement a directory scheme is to include additional status bits for each block in a particular memory module, which indicate the caches where copies of this block may be found. Then, instead of broadcasting to all caches, the memory module can send individual messages, such as an invalidate request in the write-back protocol, to only those caches that have a copy. Of course, the additional bits in the memory modules increase the cost of these modules. Different versions of directory schemes have been proposed and some have been implemented in existing multiprocessor systems.

SCI Standard

A specific approach to cache coherence has recently been standardized by the Institute of Electrical and Electronics Engineers (IEEE). It is a part of the SCI (Scalable Coherent Interface) standard,[21] which defines a multiprocessor backplane that is intended to provide fast signaling, scalable architecture, cache coherence, and simple implementation. The interconnection network uses point-to-point links, and the communication protocol is based on a single-requestor single-responder principle. A packet originates at a source node and is addressed to a single target. If a packet sent by the source is accepted by the target, the latter returns a positive acknowledgement packet. If the packet is not accepted, then a negative acknowledgment is returned, which causes a retry.

Cache coherence is achieved using a distributed directory-based protocol. A doubly-linked list is established for each cache block that contains shared data. Each processor node that caches a given block of shared data includes pointers to the previous and to the next nodes that share the block. These pointers are part of the cache-block tag. The head of this doubly-linked list has a pointer to the memory module that holds the block. When a new node accesses the memory module to read this block, the node becomes the new head of the list, and the memory directory is updated by replacing the pointer to the previous head with the address of the new head. A write access to the memory can be performed only by the head of the list. If another node wishes to perform a write, it can do so by inserting itself at the head of the list and purging the rest of the entries in the list.

The SCI cache coherence scheme scales well, because the memory directory and the processor cache-tag storage requirements do not increase as the size of the linked list increases. The disadvantage of this scheme is that this additional storage presents a costly fixed overhead that is incurred in all cases.

Although the SCI standard does not specify a particular topology for the interconnection network, the ring topology is one of the natural choices. The Exemplar multiprocessor from Convex Corporation uses a ring topology and implements the coherence protocol described above.

Cache coherence in general has been the topic of extensive research. In this section, we have briefly introduced some of the issues involved. Many subtle details are beyond the scope of this book.

10.6.3 Need for Locking and Cache Coherence

We should note that the requirement for lock guard controls on access to shared variables is independent of the need for cache coherence controls—both types of controls are needed. Consider a situation in which cache coherence is maintained by using the write-through policy accompanied by cache updating of writes to shared variables. Suppose that the contents of SUM in the example in Section 10.6.1 have been read into the caches of the two processors that execute tasks T1 and T2. If the read operations are part of an update sequence and are not made mutually exclusive by the use of a lock guard control, then the original error can still occur. If task T1 writes its new value last, as before, then SUM will contain the value 22, which is wrong. Cache coherence is maintained throughout this sequence of events. However, incorrect results are obtained because lock guard controls are not used.

10.7
MULTICOMPUTERS

In Section 10.5 we introduced the concept of multicomputers. We now examine the salient features of such systems in more detail.

A multicomputer system is structured as shown in Figure 10.4. Each processing node in the system is a self-contained computer that communicates with other processing nodes by sending messages over the network. Systems of this type are often called *message-passing* systems, in contrast to the shared-memory multiprocessors discussed previously.

In multicomputer systems, the demands on the interconnection network are less stringent than in shared-memory multiprocessor systems. A shared-memory machine must have a fast network with high bandwidth, because processor modules frequently access the remote memory modules that constitute the shared memory. A slow network would quickly become a bottleneck, and performance would severely degrade.

In a multicomputer, messages are sent much less frequently, resulting in much less traffic than in the shared-memory systems. Therefore, a simpler and less expensive network can be used. In view of this disparity in the intensity of communication, the terms *tightly-coupled* and *loosely-coupled* have also been associated with shared-memory and message-passing systems, respectively.

Any network described in Section 10.4 can be used in a multicomputer system. Since the traffic demands are relatively modest, the physical implementation of the interconnection network is likely to be inexpensive. The links in the network often involve bit-serial lines driven by I/O device interfaces. An interface circuit reads a message from the memory of the source computer using the DMA technique, converts it into a bit-serial format, and transmits it over the network to the destination computer. Source and destination addresses are included in a header of the message for routing purposes. The message is routed to the destination computer where it is written into a memory buffer by the I/O interface of that computer.

In the 1980s, hypercube-based interconnection networks were most popular. Such networks were used in several message-passing multiprocessor systems, typically using bit-serial transmission. Examples of such machines are Intel's iPSC, NCUBE's NCUBE/ten, and Thinking Machines' CM-2. Then in the early 1990s, other topologies gained popularity for both message-passing and shared-memory machines. Thinking Machines' CM-5 is an example of a message-passing machine that uses a fat tree network with a link width of four. Intel's Paragon uses a mesh network with a link width of 16. To facilitate message passing, it is useful to include a special communications unit at each node in the network. For example, the Paragon machine has a message processor that essentially frees the application processor from having to be involved in the details of message handling.

10.7.1 Local Area Networks

Because the communication demands in a multicomputer system are relatively low, we can consider replacing the specialized interconnection network with some readily available standard network that was developed for more general communication purposes. Many networks exist for interconnecting various types of computing equipment. Networks that span a small geographic area with distances not exceeding a few kilometers are called *local area networks* (LANs). Networks that cover larger areas that involve distances up to thousands of kilometers are referred to as *long-haul networks*, or *wide area networks*.

The most popular LANs use either the bus or the ring topology. The transmission media for either bus or ring LANs can be twisted wire pair, coaxial cable, or optical fiber. Bit-serial transmission is used, and rates in the range of 10 to 100 megabits per second (Mbps) are common. Only one message packet at a time can be successfully transmitted on the single shared path. Source and destination device addresses precede the data field of a packet, and appropriate delimiters indicate the start and end of the packet. In general, packets have variable lengths ranging from tens of bytes to over 1000 bytes.

A protocol that implements distributed access control is needed to ensure orderly transfer of packets between arbitrary pairs of communicating devices. We will sketch the basic ideas involved in two widely used protocols—the Ethernet bus and the token ring. These protocols are specified in detail in IEEE standards.[22]

Ethernet (CSMA/CD) Bus

The Ethernet bus access protocol, also called the Carrier Sense Multiple Access with Collision Detection (CSMA/CD) protocol, is conceptually one of the simplest protocols. Whenever an attached device has a message to transmit, it waits until it senses that the bus is idle and then begins transmission. The device then monitors the bus for 2τ seconds as it transmits its message, where τ is the end-to-end bus propagation delay. If the device does not observe any distortion of its transmitted signal during the 2τ interval, then it assumes that no other station has started transmission and continues its transmission to completion. On the other hand, if distortion is observed, caused by the beginning of a transmission from some other device, then both devices must stop transmitting. The mutually destructive distortion of the two transmitted signals is called a *collision,* and the time interval 2τ is called the *collision window.*

Messages that have been destroyed by collision must be retransmitted. If the devices involved in the collision attempt to retry immediately, their packets will almost certainly collide again. A basic strategy used to prevent collision of the retries is as follows. Each device independently waits for a random amount of time, then waits until the bus is idle and begins retransmission. If the random waits are a few multiples of 2τ, the probability of repeated collisions is reduced.

Token Ring

The token-ring protocol is used for ring networks. A single, appropriately encoded short message, called a *token*, circulates continuously around the ring. The arrival of the token at a ring node represents permission to transmit. If the node has nothing to transmit, it forwards the token to the next node downstream with as little delay as possible. If the node has data ready for transmission, it inhibits propagation of the token. Instead it transmits a packet of information preceded by an appropriately encoded header flag. As the packet is transmitted around the ring, its contents are read and copied as it travels past the destination node. The packet continues to travel around the ring until it reaches the source node, where it is discarded. When the source node completes transmitting a packet, it releases the permission token, which again starts to circulate around the ring. The packet size on a token ring is variable and is limited only by the amount of buffer memory available in each node, because the destination node must be able to store complete packets.

The main reason for considering the standard LANs in the context of multicomputer systems is not because they can be used in self-contained systems that we have been discussing, but because they can be used in conjunction with standard workstations to conveniently form a multicomputer system.

10.7.2 Network of Workstations

Today, most commercial, educational, and government organizations have a collection of workstations to meet their computing needs. These workstations are usually

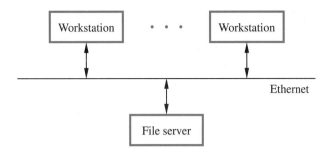

FIGURE 10.16
A typical network of workstations.

connected to a LAN that allows access to fileservers, printers, and specialized computing resources. (See Figure 10.16.)

Although each workstation is normally used as a separate computer, many workstations can be viewed as a multicomputer system. All that is needed is the software to allow parallel processing. Of course, some significant differences exist between such a system and a commercial message-passing multiprocessor machine. In particular, communication over the LAN is slower, largely because the operating system must intervene when messages have to be exchanged between programs running on different computers. This means that a network of workstations does not perform as well as a self-contained system with a specialized interconnection network. But the great advantage is that the network of workstations is usually readily available. It is certainly useful to be able to run very large applications on such systems when the workstations are not used for their normal purposes, which is typically the case at night.

10.8
PROGRAMMER'S VIEW OF SHARED MEMORY AND MESSAGE PASSING

In previous sections, we considered the hardware implications of multiprocessor systems that feature shared-memory and message-passing paradigms. Now we briefly examine how these paradigms affect the user, namely, the programmer who is implementing a parallel application. We consider a small example that involves only two processors. This keeps the discussion simple yet allows us to elaborate the key ideas.

Assume we want to compute the dot product of two N-element vectors. A sequential program for this task is outlined in Figure 10.17. It is suitable for execution on a single processor. The program is mostly self-explanatory. The **read** statements load the values of the two vectors from a disk (or some other I/O device) into the main memory. This task is done by the operating system. Let us attempt to parallelize this program to run on two processors. Evidently, the potential for parallelization lies in the loop that computes the dot product by generating the product of a pair of elements and adding the result to the previously accumulated partial dot product.

```
integer array a[1..N], b[1..N]
integer dot_product

    .

    .

read a[1..N] from vector_a
read b[1..N] from vector_b
dot_product := 0
do_dot (a, b)
print dot_product

    .

    .

do_dot (integer array x[1..N], integer array y[1..N])
    for k:= 1 to N
            dot_product := dot_product + x[k] * y[k]
    end
end
```

FIGURE 10.17
A sequential program to compute the dot product.

10.8.1 Shared Memory Case

Our first attempt to write a program for two processors is shown in Figure 10.18. As the program starts executing on one processor, it loads the vectors into memory and initializes the *dot_product* variable to 0. We achieve parallelism by having a second processor perform half of the computations needed to obtain the dot product. This is done by creating a separate thread to be executed on the second processor.

A thread is an independent path of execution within a program. Actually, the term *thread* is used to refer to a thread of control, where multiple threads execute portions of the program and can run in parallel as if they were separate programs. Thus, two or more threads can be running on different processors, executing either the same or different code. The key point is that all threads are part of a single program and run in the same address space. We should note that in the commonly used uniprocessor environment, each program has a single thread of control.

In the program in Figure 10.18, a new thread is created by the *create_thread* statement. This thread will execute the *do_dot* routine and terminate. The operating system will assign the identification number of 1 to the new thread. The first processor continues by executing the *do_dot (a,b)* statement as thread 0. The statement *id := mypid()* sets the variable *id* to the assigned identification number of the thread. Using the *id* value in the **for** loop allows simple specification of which halves of the vectors *a* and *b* should be handled by a particular thread.

Changing the accumulated value of the *dot_product* variable is the critical section in the *do_dot* routine; hence, each thread must have exclusive access to this variable. This is achieved by the locking mechanism, as discussed in Section 10.6.1. Thread 0 does not proceed past the barrier statement in the *do_dot* routine until the other thread has reached the same synchronization point. This ensures that both threads have completed their updates of the *dot_product* variable before thread 0 is allowed to print the final

```
shared integer array a[1..N], b[1..N]
shared integer dot_product
shared lock dot_product_lock
shared barrier done

 .

 .

read a[1..N] from vector_a
read b[1..N] from vector_b
dot_product := 0
create_thread (do_dot, a, b)
do_dot (a, b)
print dot_product

 .

 .

do_dot (integer array x[1..N], integer array y[1..N])
    private integer id
    id := mypid()
    for k:= (id*N/2) + 1 to (id + 1)*N/2
            lock (dot_product_lock)
                    dot_product := dot_product + x[k] * y[k]
            unlock (dot_product_lock)
    end
    barrier (done)
end
```

FIGURE 10.18
A first attempt at writing a program to compute the dot
product on two processors in a shared-memory machine.

result. The *barrier* concept can be realized in different ways. A simple approach is to
use a shared variable, such as *done* in Figure 10.18. This variable is initialized to the
number of threads (two in our example) and then decremented as each thread arrives
at the barrier.

The program in Figure 10.18 has one major flaw. The locking arrangement used
does not allow the expected parallelism to be achieved, because both threads continuously write the same shared variable, *dot_product*. Thus, the potentially parallel part of
the required computation will in fact be done serially.

To achieve the desired parallelism, we can modify the program as shown in Figure 10.19. Instead of using the shared variable, *dot_product,* in the **for** loop, a private
variable, *local_dot_product,* is introduced to accumulate the partial dot product as it is
being computed by each thread. Thus, only upon completion of the loop is it necessary
to enter a critical section where each thread updates the shared variable, *dot_product.*
This modification allows both threads to execute the **for** loop in parallel.

This example can be easily extended to a larger number of processors. All that
needs to be done is to create more threads. The loop bound expressions in the **for** loop
will determine the range of elements that each thread uses in the computation based on
the value of the assigned *id.*

```
shared integer array a[1..N], b[1..N]
shared integer dot_product
shared lock dot_product_lock
shared barrier done
.
.
.
read a[1..N] from vector_a
read b[1..N] from vector_b
dot_product := 0
create_thread (do_dot, a, b)
do_dot (a, b)
print dot_product
.
.
.
do_dot (integer array x[1..N], integer array y[1..N])
    private integer local_dot_product
    private integer id
    id := mypid()
    local_dot_product := 0
    for k:= (id*N/2) + 1 to (id + 1)*N/2
        local_dot_product := local_dot_product + x[k] * y[k]
    end
    lock (dot_product_lock)
        dot_product := dot_product + local_dot_product
    unlock (dot_product_lock)
    barrier (done)
end
```

FIGURE 10.19
An efficient program to compute the dot product on two
processors in a shared-memory machine.

The effectiveness of the program in Figure 10.19 depends on the size of the data
vectors. The larger the vectors, the more effective this approach is. For small vectors,
the overhead of creating threads and providing synchronization outweighs any benefit
that parallelism may provide.

10.8.2 Message-Passing Case

In this case the memory is distributed, and each processor can access directly only
its own memory. The desired program will run on two processors and the arrays will
have to be explicitly divided into halves, with each half being stored in the memory
of one processor. Each copy of the program will have access only to its portion of the
data. Applications of this type are called *Single Program Multiple Data* (SPDM). The
reader should note the difference between this type of application and the SIMD type

introduced in Section 10.1.1. In the SIMD type, all processors execute the same instruction at any given time.

A possible program is given in Figure 10.20. The vector data must first be loaded into the private memories of the two processors. The program that is assigned the *id* value of 0 reads the first half of vector *a* from the disk, with the help of the operating system, and it stores the data in its memory under this name. It then reads the remaining second half of vector *a* and places the data in a memory buffer called *temparray*. Next, it sends a message containing the data from this buffer to the processor that executes the program that is assigned the *id* value of 1. The same operations are then repeated for the data that constitute vector *b*. The program with the *id* value of 1 receives the second halves of vectors *a* and *b* and stores them in its memory under the same names.

The *do_dot* routine now simply computes the dot product for the N/2 elements. Note that the loop bounds are the same for both processors, because each uses the data stored in its own memory. The message-passing feature is also illustrated by the action taken when the processors complete execution of the *do_dot* routine: The program that has the *id* value of 0 will compute and print the final dot product. It will do so when it receives the message with the value of the partial dot product that was computed and sent by program 1. This value is received in a temporary buffer called *temp*.

Again, it is easy to see how this example could be extended to many processors. The vectors would have to be partitioned into portions that would be assigned to each processor for computation. One of the processors, for example, the one that executes the program with *id* = 0, would be designated to compute the final result using the data received in messages from other processors.

The overhead of establishing parallel execution on multiple processors consists of the time needed to load the copies of the program into different processors, the time used to set up the partitioned arrays in the memories associated with different processors, and the time needed to send other messages among processors. Performance benefits depend on the size of the vectors and the number of processors used.

Shared-memory and message-passing paradigms have certain strengths and weaknesses. The shared-memory environment is more natural to use, because it is an extension of the uniprocessor programming model. Hence, it is easier to write parallel programs that are reasonably efficient. Since the memory access latency may be high if data reside in remote memory modules, it is important to minimize the number of write accesses to global variables. The amount of traffic in the network may be large, causing the network to become a bottleneck. Synchronization of processes is the responsibility of the programmer and influences the performance of an application significantly.

Message passing gives a less natural programming environment, because of multiple address spaces in private memories. The time overhead of message passing is very significant; hence, the programmer must try to structure programs to minimize its effect. Since messages are relatively infrequent, the interconnection network is not likely to be a problem. Synchronization is implicit in the messages passed between processes. Perhaps the biggest advantage of message passing is that it can be supported by less expensive and more commonly available hardware.

```
integer array a[1..N/2], b[1..N/2], temparray[1..N/2]
integer dot_product
integer id
integer temp
     .

     .
id := mypid()
if (id = 0) then
            read a[1..N/2] from vector_a
            read temparray[1..N/2] from vector_a
            send (temparray[1..N/2], 1)
            read b[1..N/2] from vector_b
            read temparray[1..N/2] from vector_b
            send (temparray[1..N/2], 1)
     else receive (a[1..N/2], 0)
            receive (b[1..N/2], 0)
end
dot_product := 0
do_dot (a, b)
if (id = 1) send (dot_product, 0)
     else  receive (temp, 1)
            dot_product := dot_product + temp
            print dot_product
end
     .

     .
do_dot (integer array x[1..N/2], integer array y[1..N/2])
     for k:= 1 to N/2
            dot_product := dot_product + x[k]*y[k]
     end
end
```

FIGURE 10.20
A message-passing program to compute the dot product on
two processors.

10.9
PERFORMANCE CONSIDERATIONS

This chapter has concentrated on the design of systems that use multiple processors to reduce the time needed to run a large application. The most important performance measure is the speedup achieved on a multiprocessor system in comparison with the time it would take to run the same application on a single processor. The *speedup* is defined as

$$S_P = \frac{T_1}{T_P}$$

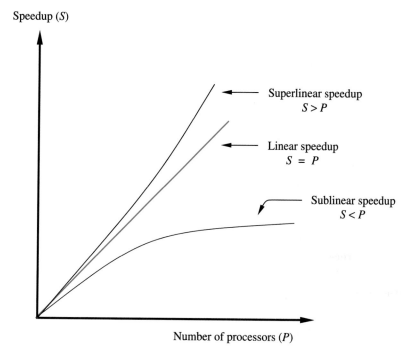

Speedup (S)

Superlinear speedup
$S > P$

Linear speedup
$S = P$

Sublinear speedup
$S < P$

Number of processors (P)

FIGURE 10.21
Speedup curves in multiprocessor systems.

where T_1 and T_P are the times needed if one or P processors are used, respectively. Figure 10.21 shows three types of speedup that may occur as a function of the number of processors in the system. Intuitively, we would expect that, as the number of processors is increased, the time needed to run an application that is parallelizable should decrease proportionately. This would give a linear speedup, where $S = P$, which is the goal in scalable systems. Unfortunately, this goal is not easy to achieve.

As the previous section shows, it is not possible to parallelize all parts of an application program. The sequential parts will take the same amount of time regardless of the number of processors used. It is the relative proportion of sequential parts that limits the achievable speedup.

Another reason why linear speedup is difficult to achieve is the overhead caused by initialization, synchronization, communication, cache coherence control, and load imbalance. Overhead tends to increase with the size of the system. We have encountered examples of such overhead in previous sections, except for load imbalance. It is usually necessary to wait for the last processor to complete a parallel task before proceeding with the next set of tasks. Hence, when a parallel task is spread over a number of processors, it is most efficient if all processors reach a given synchronization point at about the same time, in which case the load is balanced.

In practical systems the speedup achievable with most applications is sublinear, and a point is reached where adding processors no longer improves performance. Curiously, there exist some applications for which even superlinear speedup is possible, but these are not common. We give an example of such an application in the next subsection.

10.9.1 Amdahl's Law

Let us consider the improvement in performance from a quantitative point of view. An enhancement in a computer system inevitably improves some part of the system, but not the entire system. The improved performance depends on the impact of the enhanced part. This reasoning was formalized by Gene Amdahl in a well known "law".[23] It can be stated as

$$S_{new} = \frac{Old\ time}{New\ time} = \frac{1}{1 - f_{enhanced} + f_{enhanced}/S_{enhanced}}$$

where

- S_{new} is the speedup in the new system, which includes the enhancement.
- $S_{enhanced}$ is the speedup achievable if only the enhanced part of the system is used.
- $f_{enhanced}$ is the fraction of the computation time in the old system that can be improved with the enhancement made.

In terms of a multiprocessor system, this law can be restated as follows. Let f be the fraction of a computation (in terms of time) that is parallelizable, P be the number of processors in the system, and S_P the speedup achievable in comparison with sequential execution. Then we have

$$S_P = \frac{1}{1 - f + f/P} = \frac{P}{P - f(P - 1)}$$

This formula assumes that the parallelizable part is performed by all processors using perfect load balance.

Suppose that a given application is run on a 64-processor machine and that 70 percent of the application is parallelizable. Then the expected improvement is

$$S_{64} = \frac{64}{64 - 0.7 \times 63} = 3.22$$

If the same application is run on a 16-processor machine, the expected speedup would be 2.91. This indicates that the speedup is much less than the number of processors in the machine. Moreover, the difference in speedup achieved by increasing from 16 to 64 processors is minimal. Clearly, it makes little sense to use large multiprocessors for applications that have significant sequential (nonparallelizable) parts. For good speedup, the sequential parts must be very short. For an application with $f = 0.95$, the speedup in the preceding machines would be 15.42 and 9.14, respectively. Amdahl's law, in fact, states that linear speedup cannot be achieved, because almost all applications have some sections that cannot be parallelized.

This discussion assumes that each processor performs an equal amount of parallel computation. Such equal load balancing may not necessarily occur. If it is necessary to wait for the slowest processor to complete its parallel assignment before continuing with the next step, then the results will be worse than predicted by the preceding formula. However, there exist applications where the opposite may occur, namely, where the tasks performed by all processors may be terminated as soon as one processor completes its task. For example, such unusual behavior occurs in applications based on a technique known as simulated annealing. To illustrate this technique, suppose that in the design of a VLSI chip, it is desired to place the logic gates such that the total length of wires in the resulting circuit is minimized. This requires trying a large number of different placements, which can be done by assigning the best placement known at a given time to all processors as a starting point for the next iteration. Then each processor can use a different randomized approach to change the positions of the gates in search for a better placement. As soon as one processor finds a placement that is superior to the starting placement by some predetermined amount, this processor's solution can be used as the new starting point for all processors, without waiting for the other processors to also find acceptable solutions. An application of this type may exhibit superlinear speedup, because if it is performed by a single processor, this processor may spend a lot of time investigating unpromising possibilities before it reaches a good one.

10.9.2 Performance Indicators

From a user's point of view, the most important characteristics of a computer system are its cost, ease of use, reliability, and performance. Several indicators of performance are used to depict the processing capability of computers. The discussion of this issue in Section 9.3 equally applies to multiprocessor systems.

The raw power of a processor can be indicated in terms of the number of operations it can perform in one second. Two popular measures are MIPS, the number of millions of instructions executed per second, and MFLOPS (pronounced megaFLOPS), the number of millions of floating-point operations performed per second. When a manufacturer gives the MIPS and MFLOPS numbers for a given processor, these numbers indicate the processor's maximum capability. This maximum is not always achievable in practical applications. In a multiprocessor system, the total MIPS and MFLOPS are simply the sums of the values for all the processors.

Another common performance indicator is the communications capability of the interconnection network, usually given as the total bandwidth in bytes per second. This assumes an optimal situation in which sufficient data are available for transfer to keep the largest possible number of network links busy, thus maximizing the amount of data that can be transferred at one time.

While indicators such as MIPS, MFLOPS, and network bandwidth give a useful impression of what the system is capable of doing, they are not a measure of the actual performance we expect to observe when application programs are executed. Practical applications can use only a fraction of the total resources available at any given time. This fraction varies from one system to another and from one application to another. A proper comparison of two different systems is possible only if a desired set of applications is run on both systems and their performance is observed. To facilitate such comparisons, a number of *benchmark* programs have been developed. These programs are indicative of the behavior found in a variety of common applications. Comparing different systems based on benchmark programs has become widely accepted. Examples of such comparisons are given in Chapter 8 for some commercial processors.

10.10
CONCLUDING REMARKS

Multiprocessors provide a way to realize supercomputing capability at a reasonable cost. They are most cost-effective in the range of tens to hundreds of processors. Very large systems comprising thousands of processors are difficult to use fully, and their cost curtails the market demand significantly.

A particularly cost-effective possibility is to implement a multicomputer system using workstations interconnected by a local area network. This possibility will become even more attractive as local area network speeds increase.

Successful use of multiprocessors depends heavily on the availability of system software that makes good use of the available resources. An application program will not show good performance if the locality and parallelism inherent in the application are not properly exploited. The compiler must detect the opportunities for parallel execution. The operating system must schedule the execution to make good use of locality, by assigning tasks that involve a large amount of interaction to processors that are close to each other. The application programmer may provide useful hints in this respect, but it is best if the system software can do this on its own.

This chapter provides an overview of the most important aspects of multiprocessor and multicomputer systems. Many details should be studied to understand fully the capabilities of these systems and the design issues involved. For detailed study, the reader should consult books that specialize in this subject.[24–27]

PROBLEMS

10.1. Write a program loop whose instructions can be broadcast from the control processor in Figure 10.1 that will enable an array processor to iteratively compute temperatures in a plane, as discussed in Section 10.2. In addition to instructions that shift the network register contents between adjacent processing elements (PEs), assume that there are two-operand instructions for moves between PE registers and local memory and for arithmetic operations. Assume also that each PE stores the current estimate of its grid point temperature in a local memory location named CURRENT and that a few registers, R0, R1, and so on, are available for processing. Each boundary PE maintains a fixed boundary temperature value in its network register and does not execute the broadcast program. A small value stored in location EPSILON in each PE is used to determine when the local temperature has reached the required level of accuracy. At the end of each iteration of the loop, each PE must set its status bit, STATUS, to 1 if its new temperature satisfies the following condition:

$$|\text{New temperature} - [\text{CURRENT}]| < [\text{EPSILON}]$$

Otherwise, STATUS is set to 0.

10.2. Assume that a bus transfer takes T seconds and memory access time is $4T$ seconds. A read request over a conventional bus then requires $6T$ seconds to complete. How many conventional buses are needed to equal or exceed the bandwidth of a split-transaction bus that operates with the same time delays? Consider only read requests, ignore memory conflicts, and assume that all memory modules are connected to all buses in the multiple bus case. Does your answer increase or decrease if memory access time increases?

10.3. In a bus-based multiprocessor, the system bus can become a bottleneck if it does not support a high enough transfer rate. Suppose that a split-transaction bus is designed to be four times as wide as the word length of the processors used in the system. Will this increase the effective transfer rate to four times the rate of a similar bus that is only as wide as the processor word length? Explain your answer.

10.4. Assume that the cost of a 2×2 switch in a shuffle network is twice the cost of a crosspoint in a crossbar switch. There are n^2 crosspoints in an $n \times n$ crossbar switch. As n increases, the crossbar becomes more costly than the shuffle network. What is the smallest value of n for which crossbar cost is five times more costly than the shuffle network?

10.5. Shuffle networks can be built from 4×4 and 8×8 switches, for example, instead of from 2×2 switches. Draw a 16×16 ($n = 16$) shuffle network built from 4×4 switches. If the cost of a 4×4 switch is four times the cost of a 2×2 switch, compare the cost of shuffle networks built from 4×4 switches with those built from 2×2 switches for n values in the sequence 4, 4^2, 4^3, and so on. Qualitatively compare the blocking probability of these two different ways of building shuffle networks.

10.6. Suppose that each procedure of a PAR segment (see Figure 10.14) requires 1 unit of time to execute. A program consists of three sequential segments. Each segment requires k time units and must be executed on a single processor. The three sequential segments are separated by two PAR segments, each of which consists of k procedures that can be executed on independent processors. Derive an expression for speedup for this program when run on a multiprocessor with n processors. Assume $n \leq k$. What is the limiting value of the speedup when k is large and $n = k$? What does this result tell you about the effect of sequential segments in programs that have some segments with substantial parallelism?

10.7. The shortest distance a message travels in an n-dimensional hypercube is 1 hop, and the longest distance a message needs to travel is n hops. Assuming that all possible source/destination pairs are equally likely, is the average distance a message needs to travel larger or smaller than $(1 + n)/2$? Justify your answer.

10.8. A task that "busy-waits" on a lock variable by using a Test-and-Set instruction in a two-instruction loop, as in Figure 10.15, wastes bus cycles that could otherwise be used for computation. Suggest a way around this problem that involves a centralized queue of waiting tasks that is maintained by the operating system. Assume that the operating system can be called by a user task and that the operating system chooses which task is to be executed on a processor from among those ready for execution.

10.9. What are the arguments for and against invalidation and updating as strategies for maintaining cache coherence?

10.10. Section 10.6.3 argues that cache coherence controls cannot replace the need for lock variables. Can the use of lock variables replace the need for explicit cache coherence controls?

10.11. Estimate the improvement in performance that can be achieved if the program in Figure 10.19 is used rather than the program in Figure 10.18.

10.12. Modify the program in Figure 10.19 to make it suitable for execution in a four-processor machine.

10.13. Modify the program in Figure 10.20 to make it suitable for execution in a four-processor system.

10.14. For small vectors, the approach in Figure 10.19 will be worse than if the dot product is computed using a single processor. Estimate the minimum size of the vectors for which this approach leads to better performance. Make some appropriate assumptions about the amount of time it takes to perform each step in the program.

10.15. Repeat Problem 10.14 for the approach in Figure 10.20.

10.16. Shared-memory multiprocessors and message-passing multicomputers are architectures that support simultaneous execution of tasks that interact with each other. Which of these two architectures can emulate the action of the other more easily? Briefly justify your answer.

10.17. The Ethernet bus LAN protocol is really only suitable when message transmission time is significantly larger than 2τ, where τ is the end-to-end bus propagation delay. Consider the case in which transmission time is less than τ. Is it possible for a destination station to correctly receive an undistorted message, even though the source station observes a collision inside the 2τ collision window period? If not, justify your answer. If you think it is possible, give the relative locations of the source, destination, and interfering stations on the bus and describe the relevant event times.

10.18. A *mailbox memory* is a RAM memory with the following feature. A full/empty bit, F/E, is associated with each memory word location. The instruction

PUT   R0,BOXLOC,WAITSEND

is executed indivisibly as follows. The F/E bit associated with mailbox memory location BOXLOC is tested. If it is 0, denoting empty, then the contents of register R0 are written into BOXLOC, F/E is set to 1, denoting full, and execution continues with the next sequential instruction. Otherwise (i.e., for F/E = 1), no operations are performed and execution control is passed to the instruction at location WAITSEND in program memory.

(*a*) Give an appropriate definition for the instruction

GET   R0,BOXLOC,WAITREC

that is complementary to the PUT instruction.

(*b*) Suppose two tasks, T_1 and T_2, running on different processors in a multiprocessor system, pass a stream of one-word messages from T_1 to T_2 using PUT and GET instructions on a shared mailbox memory unit. Write program segments for T_1 and T_2 in assembly-language style that accomplish the same thing on a shared-memory multiprocessor system that does not have a mailbox memory unit but does have a TAS instruction as described in Section 10.6.1.

REFERENCES

1. M. J. Flynn, "Very High-Speed Computing Systems," *Proceedings of the IEEE*, vol. 54, December 1966, pp. 1901–1909.
2. D. L. Slotnick, "The Fastest Computer," *Scientific American*, vol. 224, February 1971, pp. 76–88.

3. *The Connection Machine CM-2 Technical Summary*, Thinking Machines Corp., 1990.
4. T. Blank, "The MasPar MP-1 Architecture," *COMPCON Proceedings*, 1990, pp. 20–24.
5. T. Lovett and S. Thakkar, "The Symmetry Multiprocessor System," *Proceedings of the International Conference on Parallel Processing*, vol. 1, The Pennsylvania State University Press, August 1988, pp. 303–310.
6. *The SGI POWER Challenge Multiprocessor*, Silicon Graphics Inc., 1995.
7. "Inside the GP1000," BBN Advanced Computers, Inc., October 1988.
8. "A New Direction in Scientific Computing," Intel Corporation, 1985.
9. J. P. Hayes, et al., "A Microprocessor-Based Hypercube Supercomputer," *IEEE Micro*, October 1986, pp. 6–17.
10. *Paragon XP/S Product Overview*, Intel Corporation, 1991.
11. D. Lenoski, et al., "The Stanford DASH Multiprocessor," *Computer*, vol. 25, March 1992, pp. 63–79.
12. J. Kuskin, et al., "The Stanford FLASH Multiprocessor," *Proceedings of the 21st Annual International Symposium on Computer Architecture*, Chicago, April 1994, pp. 302–313.
13. A. Agarwal, et al., "The MIT Alewife Machine: Architecture and Performance," *Proceedings of the 22nd Annual International Symposium on Computer Architecture*, Santa Margherita Ligure, Italy, June 1995, pp. 2–13.
14. W. Oed, "The Cray Research Massively Parallel Processor System Cray T3D," *Technical Report*, Cray Research GmbH, Munich, Germany, November 1993.
15. *The Connection Machine CM-5 Technical Summary*, Thinking Machines Corp., 1991.
16. *KSR-1 Technical Summary*, Kendall Square Research, 1992.
17. *Exemplar Architecture*, Convex Computer Corporation, 1994.
18. Z. G. Vranesic, M. Stumm, D. M. Lewis, and R. White, "Hector: A Hierarchically Structured Shared-Memory Multiprocessor," *Computer*, vol. 24, January 1991, pp.72–79.
19. Z. G. Vranesic, et al., "The NUMAchine Multiprocessor," *Technical Report CSRI-324*, Computer Systems Research Institute, University of Toronto, Canada, 1995.
20. W. J. Dally and P. Song, "Design of a Self-Timed Multicomputer Communication Controller," *Proceedings of the 1987 International Conference on Computer Design*, October 1987, pp. 230–234.
21. D. Gustavson, "The Scalable Coherent Interface and Related Standards Projects," *IEEE Micro*, vol. 12, January 1992, pp. 10–22.
22. *IEEE Local Area Standard 802*, IEEE, 1985.
23. G. M. Amdahl, "Validity of the Single Processor Approach to Achieving Large-Scale Computing Capabilities," *Proceedings of AFIPS Spring Joint Computer Conference*, Atlantic City, N.J., April 1967, pp. 483–485.
24. G. S. Almasi and A. Gottlieb, *Highly Parallel Computing*, 2d ed., Benjamin-Cummings, Redwood City, Calif., 1994.
25. K. Hwang, *Advanced Computer Architecture*, McGraw-Hill, New York, 1993.
26. H. S. Stone, *High-Performance Computer Architecture*, 3d ed., Addison-Wesley, Reading, Mass., 1993.
27. D. Tabak, *Multiprocessors*, Prentice-Hall, Englewood Cliffs, N.J., 1990.

Logic Circuits

Information in digital computers is represented and processed by electronic networks called *logic circuits*. These circuits operate on *binary variables* that assume one of two distinct values, usually called 0 and 1. In this appendix we will give a concise presentation of logic functions and circuits for their implementation, including a brief review of integrated circuit technology.

A.1
BASIC LOGIC FUNCTIONS

It is helpful to introduce the topic of binary logic by examining a practical problem that arises in all homes. Consider a lightbulb whose on/off status is controlled by two switches, x_1 and x_2. Each switch can be in one of two possible positions, 0 or 1, as shown in Figure A.1*a*. It can thus be represented by a binary variable. We will let the switch names serve as the names of the associated binary variables. The figure also shows an electrical power supply and a lightbulb. The way the switch terminals are interconnected determines how the switches control the light. The light will be on only if a closed path exists from the power supply through the switch network to the light-bulb. Let a binary variable f represent the condition of the light. If the light is on, $f = 1$, and if the light is off, $f = 0$. Thus, $f = 1$ means that there is at least one closed path through the network, and $f = 0$ means that there is no closed path. Clearly, f is a function of the two variables x_1 and x_2.

Let us consider some possibilities for controlling the light. First, suppose that the light is to be on if either switch is in the 1 position; that is, $f = 1$ if

$$x_1 = 1 \quad \text{and} \quad x_2 = 0$$

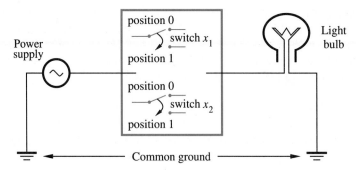

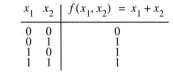

(a) Light bulb controlled by two switches

x_1	x_2	$f(x_1, x_2) = x_1 + x_2$
0	0	0
0	1	1
1	0	1
1	1	1

(b) Parallel connection (OR control)

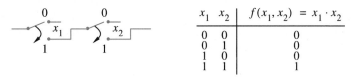

x_1	x_2	$f(x_1, x_2) = x_1 \cdot x_2$
0	0	0
0	1	0
1	0	0
1	1	1

(c) Series connection (AND control)

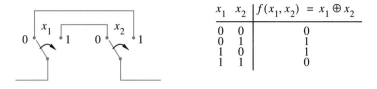

x_1	x_2	$f(x_1, x_2) = x_1 \oplus x_2$
0	0	0
0	1	1
1	0	1
1	1	0

(d) EXCLUSIVE-OR connection (EX-OR control)

FIGURE A.1
Light switch example.

or

$$x_1 = 0 \quad \text{and} \quad x_2 = 1$$

or

$$x_1 = 1 \quad \text{and} \quad x_2 = 1$$

The connections that implement this type of control are shown in Figure A.1b. A logic *truth table* that represents this situation is shown beside the wiring diagram. The table lists all possible switch settings, along with the value of f for each setting. In logic terms, this table represents the OR function of the two variables x_1 and x_2. The operation is represented algebraically by a "+" sign or a "$\vee$" sign, so that

$$f = x_1 + x_2 = x_1 \vee x_2$$

We say that x_1 and x_2 are the *input* variables and f is the *output* function.

We should point out some basic properties of the OR operation. It is commutative; that is,

$$x_1 + x_2 = x_2 + x_1$$

It can be extended to n variables, so that

$$f = x_1 + x_2 + \cdots + x_n$$

has the value 1 if any variable x_i has the value 1. This represents the effect of connecting more switches in parallel with the two switches in Figure A.1b. Also, inspection of the truth table shows that

$$1 + x = 1$$

and

$$0 + x = x$$

Now, suppose that the light is to be on only when both switches are in the 1 position. The connections for this, along with the corresponding truth-table representation, are shown in Figure A.1c. This is the AND function, which uses the symbol "$\cdot$" or "$\wedge$" and is denoted as

$$f = x_1 \cdot x_2 = x_1 \wedge x_2$$

Some basic properties of the AND operation are

$$x_1 \cdot x_2 = x_2 \cdot x_1$$
$$1 \cdot x = x$$

and

$$0 \cdot x = 0$$

The AND function also extends to n variables, with

$$f = x_1 \cdot x_2 \cdots \cdots x_n$$

having the value 1 only if all the x_i variables have the value 1. This represents the case in which more switches are connected in series with the two switches in Figure A.1c.

The final possibility that we will discuss for the way the switches determine the light status is another common situation. If we assume that the switches are at the two ends of a stairway, it should be possible to turn the light on or off from either switch. That is, if the light is on, changing either switch position should turn it off; and if it is off, changing either switch position should turn it on. Assume that the light is off when both switches are in the 0 position. Then changing either switch to the 1 position should turn the light on. Now suppose that the light is on with $x_1 = 1$ and $x_2 = 0$. Switching x_1 back to 0 will obviously turn the light off. Furthermore, it must be possible to turn the light off by changing x_2 to 1; that is, $f = 0$ if $x_1 = x_2 = 1$. The connections to implement this type of control are shown in Figure A.1d. The corresponding logic operation is called the EXCLUSIVE-OR (EX-OR) function, which is represented by the symbol "$\oplus$". Some of its properties are

$$x_1 \oplus x_2 = x_2 \oplus x_1$$

$$1 \oplus x = \overline{x}$$

and

$$0 \oplus x = x$$

where $\overline{x}$ denotes the NOT function of the variable x. This single-variable function, $f = \overline{x}$, has the value 1 if $x = 0$ and the value 0 if $x = 1$. We say that the input x is being *inverted* or *complemented*.

A.1.1 Electronic Logic Gates

The use of switches, closed or open electrical paths, and lightbulbs to illustrate the idea of logic variables and functions is convenient because of their familiarity and simplicity. The logic concepts that have been introduced are equally applicable to the electronic circuits used to process information in digital computers. The physical variables are electrical voltages and currents instead of switch positions and closed or open paths. For example, consider a circuit that is designed to operate on inputs that are at either +5 or 0 volts. The circuit outputs are also at either +5 or 0 V. Now, if we say that +5 V represents logic 1 and 0 V represents logic 0, then we can describe what the circuit does by specifying the truth table for the logic operation that it performs.

With the help of transistors, it is possible to design simple electronic circuits that perform logic operations such as AND, OR, EX-OR, and NOT. It is customary to use the name *gates* for these basic logic circuits. Standard symbols for these gates are shown in Figure A.2. A somewhat more compact graphical notation for the NOT operation is used when inversion is applied to a logic gate input or output. In such cases, the inversion is denoted by a small circle.

The electronic implementation of logic gates will be discussed in Section A.5. We will now proceed to discuss how basic gates can be used to construct logic networks that implement more complex logic functions.

A.2
SYNTHESIS OF LOGIC FUNCTIONS USING
AND, OR, AND NOT GATES

Consider the network composed of two AND gates and one OR gate that is shown in Figure A.3a. It can be represented by the expression

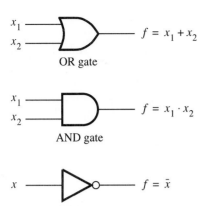

$f = x_1 + x_2$

OR gate

$f = x_1 \cdot x_2$

AND gate

$f = \bar{x}$

NOT gate

$f = x_1 \oplus x_2$

EX-OR gate

FIGURE A.2
Standard logic gate symbols.

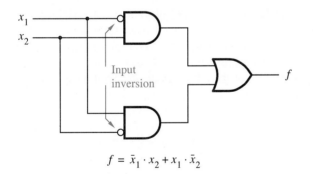

Input
inversion

$f = \bar{x}_1 \cdot x_2 + x_1 \cdot \bar{x}_2$

(a) Network for the EX-OR function

x_1	x_2	$\bar{x}_1 \cdot x_2$	$x_1 \cdot \bar{x}_2$	$f = \bar{x}_1 \cdot x_2 + x_1 \cdot \bar{x}_2$ $= x_1 \oplus x_2$
0	0	0	0	0
0	1	1	0	1
1	0	0	1	1
1	1	0	0	0

(b) Truth table construction of $\bar{x}_1 \cdot x_2 + x_1 \cdot \bar{x}_2$

FIGURE A.3
Implementation of the EX-OR
function using AND, OR, and
NOT gates.

$$f = \overline{x}_1 \cdot x_2 + x_1 \cdot \overline{x}_2$$

The construction of the truth table for this expression is shown in Figure A.3b. First, the values of the AND terms are determined for each input valuation. Then the values of the function f are determined using the OR operation. The truth table for f is identical to the truth table for the EX-OR function, so the three-gate network in Figure A.3a is an implementation of the EX-OR function using AND, OR, and NOT gates. The logic expression $\overline{x}_1 \cdot x_2 + x_1 \cdot \overline{x}_2$ is called a *sum-of-products* form because the OR operation is sometimes called the "sum" function and the AND operation the "product" function.

We should note that it would be more proper to write

$$f = ((\overline{x}_1) \cdot x_2) + (x_1 \cdot (\overline{x}_2))$$

to indicate the order of applying the operations in the expression. To simplify the appearance of such expressions, we define a hierarchy among the three operations AND, OR, and NOT. In the absence of parentheses, operations in a logic expression should be performed in the following order: NOT, AND, and then OR. Furthermore, it is customary to omit the "·" operator when there is no ambiguity.

Returning to the sum-of-products form, we will now explain how any logic function can be synthesized in this form directly from its truth table. Consider the truth table of Table A.1 and suppose we wish to synthesize the function f_1 using AND, OR, and NOT gates. For each row of the table in which $f_1 = 1$, we include a product (AND) term in the sum-of-products form. The product term includes all three input variables. The NOT operator is applied to these variables individually so that the term is 1 only when the variables have the particular valuation that corresponds to that row of the truth table. This means that if $x_i = 0$, then $\overline{x}_i$ is entered in the product term, and if $x_i = 1$, then x_i is entered. For example, the fourth row of the table has the function entry 1 for the input valuation

$$(x_1, x_2, x_3) = (0, 1, 1)$$

The product term corresponding to this is $\overline{x}_1 x_2 x_3$. Doing this for all rows in which the function f_1 has the value 1 leads to

$$f_1 = \overline{x}_1\overline{x}_2\overline{x}_3 + \overline{x}_1\overline{x}_2 x_3 + \overline{x}_1 x_2 x_3 + x_1 x_2 x_3$$

TABLE A.1
Two three-variable functions

x_1	x_2	x_3	f_1	f_2
0	0	0	1	1
0	0	1	1	1
0	1	0	0	1
0	1	1	1	0
1	0	0	0	1
1	0	1	0	1
1	1	0	0	0
1	1	1	1	0

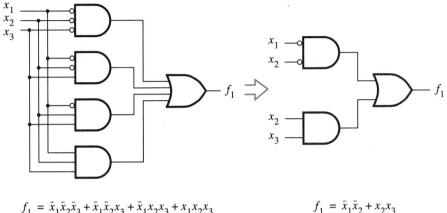

$$f_1 = \bar{x}_1\bar{x}_2\bar{x}_3 + \bar{x}_1\bar{x}_2x_3 + \bar{x}_1x_2x_3 + x_1x_2x_3 \qquad\qquad f_1 = \bar{x}_1\bar{x}_2 + x_2x_3$$

FIGURE A.4
A logic network for f_1 of Table A.1 and an equivalent minimal network.

The logic network corresponding to this expression is shown on the left side in Figure A.4. As another example, the sum-of-products expression for the EX-OR function can be derived from its truth table using this technique. This approach can be used to derive sum-of-products expressions and the corresponding logic networks for truth tables of any size.

A.3
MINIMIZATION OF LOGIC EXPRESSIONS

We have shown how to derive one sum-of-products expression for each truth table. In fact, there are many equivalent expressions and logic networks for any particular truth table. Two logic expressions or logic gate networks are equivalent if they have identical truth tables. An expression that is equivalent to the sum-of-products expression we derived for f_1 in the previous section is

$$\bar{x}_1\bar{x}_2 + x_2x_3$$

To prove this, we construct the truth table for the simpler expression and show that it is identical to the truth table for f_1 in Table A.1. This is done in Table A.2. The construction of the table for $\bar{x}_1\bar{x}_2 + x_2x_3$ is done in three steps. First, the value of the product term $\bar{x}_1\bar{x}_2$ is computed for each valuation of the inputs. Then x_2x_3 is evaluated. Finally, these two columns are ORed together to obtain the truth table for the expression. This truth table is identical to the truth table for f_1 given in Table A.1.

To simplify logic expressions we will perform a series of algebraic manipulations. The new logic rules that we will use in these manipulations are the distributive rule

$$w(y + z) = wy + wz$$

and the identity

$$w + \bar{w} = 1$$

TABLE A.2
Evaluation of the expression $\bar{x}_1\bar{x}_2 + x_2x_3$

x_1	x_2	x_3	$\bar{x}_1\bar{x}_2$	x_2x_3	$\bar{x}_1\bar{x}_2 + x_2x_3 = f_1$
0	0	0	1	0	1
0	0	1	1	0	1
0	1	0	0	0	0
0	1	1	0	1	1
1	0	0	0	0	0
1	0	1	0	0	0
1	1	0	0	0	0
1	1	1	0	1	1

Table A.3 shows the truth-table proof of the distributive rule. It should now be clear that rules such as this can always be proved by constructing the truth tables for the left-hand side and the right-hand side to show that they are identical. Logic rules, such as the distributive rule, are sometimes called *identities.* Although we will not need to use it here, another form of distributive rule that we should include for completeness is

$$w + yz = (w + y)(w + z)$$

The objective in logic minimization is to reduce the cost of implementation of a given logic function according to some criterion. More particularly, we wish to start with a sum-of-products expression derived from a truth table and simplify it to an equivalent *minimal sum-of-products* expression. To define the criterion for minimization, it is necessary to introduce a size or cost measure for a sum-of-products expression. The usual cost measure is a count of the total number of gates and gate inputs required in implementing the expression in the form shown in Figure A.4. For example, the larger expression in this figure has a cost of 21, composed of a total of 5 gates and 16 gate inputs. Input inversions are ignored in this counting process. The cost of the simpler expression is 9, composed of 3 gates and 6 inputs. We are now in a position to state that a sum-of-products expression is minimal if there is no other equivalent sum-of-products expression with a lower cost. In the simple examples that we will introduce, it is usually reasonably clear when we have arrived at a minimal expression. Thus, we will not give rigorous proofs of minimality.

TABLE A.3
Truth-table technique for proving equivalence of expressions

w	y	z	$y + z$	Left-hand side $w(y + z)$	wy	wz	Right-hand side $wy + wz$
0	0	0	0	0	0	0	0
0	0	1	1	0	0	0	0
0	1	0	1	0	0	0	0
0	1	1	1	0	0	0	0
1	0	0	0	0	0	0	0
1	0	1	1	1	0	1	1
1	1	0	1	1	1	0	1
1	1	1	1	1	1	1	1

The general strategy in performing algebraic manipulations to simplify a given expression is as follows. First, group product terms in pairs that differ only in that some variable appears complemented ($\bar{x}$) in one term and true (x) in the other. When the common subproduct consisting of the other variables is factored out of the pair by the distributive rule, we are left with the term $x + \bar{x}$, which has the value 1. Applying this procedure to the first expression for f_1, we obtain

$$
\begin{aligned}
f_1 &= \bar{x}_1\bar{x}_2\bar{x}_3 + \bar{x}_1\bar{x}_2 x_3 + \bar{x}_1 x_2 x_3 + x_1 x_2 x_3 \\
&= \bar{x}_1\bar{x}_2(\bar{x}_3 + x_3) + (\bar{x}_1 + x_1)x_2 x_3 \\
&= \bar{x}_1\bar{x}_2 \cdot 1 + 1 \cdot x_2 x_3 \\
&= \bar{x}_1\bar{x}_2 + x_2 x_3
\end{aligned}
$$

This expression is minimal. The network corresponding to it is shown in Figure A.4.

The grouping of terms in pairs so that minimization can lead to the simplest expression is not always as obvious as it is in the preceding example. A rule that is often helpful is

$$w + w = w$$

This allows us to repeat product terms so that a particular term can be combined with more than one other term in the factoring process. As an example of this, consider the function f_2 in Table A.1. The sum-of-products expression that can be derived for it directly from the truth table is

$$f_2 = \bar{x}_1\bar{x}_2\bar{x}_3 + \bar{x}_1\bar{x}_2 x_3 + \bar{x}_1 x_2 \bar{x}_3 + x_1\bar{x}_2\bar{x}_3 + x_1\bar{x}_2 x_3$$

By repeating the first product term $\bar{x}_1\bar{x}_2\bar{x}_3$ and interchanging the order of terms (by the commutative rule), we obtain

$$f_2 = \bar{x}_1\bar{x}_2\bar{x}_3 + \bar{x}_1\bar{x}_2 x_3 + x_1\bar{x}_2\bar{x}_3 + x_1\bar{x}_2 x_3 + \bar{x}_1\bar{x}_2\bar{x}_3 + \bar{x}_1 x_2\bar{x}_3$$

Grouping the terms in pairs and factoring yields

$$
\begin{aligned}
f_2 &= \bar{x}_1\bar{x}_2(\bar{x}_3 + x_3) + x_1\bar{x}_2(\bar{x}_3 + x_3) + \bar{x}_1(\bar{x}_2 + x_2)\bar{x}_3 \\
&= \bar{x}_1\bar{x}_2 + x_1\bar{x}_2 + \bar{x}_1\bar{x}_3
\end{aligned}
$$

The first pair of terms is again reduced by factoring, and we obtain the minimal expression

$$f_2 = \bar{x}_2 + \bar{x}_1\bar{x}_3$$

This completes our discussion of algebraic simplification of logic expressions. The obvious practical application of this mathematical exercise stems from the fact that networks with fewer gates and inputs are cheaper and easier to implement. Therefore, it is of economic interest to be able to determine the minimal expression that is equivalent to a given expression. The rules that we have used in manipulating logic expressions are summarized in Table A.4. They are arranged in pairs to show their symmetry as they apply to both the AND and OR functions. So far, we have not had occasion to use either involution or de Morgan's rules, but they will be found to be useful in the next section.

TABLE A.4
Rules of binary logic

Name	Algebraic identity	
Commutative	$w + y = y + w$	$wy = yw$
Associative	$(w + y) + z = w + (y + z)$	$(wy)z = w(yz)$
Distributive	$w + yz = (w + y)(w + z)$	$w(y + z) = wy + wz$
Idempotent	$w + w = w$	$ww = w$
Involution	$\overline{\overline{w}} = w$	—
Complement	$w + \overline{w} = 1$	$w\overline{w} = 0$
de Morgan	$\overline{w + y} = \overline{w}\,\overline{y}$	$\overline{wy} = \overline{w} + \overline{y}$
	$1 + w = 1$	$0 \cdot w = 0$
	$0 + w = w$	$1 \cdot w = w$

A.3.1 Minimization Using Karnaugh Maps

In our algebraic minimization of the functions f_1 and f_2 of Table A.1, it was necessary to guess the best way to proceed at certain points. For instance, the decision to repeat the term $\overline{x}_1\overline{x}_2\overline{x}_3$ as the first step in minimizing f_2 is not obvious. There is a geometric technique that can be used to quickly derive the minimal expression for a logic function of a few variables. The technique depends on a different form for presentation of the truth table, a form called the *Karnaugh map*. For a three-variable function, the map is a rectangle composed of eight squares arranged in two rows of four squares each, as shown in Figure A.5a. Each square of the map corresponds to a particular valuation of the input variables. For example, the third square of the top row represents the valuation $(x_1, x_2, x_3) = (1, 1, 0)$. Because there are eight rows in a three-variable truth table, the map obviously requires eight squares. The entries in the squares are the function values for the corresponding input valuations.

The key idea in the formation of the map is that horizontally and vertically adjacent squares correspond to input valuations that differ in only one variable. When two adjacent squares contain 1s, they indicate the possibility of an algebraic simplification. In the map for f_2 in Figure A.5a, the 1 values in the leftmost two squares of the top row correspond to the product terms $\overline{x}_1\overline{x}_2\overline{x}_3$ and $\overline{x}_1 x_2\overline{x}_3$. The simplification

$$\overline{x}_1\overline{x}_2\overline{x}_3 + \overline{x}_1 x_2\overline{x}_3 = \overline{x}_1\overline{x}_3$$

was performed earlier in minimizing the algebraic expression for f_2. This simplification can be obtained directly from the map by grouping the two 1s as shown. The product term that corresponds to a group of squares is the product of the input variables whose values are constant on these squares. If the value of input variable x_i is 0 for all 1s of a group, then $\overline{x}_i$ is entered in the product, but if x_i has the value 1 for all 1s of the group, then x_i is entered in the product. Adjacency of two squares includes the property that the left-end squares are adjacent to the right-end squares. Continuing with our discussion of f_2, the group of four 1s consisting of the left-end column and the right-end column simplifies to the single-variable term $\overline{x}_2$ because x_2 is the only variable whose value remains constant over the group. All four possible combinations of values of the other two variables occur in the group.

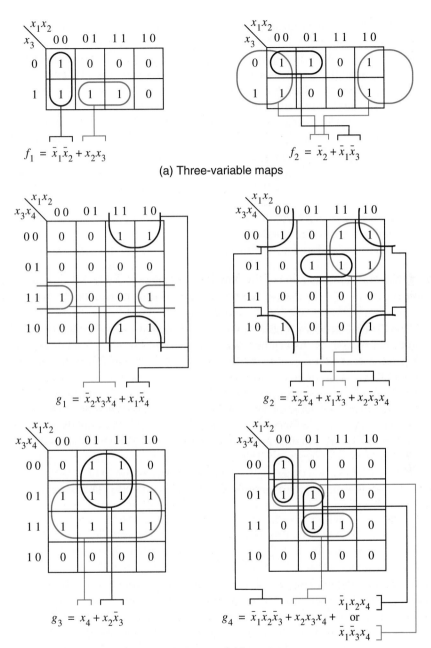

$$f_1 = \bar{x}_1\bar{x}_2 + x_2 x_3$$

$$f_2 = \bar{x}_2 + \bar{x}_1 x_3$$

(a) Three-variable maps

$$g_1 = \bar{x}_2 x_3 x_4 + x_1 \bar{x}_4$$

$$g_2 = \bar{x}_2\bar{x}_4 + x_1\bar{x}_3 + x_2\bar{x}_3 x_4$$

$$g_3 = x_4 + x_2\bar{x}_3$$

$$g_4 = \bar{x}_1\bar{x}_2\bar{x}_3 + x_2 x_3 x_4 + \begin{array}{c} \bar{x}_1 x_2 x_4 \\ \text{or} \\ \bar{x}_1\bar{x}_3 x_4 \end{array}$$

(b) Four-variable maps

FIGURE A.5
Minimization using Karnaugh maps.

Karnaugh maps can be used for more than three variables. A Karnaugh map for four variables can be obtained from 2 three-variable maps. Examples of four-variable maps are shown in Figure A.5b, along with minimal expressions for the functions represented by the maps. In addition to two- and four-square groupings, it is now possible to form eight-square groupings. Such a grouping is illustrated in the map for g_3. Note that the four corner squares constitute a valid group of four and are represented by the product term $\overline{x}_2\overline{x}_4$ in g_2. As in the case of three-variable maps, the term that corresponds to a group of squares is the product of the variables whose values do not change over the group. For example, the grouping of four 1s in the upper right-hand corner of the map for g_2 is represented by the product term $x_1\overline{x}_3$ because $x_1 = 1$ and $x_3 = 0$ over the group. The variables x_2 and x_4 have all the possible combinations of values over this group. It is also possible to use Karnaugh maps for five-variable functions. In this case, 2 four-variable maps are used, one of them corresponding to the 0 value for the fifth variable and the other corresponding to the 1 value.

The general procedure for forming groups of two, four, eight, and so on in Karnaugh maps is readily derived. Two adjacent pairs of 1s can be combined to form a group of four. Similarly, two adjacent groups of four can be combined to form a group of eight. In general, the number of squares in any valid group must be equal to 2^k, where k is an integer.

We will now consider a procedure for using Karnaugh maps to obtain minimal sum-of-products expressions. As can be seen in the maps of Figure A.5, a large group of 1s corresponds to a small product term. Thus, a simple gate implementation results from covering all the 1s in the map with as few groups as possible. In general, we should choose the smallest set of groups, picking large ones wherever possible, that cover all the 1s in the map. Consider, for example, the function g_2 in Figure A.5b. As we have already seen, the 1s in the four corners constitute a group of four that is represented by the product term $\overline{x}_2\overline{x}_4$. Another group of four exists in the upper right-hand corner and is represented by the term $x_1\overline{x}_3$. This covers all the 1s in the map except for the 1 in the square where $(x_1, x_2, x_3, x_4) = (0, 1, 0, 1)$. The largest group of 1s that includes this square is the two-square group represented by the term $x_2\overline{x}_3x_4$. Therefore, the minimal expression for g_2 is

$$g_2 = \overline{x}_2\overline{x}_4 + x_1\overline{x}_3 + x_2\overline{x}_3x_4$$

Minimal expressions for the other functions shown in the figure can be derived in a similar manner. Note that in the case of g_4 there are two possible minimal expressions, one including the term $\overline{x}_1x_2x_4$ and the other including the term $\overline{x}_1\overline{x}_3x_4$. It is often the case that a given function has more than one minimal expression.

In all our examples, it is relatively easy to derive minimal expressions. In general, there are formal algorithms for this process, but we will not consider them here.

A.3.2 Don't-Care Conditions

In many situations, some valuations of the inputs to a digital circuit never occur. For example, consider the binary-coded decimal (BCD) number representation. Four binary variables b_3, b_2, b_1, and b_0 represent the decimal digits 0 through 9, as shown in

Decimal digit represented	Binary coding $b_3\ b_2\ b_1\ b_0$				f
0	0	0	0	0	0
1	0	0	0	1	0
2	0	0	1	0	0
3	0	0	1	1	1
4	0	1	0	0	0
5	0	1	0	1	0
6	0	1	1	0	1
7	0	1	1	1	0
8	1	0	0	0	0
9	1	0	0	1	1
	1	0	1	0	d
	1	0	1	1	d
unused	1	1	0	0	d
	1	1	0	1	d
	1	1	1	0	d
	1	1	1	1	d

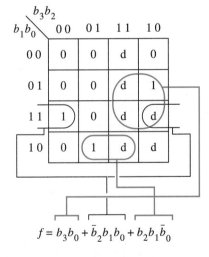

$$f = b_3 b_0 + \bar{b}_2 b_1 b_0 + b_2 b_1 \bar{b}_0$$

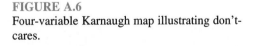

FIGURE A.6

Four-variable Karnaugh map illustrating don't-cares.

Figure A.6. These four variables have a total of 16 distinct valuations, only 10 of which are used for representing the decimal digits. The remaining valuations are not used. Therefore, any logic circuit that processes BCD data will never encounter any of these six valuations at its inputs.

Figure A.6 gives the truth table for a particular function that may be performed on a BCD digit. We do not care what the function values are for the unused input valuations; hence, they are called *don't-cares* and are denoted as such by the letter "d" in the truth table. To obtain a circuit implementation, the function values corresponding to don't-care conditions can be arbitrarily assigned to be either 0 or 1. The best way to assign them is in a manner that will lead to a minimal logic gate implementation. We should interpret don't-cares as 1s whenever they can be used to enlarge a group of 1s. Because larger groups correspond to smaller product terms, minimization is enhanced by the judicious inclusion of don't-care entries.

The function in Figure A.6 represents the following processing on a decimal digit input: The output f is to have the value 1 whenever the inputs represent a nonzero digit that is evenly divisible by 3. Three groups are necessary to cover the three 1s of the map, and don't-cares have been used to enlarge these groups as much as possible.

A.4
SYNTHESIS WITH NAND AND NOR GATES

We will now consider two other basic logic gates called NAND and NOR, which are extensively used in practice because of their simple electronic realizations. The truth table for these gates is shown in Figure A.7. They implement the equivalent of the AND and OR functions followed by the NOT function, which is the motivation for the names and standard logic symbols for these gates. Letting the arrows "↑" and "↓" denote the NAND and NOR operators, respectively, and using de Morgan's rule in Table A.4, we have

$$x_1 \uparrow x_2 = \overline{x_1 x_2} = \overline{x}_1 + \overline{x}_2$$

and

$$x_1 \downarrow x_2 = \overline{x_1 + x_2} = \overline{x}_1 \overline{x}_2$$

NAND and NOR gates with more than two input variables are available, and they operate according to the obvious generalization of de Morgan's law as

$$x_1 \uparrow x_2 \uparrow \cdots \uparrow x_n = \overline{x_1 x_2 \cdots x_n} = \overline{x}_1 + \overline{x}_2 + \cdots + \overline{x}_n$$

and

$$x_1 \downarrow x_2 \downarrow \cdots \downarrow x_n = \overline{x_1 + x_2 + \cdots + x_n} = \overline{x}_1 \overline{x}_2 \cdots \overline{x}_n$$

Logic design with NAND and NOR gates is not as straightforward as with AND, OR, and NOT gates. One of the main difficulties in the design process is that the associative rule is not valid for NAND and NOR operations. We will expand on this problem later. First, however, let us describe a simple, general procedure for synthesizing any logic function using only NAND gates. There is a direct way to translate a logic network expressed in sum-of-products form into an equivalent network composed only of NAND gates. The procedure is easily illustrated with the aid of an example. Consider the following algebraic manipulation of a logic expression corresponding to a four-input network composed of 3 two-input NAND gates:

$$(x_1 \uparrow x_2) \uparrow (x_3 \uparrow x_4) = \overline{(\overline{x_1 x_2})(\overline{x_3 x_4})}$$
$$= \overline{\overline{x_1 x_2}} + \overline{\overline{x_3 x_4}}$$
$$= x_1 x_2 + x_3 x_4$$

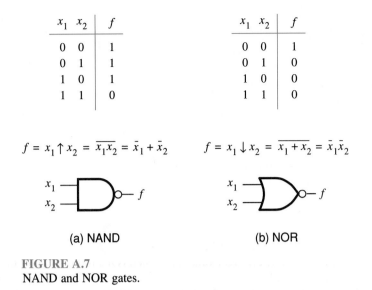

x_1	x_2	f
0	0	1
0	1	1
1	0	1
1	1	0

x_1	x_2	f
0	0	1
0	1	0
1	0	0
1	1	0

$$f = x_1 \uparrow x_2 = \overline{x_1 x_2} = \bar{x}_1 + \bar{x}_2 \qquad f = x_1 \downarrow x_2 = \overline{x_1 + x_2} = \bar{x}_1 \bar{x}_2$$

(a) NAND   (b) NOR

FIGURE A.7
NAND and NOR gates.

We have used de Morgan's rule and the involution rule in this derivation. Figure A.8 shows the logic network equivalent of this derivation. Since any logic function can be synthesized in a sum-of-products (AND-OR) form and because the preceding derivation is obviously reversible, we have the result that any logic function can be synthesized in NAND-NAND form. We can see that this result is true for functions of any number of variables. The required number of inputs to the NAND gates is obviously the same as the number of inputs to the corresponding AND and OR gates.

Let us return to the comment that the nonassociativity of the NAND operator can be an annoyance. In designing logic networks with NAND gates using the procedure illustrated in Figure A.8, a requirement for a NAND gate with more inputs than can be found on standard commercially available gates may arise. If this happens when one is

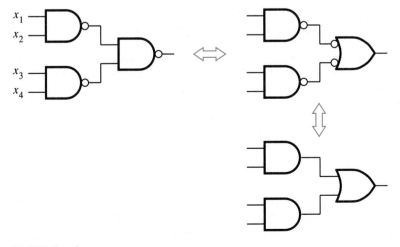

FIGURE A.8
Equivalence of NAND-NAND and AND-OR networks.

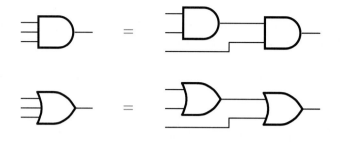

(a) Implementing three-input AND and OR functions with two-input gates

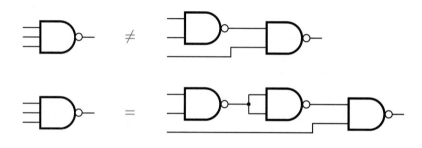

(b) Implementing a three-input NAND function with two-input gates

FIGURE A.9
Cascading of gates.

using AND and OR gates, there is no problem because the AND and OR operators are associative, and a straightforward cascade of limited fan-in gates can be used. The case of implementing three-input AND and OR functions with two-input gates is shown in Figure A.9a. The solution is not as simple in the case of NAND gates. For example, a three-input NAND function cannot be implemented by a cascade of 2 two-input NAND gates. Three gates are needed, as shown in Figure A.9b.

A discussion of the implementation of logic functions using only NOR gates proceeds in a similar manner. Any logic function can be synthesized in a product-of-sums (OR-AND) form. Such networks can be implemented by equivalent NOR-NOR networks.

The preceding discussion introduced some basic concepts in logic design. Detailed discussion of the subject can be found in any of a number of textbooks (see References 1 through 7).

It is important for the reader to appreciate that many different realizations of a given logic function are possible. For practical reasons, it is useful to find realizations that minimize the cost of implementation. It is also often necessary to minimize the propagation delay through a logic network. We introduced the concept of minimization in the previous sections to give an indication of the nature of logic synthesis and the reductions in cost that may be achieved. For example, Karnaugh maps graphically show the manipulation possibilities that lead to optimal solutions. Although it is important to understand the principles of optimization of logic networks, it is not necessary to do the optimization by hand. Sophisticated *computer-aided design* (CAD) programs exist for such synthesis. The designer needs to specify only the desired functional behavior, and the CAD software generates a cost-effective network that implements the required functionality.

A.5
PRACTICAL IMPLEMENTATION OF LOGIC GATES

Let us now turn our attention to the means by which logic variables can be represented and logic functions can be implemented in practice. The choice of a physical parameter to represent logic variables is obviously technology-dependent. In electronic circuits, either voltage or current levels can be used for this purpose.

To establish a correspondence between voltage levels and logic values or states, the concept of a *threshold* may be used. Voltages above a given threshold may be taken to represent one logic value, with voltages below that threshold representing the other. In practical situations, the voltage at any point in an electronic circuit undergoes small random variations for a variety of reasons. Because of this "noise," the logic state corresponding to a voltage level near the threshold cannot be reliably determined. To avoid such ambiguity, a "forbidden range" should be established, as shown in Figure A.10. In this case, voltages below $V_{0,max}$ represent the 0 value, and voltages above $V_{1,min}$ represent the 1 value. In subsequent discussion, we will often use the terms "low" and "high" to represent the voltage levels corresponding to logic values 0 and 1, respectively.

We will begin our discussion of electronic circuits that implement basic logic functions by considering simple circuits consisting of resistors and transistors that act as switches. These circuits belong to a "logic family" known as *resistor-transistor logic* (RTL). They are no longer used because of certain electrical limitations; however, their

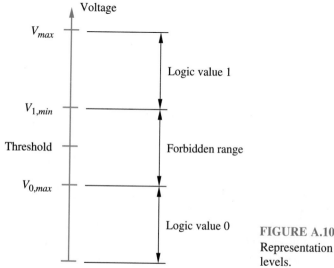

FIGURE A.10

Representation of logic values by voltage levels.

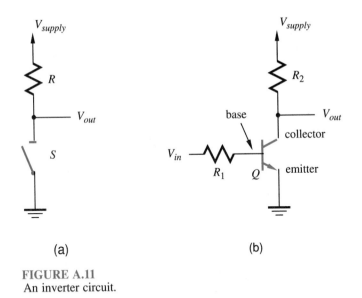

FIGURE A.11
An inverter circuit.

simplicity makes them a useful vehicle for introducing the basic concepts common to all logic families.

Consider the circuits in Figure A.11. When switch S in Figure A.11a is closed, the output voltage V_{out} is equal to 0 (ground). When S is open, the output voltage V_{out} is equal to the supply voltage. The same effect can be obtained in Figure A.11b, in which a transistor Q is used to replace the switch S. When no current is supplied to the base of the transistor (that is, when the input voltage $V_{in} = 0$), the transistor is equivalent to an open switch, and $V_{out} = V_{supply}$. As V_{in} increases, V_{out} starts to drop until it is very close to 0. The rate at which this happens is a function of the values of resistors R_1 and R_2 and the characteristics of the transistor. Through proper choice of these components, it is possible to establish the two levels $V_{1,min}$ and $V_{0,max}$ so that

$$\text{if} \quad V_{in} \leq V_{0,max}, \quad \text{then} \quad V_{out} > V_{1,min}$$

and

$$\text{if} \quad V_{in} \geq V_{1,min}, \quad \text{then} \quad V_{out} < V_{0,max}$$

Under these conditions, the circuit performs the function of a logic NOT gate.

We can now discuss the implementation of more complex logic functions. Figure A.12 shows a circuit realization for a NOR gate. In this case, V_{out} in Figure A.12a is high only when both switches S_a and S_b are open. Similarly, V_{out} in Figure A.12b is high only when both inputs V_a and V_b are low. Thus, the circuit is equivalent to a NOR gate in which V_a and V_b correspond to two logic variables x_1 and x_2. We can easily verify that a NAND gate can be obtained by connecting the transistors as shown in Figure A.13. The logic functions AND and OR can be implemented using NAND and NOR gates, respectively, followed by the inverter of Figure A.11.

It is interesting to note that NAND and NOR gates are simpler in their circuit implementations than AND and OR gates. It will be seen shortly that this is true for most

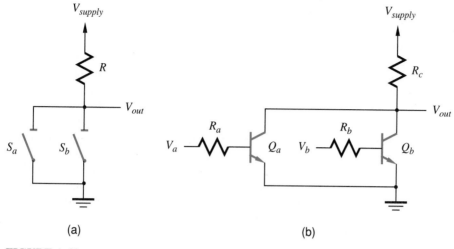

(a)   (b)

FIGURE A.12
A transistor circuit implementation of a NOR gate.

other logic families, with the notable exception of emitter-coupled logic. Hence, it is not surprising to find that practical realizations of logic functions use NAND and NOR gates extensively. Many of the examples given in this book show circuits consisting of AND, OR, and NOT gates for ease of understanding. In practice, logic circuits contain all five types of gates.

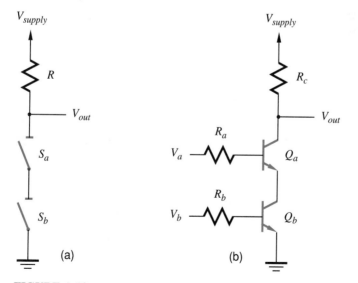

(a)   (b)

FIGURE A.13
A transistor circuit implementation of a NAND gate.

A.5.1 Logic Families

The RTL circuits are relatively slow and consume a fair amount of power, so they are no longer used. A number of other logic families have been developed to overcome these limitations. Of course, all logic families perform the same logic functions; they differ only in their electrical and physical characteristics. Although we do not intend to study these characteristics in detail, we will present a summary of those parameters that affect the choice of the logic family to be used in a given application.

Circuits belonging to different logic families exhibit a number of trade-offs among three basic properties: speed, power, and packaging density. Speed is measured by the rate at which state changes can take place at the output of any logic gate. A related parameter is the *propagation delay*, which is defined in Figure A.14. When a state change takes place at a gate input, a delay is encountered before the corresponding change at the gate output is observed. This propagation delay is usually measured between the 50-percent points of the transitions, as shown in the figure. Another important parameter is the *transition time*, which is normally measured between the 10- and 90-percent points on the waveform, as shown. The maximum speed at which a logic circuit can be operated decreases as the propagation delay through different paths within that circuit increases. The delay along any path is the sum of individual gate delays along this path.

Power consumption is the next parameter in the characterization of logic families. High power consumption requires complex and costly packaging to enable dissipation

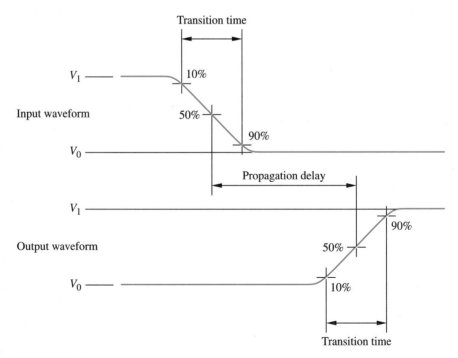

FIGURE A.14
Definition of propagation delay and transition time.

of the heat produced. The cost of the power supply is also increased. Power consumption is particularly significant in the case of *very large-scale integration* (VLSI). This is the case when a logic subsystem consisting of a large number of gates is fabricated on a single integrated circuit chip.

For a general circuit configuration such as the one in Figure A.11, it is possible to obtain a number of designs that differ in their speed and power characteristics. However, as the speed capability increases, so does the power consumption. The product of power dissipation per gate and propagation delay remains roughly constant for a given logic family technology. This power-delay product is often used as a figure of merit that describes the capabilities of a given technology.

In addition to the basic characteristics just presented, other important properties should be taken into consideration in comparing logic families. These include the following:

- *Noise immunity*—the ability to reject interference from neighboring circuits
- *Drive requirement*—the electrical load presented by a gate input to the circuit preceding it (for example, the input current in the circuit of Figure A.11b)
- *Drive capability*—the maximum amount of current that can be drawn from a gate output without serious degradation of its performance

The combination of drive requirement and drive capability determines two important parameters:

- *Fan-in*—the maximum number of inputs that a logic gate can have
- *Fan-out*—the maximum number of gates that can be driven from the output of a single gate

With the preceding considerations in mind, we shall now review some of the commonly used logic families.

Transistor-Transistor Logic (TTL)

A transistor-transistor logic (TTL) configuration for a NAND gate is shown in Figure A.15a. To understand the operation of this gate, let us consider the circuit of Figure A.15b. This circuit belongs to an earlier logic family known as *diode-transistor logic* (DTL). First consider the case when the two inputs V_a and V_b are high. Because a diode conducts current only in the forward direction, no appreciable current flows through D_1 or D_2. Diode D_3, however, is forward-biased and allows a current I_b to flow to the base of transistor Q. Thus, Q is turned on, and V_{out} is close to ground, indicating a logic value of 0. If either V_a or V_b drops to the 0 state, the corresponding diode starts to conduct. This causes the voltage at point P to drop to a value below that required to maintain the flow of I_b. Thus, transistor Q turns off, and V_{out} rises to the supply voltage. In other words, this circuit performs the NAND function.

When this DTL circuit is implemented in integrated circuit form, the three diodes D_1, D_2, and D_3 can be combined to form transistor Q_1 of Figure A.15a, reducing the chip area required for the gate. This also leads to an improvement in performance because of the higher speed with which transistor Q_2 can be changed from the on to the off state. Detailed discussion of these properties can be found in texts on electronics, such as References 8 and 9.

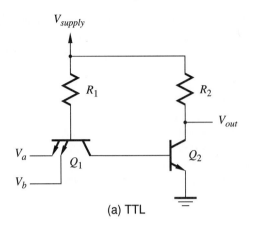

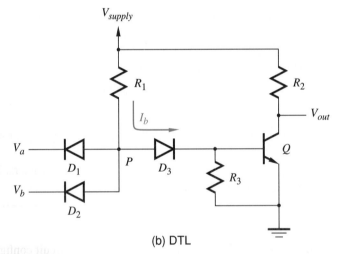

FIGURE A.15
TTL and DTL NAND gates.

To enhance the output drive capability of the circuit of Figure A.15*a* and hence to improve the fan-out, a driver stage is usually added. This yields the standard TTL circuit configuration given in Figure A.16. The output stage contains two transistors, Q_3 and Q_4. When the output is in the 0 state, transistor Q_3 is off and transistor Q_4 is on. Conversely, when the output is in the 1 state, Q_3 is on and Q_4 is off. This allows higher load currents to be handled without excessive power dissipation or reduction in speed.

Many variations of the circuit in Figure A.16 have been developed for low-power or high-speed applications. The TTL logic family was a popular choice in computer and logic applications until the 1990s, when CMOS circuits became a preferred alternative.

Complementary Metal-Oxide Semiconductor (CMOS) Logic

Numerous logic families have been developed using metal-oxide semiconductor (MOS) transistors instead of the bipolar transistors used in TTL. The differences

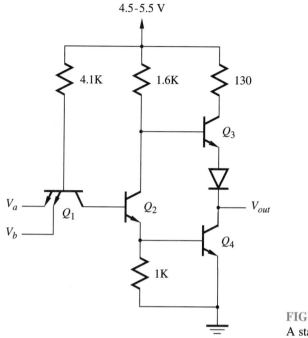

4.5-5.5 V

4.1K   1.6K   130

Q_3

V_a Q_1 Q_2 V_{out}

V_b Q_4

1K

FIGURE A.16
A standard TTL NAND gate.

between various types of transistors are of no concern for the purposes of this review. Interested readers may consult References 8 and 9. Depending on the manufacturing process, MOS transistors are known as either p- or n-channel transistors. In general, MOS circuits operate at somewhat lower speeds than bipolar circuits. However, their major advantage is that they are well suited to VLSI. Logic families based on MOS transistors are extensively used in VLSI applications.

A logic family that combines p- and n-channel MOS transistors on the same chip is known as the *complementary MOS*, or CMOS, family. The circuit configuration for a CMOS inverter is given in Figure A.17b. Operation of this inverter circuit is similar to operation of the circuit in Figure A.17a, in which the two switches S_1 and S_2 are linked so that switch S_2 is open when switch S_1 is closed, and vice versa. In the CMOS circuit, when V_{in} is high, the n-channel transistor is on and the p-channel transistor is off. Thus, the output terminal is at 0 V. As the input voltage changes from high to low, the p-channel transistor starts to conduct and the n-channel transistor turns off, causing V_{out} to rise to the supply voltage. Extension of this circuit to obtain NAND and NOR functions is straightforward. A NOR gate is illustrated in Figure A.18.

Transitions between low and high signal levels are illustrated in more detail in Figure A.19. The blue curve, known as the *transfer characteristic* of the inverter circuit, shows the output voltage as a function of the input voltage. A power supply of 5 V is assumed. The curve indicates that a rather sharp transition in output voltage takes place when the input voltage passes through the value of about 2.3 V. That is, there is a *threshold* voltage, V_t, such that $V_{out} \approx 5$ V if $V_{in} < V_t - \delta$ and $V_{out} \approx 0$ if $V_{in} > V_t + \delta$. Clearly, the value of δ is small in Figure A.19. This means that the input signal need not be exactly equal to the nominal value of either 0 or 5 V to produce the correct output

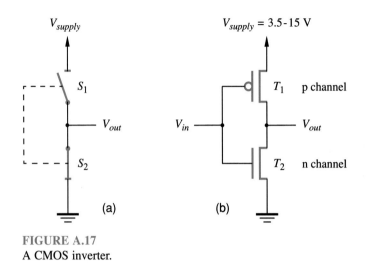

FIGURE A.17
A CMOS inverter.

signal. There is room for some error, called *noise*, in the input signal that will not cause adverse effects. The amount of noise that can be tolerated is called the *noise margin*. This margin is $5 - V_t - \delta$ volts when the logic value of the input is 1, and it is $V_t - \delta$ when the logic value of the input is 0. CMOS circuits have excellent noise margins.

Advantages of CMOS logic circuits include high noise immunity and low power consumption. The low power feature can be appreciated by inspection of Figure A.17. Consider first the case in which V_{in} is held near either 0 or V_{supply}. In either case one

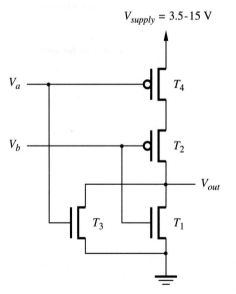

FIGURE A.18
A two-input CMOS NOR gate.

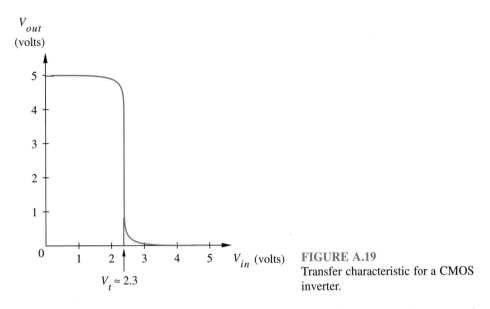

FIGURE A.19
Transfer characteristic for a CMOS inverter.

of the two transistors is in the nonconducting mode, so only a very small amount of "leakage" current exists from V_{supply} to ground, leading to very low power dissipation. While switching between the two logic states, however, there is a short period of time when both transistors are in the conducting mode. This causes a short current pulse produced with every change of state. Therefore, power dissipation in CMOS circuits is dependent on the rate at which state changes take place. In fact, it increases linearly with the frequency of operation.

Another advantage of CMOS circuits is that MOS transistors can be implemented in very small sizes and thus occupy a very small area on an integrated circuit chip. This results in two significant benefits. First, it is possible to fabricate chips containing millions of transistors, which has led to the realization of modern microprocessors and large memory chips. Second, the smaller the transistor, the faster it can be switched from one logic state to another. Thus, CMOS circuits can now be operated at speeds sufficiently high that bipolar circuits such as TTL are no longer needed for reasons of speed. Indeed, CMOS circuits have essentially replaced TTL in practical applications.

A variety of CMOS circuits have been developed to operate with power supply voltages in the range from 3.3 to 15 V. The most commonly used power supply has been 5 V. Recently, low-power circuits using $V_{supply} = 3.3$ V have emerged. They dissipate much less power (power dissipation is proportional to V_{supply}^2), which means that more transistors can be placed on a chip without causing overheating. A drawback of lower power supply voltage is reduced noise immunity.

Emitter-Coupled Logic (ECL)

The emitter-coupled logic (ECL) family provides the highest-speed logic circuits. The basic configuration of an ECL NOT gate is illustrated in Figure A.20. In this figure, current flows from the ground terminal to a negative power supply. Operation of the

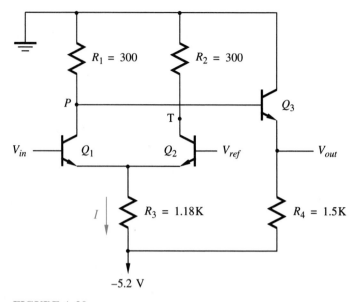

FIGURE A.20
An ECL logic inverter.

circuit can be described as follows. When the input voltage V_{in} is below the fixed reference voltage V_{ref}, transistor Q_2 is in the conducting mode and transistor Q_1 is turned off. Thus a current I flows through resistor R_2. When V_{in} rises above V_{ref}, the situation is reversed, causing the same current I to flow through R_1. Only a small change in V_{in}, of the order of a few tenths of a volt, is required for this change of state to take place. As V_{in} rises from its low state (V_L) to its high state (V_H), the voltage at point P drops from 0 to $-IR_1$. A simple voltage-level-shifting network produces output voltages of V_H and V_L when point P is at 0 and $-IR_1$, respectively.

In summary, to bring about state changes in the circuit of Figure A.20, the current I is "steered" from one branch of the circuit to the other. The use of current steering and the attendant low-voltage changes are the main reasons for the high speed of ECL logic. We should note, however, that this is accomplished at the expense of increased power consumption.

The logic levels for the ECL family are as follows:

Output $\quad V_{1,min} = -0.850$ V
$\qquad\qquad V_{0,max} = -1.500$ V
Input $\quad\;\; V_{1,min} = -1.025$ V
$\qquad\qquad V_{0,max} = -1.325$ V

Therefore, the noise margin for both the 0 and 1 states is 0.175 V.

It is interesting to note that the state of point T in the circuit of Figure A.20 is always the complement of the state of point P. Thus, at the small expense of an extra level-shifting network, both the output and its complement can be made available. This

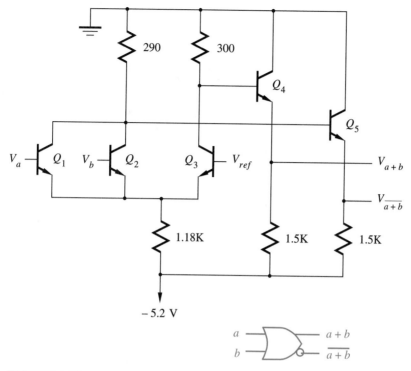

FIGURE A.21
An ECL OR-NOR gate.

is illustrated in Figure A.21, which shows the organization of an ECL OR-NOR circuit. The two outputs are represented symbolically as shown in the figure.

A.5.2 Integrated Circuit Packages

The main features of electronic circuits used to implement logic functions were discussed in previous sections. In practical design, it is necessary to use integrated circuits (ICs) that are commercially available. When ICs became available in the 1960s, there quickly developed a trend to provide logic gates in the form of standardized IC chips. An IC chip is mounted inside a sealed protective package with a number of metallic pins for external connections. Standard IC packages are available with different numbers of pins. A simple package containing four NAND gates is shown in Figure A.22. The four gates utilize common power supply and ground pins. Such ICs comprising only a few logic gates are referred to as *small-scale integrated* (SSI) *circuits.*

Much larger ICs are also available, and almost all logic circuits are now realized with such chips. They may implement useful functional blocks such as adders, multipliers, registers, encoders, and decoders. But they may also provide just an assortment of gates and programmable interconnection switches that can be configured by the designer to realize a variety of arbitrary functions using a single chip. In subsequent

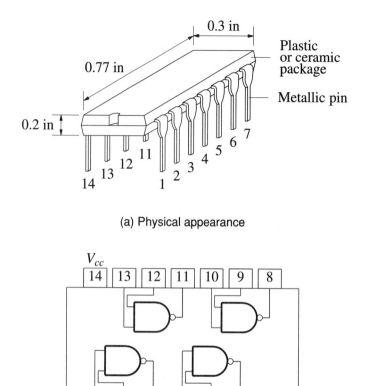

(a) Physical appearance

(b) Schematic of an integrated circuit providing four 2-input NAND gates

FIGURE A.22
A 14-pin dual in-line integrated circuit package (DIP).

sections we will discuss some commonly used functional blocks, as well as general user-programmable logic devices.

The SSI circuits provide too little functionality for the physical space that they require. Moreover, their performance is inferior because of the electrical characteristics of the pins on an IC package. In general, it is necessary to use larger transistors to provide the signals needed to drive external wires connected to pins. This increases both propagation delay and power dissipation.

A CMOS NAND gate provided as part of an IC package like the one illustrated in Figure A.22 may have a propagation delay of 5 nanoseconds. However, if a NAND circuit is used to drive a similar circuit within a large CMOS network implemented on a single IC, then the gate propagation delay may be 0.5 ns. An ECL gate in an SSI package may have a delay of 1 or 2 ns. The ECL family is not used in large ICs because of excessive power dissipation. There is a related family of circuits, known as *current mode logic* (CML), that dissipates less power than ECL and is more suitable for implementing larger circuits on a single chip. In complex integrated circuits, CML technology is about twice as fast as CMOS. Power dissipation problems restrict the use of ECL and CML to applications where high speed is of critical importance. For most applications, CMOS provides the desirable features and is the dominant technology in use today.

A.6
FLIP-FLOPS

The majority of applications of digital logic require the storage of information. For example, a circuit that controls a combination lock must remember the sequence in which the digits are dialed in order to determine whether to open the lock. Another important example is the storage of programs and data in the memory of a digital computer.

The basic electronic element for storing binary information is termed a *flip-flop*. Consider the two cross-coupled NOR gates in Figure A.23a. Let us examine this circuit, starting with the situation in which R = 1 and S = 0. Simple analysis shows that Q_a = 0 and Q_b = 1. Under this condition, both inputs to gate G_a are equal to 1. Thus, if R is changed to 0, no change will take place at the outputs Q_a and Q_b. If S is set to 1 with R equal to 0, Q_a and Q_b will become 1 and 0, respectively, and will remain in this state after S is returned to 0. Hence, this logic circuit constitutes a memory element, or a flip-flop, that remembers which of the two inputs S and R was most recently equal to 1. A truth table for this flip-flop is given in Figure A.23b. Some typical waveforms that characterize the flip-flop are shown in Figure A.23c. The arrows in Figure A.23c indicate the cause-effect relationships among the signals. Note that when the R and S inputs change from 1 to 0 at the same time, the resulting state is undefined. In practice, the flip-flop will assume one of its two stable states at random. The input valuation R = S = 1 is not used in most applications of RS flip-flops.

Because of the nature of the operation of the preceding circuit, the S and R lines are referred to as the *set* and *reset* inputs, and Q_a and Q_b are usually represented by Q and $\overline{Q}$, respectively. Furthermore, the circuit is called an *RS flip-flop*. We should note that in this context, $\overline{Q}$ should be regarded merely as a symbol representing the second output of the flip-flop rather than as the complement of Q, because the input valuation R = S = 1 yields Q = $\overline{Q}$ = 0.

A.6.1 Clocked Flip-Flops

Many applications require that the time at which a flip-flop is set or reset be controlled from an input other than R and S, termed a *clock* input. The resulting configuration is called a *clocked RS flip-flop*. A logic circuit and characteristic waveforms for such a flip-flop are given in Figure A.24. When the clock, Cl, is equal to 1, points S' and R' follow the inputs S and R, respectively. On the other hand, when Cl = 0, the S' and R' points are equal to 0, and no change in the state of the flip-flop can take place.

In technical literature, the basic storage element consisting of two cross-coupled NOR gates, such as the one in Figure A.23a, is often called a *latch*. The term

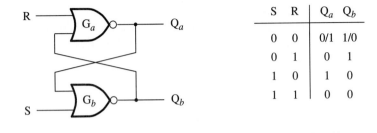

S	R	Q_a	Q_b
0	0	0/1	1/0
0	1	0	1
1	0	1	0
1	1	0	0

(a) Network   (b) Truth table

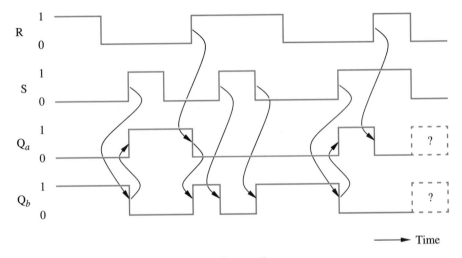

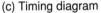

(c) Timing diagram

FIGURE A.23
An RS flip-flop.

"flip-flop" is then used to denote a circuit in which a clock input is included, such as the one in Figure A.24a.

So far we have used truth tables to describe the behavior of logic circuits. A truth table gives the output of a network for various input valuations. Logic circuits whose outputs are uniquely defined for each input valuation are referred to as *combinational circuits*. This is the class of circuits discussed in Sections A.1 to A.4. When memory elements are present, a different class of circuits is obtained. The output of such circuits is a function not only of the present valuation of the input variables but also of their previous behavior. An example of this is shown in Figure A.23. Circuits of this type are called *sequential circuits*.

Because of the memory property, a flip-flop's truth table should be modified to show the effect of its present state. Table A.5 describes the behavior of the clocked RS flip-flop, where Q_n denotes its present state. The transition to the next state, Q_{n+1}, occurs following a clock pulse. Note that for the input valuation $S = R = 1$, Q_{n+1} is undefined for reasons discussed earlier.

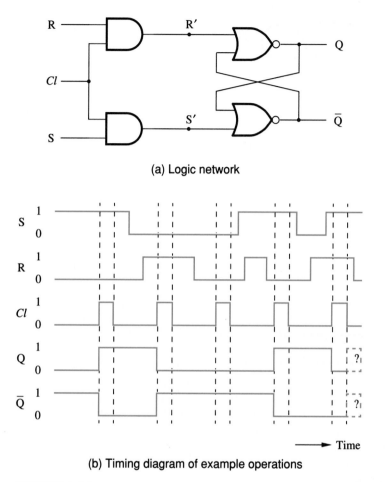

(a) Logic network

(b) Timing diagram of example operations

FIGURE A.24
Clocked RS flip-flop.

TABLE A.5
Truth table for a clocked RS flip-flop

S	R	Q_{n+1}
0	0	Q_n (no change in state)
0	1	0
1	0	1
1	1	X (undefined)

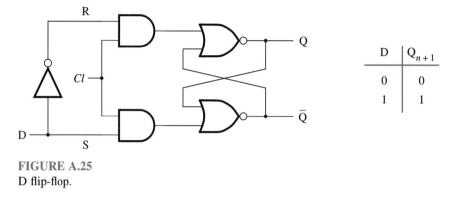

D	Q_{n+1}
0	0
1	1

FIGURE A.25
D flip-flop.

A second type of flip-flop, called the *D flip-flop,* is shown in Figure A.25. In this case, the two signals S and R are derived from a single input D. At a clock pulse, the Q output is set to 1 if D = 1 or is reset to 0 if D = 0. This means that the D flip-flop samples the D input at the time the clock is high and stores that information until a subsequent clock pulse arrives.

A.6.2 Master-Slave and Edge-Triggered Flip-Flops

In the circuit of Figure A.24 we assumed that while $Cl = 1$, the inputs S and R do not change. Inspection of the circuit reveals that the outputs will respond immediately to any change in the S or R input during this time. Similarly, for the circuit of Figure A.25, Q = D while $Cl = 1$. This is undesirable in many cases, particularly in circuits involving counters and shift registers, which will be discussed later. In such circuits, immediate propagation of logic conditions from the data inputs (R, S, and D) to the flip-flop outputs may lead to incorrect operation. The concept of a *master-slave* organization eliminates this problem. Two flip-flops can be connected to form a master-slave RS flip-flop, as shown in Figure A.26a. The first, referred to as the master, is connected to the input lines when $Cl = 1$. A 1-to-0 transition of the clock isolates the master from the input and transfers the contents of the master stage to the slave stage. The thresholds at which logic transitions occur in particular gates are arranged as in Figure A.26b. We can see that no direct path ever exists from the inputs to the outputs.

It should be noted that while $Cl = 1$, the state of the master stage is immediately affected by changes in the inputs S and R. The function of the slave stage is to hold the output of the flip-flop while the master stage is being set up to the next-state value determined by the S and R inputs. In most applications, this means that the S and R inputs should have reached the correct levels for determining the next state before the 0-to-1 transition on Cl and should hold these levels while $Cl = 1$. The new state is then transferred from the master to the slave after the 1-to-0 transition on Cl. At this point, the master stage is isolated from the inputs so that further changes in the S and R inputs will not affect this transfer. The master-stage outputs Q' and $\overline{Q}'$ are the slave-stage inputs S' and R', respectively, as shown in the figure. Examples of state transitions for various S and R input combinations are shown in Figure A.26c.

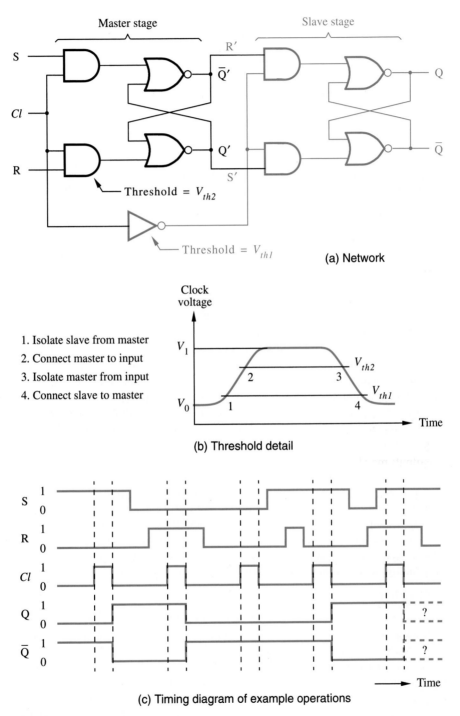

FIGURE A.26
Master-slave RS flip-flop.

TABLE A.6
Truth table for
a JK flip-flop

J	K	Q_{n+1}
0	0	Q_n
0	1	0
1	0	1
1	1	$\overline{Q}_n$

Another very useful type of flip-flop is the *JK flip-flop*. A truth table defining its operation is given in Table A.6. The first three entries in this table exhibit the same behavior as those in Table A.5, so that J and K correspond to S and R. For the input valuation $J = K = 1$, the next state is defined as the complement of the present state of the flip-flop. That is, when $J = K = 1$, the flip-flop functions as a *toggle,* or a modulo-2 counter. A JK flip-flop can be implemented using an RS flip-flop connected such that

$$S = J\overline{Q} \quad \text{and} \quad R = KQ$$

This means that feedback connections are required from the outputs Q and $\overline{Q}$ to the inputs R and S. It is important, therefore, that the flip-flop not allow input changes to be propagated immediately to the output. Otherwise, a steady state can never be reached when $J = K = 1$, because a change in the output causes a change in the input. This leads to a further change in the output, and so on. In other words, the circuit will oscillate. A master-slave organization can be used to guarantee proper operation. Figure A.27a gives an implementation of a master-slave JK flip-flop derived by adding the appropriate feedback connections to the master-slave RS flip-flop shown in Figure A.26. The remainder of Figure A.27 shows how a JK flip-flop can be constructed using NAND gates only. Figure A.27b illustrates the implementation of a clocked RS flip-flop using NAND gates. The reader should verify that the NAND network operates as desired. Figure A.27c shows how two NAND gate flip-flops can be used to implement the JK flip-flop. Two additional control inputs are shown in this implementation. These are Preset and Clear, which force the flip-flop to the 1 or 0 state, respectively, independent of the J, K, and *Cl* inputs. When both the Preset and Clear inputs are equal to 0, the flip-flop is controlled by the other inputs in the normal way. When Preset $= 1$, the flip-flop is forced to the 1 state, and when Clear $= 1$, the flip-flop is forced to the 0 state. These additional controls are also often incorporated in the other flip-flop types.

Edge-Triggering

A slightly different approach to the control of data transfer from the input to the output of a flip-flop is known as *edge-triggering*. In this case, data present at the input are transferred to the output only at a transition in the clock signal. The input and output are isolated from each other at all other times. The terms *leading (positive) edge-triggered* and *trailing (negative) edge-triggered* describe flip-flops in which data transfer takes place at the 0-to-1 and the 1-to-0 clock transitions, respectively. For proper operation, edge-triggered flip-flops require the triggering edge of the clock pulse to be well defined and to have a very short transition time.

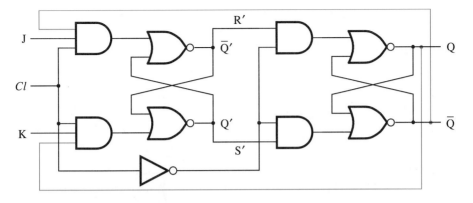

(a) Implementation of a JK flip-flop from a master-slave RS flip-flop

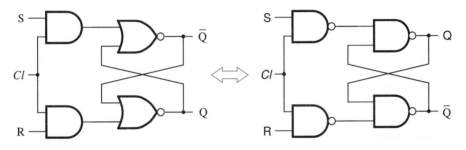

(b) NAND gate implementation of a clocked RS flip-flop

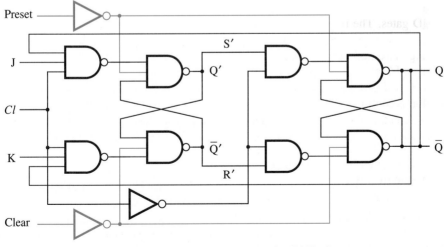

(c) NAND gate implementation of a JK flip-flop

FIGURE A.27
Master-slave JK flip-flops.

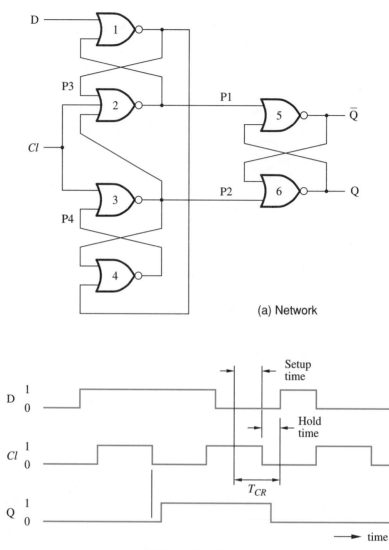

(a) Network

(b) Example of timing

FIGURE A.28
A negative edge-triggered D flip-flop.

An example of a negative edge-triggered D flip-flop is given in Figure A.28a. Let us consider the operation of this flip-flop. If $Cl = 1$, the outputs of gates 2 and 3 are both 0. Therefore, the flip-flop outputs Q and $\overline{Q}$ maintain the current state of the flip-flop. It is easy to verify that during this period, points P3 and P4 immediately respond to changes at D. Point P3 is kept equal to $\overline{D}$, and P4 is maintained equal to D. When Cl drops to 0, these values are transmitted to P1 and P2 by gates 2 and 3, respectively. Thus, the output latch, consisting of gates 5 and 6, acquires the new state to be stored.

We now verify that while $Cl = 0$, further changes at D do not change points P1 and P2. Consider two cases. First, suppose D = 0 at the trailing edge of Cl. The 1 at P2 maintains an input of 1 at each of the gates 2 and 4, holding P1 and P2 at 0 and 1, respectively, independent of further changes in D. Second, suppose D = 1 at the trailing edge of Cl. The 1 at P1 means that further changes at D cannot affect the output of gate 1, which is maintained at 0.

When Cl goes to 1 at the start of the next clock pulse, points P1 and P2 are again forced to 0, isolating the output from the remainder of the circuit. Points P3 and P4 then follow changes at D, as we have previously described.

An example of the operation of this type of D flip-flop is shown in Figure A.28b. The state acquired by the flip-flop upon the 1 to 0 transition of Cl is equal to the value on the D input immediately preceding this transition. However, there is a critical time period T_{CR} around the trailing edge of Cl during which the value on D should not change. This region is split into two parts, the *setup time* before the clock edge and the *hold time* after the clock edge, as shown in the figure. The timing diagram shows that the output Q changes slightly after the negative edge of the clock. This is the effect of the propagation delay through the NOR gates.

Other flip-flop types are available in the edge-triggered configuration, but we will not discuss their details.

We have introduced a number of flip-flop configurations that differ in their data input and clock requirements. The data input can take the form of RS, D, and JK inputs. Clocking may consist of simple input gating, edge-triggering, or a master-slave arrangement. This gives considerable flexibility in the choice of a particular type of flip-flop for a given application. In general, the input configuration is chosen to simplify any external logic circuitry that may be required. Choice of the clocking arrangement is dependent upon the timing constraints.

A.7
REGISTERS AND SHIFT REGISTERS

An individual flip-flop can be used to store one bit. However, in machines in which data are handled in words consisting of many bits (perhaps as many as 64), it is convenient to arrange a number of flip-flops into a common structure called a *register*. The operation of all flip-flops in a register is synchronized by a common clock. Thus, data are written (loaded) into or read from all flip-flops at the same time.

Processing of digital data often requires the capability to shift and rotate the data, so it is necessary to provide the hardware with this facility. A simple mechanism for realizing both operations is a register whose contents may be shifted to the right or left one bit position at a time. As an example, consider the 4-bit shift register in Figure A.29. It consists of JK flip-flops connected so that each clock pulse will cause the transfer of the contents (state) of F_i to F_{i+1}, effecting a "right shift." Data are shifted serially into and out of the register.

Proper operation of a shift register requires that its contents be shifted exactly one position for each clock pulse. This places a constraint on the type of flip-flops that can be used. Flip-flops that have simple input gating, as in Figures A.24 and A.25, are not suitable for this purpose. While the clock is high, the data applied to the input of these flip-flops quickly propagate to output. From there, the data propagate through the next flip-flop in the same manner. Hence, there is no control over the number of shifts

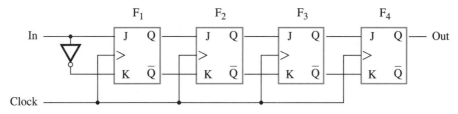

FIGURE A.29
A simple shift register.

that will take place during a single clock pulse. This number depends on the propagation delays of the flip-flops and the duration of the clock pulse. The solution to the problem is to use either the master-slave or the edge-triggered flip-flops described in Section A.6.2. In the remainder of this appendix we will assume that one of these two types is used.

Observe that we have used an arrowhead, instead of the label Cl, to denote the clock input to the flip-flops in Figure A.29. This is a standard symbol for a positive edge-triggered flip-flop. To denote a negative edge-triggered flip-flop, a small circle is used (in addition to the arrowhead) on the clock input.

A particularly useful form of a shift register is one that can be loaded and read in parallel. This can be accomplished with some additional gating as illustrated in Figure A.30, which shows a 4-bit register constructed with RS flip-flops. The register can be

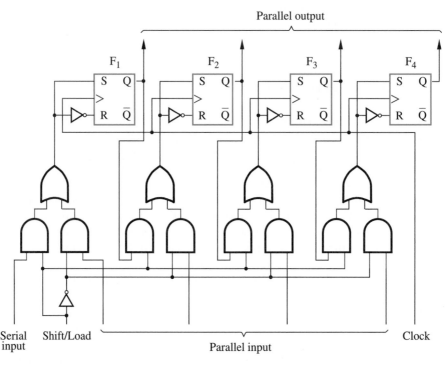

FIGURE A.30
Parallel-access shift register.

loaded either serially or in parallel. When the register is clocked, a shift takes place if Shift/Load = 1; otherwise, a parallel load is performed.

A.8
COUNTERS

In the preceding section we discussed the applicability of flip-flops in the construction of shift registers. They are equally useful in the implementation of *counter* circuits. It is hardly necessary to justify the need for counters in digital machines. In addition to being hardware mechanisms for realizing ordinary counting functions, counters are also used to generate control and timing signals. A counter driven by a high-frequency clock can be used to produce signals whose frequencies are submultiples of the original clock frequency. In such applications a counter is said to be functioning as a *scaler*.

A simple four-stage (or 4-bit) counter constructed with JK flip-flops is shown in Figure A.31. Recall that when the J and K inputs are both equal to 1, the flip-flop acts as a toggle; that is, its state changes with each successive clock pulse. Thus, two clock pulses will cause F_1 to change from the 1 state to the 0 state and back to the 1 state or from 0 to 1 to 0. This means that the output waveform of F_1, denoted in the figure as

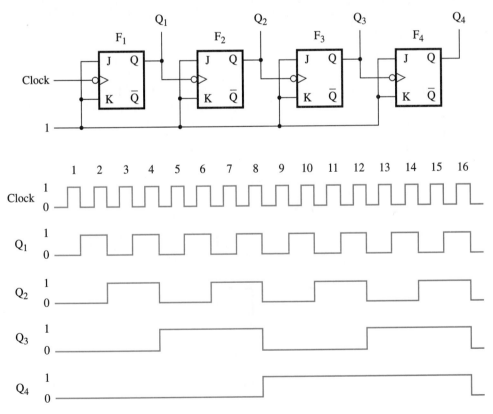

FIGURE A.31
A four-stage counter and associated signal waveforms.

Q_1, has half the frequency of the clock. Similarly, because F_2 is driven by the output of F_1, the waveform at Q_2 has half the frequency of Q_1, or one-fourth the frequency of the clock. Note that we have assumed that the trailing edge of the clock input to each flip-flop triggers the change of its state.

Such a counter is often called a *ripple counter* because the effect of an input clock pulse ripples through the counter. For example, the trailing edge of pulse 8 will change the state of F_1 from 1 to 0. This change in Q_1 will then force Q_2 from 1 to 0. Next, Q_3 is changed from 1 to 0, which in turn forces Q_4 from 0 to 1. If each flip-flop introduces some delay Δ, then the delay in setting Q_4 is 4Δ. Such delays can be a problem when very fast operation of counter circuits is required. In many applications, however, these delays are small in comparison with the length of the clock pulses and can be neglected.

With the addition of some extra logic gates, it is possible to construct a "synchronous" counter in which each stage is under the control of the common clock so that all flip-flops can change their states simultaneously. Such counters are capable of operation at higher speed because the total propagation delay is reduced considerably.

A.9
DECODERS

Much of the information in computers is handled in a highly encoded form. In an instruction, an n-bit field may be used to denote 1 out of 2^n possible choices for the action to be taken. To perform the desired action, the encoded instruction must first be decoded. A circuit capable of accepting an n-variable input and generating the corresponding output signal on one out of 2^n output lines is called a *decoder*. A simple example of a two-input to four-output decoder is given in Figure A.32. One of the four output lines is selected by the inputs x_1 and x_2, as indicated in the figure. The selected output has the logic value 1, and the remaining outputs have the value 0.

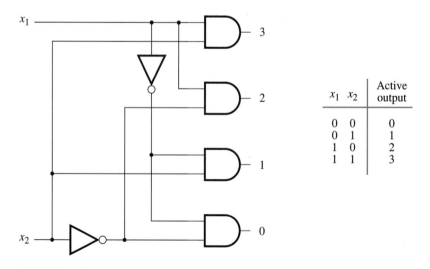

x_1	x_2	Active output
0	0	0
0	1	1
1	0	2
1	1	3

FIGURE A.32
A two-input to four-output decoder.

So far, we have considered only the simplest kind of decoders, but many others exist. For example, using information in BCD form often requires decoding circuits in which a four-variable BCD input is used to select 1 out of 10 possible outputs. As another specific example, let us consider a decoder suitable for driving a seven-segment display. Figure A.33 shows the structure of a seven-segment element used for display purposes. We can easily see that any decimal number from zero to nine can be displayed with this element simply by turning some segments on (light) while leaving others off (dark). The necessary functions are indicated in the table. They can be realized using the decoding circuit shown in the figure. Note that the circuit is constructed with NAND gates. We encourage the reader to verify that the circuit implements the required functions.

A.10
MULTIPLEXERS

In the preceding section we saw that decoders select one output line on the basis of input signals. The selected output line has logic value 1, while the other outputs have the value 0. Another class of very useful selector circuits exists, in which any one of n inputs can be selected to appear as the output. The choice is governed by a set of "select" inputs. Such circuits are called *multiplexers*. An example of a multiplexer circuit is shown in Figure A.34. It has two select inputs, w_1 and w_2. Their four possible valuations are used to select one of four inputs, x_1, x_2, x_3, or x_4, to appear as the output z. A simple logic circuit that can implement the required operation is also given. Obviously, the same structure can be used to realize larger multiplexers, in which k select inputs are used to connect one of the 2^k data inputs to the output.

The obvious application of multiplexers is in the gating of data that may come from a number of different sources. For example, loading a 16-bit data register from one of four distinct sources can be accomplished with 16 four-input multiplexers.

Multiplexers are also very useful as basic elements for implementing logic functions. Consider a function f defined by the truth table of Figure A.35. It can be represented as shown in the figure by factoring out the variables x_1 and x_2. Note that for each valuation of x_1 and x_2, the function f corresponds to one of four terms: 0, 1, x_3, or $\overline{x}_3$. This suggests the possibility of using a four-input multiplexer circuit, in which x_1 and x_2 are the two select inputs that choose one of the four data inputs. Then, if the data inputs are connected to 0, 1, x_3, or $\overline{x}_3$ as required by the truth table, the output of the multiplexer will correspond to the function f. The approach is completely general. Any function of three variables can be realized with a single four-input multiplexer. Similarly, any function of four variables can be implemented with an eight-input multiplexer, and so on.

A.11
PROGRAMMABLE LOGIC DEVICES (PLDs)

Sections A.2 and A.3 showed how a given switching function can be represented in terms of sum-of-products expressions and implemented by corresponding AND-OR

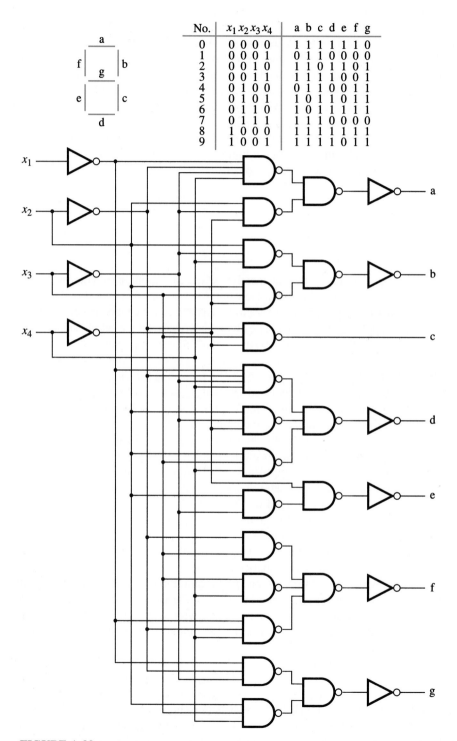

No.	$x_1\, x_2\, x_3\, x_4$	a b c d e f g
0	0 0 0 0	1 1 1 1 1 1 0
1	0 0 0 1	0 1 1 0 0 0 0
2	0 0 1 0	1 1 0 1 1 0 1
3	0 0 1 1	1 1 1 1 0 0 1
4	0 1 0 0	0 1 1 0 0 1 1
5	0 1 0 1	1 0 1 1 0 1 1
6	0 1 1 0	1 0 1 1 1 1 1
7	0 1 1 1	1 1 1 0 0 0 0
8	1 0 0 0	1 1 1 1 1 1 1
9	1 0 0 1	1 1 1 1 0 1 1

FIGURE A.33
A BCD–to–seven-segment display decoder.

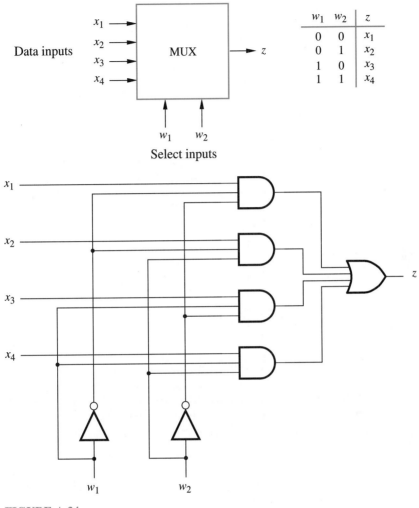

w_1	w_2	z
0	0	x_1
0	1	x_2
1	0	x_3
1	1	x_4

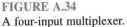

FIGURE A.34
A four-input multiplexer.

gate networks. Section A.10 showed how multiplexers can be used to realize switching functions. In this section we will consider another class of circuits that can be used for the same purpose. These circuits consist of arrays of switching elements that can be programmed to allow implementation of sum-of-products expressions. They are called *programmable logic devices* (PLDs).

Figure A.36 shows the block diagram of a PLD. It has n input variables $(x_1, \ldots, x_n)$ and m output functions $(f_1, \ldots, f_m)$. Each function f_i is realized as a sum of product terms that involve the input variables. The variables $x_1, \ldots, x_n$ are presented in true and complemented form to the AND array, where up to k product terms are formed. These are then gated into the OR array, where the output functions are formed. Two commonly used types of PLDs are described in the remainder of this section.

x_1	x_2	x_3	f
0	0	0	0 ⎫
0	0	1	0 ⎭
0	1	0	0 ⎫
0	1	1	1 ⎭
1	0	0	1 ⎫
1	0	1	1 ⎭
1	1	0	1 ⎫
1	1	1	0 ⎭

x_1	x_2	f
0	0	0
0	1	x_3
1	0	1
1	1	$\bar{x}_3$

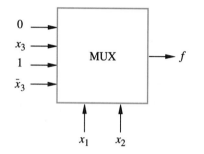

FIGURE A.35
Multiplexer implementation of a logic function.

A.11.1 Programmable Logic Array (PLA)

A circuit in which connections to both the AND and the OR arrays can be programmed is called a *programmable logic array* (PLA). Figure A.37 illustrates the functional structure of a PLA using a simple example. The programmable connections must be such that if no connection is made to a given input of an AND gate, the input behaves as if a logic value of 1 is driving it (that is, this input does not contribute to the product

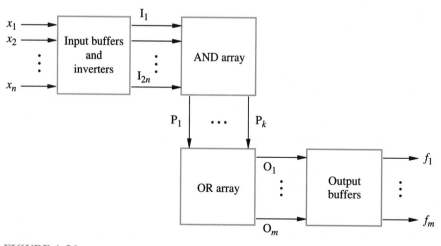

FIGURE A.36
A block diagram for a PLD.

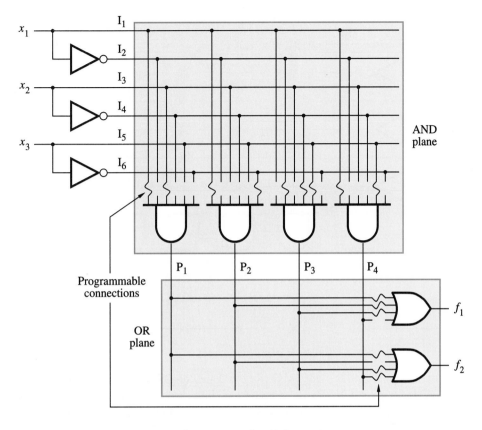

FIGURE A.37
Functional structure of a PLA.

$$f_1 = x_1 x_2 + x_1 \bar{x}_3 + \bar{x}_1 \bar{x}_2 x_3$$
$$f_2 = x_1 x_2 + \bar{x}_1 \bar{x}_2 x_3 + x_1 \bar{x}_3$$

term realized by this gate). Similarly, if no connection is made to a given input of an OR gate, this input must have no effect on the output of the gate (that is, the input must behave as if a logic value of 0 is driving it).

Programmed connections may be realized in different ways. In one method programming consists of blowing fuses in positions where connections are not required. This is done by applying higher-than-normal current. Another possibility is to use transistor switches controlled by erasable memory elements (see Section 5.3 on EPROM memory circuits) to provide the connections as desired. This allows the PLA to be reprogrammable.

The simple PLA in Figure A.37 can generate up to four product terms from three input variables. Two output functions may be implemented using these product terms. Some of the product terms may be used in more than one output function. The PLA is configured to realize the following two functions:

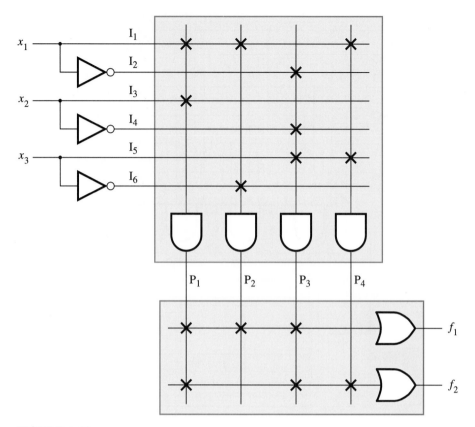

FIGURE A.38
A simplified sketch of the PLA in Figure A.37.

$$f_1 = x_1 x_2 + x_1 \overline{x}_3 + \overline{x}_1 \overline{x}_2 x_3$$
$$f_2 = x_1 x_2 + x_1 x_3 + \overline{x}_1 \overline{x}_2 x_3$$

Only four product terms are needed, because two terms can be shared by both functions. Practical PLAs come in much larger sizes.

Although Figure A.37 depicts clearly the basic functionality of a PLA, this style of presentation is awkward for describing a larger PLA. It has become customary in technical literature to represent the product and sum terms by means of corresponding gate symbols that have only one symbolic input line. An × is placed on this line to represent each programmed connection. This drawing convention is used in Figure A.38 to represent the PLA example from Figure A.37. In general, a programmable connection can be made at any crossing of a vertical line and a horizontal line in the diagram, to implement arbitrary functions of input variables.

The PLA structure is very efficient in terms of the area needed for its implementation on an integrated circuit chip. For this reason, such structures are often used for implementing control circuits in processor chips. In this case, the desired connections are put in place as the last step in the manufacturing process, rather than making them programmable after the chip has been fabricated.

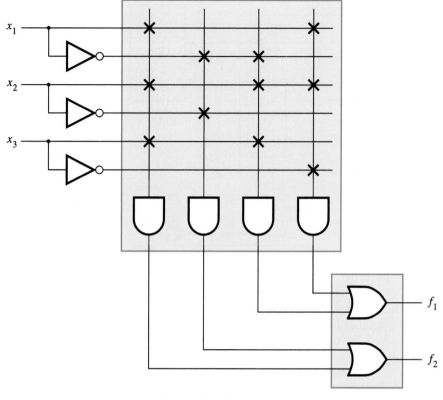

$$f_1 = x_1 x_2 \bar{x}_3 + \bar{x}_1 x_2 x_3$$

$$f_2 = \bar{x}_1 \bar{x}_2 + x_1 x_2 x_3$$

FIGURE A.39
An example of a PAL.

A.11.2 Programmable Array Logic (PAL)

In a PLA, the inputs to both the AND array and the OR array are programmable. A similar device, in which the inputs to the AND array are programmable but the connections to the OR gates are fixed, has found great popularity in practical applications. Such devices are known as *programmable array logic* (PAL) chips.

Figure A.39 shows a simple example of a PAL that can implement two functions. The number of AND gates connected to each OR gate in a PAL determines the maximum number of product terms that can be realized in a sum-of-products representation of a given function. The AND gates are permanently connected to specific OR gates, which means that a particular product term cannot be shared among output functions.

PAL chips are available in various configurations. A substantial number of input variables and output functions can be provided, allowing large functions to be realized. The versatility of a PAL may be enhanced further by including flip-flops in the outputs

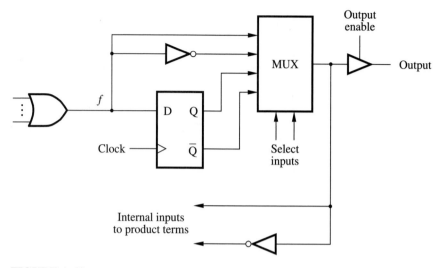

FIGURE A.40
An example of the output of a PAL element.

from the OR gates. Such PAL chips enable the designer of a digital system to implement a relatively complex logic network using a single chip.

Figure A.40 indicates the kind of flexibility that can be provided. A multiplexer is used to choose whether a true, complemented, or stored (from the previous clock cycle) value of f is to be presented at the output pin of the PAL chip. The select inputs to the multiplexer can be set as programmable connections. The output pin is driven by a three-state driver (see Section 3.1 for a discussion of such drivers), under control of the Output-enable signal. Note that the signal from the output of the multiplexer is also made available as an internal input that can be used in product terms that feed other OR gates in the PAL. This facilitates the realization of circuits that have several levels (stages) of logic gates.

A.12
FIELD-PROGRAMMABLE GATE ARRAYS

PAL chips provide general functionality but are somewhat limited in size because an output pin is provided for each sum-of-products circuit. A more powerful class of programmable devices has been developed to overcome these size limitations. They are known as *field-programmable gate arrays* (FPGAs). Figure A.41 shows a conceptual block diagram of an FPGA. It consists of an array of logic blocks (indicated as black boxes) that can be connected by general interconnection resources. The *interconnect*, shown in blue, consists of segments of wire and programmable switches. The switches are used to connect the logic blocks to the wire segments, and to establish connections between different wire segments as desired. This allows a large degree of routing flexibility on the chip. Input and output buffers are provided for access to the pins of the chip.

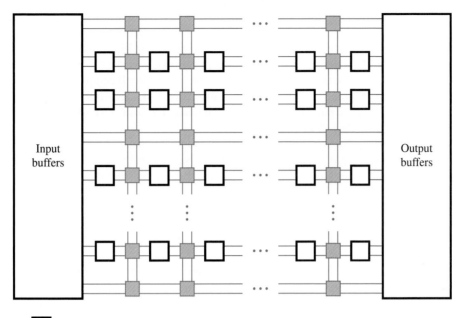

 Logic block

Interconnection switches

FIGURE A.41
A conceptual block diagram of an FPGA.

There are a variety of designs for the logic blocks and the interconnect structure. A logic block may be just a simple multiplexer-based circuit capable of implementing logic functions as discussed in Section A.10. Another popular design uses a simple lookup table as a logic block. For example, a four-input lookup table can be implemented in the form of a 16-bit memory circuit in which the truth table of a logic function is stored. Each memory bit corresponds to one combination of the input variables. Such a lookup table can be programmed to implement any function of four variables. The logic blocks may contain flip-flops to provide additional flexibility of the type encountered in Figure A.40. Some FPGAs use much larger logic blocks that are similar in functionality to a PAL. Thus, a single FPGA may have the functionality of a number of PAL chips.

From the user's point of view, there are two major differences between FPGAs and PALs. The FPGA chips have much greater functionality and can be used to implement rather large logic networks. Hundreds of logic blocks can be included on an FPGA chip. In contrast, a PAL contains a much smaller number of sum-of-products circuits. The second important consideration is the speed of these devices. Since programmable switches are used to establish all connections in the interconnect, an FPGA will inevitably have significantly longer propagation delays compared with a less flexible device such as a PAL.

The growing popularity of FPGAs is due to the fact that they allow a designer to implement very complex logic networks on a single chip without having to design and fabricate a custom VLSI chip, which is both expensive and time-consuming. Using CAD tools, it is possible to generate an FPGA design in a matter of days, rather than the months needed to produce a custom-designed VLSI chip. The FPGA implementations are also attractive in terms of cost. Even the largest FPGAs cost only a few hundred dollars, and the cost associated with the design time is very small compared to the cost of designing a custom chip. We should keep in mind that PALs are even less expensive than FPGAs, but a large number of PALs may be needed to realize a complex network that can fit into a single FPGA chip.

An introductory discussion of programmable logic devices can be found in many modern books on logic design. For a more extensive treatment of these devices, the reader may consult specialized books[10-13] and manufacturers' literature.

A.13
SEQUENTIAL CIRCUITS

A combinational circuit is one whose output is determined entirely by its present inputs. Examples of such circuits are the decoders and multiplexers presented in Sections A.9 and A.10. A different class of circuits are those whose outputs depend on both the present inputs and on the sequence of previous inputs. They are called *sequential circuits*. Such circuits can be in different *states,* depending on what the sequence of inputs has been up to a given time. The state of a circuit determines the behavior when various input patterns are applied to the circuit. We encountered two specific forms of such circuits in Sections A.7 and A.8, called shift registers and counters. In this section, we will introduce more examples of sequential circuits, provide a general form for them, and give a brief introduction to the design of these circuits.

A.13.1 An Example of an Up/Down Counter

Figure A.31 shows the configuration of an up counter, implemented with four JK flip-flops, which counts in the sequence 0, 1, 2, ..., 15, 0, ... A similar circuit can be used to count in the down direction, that is, 0, 15, 14, ..., 1, 0, ... (see Problem A.23). These simple circuits are made possible by the toggle feature of JK flip-flops.

We now consider the possibility of implementing such counters with D flip-flops. As a specific example, we will design a counter that counts either up or down, depending on the value of an external control input. To keep the example small, let us restrict the size to a mod-4 counter, which requires only 2 state bits to represent the four possible count values. We will show how this counter can be designed using general techniques for the synthesis of sequential circuits. The desired circuit will count up if an input signal x is equal to 0 and down if x is 1. The count will change on the negative edge of the clock signal. Let us assume that we are particularly interested in the state when the count is equal to 2. Thus, an output signal, z, should be asserted when the count is equal to 2; otherwise $z = 0$.

The desired counter can be implemented as a sequential circuit. In order to determine what the new count will be when a clock pulse is applied, it is sufficient to know the value of x and the present count. It is not necessary to know what the actual sequence of previous input values has been, as long as we know the present count that has been reached. This count value is said to determine the *present state* of the circuit, which is all that the circuit remembers about previous input values. If the present count is 2 and $x = 0$, the next count will be 3. It makes no difference whether the count of 2 was reached counting down from 3 or up from 1.

Before we show a circuit implementation, let us depict the desired behavior of the counter by means of a state diagram. The counter has four distinct states: S0, S1, S2, and S3. A *state diagram* is a graph in which states are represented as circles (sometimes called nodes). Transitions between states are indicated by labeled arrows. The label associated with an arrow specifies the value of the input x that will cause this particular transition to occur and the value of the output produced as a result. Figure A.42 shows the state diagram of our up/down counter. For example, the arrow emanating from state S1 (count $= 1$) for an input $x = 0$ points to state S2, thus specifying the transition to state S2. It also indicates that the output z must be equal to 0 while the circuit is in state S1 and the value of x is 0. An arrow from S2 to S3 specifies that when $x = 0$ the next clock pulse will cause a transition from S2 to S3, and that the output z should be 1 while the circuit is in state S2.

Note that the state diagram describes the functional behavior of the counter, without any reference to how it is implemented. Figure A.42 can be used to describe an electronic digital circuit, a mechanical counter, or a computer program that behaves in this way. Such diagrams are a powerful means of describing any system that exhibits sequential behavior.

A different way of presenting the information in a state diagram is to use a *state table*. Figure A.43 gives the state table for the example in Figure A.42. The table indicates transitions from all present states to the *next states*, as required by the applied input

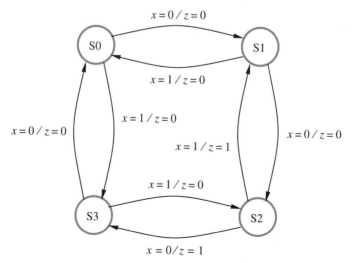

FIGURE A.42

State diagram of a mod-4 up/down counter that detects the count of 2.

Present state	Next state		Output z	
	x = 0	x = 1	x = 0	x = 1
S0	S1	S3	0	0
S1	S2	S0	0	0
S2	S3	S1	1	1
S3	S0	S2	0	0

FIGURE A.43
State table for the example of the up/down counter.

x. The output signal, z, is determined by the present state of the circuit and the value of the applied input, x.

Having specified the desired up/down counter in general terms, we will now consider its physical realization. Two bits are needed to encode the four states that indicate the count. Let these bits be y_2 (high-order) and y_1 (low-order). The states of the counter are determined by the values of y_2 and y_1, which we will write in the form $y_2 y_1$. We will assign values to $y_2 y_1$ for each of the four states as follows: S0 = 00, S1 = 01, S2 = 10, and S3 = 11. We have chosen the assignment such that the binary number $y_2 y_1$ represents the count in an obvious way. The variables y_2 and y_1 are called the *state variables* of the sequential circuit. Using this *state assignment,* the state table for our example is as shown in Figure A.44. Note that we are using the variables Y_1 and Y_2 to denote the next state in the same manner as y_1 and y_2.

It is important to note that we could have chosen a different assignment of $y_2 y_1$ values to the various states. For example, a possible state assignment is: S0 = 10, S1 = 11, S2 = 01, and S3 = 00. For a counter circuit, this assignment is less intuitive than the one in Figure A.44, but the resultant circuit will work properly. Different state assignments usually lead to different costs in implementing the circuit (see Problem A.28).

Present state	Next state		Output z	
	x = 0	x = 1	x = 0	x = 1
$y_2 y_1$	$Y_2 \ Y_1$	$Y_2 \ Y_1$		
0 0	0 1	1 1	0	0
0 1	1 0	0 0	0	0
1 0	1 1	0 1	1	1
1 1	0 0	1 0	0	0

FIGURE A.44
State assignment for the example in Figure A.43.

Our intention in this example is to use D flip-flops to store the values of the two state variables between successive clock pulses. The output, Q, of a flip-flop is the present-state variable y_i, and the input, D, is the next-state variable Y_i. Note that Y_i is a function of y_2, y_1, and x, as indicated in Figure A.44. From the figure, we see that

$$Y_2 = \overline{x}\,\overline{y}_2 y_1 + \overline{x} y_2 \overline{y}_1 + x \overline{y}_2 \overline{y}_1 + x y_2 y_1$$
$$= x \oplus y_2 \oplus y_1$$
$$Y_1 = \overline{x}\,\overline{y}_2 \overline{y}_1 + \overline{x} y_2 \overline{y}_1 + x \overline{y}_2 \overline{y}_1 + x y_2 \overline{y}_1$$
$$= \overline{y}_1$$

The output z is determined as

$$z = y_2 \overline{y}_1$$

These expressions lead to the circuit shown in Figure A.45.

A.13.2 Timing Diagrams

To fully understand the operation of the counter circuit, it is useful to consider its timing diagram. Figure A.46 gives an example of a possible sequence of events. It assumes that state transitions (changes in flip-flop values) occur on the negative edge of the clock

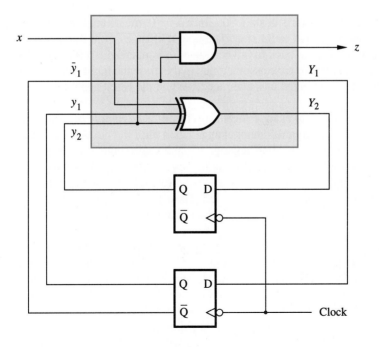

FIGURE A.45
Implementation of the up/down counter.

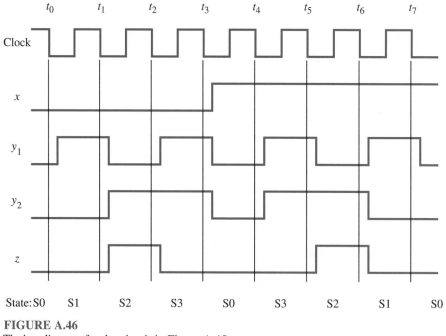

FIGURE A.46
Timing diagram for the circuit in Figure A.45.

and that the counter starts in state S0. Since $x = 0$, the counter advances to state S1 at t_0, then to S2 at t_1, and to S3 at t_2. The output changes from 0 to 1 when the counter enters state S2. It goes back to 0 when state S3 is reached. At the end of S3, at t_3, the counter goes to S0. We have assumed that at this time the input x changes to 1, causing the counter to count in the down sequence. When the count again reaches S2, at t_5, the output z goes to 1.

Note that all signal changes occur just after the beginning of a clock period (at the negative edge), and signals do not change again until the next clock period. The delay from the clock edge to the time at which variables y_i change is the propagation delay of the flip-flops used to implement the counter circuit (see Figure A.28). It is important to note that the input x is also assumed to be controlled by the same clock, and it changes only near the beginning of a clock period. These are essential features of circuits where all changes are controlled by a clock. Such circuits are called *synchronous sequential circuits*.

Another important observation concerns the relationship between the labels used in the state diagram in Figure A.42 and the timing diagram. For example, consider the clock period between t_1 and t_2. During this clock period, the machine is in state S2 and the input value is $x = 0$. This situation is described in the state diagram by the arrow emanating from state S2 labeled $x = 0$. Since this arrow points to state S3, the timing diagram shows y_2 and y_1 changing to the values corresponding to state S3 at the next clock edge, t_2. The output value associated with the arrow gives the value of z while the counter is in state S2.

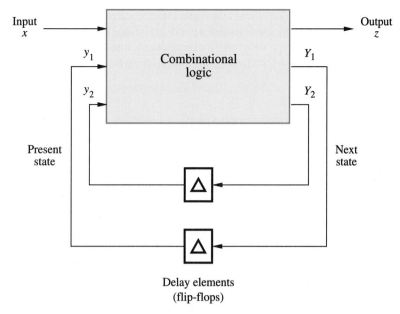

FIGURE A.47
A formal model of a finite state machine.

A.13.3 The Finite State Machine Model

The specific example of the up/down counter implemented as a synchronous sequential circuit with flip-flops and combinational logic gates, as shown in Figure A.45, is easily generalized to the formal *finite state machine* model given in Figure A.47. In this model, the time delay through the delay elements is equal to the duration of the clock cycle. This is the time that elapses between changes in Y_i and the corresponding changes in y_i. The model assumes that the combinational logic block has no delay; hence, the outputs z, Y_1, and Y_2 are instantaneous functions of the inputs x, y_1, and y_2. In an actual circuit, some delay will be introduced by the circuit elements, as shown in Figure A.46. The circuit will work properly if the delay through the combinational logic block is short with respect to the clock cycle. The next-state outputs Y_i must be available in time to cause the flip-flops to change to the desired next state at the end of the clock cycle. Also, while the output z may not be at the desired value during all of the clock cycle, it must reach this value well before the end of the cycle.

Inputs to the combinational logic block consist of the flip-flop outputs, y_i, which represent the present state, and the external input, x. The outputs of the block are the inputs to the flip-flops, which we have called Y_i, and the external output, z. When the active clock edge arrives marking the end of the present clock cycle, the values on the Y_i lines are loaded into the flip-flops. They become the next set of values of the state variables, y_i. Since these signals are connected to the input of the combinational block, they, along with the next value of the external input x, will produce new z and Y_i values. A clock cycle later, the new Y_i values are transferred to y_i, and the process repeats. In other words, the flip-flops constitute a feedback path from the output to the input of the combinational block, introducing a delay of one clock period.

Although we have shown only one external input, one external output, and two state variables in Figure A.47, it is clear that multiple versions are possible for any of the three types of variables.

A.13.4 Synthesis of Finite State Machines

Let us summarize how to design a synchronous sequential circuit having the general organization in Figure A.47, based on a state diagram like that in Figure A.42. The design, or synthesis, process involves the following steps:

1. Develop an appropriate state diagram or state table.
2. Determine the number of flip-flops needed, and choose a suitable type of flip-flop.
3. Determine the values to be stored in these flip-flops for each state in the state diagram. This is referred to as state assignment.
4. Develop the state-assigned state table.
5. Derive a truth table for the combinational logic block.
6. Find a suitable circuit implementation for the combinational logic block.

Example

As a further example of a finite state machine that has both inputs and outputs, consider a coin-operated vending machine. For simplicity, let us assume that the machine accepts only quarters and dimes. The quarters or dimes are applied as inputs until a total of 30 cents or more is deposited. When this total is reached, an output (merchandise) is provided. No change is provided if more than 30 cents is deposited. Let binary inputs x_1 and x_2 represent coins being deposited, such that $x_1 = 1$ or $x_2 = 1$ if a quarter or a dime is deposited, respectively. Otherwise, these inputs are equal to 0. Only one coin is deposited at a time, so that input combination $x_1 x_2 = 11$ never occurs. Also, let a binary output z represent merchandise provided by the machine, such that $z = 0$ for no merchandise and $z = 1$ for merchandise provided.

The first task in designing a logic circuit for the vending machine is to draw a state diagram or a state table. It is best to give a word description of each state needed and then decide later how many flip-flops will be needed to represent the required number of states. The states represent the total amount of money deposited at any point in the process. Based on the fact that dimes or quarters can be deposited in any order until the total is equal to or greater than 30 cents, the states needed are

S0 = nothing deposited (the "start" state)
S1 = 10 cents
S2 = 20 cents
S3 = 25 cents

We do not need any more states because when the present state is either S2 or S3, either a dime or a quarter will suffice as the present input to generate the $z = 1$ output and move to state S0 to start again.

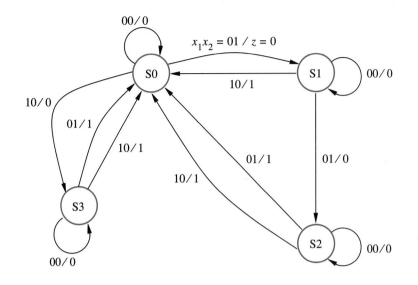

$x_1 = 1 \sim$ quarter deposited

$x_2 = 1 \sim$ dime deposited

$z = 1 \sim$ dispense merchandise
(i.e., a total of 30 cents deposited)

Input combination $x_1 x_2 = 11$ cannot occur

FIGURE A.48
State diagram for the vending machine example.

A state diagram description of the desired behavior for the vending machine is given in Figure A.48. Note that the input $x_1 x_2 = 11$ does not appear because both a quarter and a dime cannot be deposited at the same time. Also notice that each state has an arrow looping back to itself labeled 00/0. This indicates that if no coins are being deposited during a clock cycle, the circuit stays in its present state.

Only four states are needed for this machine. This will require two flip-flops. If we label them y_2 and y_1, and assign their values to represent the states as $S0 = 00$, $S1 = 01, S2 = 10$, and $S3 = 11$, Figure A.49 shows the resultant assigned state table. We have used dashes in the table to indicate that the input combination of $x_1 x_2 = 11$ does not appear. These entries are don't-care conditions, which we can take advantage of in the design of the combinational logic block, which will be discussed next.

This completes the first four steps in the synthesis procedure. We now go to step 5. The assigned state table in Figure A.49 leads directly to the truth table in Figure A.50, which specifies the functions of the combinational logic block. From the table, it is easy to derive the following expressions that give the implementation of the logic block:

$$Y_2 = \overline{x}_1 \overline{x}_2 y_2 + x_2 \overline{y}_2 y_1 + x_1 \overline{y}_2 \overline{y}_1$$
$$Y_1 = \overline{x}_1 \overline{x}_2 y_1 + \overline{y}_2 \overline{y}_1 (x_1 + x_2)$$
$$z = y_2(x_1 + x_2) + x_1 y_1$$

Present state	Next state				Output z			
	$x_1x_2 = 00$	$x_1x_2 = 01$	$x_1x_2 = 10$	$x_1x_2 = 11$	$x_1x_2 = 00$	$x_1x_2 = 01$	$x_1x_2 = 10$	$x_1x_2 = 11$
y_2y_1	Y_2Y_1	Y_2Y_1	Y_2Y_1	Y_2Y_1				
S0 0 0	0 0	0 1	1 1	-	0	0	0	-
S1 0 1	0 1	1 0	0 0	-	0	0	1	-
S2 1 0	1 0	0 0	0 0	-	0	1	1	-
S3 1 1	1 1	0 0	0 0	-	0	1	1	-

FIGURE A.49
Assigned state table for the vending machine example.

x_1	x_2	y_2	y_1	Y_2	Y_1	z
0	0	0	0	0	0	0
0	0	0	1	0	1	0
0	0	1	0	1	0	0
0	0	1	1	1	1	0
0	1	0	0	0	1	0
0	1	0	1	1	0	0
0	1	1	0	0	0	1
0	1	1	1	0	0	1
1	0	0	0	1	1	0
1	0	0	1	0	0	1
1	0	1	0	0	0	1
1	0	1	1	0	0	1
1	1	0	0	d	d	d
1	1	0	1	d	d	d
1	1	1	0	d	d	d
1	1	1	1	d	d	d

FIGURE A.50
Combinational logic specification for the vending machine circuit.

Observe that the logic terms $\overline{x}_1\overline{x}_2$, $\overline{y}_1\overline{y}_2$, and $(x_1 + x_2)$ appear in more than one of the expressions. This leads to a cost saving in the implementation of the block.

Sequential circuits can easily be implemented with PALs and FPGAs, because these devices contain flip-flops as well as combinational logic gates. Modern computer-aided design tools can be used to synthesize sequential circuits directly from a specification given in terms of a state diagram.

Note that the next-state and output entries in Figure A.49 are the same for states S2 and S3 for all input combinations where a change of state occurs. This implies that two different states are not really needed to represent the totals 20 cents and 25 cents. One state would be sufficient, because from either of these total deposits, the next coin deposited will cause merchandise to be provided ($z = 1$) and will cause a return to the starting state S0. Thus, states S2 and S3 are *equivalent* and can be replaced by a single state. This means that only three states are needed to implement the machine. Two flip-flops are still required. However, in more general situations, a reduction in the number of states through state equivalences often leads to fewer flip-flops and simpler circuits.

Another economy that can be achieved in implementing sequential circuits is in the combinational logic required. Different state assignments will lead to different logic specifications, some of which may require fewer gates than others. We will not develop these ideas further, but the reader should appreciate that there are many interesting aspects to the economical design and implementation of sequential circuits.

Finally, we should note that other types of flip-flops can be used to represent state variables. We have used the D flip-flops here to keep the presentation as simple as possible. By using other, more flexible types, such as JK flip-flops, the required combinational logic can sometimes be reduced. See Problems A.31 and A.32 for an exploration of this possibility.

The preceding introduction to sequential circuits is based on the type of circuits that operate under the control of a clock. It is also possible to implement sequential circuits without using a clock. Such circuits are called *asynchronous sequential circuits*. Their design is not as straightforward as that of the synchronous sequential circuits. For a complete treatment of both types of sequential circuits, consult one of many books that specialize in logic design.[1-7]

A.14
CONCLUDING REMARKS

The main purpose of this appendix is to acquaint the reader with the basic concepts in logic design and to provide an indication of the circuit configurations commonly used in the construction of computer systems. Familiarity with this material will lead to a much better understanding of the architectural concepts discussed in the main chapters of the book. As we have said in several places, the detailed design of logic networks is done with the help of CAD tools. These tools take care of many details and can be used very effectively by a knowledgeable designer.

IC technology and CAD tools have revolutionized logic design. A variety of IC components are commercially available at ever-decreasing costs, and new developments and technological improvements are constantly occurring. In this appendix we introduced some of the basic components that are useful in the design of digital systems.

From the designer's point of view, the important parameters are the cost and speed of the resultant circuits. Both of these measures are improved by making the number of IC packages used as low as possible. This can be achieved if large chips are used, which are capable of implementing complex logic networks on a single chip. In particular, the PAL and FPGA devices offer effective solutions in many applications.

Two other design objectives are becoming increasingly important. The ability to easily test the resultant circuits simplifies both the task of proving that newly produced equipment works correctly and the task of repairing it when it fails. Furthermore, it is often desirable to increase the reliability of a system with the help of additional, redundant logic circuits (for example, by duplicating some parts). Both of these objectives are likely to lead to increased component cost. It is the designer's job to arrive at a satisfactory trade-off between these considerations. A number of specialized books are available that deal with the subject of testing and fault tolerance.[14-17]

PROBLEMS

A.1. Implement the COINCIDENCE function in sum-of-products form, where COINCIDENCE = $\overline{\text{EX-OR}}$.

A.2. Prove the following identities by using algebraic manipulation and also by using truth tables.

(a) $\overline{a \oplus b} \oplus c = \overline{a}\overline{b}\overline{c} + ab\overline{c} + \overline{a}bc + a\overline{b}c$
(b) $x + w\overline{x} = x + w$
(c) $x_1\overline{x}_2 + \overline{x}_2 x_3 + x_3\overline{x}_1 = x_1\overline{x}_2 + x_3\overline{x}_1$

A.3. Derive minimal sum-of-products forms for the 4 three-variable functions f_1, f_2, f_3, and f_4 given in Figure PA.1. Is there more than one minimal form for any of these functions? If so, derive all of them.

x_1	x_2	x_3	f_1	f_2	f_3	f_4
0	0	0	1	1	d	0
0	0	1	1	1	1	1
0	1	0	0	1	0	1
0	1	1	0	1	1	d
1	0	0	1	0	d	d
1	0	1	0	0	0	d
1	1	0	1	0	1	1
1	1	1	1	1	1	0

FIGURE PA.1
Logic functions for Problem A.3.

A.4. Find the simplest sum-of-products form for the function f using the don't-care condition d, where

$$f = x_1(x_2\overline{x}_3 + x_2x_3 + \overline{x}_2\overline{x}_3x_4) + x_2\overline{x}_4(\overline{x}_3 + x_1)$$

and

$$d = x_1\overline{x}_2(x_3x_4 + \overline{x}_3\overline{x}_4) + \overline{x}_1\overline{x}_3x_4$$

A.5. Two 2-bit numbers $A = a_1a_0$ and $B = b_1b_0$ are to be compared by a four-variable function $f(a_1, a_0, b_1, b_0)$. The function f is to have the value 1 whenever

$$v(A) \le v(B)$$

where $v(X) = x_1 \times 2^1 + x_0 \times 2^0$ for any 2-bit number. Assume that the variables A and B are such that $|v(A) - v(B)| \le 2$. Synthesize f using as few gates as possible.

A.6. Repeat Problem A.5 for the requirement that $f = 1$ whenever

$$v(A) > v(B)$$

subject to the input constraint

$$v(A) + v(B) \le 4$$

A.7. Implement the following function with no more than six NAND gates, each having three inputs.

$$f = x_1x_2 + x_1x_2x_3 + \overline{x}_1\overline{x}_2\overline{x}_3x_4 + \overline{x}_1\overline{x}_2x_3\overline{x}_4$$

Assume that both true and complemented inputs are available.

A.8. Show how to implement the following function using six or fewer two-input NAND gates. Complemented input variables are not available.

$$f = x_1x_2 + \overline{x}_3 + \overline{x}_1x_4$$

A.9. Implement the following function as economically as possible using only NAND gates. Assume that complemented input variables are not available.

$$f = (x_1 + x_3)(\overline{x}_2 + \overline{x}_4)$$

A.10. A number code in which consecutive numbers are represented by binary patterns that differ in one bit position only is called Gray code. A truth table for a 3-bit Gray code to binary code converter is shown in Figure PA.2a.

(a) Implement the three functions f_1, f_2, and f_3 using only NAND gates.
(b) A lower-cost network for performing this code conversion can be derived by noting the following relationships between the input and output variables.

$$f_1 = a$$
$$f_2 = f_1 \oplus b$$
$$f_3 = f_2 \oplus c$$

3-bit Gray code inputs			Binary code outputs		
a	b	c	f_1	f_2	f_3
0	0	0	0	0	0
0	0	1	0	0	1
0	1	1	0	1	0
0	1	0	0	1	1
1	1	0	1	0	0
1	1	1	1	0	1
1	0	1	1	1	0
1	0	0	1	1	1

(a) Three-bit Gray code

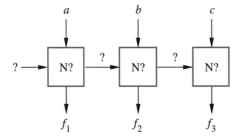

(b) Code conversion network

FIGURE PA.2
Gray code example for Problem A.10.

Using these relationships, specify the contents of a combinational network N that can be repeated, as shown in Figure PA.2b, to implement the conversion. Compare the total number of NAND gates required to implement the conversion in this form to the number required in part a.

A.11. In the production of ICs it is desirable to have circuits with as few wire crossovers as possible. Implement the EX-OR function using only NAND gates, so that there are no wire crossovers inside the box shown in Figure PA.3.

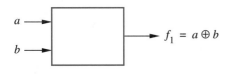

FIGURE PA.3
Combinational network for the EX-OR function.

A.12. Figure A.33 defines a BCD to seven-segment display decoder. Give an implementation for this truth table using AND, OR, and NOT gates. Verify that the same functions are correctly implemented by the NAND gate circuits shown in the figure.

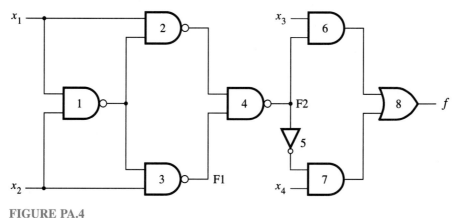

FIGURE PA.4
A faulty network.

A.13. In the logic network shown in Figure PA.4, gate 3 fails and produces the logic value 1 at its output F1 regardless of the inputs. Redraw the network, making simplifications wherever possible, to obtain a new network that is equivalent to the given faulty network and that contains as few gates as possible. Repeat this problem, assuming that the fault is at position F2, which is stuck at a logic value 0.

A.14. The circuit configuration for a CMOS two-input NOR gate is given in Figure A.18. Show how the four MOS transistors can be connected to obtain a two-input NAND gate.

A.15. The ECL logic family provides considerable flexibility in implementing logic functions by allowing gate outputs to be tied together. By inspection of the circuit configuration for an ECL NOR gate, derive the logic expressions for the functions f_1 to f_4 in Figure PA.5.

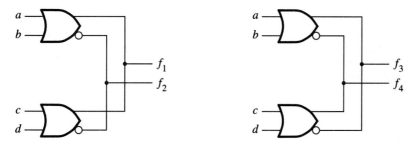

FIGURE PA.5
Wired output configurations.

A.16. Logic circuits for JK master-slave flip-flops are given in Figure A.27. Draw the waveforms at S', R', Q, and $\overline{Q}$ for the input waveforms shown in Figure PA.6, assuming that the flip-flop is initially in the 0 state.

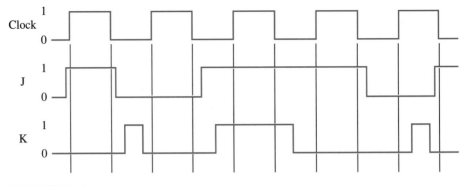

FIGURE PA.6
Input waveforms for a JK flip-flop.

A.17. Derive the truth table for the NAND gate circuit in Figure PA.7. Compare it to the truth table in Figure A.23*b* and then verify that the equivalence shown in Figure A.27*b* is correct.

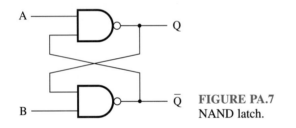

FIGURE PA.7
NAND latch.

A.18. Compute both the setup time and the hold time in terms of NOR gate delays for the negative edge-triggered D flip-flop shown in Figure A.28.

A.19. Figure A.29 shows a shift register network that shifts the data to the right one place at a time under the control of a clock signal. Modify this shift register to make it capable of shifting data either one or two places at a time under the control of the clock and an additional control input ONE/TWO.

A.20. A 4-bit shift register that has three inputs—INITIALIZE, RIGHT/LEFT, and CLOCK—is required. When INITIALIZE is set to 1, the binary number 1000 should be loaded into the register independently of the clock input. When INITIALIZE = 0, pulses at the CLOCK input should rotate this pattern. The pattern moves right or left when the RIGHT/LEFT input is equal to 1 or 0, respectively. Give a suitable design for this register using JK flip-flops that have PRESET and CLEAR inputs as shown in Figure A.27.

A.21. Derive a three-input to eight-output decoder network, with the restriction that the gates to be used cannot have more than two inputs.

A.22. JK flip-flops are useful in constructing counters because of their toggle effect when J = K = 1. Isolating this feature in a separate storage circuit leads to a "T" flip-flop, shown in Figure PA.8.

T	Q_{n+1}
0	Q_n
1	$\overline{Q}_n$

FIGURE PA.8
A T flip-flop.

(a) Derive a T flip-flop using a D flip-flop and any additional logic gates that may be required.

(b) Construct a modulo-8 counter using the T flip-flops.

A.23. Figure A.31 shows a four-stage up counter. A counter that counts in the opposite direction (that is, 15, 14, ..., 1, 0, 15, ...) is called a down counter. A counter capable of counting in both directions under the control of an UP/DOWN signal is called an up/down counter. Show a logic diagram for a four-stage up/down counter that can also be preset to any state through parallel loading of its flip-flops from an external source. A LOAD/COUNT control is used to determine whether the counter is being loaded or is operating as a counter.

A.24. A switching function to be implemented is described by the expression

$$f(x_1, x_2, x_3, x_4) = x_1 x_3 \overline{x}_4 + \overline{x}_1 \overline{x}_3 x_4 + \overline{x}_2 \overline{x}_3 \overline{x}_4$$

(a) Show an implementation of f in terms of an eight-input multiplexer circuit.

(b) Can f be realized with a four-input multiplexer circuit? If so, show how.

A.25. Repeat Problem A.24 for

$$f(x_1, x_2, x_3, x_4) = x_1 \overline{x}_2 x_3 + x_2 x_3 x_4 + \overline{x}_1 \overline{x}_4$$

A.26. (a) What is the total number of distinct functions, $f(x_1, x_2, x_3)$, of three binary variables?

(b) How many of these functions are implementable with one PAL circuit of the type shown in Figure A.39?

(c) What is the smallest change in the circuit in Figure A.39 that should be made to allow any three-variable function to be implemented with a single PAL circuit?

A.27. Consider the PAL circuit in Figure A.39. Suppose that the circuit is modified by adding a fourth input variable, x_4, which is connected in its uncomplemented and complemented forms to all four AND gates in the same way as the variables x_1, x_2, and x_3.

(a) Can this modified PAL be used to implement the function

$$f = x_1 \overline{x}_2 \overline{x}_3 + \overline{x}_1 x_2 \overline{x}_3 + \overline{x}_1 \overline{x}_2 x_3$$

If so, show how.

(b) How many functions of three variables cannot be implemented with this PAL?

A.28. Complete the design of the up/down counter in Figure A.43 by using the state assignment S0 = 10, S1 = 11, S2 = 01, and S3 = 00. How does this design compare with the one given in Section A.13.1?

A.29. Design a 2-bit synchronous counter of the general form shown in Figure A.45 that counts in the sequence . . . , 0, 3, 1, 2, 0, ... Use D flip-flops. This circuit has no external inputs, and the outputs are the flip-flop values themselves.

A.30. Repeat Problem A.29 for a 3-bit counter that counts in the sequence . . . , 0, 1, 2, 3, 4, 5, 0, . . . , taking advantage of the unused count values 6 and 7 as don't-care conditions in designing the combinational logic.

A.31. In Section A.13, D flip-flops were used in the design of synchronous sequential circuits. This is the simplest choice in the sense that the logic function values for a D input are directly determined by the desired next-state values in the state table. Suppose that JK flip-flops are to be used instead of D flip-flops. Describe, by the construction of a table, how to determine the binary value for each of the J and K inputs for a flip-flop as a function of each possible required transition from present state to next state for that flip-flop. (*Hint:* The table should have four rows, one for each of the transitions $0 \to 0$, $0 \to 1$, $1 \to 0$, and $1 \to 1$; and each J and K entry is to be 0, 1, or "don't care," as required.) Apply the information in your table to the design of individual combinational logic functions for each J and K input for each of the two flip-flops of the 2-bit binary counter of Problem A.29. How does the simplicity of the logic required compare to that needed for the design of the counter using D flip-flops?

A.32. Repeat Problem A.30 using JK flip-flops instead of D flip-flops. The general procedure for doing this is provided by the answer to Problem A.31.

A.33. In the vending machine example used in Section A.13.4 to illustrate the finite state machine model, a single binary output, z, was used to indicate the dispensing of merchandise. Change was not provided as an output. The purpose of this problem is to expand the output to include providing proper change. Assume that the only input sequences of dimes and quarters are: 10-10-10, 10-25, 25-10, and 25-25. Coincident with the last coin input, the outputs to be provided for these sequences are 0, 5, 5, and 20, respectively. Use two new binary outputs, z_2 and z_3, to represent the three distinct outputs. (This does not correspond directly to coins in use, but it keeps the problem simple.)

(*a*) Specify the new state table that incorporates the new outputs.
(*b*) Develop the logic expressions for the new outputs z_2 and z_3.
(*c*) Are there any equivalent states in the new state table?

A.34. Finite state machines can be used to detect the occurrence of certain subsequences in the sequence of binary inputs applied to the machine. Such machines are called *finite state recognizers*. Suppose that a machine is to produce a 1 as its output coincident with the second 1 in the pattern 011 whenever that subsequence occurs in the input sequence applied to the machine.

(*a*) Draw the state diagram for this machine.
(*b*) Make a state assignment for the required number of flip-flops and construct the assigned state table, assuming that D flip-flops are to be used.
(*c*) Derive the logic expressions for the output and the next-state variables.

A.35. Repeat part *a* only of Problem A.34 for a machine that is to recognize the occurrence of either of the subsequences 011 and 010 in the input sequence, including the cases where overlap occurs. For example, the input sequence 110101011 ... is to produce the output sequence 000010101 ....

REFERENCES

1. R. H. Katz, *Contemporary Logic Design,* Benjamin Cummings, Redwood City, Calif., 1994.
2. J. P. Hayes, *Digital Logic Design,* Addison-Wesley, Reading, Mass., 1993.
3. F. H. Hill and G. R. Peterson, *Computer Aided Logical Design with Emphasis on VLSI,* 4th ed., Wiley, New York, 1993.
4. C. H. Roth, *Fundamentals of Logic Design,* 4th ed., West, St. Paul, Minn., 1992.
5. M. M. Mano, *Digital Design,* 2d ed., Prentice-Hall, Englewood Cliffs, N.J., 1991.
6. R. S. Sandige, *Modern Digital Design,* McGraw-Hill, New York, 1990.
7. E. J. McCluskey, *Logic Design Principles,* Prentice-Hall, Englewood Cliffs, N.J., 1986.
8. A. S. Sedra and K. C. Smith, *Microelectronic Circuits,* 3d ed., Saunders, Philadelphia, 1991.
9. D. A. Hodges and H. G. Jackson, *Analysis and Design of Digital Integrated Circuits,* McGraw-Hill, New York, 1988.
10. J. H. Jenkins, *Designing with FPGAs and CPLDs,* Prentice-Hall, Englewood Cliffs, N.J., 1994.
11. S. M. Trimberger, *Field-Programmable Gate Array Technology,* Kluwer, Boston, 1994.
12. S. D. Brown, R. J. Francis, J. Rose, and Z. G. Vranesic, *Field-Programmable Gate Arrays,* Kluwer, Boston, 1992.
13. P. K. Lala, *Digital System Design Using Programmable Logic Devices,* Prentice-Hall, Englewood Cliffs, N.J., 1990.
14. V. N. Yarmolik, *Fault Diagnosis of Digital Circuits,* Wiley, Chichester, England, 1994.
15. B. W. Johnson, *Design and Analysis of Fault-Tolerant Digital Systems,* Addison-Wesley, Reading, Mass., 1989.
16. A. J. Miczo, *Digital Logic Testing and Simulation,* Wiley, New York, 1986.
17. D. K. Pradhan, *Fault-Tolerant Computing,* Prentice-Hall, Englewood Cliffs, N.J., 1986.

PowerPC Instruction Set

This appendix gives a portion of the instruction set of the PowerPC processors. Enough instructions are included here to enable the reader to write simple programs and to appreciate the variety of instructions available. The PowerPC architecture is defined as a 64-bit architecture with a 32-bit subset. This appendix discusses only the 32-bit subset, which is implemented in PowerPC models 603 and 604. The full 64-bit architecture is implemented in model 620.

The PowerPC has a large number of instructions, because instructions that perform the same operation on different operand sizes or have different addressing modes have distinct OP-code mnemonics. In the following tables, instructions are grouped together whenever they share some feature, such as performing the same function on operands of different sizes or having the same addressing mode. Because OP-code mnemonics follow regular patterns, they are easily deciphered. For example, all Load and Store instructions that use the indexed mode have mnemonics that end with the letter X.

INSTRUCTION FORMAT

Knowing the format of the instruction OP-code word is helpful in understanding the instruction set of the PowerPC. Figure B.1 shows the formats used in the instructions described in this appendix. The operand names used in the description of various instructions, such as RD or I16, refer to fields in the instruction word, as shown in the figure. Most instructions that have an immediate operand use format 1. A 6-bit OP-code field specifies both the operation to be performed and the addressing mode to be used. Next are two 5-bit fields. The first identifies the destination register, RD, where the result is to be stored. In some cases, such as in Store instructions, this field names

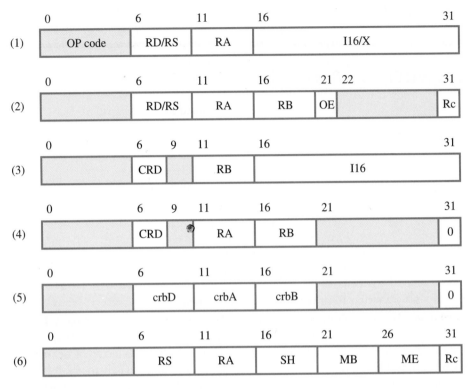

FIGURE B.1
Instruction word formats. Shaded areas contain OP-code information. Bits OE and Rc enable setting the flags in the XER and CR registers, respectively.

the source register, RS. The second 5-bit field gives the number of a second register, RA, which either contains another operand or is used in computing the effective address of an operand. The remaining 16 bits of the instruction word contain a 16-bit value. This value is either an immediate operand, I16, or the offset value, X, of an index addressing-mode specification.

Instructions that name three registers as operands use format 2. This format contains a third 5-bit register that identifies a third register referred to as RB in instruction descriptions. Bits 31 and 21 of the instruction word indicate whether the instruction affects the condition register, CR, and the exception register, XER, respectively. These bits are set to 1 when the suffixes "." and "o" are used in the assembler mnemonic of the instruction OP-code. The remainder of the instruction word gives additional information about the instruction. This portion of the instruction word can be viewed as a sub-opcode field, because the 6 bits in the first OP-code field are not sufficient to give a unique code to all instructions.

The conventions that we use in describing the instruction set of the PowerPC are summarized in Table B.10. Most of the instructions are introduced in Part III of Chapter 2. In the following sections, we comment only on some instructions that have not been described before.

LOAD AND STORE INSTRUCTIONS

Table B.1 gives the Load and Store instructions, which move data between the registers and the main memory. The addressing modes for these instructions are given in Table B.2.

The Load Multiple Word (LMW) instruction loads as many words from memory as needed to fill all registers, from the register named in the RD field through register R31. It uses the immediate index mode. For example, if R1 contains the value 3500, the instruction

LMW R20,40(R1)

transfers 12 words from locations 3540, 3544, . . . ,3584 into registers R20, R21, . . . , R31, respectively. A similar instruction, STMW, stores the contents of the registers into successive memory locations.

String instructions transfer string data from successive memory byte locations into registers, and vice versa. For example, the Load-string-word-immediate instruction

LSWI RD,RA,NB

transfers a byte string from memory, starting at location [RA]. The number of bytes transferred is NB, where NB is a 5-bit immediate operand. If NB = 0, 32 bytes are transferred. Bytes are loaded from left to right into successive registers, starting with register RD and wrapping around to register R0 if the register number exceeds 31. The instruction

LSWX RD,RA,RB

performs the same function, except that the initial memory address is [RA] + [RB]. The number of bytes to be transferred is taken from register XER, bits 25 through 31. Two Store-string instructions, STWI and STWX, transfer byte strings from the registers to the memory. Their operands are similar to those used in the corresponding Load-string instructions.

Floating-point registers are loaded or stored using the instructions in the bottom two rows of the table.

INTEGER ARITHMETIC INSTRUCTIONS

Table B.3 shows several Add and Subtract instructions. Different versions are provided for register and immediate operands, for a shifted 16-bit immediate operand, and for multiple precision. Note that, for subtract operations in 2's complement, a carry of 1 results when there is no borrow. For example, the operation $6 - 2$ using 2's-complement representation and 4-bit numbers yields $0110 + 1110 = 0100$, with a carry of 1.

For multiplication operations, MULLW provides the correct low-order, 32-bit product for both signed and unsigned operands. If the suffix "o" is used, the overflow bit in XER is set or cleared based on whether the operands are interpreted as signed or unsigned. Separate instructions are provided for signed and unsigned operands for computing the high-order half of the product.

TABLE B.1
Load and Store instructions

Name	Mnemonics for different addressing modes	Description
Load byte and zero	LBZ, LBZX LBZU, LBZUX	Load one byte into bits 24 through 31 of register RD and fill bits 0 through 23 with 0s.
Load half word and zero	LHZ, LHZX LHZU, LHZUX	Load one half word into bits 16 through 31 of register RD and fill bits 0 through 15 with 0s.
Load word	LWZ, LWZX LWZU, LWZUX	Load one word into register RD.
Load half word algebraic	LHA, LHAX LHAU, LHAUX	Load half word sign-extended to 32 bits into register RD.
Store byte	STB, STBX STU, STUX	Store the low-order byte of register RS in memory.
Store half word	STH, STHX STHU, STHUX	Store the low-order half word register RS in memory.
Store word	STW, STWX STWU, STWUX	Store register RS in memory.
Load multiple words	LMW	Load successive words from memory into registers RD, R(D + 1), ..., R31.
Store multiple words	STMW	Store registers RD, R(D + 1), ..., R31 into successive memory words.
Load string/ Store string	LSWI, LSWX STSWI, STSWX	See text.
Load floating-point single	LFS, LFSX LFSU, LFSUX	Load a 32-bit number into floating-point register FRD.
Store floating-point single	STFS, STFSX, STFSU, STFSUX	Store floating-point register FRD in memory.

(See Table B.2 for operand specification and addressing modes.)

TABLE B.2
Addressing modes for Load and Store instructions

Mnemonic	Operand syntax	Effective address
LBZ, LHZ, LWZ, LHA, STB, STH, STW, LMW, STMW	RD,X(RA)	[RA] + exts(X)
LBZX, LHZX, LWZX, LHAX, STBX, STHX, STWX, STSWX	RD,RA,RB	[RA] + [RB]
LBZU, LHZU, LHWU, LHAU, STBU, STHU, STWU	RD,X(RA)	[RA] + exts(X) RA ← effective address
LBZUX, LHZUX, LWZUX, LHAUX, STBUX, STHUX, STWUX	RD,RA,RB	[RA] + [RB] RA ← effective address
LSWI, STSWI	RD,RA,NB	[RA]
LSWX, STSWX	RD,RA,RB	[RA] + [RB]
LFS, STFS	FRD,X(RA)	[RA] + exts(X)
LFSX, STFSX	FRD,RA,RB	[RA] + [RB]
LFSU, STFSU	FRD,X(RA)	[RA] + exts(X) RA ← effective address
LFSX, STFSX	FRD,RA,RB	[RA] + [RB] RA ← effective address

Load and Store instructions that use an offset, X, to determine the effective address use format 1. Instructions that have three register operands use format 2.

Divide instructions produce a quotient such that the sign of the remainder is always the same as the sign of the dividend. For example, the operation $-\frac{43}{5}$ yields a quotient of -8 (the remainder is -3), not -9 (a remainder of $+2$). The quotient is recorded in the destination register and the remainder is lost.

LOGIC INSTRUCTIONS

Several versions are available for each logic operation, as Table B.4 shows. All instructions produce a 32-bit result. However, some operate only on 8 or 16 bits of one of their source operands, extending it with zeros either to the right or to the left.

TABLE B.3
Integer arithmetic instructions

Instruction		Name	Description
ADDx	RD,RA,RB	Add	RD ← [RA] + [RB]
ADDCx	RD,RA,RB	Add carrying	RD ← [RA] + [RB]; CA ← carry
ADDEx	RD,RA,RB	Add extended	RD ← [RA] + [RB] + [CA]
ADDI	RD,RA,I16	Add immediate	RD ← [RA] + exts(I16)
ADDIC[.]	RD,RA,I16	Add immediate carrying	RD ← [RA] + exts(I16); CA ← carry
ADDIS	RD,RA,I16	Add immediate shifted	RD ← [RA] + extzr(I16)
ADDMEx	RD,RA,RB	Add minus one extended	RD ← [RA] − 1 + [CA]
ADDZEx	RD,RA,RB	Add to zero extended	RD ← [RA] + [CA]
SUBFx	RD,RA,RB	Subtract from	RD ← [RB] − [RA]
SUBFCx	RD,RA,RB	Subtract from carrying	RD ← [RB] − [RA]; CA ← carry
SUBFEx	RD,RA,RB	Subtract from extended	RD ← [RB] − [RA] − bitc([CA])
SUBFIC[.]	RD,RA,I16	Subtract from immediate carrying	RD ← exts(I16) − [RA]; CA ← carry
SUBFMEx	RD,RA,RB	Subtract from minus one extended	RD ← −1 − [RA] − bitc([CA])
SUBFZEx	RD,RA,RB	Subtract from zero extended	RD ← 0 − [RA] − bitc([CA])
NEGx	RD,RA	Negate	RD ← −[RA]

(Continued)

TABLE B.3
(Continued)

Instruction		Name	Description
MULLW*x*	RD,RA,RB	Multiply low	RD ← low-order 32 bits of [RA] × [RB]; The operands are interpreted as signed.
MULHW[.]	RD,RA,RB	Multiply high word	RD ← high-order 32 bits of [RA] × [RB]; The operands are interpreted as signed.
MULHWU[.]	RD,RA,RB	Multiply high word unsigned	RD ← high-order 32 bits of [RA] × [RB]; The operands are interpreted as unsigned.
MULLI*x*	RD,RA,I16	Multiply low immediate	RD ← low-order 32 bits of [RA] × I16; The operands are interpreted as signed.
DIVW*x*	RD,RA,RB	Divide word	RD ← quotient of [RA]/[RB]; The operands are interpreted as signed integers; the remainder is lost.
DIVWU*x*	RD,RA,RB	Divide word unsigned	RD ← quotient of [RA]/[RB]; The operands are interpreted as unsigned integers; the remainder is lost.
CMPW	CRD,RA,RB	Compare word	Set condition flags LT, GT, or EQ in field CRD of register CR if [RA] is $<$, $>$, or $=$ [RB]; copy flag SO from XER into field CRD.
CMPWI	CRD,RA,I16	Compare word immediate	Set flags based on [RA] $<$, $>$, or $=$ exts(I16).
CMPL	CRD,0,RA,RB	Compare logical	Set flags based on unsigned([RA]) $<$, $>$, or $=$ unsigned([RB]).
CMPLI	CRD,0,RA,I16	Compare logical immediate	Set flags based on unsigned([RA]) $<$, $>$, or $=$ extz(I16).

Except for Compare, all integer arithmetic instructions with an immediate operand use format 1. Instructions with three register operands use format 2. Compare instructions use either format 3 or format 4, as appropriate.

TABLE B.4
Logic instructions

Instruction	Name	Description
AND[.] RA,RS,RB	And	RA ← [RS] $\wedge$ [RB]
ANDC[.] RA,RS,RB	And with complement	RA ← [RS] $\wedge$ bitc([RB])
ANDI. RA,RS,I16	And immediate	RA ← [RS] $\wedge$ exzl(I16)
ANDIS. RA,RS,I16	And immediate shifted	RA ← [RS] $\wedge$ exzr(I16)
NAND[.], NOR[.], OR[.], ORC[.], ORI, ORIS, XOR[.], XORI, XORIS		Similar to corresponding AND instruction.
EQV[.] RA,RS,RB	Equivalent	RA ← bitc([RS] $\oplus$ [RB])
EXTSB[.] RA,RS	Extend sign byte	RA ← exts($[RS]_{24-31}$)
EXTSH[.] RA,RS	Extend sign half word	RA ← exts($[RS]_{16-31}$)
CNTLZWx RA,RS	Count leading zeros word	RA ← Number of leading 0s in [RS]
CRAND crbD,crbA,crbB	Condition register AND	CR_{crbD} ← $[CR_{crbA}]$ $\wedge$ $[CR_{crbB}]$; Each operand consists of a single bit in the control register.
CRANDC, CRNAND, CRNOR, CROR, CRORC, CRXOR, CREQV		Same as CRAND, but different logic operation.

Logical instructions with an immediate operand use format 1, and those that name three registers use format 2. Instructions that operate on the condition register, CR, use format 5.

The condition register instructions perform a logic operation on two bits of register CR. They deposit the result in a third bit location.

ROTATE AND SHIFT INSTRUCTIONS

Rotate and Shift instructions are given in Table B.5. The Rotate instructions extract a field of arbitrary size from one register, rotate it left any number of bit locations, and deposit the result in the destination register. The shift instructions perform either a logical or an algebraic shift.

TABLE B.5
Rotate and Shift instructions

Instruction	Name	Description
RLWINMx RA,RS,SH,MB,ME	Rotate left word immediate then AND with mask	Set $M = 0\ldots01\ldots10\ldots0$, where the beginning (leftmost) and end of the block of 1s are defined by MB and ME, respectively. TEMP ← [RS] rotated left SH bits. RA ← $M \wedge$ TEMP
RLWIMLx RA,RS,SH,MB,ME	Rotate left word immediate then mask insert	Set $M = 0\ldots01\ldots10\ldots0$, where the beginning (leftmost) and end of the block of 1s are defined by MB and ME, respectively. TEMP ← [RS] rotated left SH bits. Copy the field corresponding to the block of 1s in the mask M from TEMP into register RA. Leave other bits in RA unchanged. RA_{MB-ME} ← $TEMP_{MB-ME}$
RLWNMx RA,RS,RB,MB,ME	Rotate left word then AND with mask	Set $M = 0\ldots01\ldots10\ldots0$, where the beginning (leftmost) and end of the block of 1s are defined by MB and ME, respectively. TEMP ← [RS] rotated left [RB] bits; RA ← $M \wedge$ TEMP
SLWx RA,RS,RB	Shift left word	RA ← [RS] shifted left [RB] bit positions. Vacated bits are filled with 0s.
SRAWx RA,RS,SH	Shift right algebraic word	RA ← [RS] shifted right [RB] bit positions and sign-extended.
SRAWLx RA,RS,SH	Shift right algebraic word immediate	RA ← [RS] shifted right SH bit positions and sign-extended.
SRWx RA,RS,RB	Shift right word	RA ← [RS] shifted right [RB] bit positions. Vacated bits are filled with 0s.

Rotate and Shift instructions use format 6. The MB and ME fields are used as operands in the Rotate instructions. They are used as a sub-opcode in the shift instructions.

TABLE B.6
Selected floating-point instructions

Instruction	Name	Description
FADDSx FRD,FRA,FRB	Floating add single	FRD ← [FRA] + [FRB] The sum is normalized and rounded to a 32-bit floating-point number.
FSUBSx FRD,FRA,FRB	Floating subtract single	FRD ← [FRB] − [FRA] The result of subtraction is normalized and rounded to a 32-bit floating-point number.
FMULSx FRD,FRA,FRC	Floating multiply single	FRD ← [FRA] × [FRC] The product is normalized and rounded to a 32-bit floating-point number.
FDIVSx FRD,FRA,FRB	Floating divide single	FRD ← [FRA]/[FRB] The quotient is normalized and rounded to a 32-bit floating-point number. No remainder is kept.
FMADDSx FRD,FRA,FRC,FRB	Floating multiply-add single	FRD ← [FRA] × [FRC] + [FRB] The result is normalized and rounded to a 32-bit floating-point number.
FMSUBSx FRD,FRA,FRC,FRB	Floating multiply-subtract single	FRD ← [FRA] × [FRC] − [FRB] The result is normalized and rounded to a 32-bit floating-point number.

Floating-point instructions use format 2. Register FRC is given in bits 21 through 25.

FLOATING-POINT INSTRUCTIONS

A few examples of floating-point instructions are given in Table B.6. In addition to the basic four arithmetic operations, some of these instructions perform more complex operations, such as the combined multiply-add and multiply-subtract instructions shown in the table.

BRANCH INSTRUCTIONS

The PowerPC branch instructions can test many conditions. A subset of frequently used branch instructions is given in Tables B.7 and B.8. Unconditional branch instructions

TABLE B.7
Selected conditional branch instructions

Condition	LR Unaffected		Update LR	
	Relative	Absolute	Relative	Absolute
Unconditional	B	BA	BL	BLA
Less than (LT = 1)	BLT	BLTA	BLTL	BLTLA
Less than (GT = 0) or equal to	BLE	BLEA	BLEL	BLELA
Equal (EQ = 1)	BEQ	BEQA	BEQL	BEQLA
Greater than or equal to (LT = 0)	BGE	BGEA	BGEL	BGELA
Greater than (GT = 1)	BGT	BGTA	BGTL	BGTLA
Not equal (EQ = 0)	BNE	BNEA	BNEL	BNELA
Decrement CTR, Branch if CTR = 0	BDZ	BDZA	BDZL	BDZLA
Decrement CTR, Branch if CTR ≠ 0	BDNZ	BDNZA	BDNZL	BDNZLA

have a 24-bit immediate operand. This operand is extended to a 32-bit quantity by appending eight zeros to the right, and then it is used to compute the target address. The extended operand is either used directly as an absolute address, or it is treated as a relative address. In the latter case, it is added to the contents of the program counter to produce the target address. The choice between these two modes is specified by the instruction mnemonic, as shown in the table.

The same options exist with conditional branch instructions, except that the immediate operand is only 16 bits long. This operand is interpreted as a signed value representing the number of words between the target address and the current instruction location. Two zeros are appended to the right and the number is sign-extended to produce a 32-bit offset. This offset is then added to the program counter to obtain the target address.

The conditions given in Tables B.7 and B.8 refer to the flags in the condition register. The last two instructions in each table decrement the Count register, CTR, and test the result. Other instructions that are not shown here perform various combinations of tests on the Count register and the condition flags.

TABLE B.8
Branch to LR and CTR

Condition	LR Unaffected		Update LR	
	to LR	to CTR	to LR	to CTR
Unconditionally	BLR	BCTR	BLRL	BCTRL
Less than (LT = 1)	BLTLR	BLTCTR	BLTLRL	BLTCTRL
Less than (GT = 0) or equal to	BLELR	BLECTR	BLELRL	BLECTRL
Equal (EQ = 1)	BEQLR	BEQCTR	BEQLRL	BEQCTRL
Greater than or equal to (LT = 0)	BGELR	BGECTR	BGELRL	BGECTRL
Greater than (GT = 1)	BGTLR	BGTCTR	BGTLRL	BGTCTRL
Not equal (EQ = 0)	BNELR	BNECTR	BNELRL	BNECTRL
Decrement CTR, Branch if CTR = 0	BDZLR	—	BDZLRL	—
Decrement CTR, Branch if CTR ≠ 0	BDNZLR	—	BDNZLRL	—

Instructions that load the Link register, LR, are, in effect, subroutine calls, as explained in Section 2.20. Return from subroutine is made possible by the instructions that branch to the Link register; that is, their target address is the contents of the Link register.

PROCESSOR CONTROL INSTRUCTIONS

The PowerPC has many control instructions in this class. A few of them are shown in Table B.9. These instructions enable data to be transferred between one of the general-purpose registers and either the machine status register, MSR, or one of the special-purpose registers. The latter include the exception register, XER, the Link register, LR, and the Count register, CTR.

Other processor control instructions perform a variety of control operations, including cache control and memory management.

TABLE B.9
Processor control instructions

Instruction		Name	Description
MTMSR	RS	Move to machine status register	MSR ← [RS]
MFMSR	RD	Move from machine status register	RD ← [MSR]
MTSPR	SPR,RS	Move to special-purpose register	SPR ← [RS]
MFSPR	SPR,RS	Move from special-purpose register	RD ← [SPR] The SPR field denotes one of the special-purpose registers. User-level registers are encoded as follows: 1 XER register 8 LR register 9 CTR register

TABLE B.10
Conventions used to describe the PowerPC instruction set

Symbol	Description
CA	Carry flag in register XER.
I16	A 16-bit immediate operand, given in the instruction word.
X	A 16-bit offset given in the instruction word, used as an index in effective address calculations.
RA, RB, RD, RS	Any of the general-purpose registers R0 through R31. The name used indicates the location of the operand in the instruction word, as given in Figure B.1.
SPR	One of the special-purpose registers. User-level special-purpose registers are encoded as follows: 1 XER register 8 LR register 9 CTR register
[Reg/Loc]	Contents of named register or memory location.
x	The suffix x may take any of the following values: blank No condition flags are affected . The LT, GT, EQ, and SO flags in CR are updated based on the result of the instruction o The OV and SO flags in XER are updated based on the result of the instruction .o Both the CR and the XER flags are updated based on the result of the instruction
[.]	A "." suffix may be used, in which case the CR flags are updated based on the result of the instruction.
bitc(X)	Bit-by-bit complement of X.
cmpl(X)	Two's complement of X.
exts(X)	The value X is extended to a longer word by duplicating the sign bit.
extzl(X)	The value X is extended to a longer word by appending zeros on the left.
extzr(X)	The value X is extended to a longer word by appending zeros on the right.

Instruction Set for Motorola 68000 Microprocessor

This appendix contains a summary of the instructions for the 68000 microprocessor. Chapter 2 gives an introductory discussion of the main characteristics of this microprocessor including a description of the register structure and the addressing modes, summarized in Figure 2.21 and Table 2.1, respectively. Note that Table 2.1 includes the assembler syntax for the addressing modes.

The general format for encoding the address field for an operand is shown in Table C.1. A 6-bit field specifies the addressing mode and the register involved. For the modes in which it is not necessary to specify a particular register, all 6 bits are used to specify the addressing mode.

The names of addressing modes in Table C.1 are consistent with those used in this book. Some of these names differ from those used in Motorola literature, however. Because the reader will find it useful to consult the manufacturer's data sheets and user manuals, we summarize the differences in the terminology in Table C.2. The Motorola terminology is highly descriptive but somewhat awkward to use for discussion.

The 68000 instructions are presented in this appendix in the form of a table. To keep the table reasonably small, extensive notational abbreviations are used. Table C.3 gives the notational symbols and their meanings. Note that symbols that correspond to bit patterns in the OP-code field have one letter for each bit position involved.

Table C.4 provides a complete list of the available instructions. The addressing modes allowed for each instruction are indicated in a matrix format. For each source (destination) addressing mode provided, all destination (source) addressing modes permitted are denoted with an x. For example, for the AND instruction, if the source is a data register, the destination mode may be (An), (An)+, −(An), d(An), d(An,Xi), Abs.W, or Abs.L. Moreover, if the destination is a data register, the source can be specified in any of the 11 modes shown in the table.

The OP-code column shows the actual bit pattern of the first 16-bit word of an instruction. Instructions that have immediate source data use a second word for 8- and 16-bit operands, and a second and third word for 32-bit operands. For the indexed and relative addressing modes, the required index value (that is, the displacement) is given in the word that follows the OP code.

TABLE C.1
Address field encoding for 68000

Address field

| Mode | Register |

5 4 3 2 1 0

Addressing mode	Mode field	Register field
Data register direct	000	Register number
Address register direct	001	Register number
Address register indirect	010	Register number
Autoincrement	011	Register number
Autodecrement	100	Register number
Indexed basic	101	Register number
Indexed full	110	Register number
Absolute short	111	000
Absolute long	111	001
Relative basic	111	010
Relative full	111	011
Immediate or status register	111	100

Shift and Rotate instructions can specify a count of the number of bit positions by which the operand is to be shifted or rotated. The count can be given as the contents of a data register or as an immediate 3-bit value within the OP code. If a memory operand is involved, however, then the count is always equal to 1.

Branch instructions are listed in Table C.5. The branch offset (the displacement) is a signed 2's-complement number that specifies the relative distance in bytes. For conditional branch instructions, as well as for Scc (Set on condition) instructions, the condition code suffix possibilities (cc) are shown in Table C.6. This table also indicates the condition that is tested to determine if a branch is to be taken.

The operation performed for a given instruction is indicated in Tables C.4 and C.5. For most instructions, the action taken is obvious. However, for a few instructions,

TABLE C.2
Differences from Motorola terminology

Terminology used in this text	Motorola terminology
Autoincrement	Address register indirect with postincrement
Autodecrement	Address register indirect with predecrement
Indexed basic	Address register indirect with displacement
Indexed full	Address register indirect with index
Relative basic	Program counter with displacement
Relative full	Program counter with index

TABLE C.3
Notation for Table C.4

Symbol	Meaning
s	Source operand
d	Destination operand
An	Address register n
Dn	Data register n
Xn	An address or data register, used as an index register
PC	Program counter
SP	Stack pointer
SR	Status register
CCR	Condition code flags in SR
AAA	Address register number
DDD	Data register number
rrr	Source register number
RRR	Destination register number
eeeeee	Effective address of the source operand
EEEEEE	Effective address of the destination operand
MMM	Effective address mode of destination
CCCC	Specification for a condition code test
P...P	Displacement
Q...Q	Quick immediate data
SS	Size: 00 ≡ byte, 01 ≡ word, 10 ≡ long word (for most instructions) 01 ≡ byte, 11 ≡ word, 10 ≡ long word (for MOVE and MOVEA instructions)
VVVV	Trap vector number
u	Condition code flag state is undefined (meaningless)
d(An)	Indexed basic addressing mode
d(An,Xi)	Indexed full addressing mode
d(PC)	Relative basic addressing mode
d(PC,Xi)	Relative full addressing mode

additional comments are in order. The instructions labeled with an asterisk in the mnemonic column are discussed further in the following paragraphs.

BCHG, BCLR, BSET, and BTST

All of these instructions test a specified bit of the destination operand. The number of the bit position to be tested (bit#) is indicated either as the contents of a data register or as an immediate value within the instruction. The test is made by loading the complement of the tested bit into the condition flag Z.

MOVEM

This instruction moves the contents of one or more registers to or from consecutive memory locations. The registers involved in the transfer are specified in the second word of the instruction. Bits 0 through 7 correspond to D0 through D7, and bits 8 through 15 correspond to A0 through A7. This arrangement is valid for all addressing modes except the autodecrement mode, in which case the order of registers is reversed.

TABLE C.4
68000 instruction set

Mnemonic (Name)	Size	Addressing mode		Dn	An	(An)	(An)+	-(An)	d(An)	d(An,Xi)	Abs.W	Abs.L	d(PC)	d(PC,Xi)	Immed	SR or CCR
ABCD (Add BCD)	B	s = Dn	d =	x												
		s = −(An)	d =					x								
ADD (Add)	B,W,L	s = Dn	d =			x	x	x	x	x	x	x				
		d = Dn	s =	x	x	x	x	x	x	x	x	x	x	x	x	
ADDA (Add address)	W	d = An	s =	x	x	x	x	x	x	x	x	x	x	x	x	
	L	d = An	s =	x	x	x	x	x	x	x	x	x	x	x	x	
ADDI (Add immediate)	B,W,L	s = Immed	d =	x		x	x	x	x	x	x	x				
ADDQ (Add quick)	B,W,L	s = Immed3	d =	x	x	x	x	x	x	x	x	x				
ADDX (Add extended)	B,W,L	s = Dn	d =	x												
		s = −(An)	d =					x								
AND (Logical AND)	B,W,L	s = Dn	d =			x	x	x	x	x	x	x				
		d = Dn	s =	x		x	x	x	x	x	x	x	x	x	x	
ANDI (AND immediate)	B,W,L	s = Immed	d =	x		x	x	x	x	x	x	x				x
ASL (Arithmetic shift left)	B,W,L	count = [Dn]	d =	x												
		count = QQQ	d =	x												
		count = 1	d =			x	x	x	x	x	x					
ASR (Arithmetic shift right)	B,W,L	count = [Dn]	d =	x												
		count = QQQ	d =	x												
		count = 1	d =			x	x	x	x	x	x					
BCHG* (Test a bit and change it)	B	bit# = [Dn]	d =			x	x	x	x	x	x	x				
		bit# = Immed	d =			x	x	x	x	x	x	x				
	L	bit# = [Dn]	d =	x												
		bit# = Immed	d =	x												
BCLR* (Test a bit and clear it)	B	bit# = [Dn]	d =			x	x	x	x	x	x	x				
		bit# = Immed	d =			x	x	x	x	x	x	x				
	L	bit# = [Dn]	d =	x												
		bit# = Immed	d =	x												

OP code $b_{15} \ldots b_0$	Operation performed	Condition flags				
		X	N	Z	V	C
1100 RRR1 0000 0rrr 1100 RRR1 0000 1rrr	$d \leftarrow [s] + [d] + [X]$ Binary-coded decimal addition	x	u	x	u	x
1101 DDD1 SSEE EEEE 1101 DDD0 SSee eeee	$d \leftarrow [Dn] + [d]$ $Dn \leftarrow [s] + [Dn]$	x x	x x	x x	x x	x x
1101 AAA0 11ee eeee 1101 AAA1 11ee eeee	$An \leftarrow [s] + [An]$					
0000 0110 SSEE EEEE	$d \leftarrow s + [d]$	x	x	x	x	x
0101 QQQ0 SSEE EEEE	$d \leftarrow QQQ + [d]$	x	x	x	x	x
1101 RRR1 SS00 0rrr 1101 RRR1 SS00 1rrr	$d \leftarrow [s] + [d] + [X]$ Multiprecision addition	x	x	x	x	x
1100 DDD1 SSEE EEEE 1100 DDD0 SSee eeee	$d \leftarrow [Dn] \wedge [d]$		x	x	0	0
0000 0010 SSEE EEEE	$d \leftarrow s \wedge [d]$		x	x	0	0
1110 rrr1 SS10 0DDD 1110 QQQ1 SS00 0DDD 1110 0001 11EE EEEE	(rotate diagram: C ← operand ← 0, X ←)	x	x	x	x	x
1110 rrr0 SS10 0DDD 1110 QQQ0 SS00 0DDD 1110 0000 11EE EEEE	(rotate diagram: → operand → C, → X)	x	x	x	x	x
0000 rrr1 01EE EEEE 0000 1000 01EE EEEE 0000 rrr1 01EE EEEE 0000 1000 01EE EEEE	$Z \leftarrow \overline{(\text{bit\# of d})}$; then complement the tested bit in d.			x		
0000 rrr1 10EE EEEE 0000 1000 10EE EEEE 0000 rrr1 10EE EEEE 0000 1000 10EE EEEE	$Z \leftarrow \overline{(\text{bit\# of d})}$; then clear the tested bit in d.			x		

TABLE C.4
(*Continued*)

Mnemonic (Name)	Size	Addressing mode		Dn	An	(An)	(An)+	-(An)	d(An)	d(An,Xi)	Abs.W	Abs.L	d(PC)	d(PC,Xi)	Immed	SR or CCR
BSET* (Test a bit and set it)	B	bit# = [Dn]	d =			x	x	x	x	x	x	x				
		bit# = Immed	d =			x	x	x	x	x	x	x				
	L	bit# = [Dn]	d =	x												
		bit# = Immed	d =	x												
BTST* (Test a bit)	B	bit# = [Dn]	d =			x	x	x	x	x	x	x				
		bit# = Immed	d =			x	x	x	x	x	x	x				
	L	bit# = [Dn]	d =	x												
		bit# = Immed	d =	x												
CHK (Check register against bounds)	W	d = Dn	s =	x		x	x	x	x	x	x	x	x	x	x	
CLR (Clear)	B,W,L		d =	x		x	x	x	x	x	x	x				
CMP (Compare)	B,W,L	d = Dn	s =	x	x	x	x	x	x	x	x	x	x	x	x	
CMPA (Compare address)	W	d = An	s =	x	x	x	x	x	x	x	x	x	x	x	x	
	L	d = An	s =	x	x	x	x	x	x	x	x	x	x	x	x	
CMPI (Compare immediate)	B,W,L	s = Immed	d =	x		x	x	x	x	x	x	x				
CMPM (Compare memory)	B,W,L	s = (An)+	d =				x									
DIVS (Divide signed)	W	d = Dn	s =	x		x	x	x	x	x	x	x	x	x	x	
DIVU (Divide unsigned)	W	d = Dn	s =	x		x	x	x	x	x	x	x	x	x	x	
EOR (Exclusive OR)	B,W,L	s = Dn	d =	x		x	x	x	x	x	x	x				
EORI (Exclusive OR immediate)	B,W,L	s = Immed	d =	x		x	x	x	x	x	x	x				x
EXG (Exchange)	L	s = Dn	d =	x	x											
		s = An	d =	x	x											
EXT (Sign extend)	W		d =	x												
	L		d =	x												

OP code $b_{15} \ldots b_0$	Operation performed	Condition flags X	N	Z	V	C
0000 rrr1 11EE EEEE 0000 1000 11EE EEEE 0000 rrr1 11EE EEEE 0000 1000 11EE EEEE	$Z \leftarrow (\overline{\text{bit\# of d}})$; then set to 1 the tested bit in d.			x		
0000 rrr1 00EE EEEE 0000 1000 00EE EEEE 0000 rrr1 00EE EEEE 0000 1000 00EE EEEE	$Z \leftarrow (\overline{\text{bit\# of d}})$			x		
0100 DDD1 10ee eeee	If [Dn] < 0 or [Dn] > [s], then raise an interrupt.		x	u	u	u
0100 0010 SSEE EEEE	$d \leftarrow 0$	0	1	0	0	
1011 DDD0 SSee eeee	[d] − [s]		x	x	x	x
1011 AAA0 11ee eeee 1011 AAA1 11ee eeee	[An − [s]		x	x	x	x
0000 1100 SSEE EEEE	[d] − [s]		x	x	x	x
1011 RRR1 SS00 1rrr	[d] − [s]		x	x	x	x
1000 DDD1 11ee eeee	$d \leftarrow [d] \div [s]$, using 32 bits of d and 16 bits of s.		x	x	x	0
1000 DDD0 11ee eeee	$d \leftarrow [d] \div [s]$, using 32 bits of d and 16 bits of s.		x	x	x	0
1011 rrr1 SSEE EEEE	$d \leftarrow [Dn] \oplus [d]$		x	x	0	0
0000 1010 SSEE EEEE	$d \leftarrow s \oplus [d]$		x	x	0	0
1100 DDD1 0100 0DDD 1100 AAA1 0100 1AAA 1100 DDD1 1000 1AAA	$[s] \leftrightarrow [d]$					
0100 1000 1000 0DDD 0100 1000 1100 0DDD	(bits 8–15 of d) ← (bit 7 of d) (bits 16–31 of d) ← (bit 15 of d)		x x	x x	0 0	0 0

TABLE C.4
(*Continued*)

Mnemonic (Name)	Size	Addressing mode		Dn	An	(An)	(An)+	−(An)	d(An)	d(An,Xi)	Abs.W	Abs.L	d(PC)	d(PC,Xi)	Immed	SR or CCR
JMP (Jump)			d =			x			x	x	x	x	x	x		
JSR (Jump to subroutine)			d =			x			x	x	x	x	x	x		
LEA (Load effective address)	L	d = An	s =			x			x	x	x	x	x	x		
LINK (Link and allocate)		disp = Immed	s =	x												
LSL (Logical shift left)	B,W,L	count = [Dn]	d =	x												
		count = QQQ	d =	x												
	W	count = I	d =			x	x	x	x	x	x	x				
LSR (Logical shift right)	B,W,L	count = [Dn]	d =	x												
		count = QQQ	d =	x												
	W	count = I	d =			x	x	x	x	x	x	x				
MOVE (Move)	B,W,L	s = Dn	d =	x		x	x	x	x	x	x	x				
		s = An	d =	x		x	x	x	x	x	x	x				
		s = (An)	d =	x		x	x	x	x	x	x	x				
		s = (An)+	d =	x		x	x	x	x	x	x	x				
		s = −(An)	d =	x		x	x	x	x	x	x	x				
		s = d(An)	d =	x		x	x	x	x	x	x	x				
		s = d(An, Xi)	d =	x		x	x	x	x	x	x	x				
		s = Abs.W	d =	x		x	x	x	x	x	x	x				
		s = Abs.L	d =	x		x	x	x	x	x	x	x				
		s = d(PC)	d =	x		x	x	x	x	x	x	x				
		s = d(PC, Xi)	d =	x		x	x	x	x	x	x	x				
		s = Immed	d =	x		x	x	x	x	x	x	x				
	W	d = CCR	s =	x		x	x	x	x	x	x	x	x	x	x	
		d = SR	s =	x		x	x	x	x	x	x	x	x	x	x	
		s = SR	d =	x		x	x	x	x	x	x	x				
	L	s = SP	d =		x											
		d = SP	s =		x											
MOVEA (Move address)	W,L	d = An	s =	x	x	x	x	x	x	x	x	x	x	x	x	

OP code $b_{15}\ldots b_0$	Operation performed	Condition flags				
		X	N	Z	V	C
0100 1110 11EE EEEE	PC ← effective address of d					
0100 1110 10EE EEEE	SP ← [SP] − 4; [SP ← [PC]; PC ← effective address of d					
0100 AAA1 11ee eeee	An ← effective address of s					
0100 1110 0101 0AAA	SP ← [SP] − 4; [SP] ← [An]; An ← [SP]; SP ← [SP] + disp					
1110 rrr1 SS10 1DDD 1110 QQQ1 SS00 1DDD 1110 0011 11EE EEEE	[C] ←— operand ←— O [X] ←	x	x	x	0	x
1110 rrr0 SS10 1DDD 1110 QQQ0 SS00 1DDD 1110 0010 11EE EEEE	O —→ operand —→ [C] —→ [X]	x	x	x	0	x
00SS RRRM MMee eeee	d ← [s]		x	x	0	0
0100 0100 11ee eeee	CCR ← [s]	x	x	x	x	x
0100 0110 11ee eeee	SR ← [s]	x	x	x	x	x
0100 0000 1EEE EEEE	d ← [SR]					
0100 1110 0110 1AAA	d ← [SP]					
0100 1110 0110 0AAA	SP ← [d]					
00SS AAA0 01ee eeee	An ← [s]					

TABLE C.4
(Continued)

Mnemonic (Name)	Size	Addressing mode	Dn	An	(An)	(An)+	-(An)	d(An)	d(An,Xi)	Abs.W	Abs.L	d(PC)	d(PC,Xi)	Immed	SR or CCR
MOVEM* (Move multiple registers)	W	s = Xn d =			x		x	x	x	x	x				
		d = Xn s =			x	x		x	x	x	x	x	x		
	L	s = Xn d =			x			x	x	x	x				
		d = Xn s =			x	x		x	x	x	x	x	x		
MOVEP* (Move peripheral data)	W	s = Dn d =						x							
	L	s = Dn d =						x							
	W	s = d(An) d =	x												
	L	s = d(An) d =	x												
MOVEQ (Move quick)	L	s = Immed8 d =	x												
MULS (Multiply signed)	W	d = Dn s =	x		x	x	x	x	x	x	x	x	x	x	
MULU (Multiply unsigned)	W	d = Dn s =	x		x	x	x	x	x	x	x	x	x	x	
NBCD (Negate BCD)	B	d =	x		x	x	x	x	x	x	x				
NEG (Negate)	B,W,L	d =	x		x	x	x	x	x	x	x				
NEGX (Negate extended)	B,W,L	d =	x		x	x	x	x	x	x	x				
NOP (No operation)															
NOT (Complement)	B,W,L	d =	x		x	x	x	x	x	x	x				
OR (Logical OR)	B,W,L	s = Dn d =			x	x	x	x	x	x	x				
		d = Dn s =	x		x	x	x	x	x	x	x	x	x	x	
ORI (OR immediate)	B,W,L	s = Immed d =	x		x	x	x	x	x	x	x				x
PEA (Push effective address)	L	s =			x			x	x	x	x	x	x		

OP code $b_{15} \ldots b_0$	Operation performed	Condition flags				
		X	N	Z	V	C
0100 1000 10EE EEEE 0100 1100 10ee eeee 0100 1000 11EE EEEE 0100 1100 11ee eeee	$d \leftarrow [Xn]$ ⎫ A second word is $Xn \leftarrow [s]$ ⎪ used to specify $d \leftarrow [Xn]$ ⎬ the registers $Xn \leftarrow [s]$ ⎭ involved.					
0000 DDD1 1000 1AAA 0000 DDD1 1100 1AAA 0000 DDD1 0000 1AAA 0000 DDD1 0100 1AAA	Alternate bytes of $d \leftarrow [Dn]$ $Dn \leftarrow$ alternate bytes of d					
0111 DDD0 QQQQ QQQQ	$Dn \leftarrow QQQQQQQQ$		x	x	0	0
1100 DDD1 11ee eeee	$Dn \leftarrow [s] \times [Dn]$		x	x	0	0
1100 DDD0 11ee eeee	$Dn \leftarrow [s] \times [Dn]$		x	x	0	0
0100 1000 00EE EEEE	$d \leftarrow 0 - [d] - [X]$ using BCD arithmetic	x	u	x	u	x
0100 0100 SSEE EEEE	$d \leftarrow 0 - [d]$	x	x	x	x	x
0100 0000 SSEE EEEE	$d \leftarrow 0 - [d] - [X]$	x	x	x	x	x
0100 1110 0111 0001	none					
0100 0110 SSEE EEEE	$d \leftarrow \overline{[d]}$		x	x	0	0
1000 DDD1 SSEE EEEE 1000 DDD0 SSee eeee	$d \leftarrow [s] \vee [d]$		x	x	0	0
0000 0000 SSEE EEEE	$d \leftarrow s \vee [d]$		x	x	0	0
0100 1000 01ee eeee	$SP \leftarrow [SP] - 4$ $[SP] \leftarrow$ effective address of s					

TABLE C.4
(*Continued*)

Mnemonic (Name)	Size	Addressing mode		Dn	An	(An)	(An)+	−(An)	d(An)	d(An,Xi)	Abs.W	Abs.L	d(PC)	d(PC,Xi)	Immed	SR or CCR
RESET																
ROL (Rotate left without X)	B,W,L	count = [Dn]	d =	x												
	B,W,L	count = QQQ	d =	x												
	W	count = 1	d =			x	x	x	x	x	x	x				
ROR (Rotate right without X)	B,W,L	count = [Dn]	d =	x												
	B,W,L	count = QQQ	d =	x												
	W	count = 1	d =			x	x	x	x	x	x	x				
ROXL (Rotate left with X)	B,W,L	count = [Dn]	d =	x												
	B,W,L	count = QQQ	d =	x												
	W	count = 1	d =			x	x	x	x	x	x	x				
ROXR (Rotate right with X)	B,W,L	count = [Dn]	d =	x												
	B,W,L	count = QQQ	d =	x												
	W	count = 1	d =			x	x	x	x	x	x	x				
RTE (Return from exception)																
RTR (Return and restore CCR)																
RTS (Return from subroutine)																
SBCD (Subtract BCD)	B	s = Dn	d =	x												
		s = −(An)	d =					x								
Scc (Set on condition)	B		d =	x		x	x	x	x	x	x	x				

OP code $b_{15} \ldots b_0$	Operation performed	Condition flags				
		X	N	Z	V	C
0100 1110 0111 0000	Assert RESET output line.					
1110 rrr1 SS11 1DDD 1110 QQQ1 SS01 1DDD 1110 0111 11EE EEEE	$\boxed{C} \leftarrow \boxed{\text{operand}} \leftarrow$		x	x	0	x
1100 rrr1 SS11 1DDD 1110 QQQ0 SS01 1DDD 1110 0111 11EE EEEE	$\rightarrow \boxed{\text{operand}} \rightarrow \boxed{C}$		x	x	0	x
1110 rrr1 SS11 0DDD 1110 QQQ1 SS01 0DDD 1110 0101 11EE EEEE	$\boxed{C} \leftarrow \boxed{\text{operand}} \leftarrow \boxed{X}$	x	x	x	0	x
1110 rrr0 SS11 0DDD 1110 QQQ0 SS01 0DDD 1110 0100 11EE EEEE	$\boxed{X} \rightarrow \boxed{\text{operand}} \rightarrow \boxed{C}$	x	x	x	0	x
0100 1110 0111 0011	$SR \leftarrow [[SP]];$ $SP \leftarrow [SP] + 2;$ $PC \leftarrow [[SP]];$ $SP \leftarrow [SP] + 4;$	x	x	x	x	x
0100 1110 0111 0111	$CCR \leftarrow [[SP]];$ $SP \leftarrow [SP] + 2;$ $PC \leftarrow [[SP]];$ $SP \leftarrow [SP] + 4;$	x	x	x	x	x
0100 1110 0111 0101	$PC \leftarrow [[SP]];$ $SP \leftarrow [SP] + 4$					
1000 RRR1 0000 0rrr 1000 RRR1 0000 1rrr	$d \leftarrow [d] - [s] - [X]$ Binary-coded decimal subtraction	x	u	x	u	x
0101 CCCC 11EE EEEE	Set all 8 bits of d to 1 if cc is true, otherwise clear them to 0.					

TABLE C.4
(*Continued*)

Mnemonic (Name)	Size	Addressing mode		Dn	An	(An)	(An)+	−(An)	d(An)	d(An,Xi)	Abs.W	Abs.L	d(PC)	d(PC,Xi)	Immed	SR or CCR
STOP (Load SR and stop)			s =												x	
SUB (Subtract)	B,W,L	s = Dn	d =			x	x	x	x	x	x	x				
		d = Dn	s =	x	x	x	x	x	x	x	x	x	x	x	x	
SUBA (Subtract address)	W	d = An	s =	x	x	x	x	x	x	x	x	x	x	x	x	
	L	d = An	s =	x	x	x	x	x	x	x	x	x	x	x	x	
SUBI (Subtract immediate)	B,W,L	s = Immed	d =	x		x	x	x	x	x	x	x				
SUBQ (Subtract quick)	B,W,L	s = Immed3	d =	x	x	x	x	x	x	x	x	x				
SUBX (Subtract extended)	B,W,L	s = Dn	d =	x												
		s = −(An)	d =					x								
SWAP (Swap register halves)	W		d =	x												
TAS (Test and set)	B		d =	x		x	x	x	x	x	x	x				
TRAP (Trap)																
TRAPV (Trap on overflow)																
TST (Test)	B,W,L		d =	x		x	x	x	x	x	x	x				
UNLK (Unlink)					x											

OP code $b_{15}\ldots b_0$	Operation performed	Condition flags				
		X	N	Z	V	C
0100 1110 0111 0010	SR ← s; wait for interrupt.	x	x	x	x	x
1001 DDD1 SSEE EEEE 1001 DDD0 SSee eeee	d ← [d] − [s]	x	x	x	x	x
1001 AAA0 11ee eeee 1001 AAA1 11ee eeee	An ← [An] − [s]					
0000 0100 SSEE EEEE	d ← [d] − s	x	x	x	x	x
0101 QQQ1 SSEE EEEE	d ← [d] − QQQ	x	x	x	x	x
1001 RRR1 SS00 0rrr 1001 RRR1 SS00 1rrr	d ← [d] − [s] − [X]	x	x	x	x	x
0100 1000 0100 0DDD	$[Dn]_{31-16} \leftrightarrow [Dn]_{15-0}$		x	x	0	0
0100 1010 11EE EEEE	Test d and set N and Z flags; set bit 7 of d to 1.		x	x	0	0
0100 1110 0100 VVVV	SP ← [SP] − 4; [SP] ← [PC]; SP ← [SP] − 2; [SP] ← [SR]; PC ← vector					

0100 1110 0111 0110	If V = 1, then
	    SP ← [SP] − 4;
	    [SP] ← [PC];
	    SP ← [SP] − 2;
	    [SP] ← [SR];
	    PC ← TRAPV vector					

0100 1010 SSEE EEEE	Test d and set N and Z flags.		x	x	0	0
0100 1110 0101 1AAA	SP ← [An]; An ← [[SP]]; SP ← [SP] + 4					

TABLE C.5
68000 branch instructions

Mnemonic (Name)	Displacement size	OP code	Operation performed
BRA (Branch always)	8	0100 0000 PPPP PPPP	PC ← [PC] + disp
	16	0110 0000 0000 0000 PPPP PPPP PPPP PPPP	
Bcc (Branch conditionally)	8	0110 CCCC PPPP PPPP	If cc is true, then
	16	0110 CCCC 0000 0000 PPPP PPPP PPPP PPPP	PC ← [PC] + disp
BSR (Branch to subroutine)	8	0110 0001 PPPP PPPP	SP ← [SP] − 4; [SP] ← [PC];
	16	0110 0001 0000 0000 PPPP PPPP PPPP PPPP	PC ← [PC] + disp
DBcc (Decrement and branch conditionally)	16	0101 CCCC 1100 1DDD PPPP PPPP PPPP PPPP	If cc is false, then Dn ← [Dn] − 1; If [Dn] ≠ −1, then PC ← [PC] + disp
DBRA (Decrement and branch)	The assembler interprets this instruction as DBF (see the DBcc entry).		

MOVEP

This instruction is useful for data transfers between the 68000 and 8-bit peripheral devices. The data are transferred in bytes, with the memory address incremented by 2 after each byte. Thus, if the starting address is even, all bytes are transferred to or from even-numbered address locations by means of the high-order eight lines of the data bus. Similarly, if the starting address is odd, then all transfers are done via the low-order eight lines of the data bus. The high-order byte of a data register is transferred first and the low-order byte is transferred last.

As Chapter 2 points out, the 68000 has two basic modes of operation. In the supervisor mode, all instructions can be used. In the user mode, some instructions cannot be executed. Instructions that can be used in the supervisor mode only are called privileged instructions. These are

- ANDI, EORI, ORI, and MOVE instructions when the destination is the status register SR
- MOVE instruction, which moves the contents of the user stack pointer to or from an address register
- RESET, RTE, and STOP instructions

The information presented in this appendix should enable the reader to write and debug assembly-language programs for the 68000. The size and structure of assembled

TABLE C.6
Condition codes for Bcc, DBcc, and Scc instructions

Machine code CCCC	Condition suffix cc	Name	Test condition
0000	T	True	Always true
0001	F	False	Always false
0010	HI	High	$C \vee Z = 0$
0011	LS	Low or same	$C \vee Z = 1$
0100	CC	Carry clear	$C = 0$
0101	CS	Carry set	$C = 1$
0110	NE	Not equal	$Z = 0$
0111	EQ	Equal	$Z = 1$
1000	VC	Overflow clear	$V = 0$
1001	VS	Overflow set	$V = 1$
1010	PL	Plus	$N = 0$
1011	MI	Minus	$N = 1$
1100	GE	Greater or equal	$N \oplus V = 0$
1101	LT	Less than	$N \oplus V = 1$
1110	GT	Greater than	$Z \vee (N \oplus V) = 0$
1111	LE	Less or equal	$Z \vee (N \oplus V) = 1$

T and F suffixes cannot be used in the Bcc instruction.

instructions can be determined on the basis of the OP codes given and the addressing modes employed. Lack of space has prevented the inclusion of timing information, such as the number of machine cycles needed to execute a given instruction. This information, as well as further details about the instruction set, can be found in the manufacturer's literature.

APPENDIX D

Character Codes and Number Conversion

D.1
CHARACTER CODES

Information storage and processing in digital computers involves coding the individual items of information by using several binary variables. In most scientific computers, positive and negative numbers are represented in some variation of the binary number system. The most usual formats are presented in Chapter 6, where both integer and floating-point numbers are discussed.

In computers used mainly for business data processing, it is useful to represent and process numbers in the base-10 (decimal) format. Table D.1 gives the most usual coding for individual digits, called the binary-coded decimal (BCD) code. This code is simply the first 10 values (0–9) of the 4-bit binary number system. Strings of these 4-bit code values can be used to represent any desired range of positive and negative integers, with an appropriate code used for the sign position.

TABLE D.1
BCD encoding of decimal digits

Decimal digit	BCD code
0	0000
1	0001
2	0010
3	0011
4	0100
5	0101
6	0110
7	0111
8	1000
9	1001

Alphabetic characters (A–Z), operators, punctuation symbols, and control characters (+ − / , : ; LF CR EOT), as well as numbers, must be represented for text storage and editing and for high-level language input, processing, and output operations. Two standard codes for this purpose are the American Standards Committee on Information Interchange (ASCII) code and the Extended Binary Coded Decimal Interchange Code (EBCDIC). The standard ASCII code is a 7-bit code, and the EBCDIC code is an 8-bit code. Tables D.2 and D.3 show the standard ASCII and EBCDIC codes, respectively. In modern computing, the ASCII code is by far the most frequently used.

TABLE D.2
The 7-bit ASCII code

Bit positions 3210	Bit positions 654							
	000	001	010	011	100	101	110	111
0000	NUL	DLE	SPACE	0	@	P	'	p
0001	SOH	DC1	!	1	A	Q	a	q
0010	STX	DC2	"	2	B	R	b	r
0011	ETX	DC3	#	3	C	S	c	s
0100	EOT	DC4	$	4	D	T	d	t
0101	ENQ	NAK	%	5	E	U	e	u
0110	ACK	SYN	&	6	F	V	f	v
0111	BEL	ETB	'	7	G	W	g	w
1000	BS	CAN	(	8	H	X	h	x
1001	HT	EM	)	9	I	Y	i	y
1010	LF	SUB	*	:	J	Z	j	z
1011	VT	ESC	+	;	K	[	k	{
1100	FF	FS	,	<	L	\	l	|
1101	CR	GS	−	=	M	]	m	}
1110	SO	RS	.	>	N	^	n	~
1111	SI	US	/	?	O	—	o	DEL

NUL	Null/Idle	SI	Shift in
SOH	Start of header	DLE	Data link escape
STX	Start of text	DC1-DC4	Device control
ETX	End of text	NAK	Negative acknowledgement
EOT	End of transmitted	SYN	Synchronous idle
ENQ	Enquiry	ETB	End of transmitted block
ACK	Acknowledgment	CAN	Cancel (error in data)
BEL	Audible signal	EM	End of medium
BS	Back space	SUB	Special sequence
HT	Horizontal tab	ESC	Escape
LF	Line feed	FS	File separator
VT	Vertical tab	GS	Group separator
FF	Form feed	RS	Record separator
CR	Carriage return	US	Unit separator
SO	Shift out	DEL	Delete/Idle

Bit positions of code format = | 6 | 5 | 4 | 3 | 2 | 1 | 0 |

TABLE D.3
The 8-bit EBCDIC code

Bit positions 3210	\[Bit positions 7654\] 0000	0001	0010	0011	0100	0101	0110	0111	1000	1001	1010	1011	1100	1101	1110	1111
0000	NULL				SP	&	–									0
0001							/		a	j			A	J		1
0010									b	k	s		B	K	S	2
0011									c	l	t		C	L	T	3
0100	PF	RES	BYP	PN					d	m	u		D	M	U	4
0101	HT	NL	LF	RS					e	n	v		E	N	V	5
0110	LC	BS	EOB	UC					f	o	w		F	O	W	6
0111	DEL	IL	PRE	EOT					g	p	x		G	P	X	7
1000									h	q	y		H	Q	Y	8
1001									i	r	z		I	R	Z	9
1010			SM		¢	!		:								
1011					.	$	,	#								
1100					<	*	%	@								
1101					(	)	_	'								
1110					+	;	>	=								
1111							¬	?	"							

NULL	Null/Idle	NL	New line	PRE	Prefix
PF	Punch off	BS	Backspace	SM	Set mode
HT	Horizontal tab	IL	Idle	PN	Punch on
LC	Lowercase	BYP	Bypass	RS	Reader stop
DEL	Delete	LF	Line feed	UC	Uppercase
RES	Restore	EOB	End of block	EOT	End of transmission
				SP	Space

Bit positions of code format = 7 6 5 4 3 2 1 0

543

In many applications, it is preferable to use 8-bit quantities; thus, the basic ASCII code is often extended to 8-bits. A common way of doing this is to set the high-order bit position, bit 7, to zero. Another popular possibility is to use bit 7 as a parity bit for the encoded character.

Some comments about the structure of the ASCII and EBCDIC codes are helpful. Note that in both codes the low-order 4 bits of the decimal character codes (0–9) are the BCD codes of Table D.1. This facilitates two operations. First, two characters that represent decimal digits can be compared to determine which is larger. This can be done with the same type of logic circuits that are used to perform the standard arithmetic operations on binary numbers. This is helpful when strings of decimal numbers must be sorted into numerical order. Second, when it is determined by context that consecutive 7- or 8-bit codes in some input string represent a decimal number that is to be stored and processed as a single entity, then it is sometimes practical to remove the leftmost 3 or 4 bits of each digit code and compress the number being represented into a string of 4-bit BCD digits. This compression or packing of data requires starting and ending delimiters, but it is justified in many situations in which storage space requirements are a concern. Similar comments apply to the codes for the alphabetic characters. The fact that their binary bit patterns are in numerical sequence facilitates alphabetic sorting.

D.2
DECIMAL-TO-BINARY CONVERSION

This section shows how to convert a fixed-point decimal number to its binary equivalent. The value, V, represented by the binary number

$$B = b_n b_{n-1} \cdots b_0 \cdot b_{-1} b_{-2} \cdots b_{-m}$$

is given by

$$V(B) = b_n \times 2^n + b_{n-1} \times 2^{n+1} + \cdots + b_0 \times 2^0$$
$$+ b_{-1} \times 2^{-1} + b_{-2} \times 2^{-2} + \cdots + b_{-m} \times 2^{-m}$$

To convert a fixed-point decimal number into binary, the integer and fraction parts are handled separately. First, the integer part is converted as follows. It is divided by 2. The remainder is the least significant bit of the integer part of the binary representation. The quotient is again divided by 2, and the remainder is the next bit of the binary representation. The process is repeated up to and including the step in which the quotient becomes 0.

Second, the fraction part is converted by multiplying it by 2. The part of the product to the left of the decimal point, which is either 0 or 1, is a bit in the binary representation. The fractional part of the product is again multiplied by 2, generating the next bit of the binary representation. The first bit generated is the bit immediately to the right of the binary point. The next bit generated is the second bit to the right, and so on. The process is repeated until the required accuracy is attained.

Convert $(927.45)_{10}$

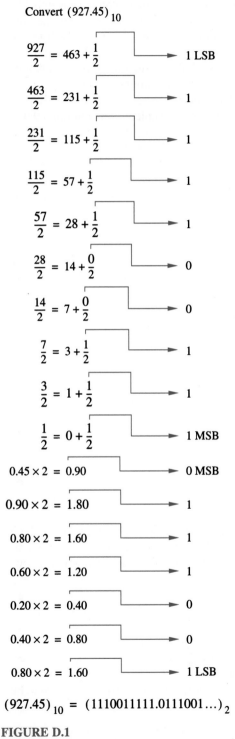

$$\frac{927}{2} = 463 + \frac{1}{2} \qquad \longrightarrow \quad 1 \text{ LSB}$$

$$\frac{463}{2} = 231 + \frac{1}{2} \qquad \longrightarrow \quad 1$$

$$\frac{231}{2} = 115 + \frac{1}{2} \qquad \longrightarrow \quad 1$$

$$\frac{115}{2} = 57 + \frac{1}{2} \qquad \longrightarrow \quad 1$$

$$\frac{57}{2} = 28 + \frac{1}{2} \qquad \longrightarrow \quad 1$$

$$\frac{28}{2} = 14 + \frac{0}{2} \qquad \longrightarrow \quad 0$$

$$\frac{14}{2} = 7 + \frac{0}{2} \qquad \longrightarrow \quad 0$$

$$\frac{7}{2} = 3 + \frac{1}{2} \qquad \longrightarrow \quad 1$$

$$\frac{3}{2} = 1 + \frac{1}{2} \qquad \longrightarrow \quad 1$$

$$\frac{1}{2} = 0 + \frac{1}{2} \qquad \longrightarrow \quad 1 \text{ MSB}$$

$$0.45 \times 2 = 0.90 \qquad \longrightarrow \quad 0 \text{ MSB}$$

$$0.90 \times 2 = 1.80 \qquad \longrightarrow \quad 1$$

$$0.80 \times 2 = 1.60 \qquad \longrightarrow \quad 1$$

$$0.60 \times 2 = 1.20 \qquad \longrightarrow \quad 1$$

$$0.20 \times 2 = 0.40 \qquad \longrightarrow \quad 0$$

$$0.40 \times 2 = 0.80 \qquad \longrightarrow \quad 0$$

$$0.80 \times 2 = 1.60 \qquad \longrightarrow \quad 1 \text{ LSB}$$

$$(927.45)_{10} = (1110011111.0111001\dots)_2$$

FIGURE D.1
Conversion from decimal to binary.

Figure D.1 shows an example of conversion from $(927.45)_{10}$ to binary. Note that conversion of the integer part is always exact, but the binary fraction for an exact decimal fraction may not be exact. For example, the fraction $(0.45)_{10}$ used in Figure D.1 does not have an exact binary equivalent. This is obvious from the pattern developing in the figure. In such cases, the binary fraction is generated to some desired level of accuracy. In general, the maximum absolute error, e, in generating a k-bit fractional representation is bounded as $e \leq 2^{-k}$. Of course, some decimal fractions have an exact binary representation. For example, $(0.25)_{10}$ equals $(0.01)_2$.

INDEX

Accumulator, **28**, 344
Access time:
  main memory, 5, 209
  magnetic disk, 385
Adder:
  BCD, 297
  carry lookahead, **263**
  circuit, **261**
  full-adder, **259**
  half-adder, **296**
  propagation delay, 262
  ripple-carry, **260**
Addition, 259–268
  carry, 259
  carry-save, **280**
  end-around carry, **298**
  floating-point, **289**
  generate function, 262
  modular, 265
  overflow, 34, **260**, 267
  propagate function, 262
  sum, 259
Address pointer, **36**, 345
Address space, **22**, 153, 347
Addressing mode, 24, **34**
  absolute, **35**, 87
  autodecrement, **40**, 321
  autoincrement, **39**, 321
  immediate, **35**
  in pipelining, 322
  index, 36–39, 341
  indirect, **35**, 341
  PowerPC, 82, 90
  register, 34
  relative, 61
  68000, 60
  68020, 341
Alpha processors, 352
  performance, 354
Alphanumeric characters, 3, **31**, 541
Alphanumeric displays, 378
  ASCII, 31, 71, 542
  EBCDIC, 3, 543
Amdahl's law, **434**
Application program, 11
Arbitration, 177 (*see also* Bus)
  centralized, 179
  distributed, 179

  on SCSI bus, 198
Architecture, 1, 339
Arithmetic, 257–293
  floating-point (*see* Floating point)
  multiple-precision, 269
  (*see also* Addition; Division; Multiplication;
    Subtraction)
  Arithmetic and logic unit (ALU), 5
  array, 401
  array processor, **400**
  ASCII (American Standards Committee on
    Information Exchange) code, 3, 31, 71,
    372, 542
Assembler, **41**
  two-pass, **45**
Assembler commands, 42
Assembly language, 41–46
  mnemonics, 41
  68000, 66
  syntax, **41**, 62, 88
Associative search, 228
Asynchronous transfer, 115
Asynchronous transmission, 371, 373
Autovector, 170

Backplane, 199
  standards (*see* Standards)
Bandwidth, 373 (*see also* Bit rate)
Barrier synchronization, 429
Baud rate, 372
BCD (*see* Binary-coded decimal)
BBN Butterfly, 408
Benchmark program, 354, 435
Big-endian, **25**, 81, 208
Binary-coded decimal (BCD), 3, 73, 341, 541
  addition, 297
  packed, 73
Binary variable, 441
Bit, 3
Bit map, 379
Bit-ORing, **138**
Bit rate, 193 (*see also* Baud rate)
Booth algorithm, **274**
  bit-pair recoding, 278
Branch:
  delay slot, 314
  delayed, 313